NO
LASTING
CITY

NO
LASTING
CITY

Essays on Theology, Politics, and Culture

FREDERICK CHRISTIAN BAUERSCHMIDT

Published by Word on Fire Academic, an imprint of
Word on Fire, Elk Grove Village, IL 60007
© 2023 by Word on Fire Catholic Ministries
Printed in the United States of America
All rights reserved.

Cover design by Michael Stevens, typesetting by Clark Kenyon,
and interior art direction by Nicolas Fredrickson

ISBN: 978-1-68578-046-3

Library of Congress Control Number: 2023941915

In memoriam
Angela Russell Christman
(1958–2020)

Fecisti nos ad te
et inquietum est cor nostrum
donec requiescat in te

Contents

An Image Gallery appears after page 330

Introduction

The essays collected here represent attempts I have made over the past twenty-five years to think through how theology relates to politics and culture. They might seem like a bit of a diversion from much of my published work, which has been in large part focused on the Middle Ages, particularly the twelfth through the fifteenth centuries. But I have never seen study of the past as an end in itself. Like most people, my main desire is to understand the world around me and my place in it, which is what I think Aristotle meant when he said that all philosophy begins in wonder. Moreover, I don't have a natural affinity for the Middle Ages (and suspect those who claim that they do are fooling themselves just a bit). I find it is only with some effort that I can understand how medieval people thought and felt. I have no desire to have lived in those times, and I don't particularly want to reshape my own times to be more like them.

I have spent time studying the Middle Ages not for their own sake, but because I believe that one of the most useful tools for understanding the present is to try to view it from that foreign country that we call the past. Not unlike a hitherto unknown culture encountered in some distant land, the past holds up a mirror to us in which we might catch a glimpse of our own world and how we are positioned within it. Indeed, the past can be more useful in this regard than some contemporary alien culture, because while being different, it is also the soil from which our present grows and in which, for good or for ill, it remains rooted. Study of the past forces us to reckon with the fact that what for us goes without saying was not necessarily presumed by our ancestors; indeed, what many of us presume without argument would, in some cases, have been for them quite unthinkable (a godless world? gender as a social construct? the natural equality of all people?). To explore the past is to realize not simply how strange the past is, but how strange our present world is when viewed from the past.

This interest in the present has never been particularly hidden in my writing. After all, I wrote a book on Julian of Norwich that ended with an appeal to Dorothy Day, followed by a book on Thomas Aquinas that concluded with the question of how the theology of the past can be made relevant today. But sometimes I have tried to make the present interest of my work even more explicit, and the essays in this volume for the most part place the present in the foreground. Of course, due to the inevitable limits of anyone's base of knowledge, there are a lot of thinkers from the past who figure in these essays: Augustine, Thomas Aquinas, Julian of Norwich, the painters known as the "Flemish Primitives," and so forth. But modern figures are engaged as well: William James and Max Weber, Hans Urs von Balthasar and Edward Schillebeeckx, Walter Benjamin and Michel de Certeau. And the aim of each essay is to explore present questions concerning theology, politics, and culture. How are theology and ethics related? How should we understand the secularization of the West? What political purposes do certain forms of spirituality serve? How can theology take place within the realm of the visual and literary arts? These are questions about how we live now, not questions about the past, even though glancing backward can be useful as we move forward.

***

The essays in this book are organized under three headings: Theology, Politics, and Culture. The essays in the "Theology" section develop positions on certain fundamental questions that provide a theological framework for the other essays.

The first essay, "Confessions of an Evangelical Catholic," deals with issues of theological anthropology and what difference it makes if one takes seriously the claim of the Second Vatican Council that "it is only in the mystery of the Word incarnate that light is shed on the mystery of humankind."[1] It is my attempt to give the "anthropological turn" that Catholic theology took during the twentieth century something of a Christological corrective. This essay also allows me to make some remarks on what in the twentieth century is probably the principal issue in Catholic theology: the relationship between nature and grace. I do not pretend that what I say here is the last word on the topic, which continues to be debated into the twenty-first century. It is rather an attempt to sketch a position that is compatible with what is sometimes called "evangelical Catholicism."

The second essay, "Aesthetics: The Theological Sublime," grapples with the claim that we live in a time that is aptly described as "postmodernity" and tries to discern what Christians can and cannot make use of in postmodern thought. In the late twentieth century (which my undergraduate students call, disconcertingly, "the 1900s") this seemed an extraordinarily pressing question. Today, despite its connotations of futurity, "postmodernity" seems slightly passé, its genial relativism replaced by a new kind of strident moralism. Fortunately, this essay does not overinvest in the enduring relevance of postmodernity but rather presents Christianity as possessing its own sort of critique of modern thought. At the same time, I do believe that the postmodern critique of master narratives, especially the master narrative of

1. Vatican Council II, *Gaudium et Spes* 22, in *Decrees of the Ecumenical Councils*, ed. Norman Tanner (Washington, DC: Georgetown University Press, 1990), 2:1081.

Enlightenment modernity, retains a certain usefulness, helping to free theology from subservience to a putatively more "neutral" secular discourse. It is probably this aspect of the essay that warranted its inclusion in the volume *Radical Orthodoxy*.[2] And while I do not typically apply the label "radically orthodox" to myself, this essay displays my intellectual debt to John Milbank and others in this movement. It likewise shows my debt to Hans Urs von Balthasar, even if I now find dubious some of his more adventurous claims about the inner life of God and feel somewhat more kindly toward the bête noire of Balthasarians, Karl Rahner.

The third essay, "Doctrine: Knowing and Doing," tries to map the relationship between ethical discourse and doctrinal discourse, suggesting that one cannot and ought not draw too sharp a line between the two. It might be thought of as an updated version of Thomas Aquinas's claim that theology is both a speculative and a practical discipline, and that theology does not become less practical the more speculative it becomes, nor more practical the less speculative it becomes. Here the past proves useful as a mirror for the present, as Augustine's debate with the Donatists is used to show how thinking and doing are so mutually implicating that we cannot really say where speculation leaves off and practice begins.

Essay four, "The Trinity and Politics," in some ways continues this topic, in this case looking at the ways in which the doctrine of the Trinity has been used in various political theologies. While still holding to the simultaneously speculative and practical nature of theology, this essay puts more emphasis on the irreducibility of the speculative. That is to say, the doctrine of the Trinity first of all tells us something true about God, and we should not fall into the trap of thinking that the doctrine of the Trinity is about anything other than God—something more

2. John Milbank, Catherine Pickstock, and Graham Ward, eds., *Radical Orthodoxy: A New Theology* (London: Routledge, 1999).

"practical," such as striking a balance among various sorts of moral knowledge or providing a blueprint for human social relations. Trinitarian doctrine orients us toward the truth of God, providing rules for ordering our speaking and thinking about how the Father saves us through the Son in the Spirit by drawing us into God's own eternal life. This belief, like all beliefs, has practical consequences, which are at work in the doctrine itself. In other words, the doctrine of the Trinity is politically relevant because it tells us of our highest good, and how that good has come to dwell among us in the missions of Christ and the Spirit, and not because it tells us some practical thing encoded within the doctrine.

The fifth essay, "Christendom and the Marian Path of the Church," presents another way in which doctrine and practice can intertwine by offering the perhaps odd pairing of secularization theory and Mariology. While the meaning of "secularization" is contested, it seems obvious that something has changed in the Western world, and that this something has to do with the place of Christianity in Western societies. The shorthand for this change is "the end of Christendom." How do we understand what this change means for the Church? I suggest that if one employs something like patristic "figural" reading to the life of Mary—so that Mary's story provides the key for reading the story of the Church—we can better understand where the Church is within the arc of her story, which might help us be more hopeful of the future and less nostalgic for the past glories that (we imagine) were Christendom.

The second section, "Politics," focuses on the question of modernity and freedom. Essay six, "Order, Freedom, and 'Kindness'" offers a genealogy of modern freedom and points to Julian of Norwich's account of "kindness" as offering an alternative to freedom understood as a contentless capacity for choice. Since writing this essay, I have become more wary of such genealogies, worried that they are simply "just-so stories" that narrate the past in such a way as to arrive at precisely the denunciation of features of the present that we have already decided on other grounds are worthy of denunciation.[3] While I don't think that my claims about how the ideas of William of Ockham are related to modern notions of liberty are entirely false, I am now more interested in Julian's notion of "kindness" as a positive proposal than as a path not taken in the genealogy of modernity. I suppose what I would say of genealogies is what Reinhold Niebuhr said of biblical symbols: they should be taken seriously, but not literally. That is, they can be interesting and illuminating, but they are to history what a Hollywood biopic is to a person's life. They are more concerned with telling a compelling story than with the messy complexities of history. One should use genealogies with caution.

The seventh and eighth essays, "Making Religion Safe for Democracy" and "The Politics of Disenchantment," together offer an account of how two seminal modern thinkers, William James and Max Weber, use the category of "mysticism" to secure politics as a space that is free from the baleful effects of religion while still allowing that religion remains an important part of human experience. My interest in early twentieth-century discussions of mysticism grew out of my work on Julian of Norwich, whose work gained a broad popular audience precisely at the time that thinkers like James and Weber were constructing "mysticism" as the essential core of religion, a core that was by its very nature inward and private and therefore politically harmless. My own "political" reading of Julian was developed precisely in opposition to such accounts of mysticism, though engagement with them remained implicit in my book on Julian.[4] These two essays make that engagement explicit and, in the case of Weber, show

---

3. I sketch a critique of the practice of genealogy in my review of Thomas Pfau's *Minding the Modern* in *Commonweal* 142, no. 3 (Spring 2015): 32–35.

4. Frederick Christian Bauerschmidt, *Julian of Norwich and the Mystical Body Politic of Christ* (South Bend, IN: The University of Notre Dame Press, 1999).

how his construal of mysticism is still at work in contemporary political theology.

Essay nine, "All Things Counter, Original, Spare, Strange," is something of an olive branch to modern liberalism. It represents a bit of rethinking on my part regarding how metaphysical vision might be related to political theory. If essay two seeks to blur the line between the speculative and the practical, this essay tries to draw it back in, at least as a dotted line, by recognizing a certain looseness of fit between metaphysics and politics. I do not endorse David Hume's view that "ought" can never be derived from "is," and so I still think John Rawls is wrong in suggesting that one's "political conception" can or should be independent of one's "comprehensive worldview," but I judge Rawls to be correct in thinking that the burdens of judgment are such that the political pie might get sliced in a variety of ways even by those who share the same comprehensive worldview. In other words, one should be wary of reading policy proposals off the Nicene Creed. Liberal democracy may not be the reign of God, but, as recent years have shown us, certain formalistic processes enshrined in liberal democracies, such as the peaceful transfer of political power, are also not nothing.

The third section, "Culture," collects essays that attempt to find theology in unexpected places. Essay ten, "Walking in the Pilgrim City," uses the work of Michel de Certeau to think about Christianity as a cultural practice that might find lodging in a variety of different places, but which, like Jesus himself, has no place to lay its head (Luke 9:58). This is the oldest essay in this collection (it was published the same year I earned my PhD) but seems to me to retain its value inasmuch as it attempts to work out some basic ideas that I have continued to presume in writing about theology and politics. In particular, it tries to explain why thinking of the Church as a "politics" did not involve Christians trying to lay their hands on the levers of power. The politics of the Church can be exercised even when the Church is stripped of all power; indeed, that might be when it can best be exercised. Moreover, it shows how different sorts of cultural production by Christians can embody a politics without ever talking about elections or policies.

The eleventh essay, "The Catholic Intellectual Tradition: Medieval Lessons," presents a high-level overview of what medieval intellectual culture can tell us about how we might think about the Catholic intellectual tradition today. It is a plea for Catholics to find a way to hold fast to that tradition without retreating into a defensive posture vis-à-vis secular culture. The Middle Ages is exemplary for the confidence with which it sought to "take every thought captive to obey Christ" (2 Cor. 10:5). But the medieval approach cannot simply be replicated today, not least because the cultural conditions that we call "Christendom" are irretrievable (if such a retrieval were even desirable). Nevertheless, there are medieval lessons to be learned, and this essay seeks to suggest what those might be.

Essay twelve, "Startling Figures and Wingless Chickens," looks at the fiction of Flannery O'Connor in order to reflect on how one goes about proclaiming Christ in a world that believes it has outgrown him. O'Connor embraced modernist literary techniques but put them to work in service to Catholic dogma—particularly the Church's teachings on the fallen human condition and the redemptive possibilities of grace. She did this, however, with such great artistry—never turning her stories into containers for dogmatic statements—that many of her readers had no idea that she was a deeply devout Christian. Yet her stories work a weird alchemy that unsettles modern complacencies and opens us up to the disruptive workings of grace in our world.

The thirteenth, fourteenth, and fifteenth essays all focus on Renaissance paintings. "The Lamb of God in the Age of Mechanical Reproduction" looks at Jan van Eyck's *Lamb of God* (often called *The Adoration of the Mystic Lamb* or *The Ghent Altarpiece*) in conversation with Walter Benjamin as a meditation on what becomes of art once it is severed from its roots in ritual. The essay on Masaccio's *Trinity* explores how both iconography and spatial construction can be used to encode a rich theology of the triune God. The final essay, a brief meditation on Hans Memling's *St. John Altarpiece*, explores how even amid human suffering and the drab routine of everyday life the longed-for peace of the heavenly city is always on the verge of being revealed.

***

Aside from some minor tweaks of wording (in order not to embarrass the good editors at Word on Fire Academic with my solecisms) and an attempt to regularize citations, I have left these essays more or less in the form that they originally appeared. They were written over the course of some twenty-five years, and it would be odd if I had changed none of my opinions in that time. We human beings are, after all, pilgrim wanderers, always moving forward. But I have not tried to update them to completely match my present views. *Quod scripsi, scripsi.* There are a few specific things I said that I would now not say. For example, I was wrong to say in the essay on William James that the young Schleiermacher was interested in religion in general but not in any specific religion, and in the essay on doctrine I now think that it is unfair to Lonergan to identify his sophisticated account of theological method with a slogan like "doctrine divides; service unites" and that his notion of "constitutive meaning" might not be all that different from what I call "theological ecology" in that essay. In terms of overall tone, I am struck by how some of the older essays display such a fierce desire to defeat intellectual opponents. This is a desire that has moderated in me over the years, and I now try to be a bit more charitable toward those with whom I disagree. I am also struck by how I have become more chastened in what I hope for from the Church. I still believe her to be the Body of Christ and the temple of the Spirit, and I likewise believe that the gates of hell will not prevail against her. But twenty years of scandals, some involving figures that I had held up as exemplary in their witness, have left me feeling that the holiness of the Church might be much more hidden and mysterious than I had previously reckoned.

Our views change, we hope, because we grow wiser and not simply because we grow weary. Any growth in wisdom that may have occurred in me cannot be ascribed to my own effort but to those who have patiently loved me even in my foolishness. To these friends, family, and colleagues I owe a debt of gratitude. I would mention in particular my late colleague Angela Russell Christman, a scholar of the early Church, a lover of art and nature, and a true friend. Our quarter century of conversation enriched my life beyond measure. She died too young and suffered much, but she was faithful to the end. In her living and her dying she taught me many things about being a Christian. I dedicate this book to her memory.

Theology: Orienting

1

Confessions of an Evangelical Catholic

Five Theses Related to Theological Anthropology

In the final session of the Second Vatican Council, the bishops assembled issued the Pastoral Constitution *Gaudium et Spes*, which, in the spirit of *aggiornamento,* sought to bring about a *rapprochement* between the Church and the modern world. During the debate on the Constitution—at that point called Schema 13—Gregory Baum wrote in *Commonweal* that it had found "a new method of speaking to Christians and non-Christians alike. . . . The authors of the schema, therefore, are convinced that if they announce the mystery of man and his solidarity here on earth as it is revealed in the Christian Gospel, the people of the world, called as they are by the Spirit, may well understand such language."[1] Not the authority of the Church, nor even the natural law that is accessible to human reason, but rather "man" was assuming his place as the common ground of future dialogue between the Church and the modern world. Seemingly, in *Gaudium et Spes*, the Church was endorsing the anthropological starting point in theology, which found its

* This essay was originally published as "Confessions of an Evangelical Catholic: Five Theses Related to Theological Anthropology." *Communio: International Catholic Review* 31, no. 1 (Spring 2004): 67–84.

1. Gregory Baum, "On the Modern World," *Commonweal* 83, no. 4 (October 29, 1965): 117–19, at 118.

genesis in the "method of immanence" of Maurice Blondel and its chief proponent in Karl Rahner.[2]

Meanwhile, at just about the same time, Michel Foucault was offering a rather different assessment of "man's" future, writing: "man is neither the oldest nor the most constant problem that has been posed for human knowledge. . . . As the archeology of our thought easily shows, man is an invention of recent date. And one perhaps nearing its end." If the conditions that produced "man" as the subject of the human sciences were to disappear, "then one can certainly wager that man would be erased, like a face drawn in the sand at the edge of the sea."[3] Rather than being the firm basis for dialogue, "man" was at best a contested territory and perhaps only an ephemeral image, even now in the process of being obliterated by vast, impersonal historical forces.

For some, among whom I must number myself, time seems to have proved Foucault to be the more prescient prophet. Contrary to the hopes that flourished in the immediate wake of the council, the ground constituted by "man" has proved to be more contested than common. Perhaps the simple fact that some readers wince to see "man" used as a generic term for human beings indicates the difficulty today of trying to encompass the human *qua* human without arousing ideological suspicion. The modern "man" of which *Gaudium et Spes* speaks appears today to be, in fact, quite parochial: not only male but also European, bourgeois, and university educated.[4] As the modern cosmopolitan utopia devolves into multicultural identity politics, we cast a jaundiced eye upon

---

2. See Maurice Blondel, "The Letter on Apologetics," in *The Letter on Apologetics and History and Dogma*, trans. Alexander Dru and Illtyd Trethowan (London: Harvill, 1964). For Rahner, see, for example, "Theology and Anthropology," in *Theological Investigations IX: Writings of 1965–1967 I*, trans. Graham Harrison (New York: Herder, 1972), 28–45.

3. Michel Foucault, *The Order of Things: An Archaeology of the Human Sciences*, trans. Alan Sheridan (New York: Vintage, 1973), 386–87.

4. For a critique of what one might call the "Eurocentrism" of Dietrich Bonhoeffer that, *mutatis mutandis*, could be applied to *Gaudium et Spes*, see Gustavo Gutiérrez, "The Limitations of Modern Theology: On a Letter of Dietrich Bonhoeffer," in *Essential Writings*, ed. James B. Nickoloff (Minneapolis, MN: Fortress, 1996), 35–42.

claims that beneath our differences of gender, race, language, and culture—"under the skin," as it were—we are fundamentally the same. In the post-Foucauldian, post-humanist climate in which at least academics like me live, the Fathers of the Second Vatican Council, in their appeal to "man" as common ground, seem to be a day late and a dollar short.

If the Church is to speak and listen to the world today, it seems that the basis will have to be something other than the "man" of *Gaudium et Spes*; perhaps it should be what it always has been: Christ and his Gospel. If we wish to speak to the world about human existence, we do it by speaking of the man Jesus. This claim does not originate from any desire to "go back" to what some see as the dark days of the nineteen-and-a-half centuries prior to the Second Vatican Council, nor it is a retreat from theological anthropology. Rather, this claim springs from a recognition that the world has moved on and that Foucault was right: claims about what it means to be human are not neutral scientific claims but rather are shaped by highly particular beliefs, practices, institutions, and narratives. The "man" of modernity was a recent invention that has now eroded beyond recognition because of the erosion of the conditions that produced him. So, if the Church is to speak about humanity, it must not appeal to that face now washed away but to the face of Christ.

The claim that we speak about humanity by speaking about Christ, and not vice versa, is found in *Gaudium et Spes* itself: "it is only in the mystery of the Word incarnate that light is shed on the mystery of humankind."[5] This quotation is, of course, the key text in John Paul II's interpretation of the Second Vatican Council, and I think that his choice of this text is an inspired one for the Church's mission of bringing Christ and his Gospel to the world. It defines, I would argue, a certain kind of "evangelical

---

5. Vatican Council II, *Gaudium et Spes* 22, in *Decrees of the Ecumenical Councils*, ed. Norman Tanner (Washington, DC: Georgetown University Press, 1990), 2:1081.

Catholicism." In the American context, this term has been used by William Portier and others to refer to Catholics for whom the key historical/sociological moment is not the Second Vatican Council but the dissolution of the immigrant Catholic subculture of the Church in America, the "de-ghettoizing" of the Church, often identified with the election of John F. Kennedy as president, by which Catholics were allowed fully to embrace their American identity.[6] This dissolution caused an identity crisis for some Catholics. No longer given an identity by life within Catholic enclaves, evangelical Catholics are those who consciously choose to identify as Catholic and who often see such a choice as involving some kind of disaffiliation from American culture, particularly from the standard political spectrum of left and right, in order to live the fullness of the Catholic faith. They are inclined to look to figures such as Dorothy Day, who made common cause on questions of labor and race with the radical left of her day but who could also write, "my nature is such that gratitude alone, gratitude for the faith, that most splendid gift, a gift not earned by me, a gratuitous gift, is enough to bind me in holy obedience to Holy Mother Church and her commands."[7] Evangelical Catholics, rather than embracing assimilation, see the teachings of the Church as defining a distinctive, Christocentric account of human flourishing that to some degree sets Catholics apart.

While I find intriguing and helpful Portier's suggestion that the emergence in America of this new "style" of Catholicism is connected to the dissolution of the American Catholic subculture, what I would like to focus on here is not the distinctively

6. William L. Portier, "Here Come the Evangelical Catholics," *Communio* 31, no. 1 (Spring 2004): 35–66. Portier mentions in his essay Catholics coming out of the charismatic movement, admirers of Dorothy Day, and Catholic students of Stanley Hauerwas (of which I am one). Robert Barron has identified his own approach to Catholicism with this term; see "The Evangelical Path of Word on Fire," March 2, 2021, https://www.wordonfire.org. I would note that the term "evangelical catholic" is also used by some Protestants, particularly Lutherans, who wish to reclaim the sacramental and liturgical heritage of the churches of the Reformation.

7. Dorothy Day, *By Little and By Little: The Selected Writings of Dorothy Day*, ed. Robert Ellsberg (New York: Knopf, 1983), 172–73.

American and post-subculture qualities of evangelical Catholicism but rather how evangelical Catholicism is part of a larger theological tradition: a tradition extended both in time (beyond our present moment) and space (beyond the national and cultural boundaries of the United States). What is *theologically* distinctive about the evangelical style of Catholicism is a particular theological anthropology: one that is transformed by Christology, such that it is the humanity of Christ that is the concrete norm for all discussions of human nature. Therefore, in what follows I would like to offer five theses that I think characterize evangelical Catholicism theologically. I realize that not every Catholic who fits within Portier's more sociological definition of "evangelical Catholicism" will agree with all, or even any, of these theses. So, I offer them as the *confessio* of a self-identified evangelical Catholic, trying to explain what I mean by them and how they form a persistent thread in the Catholic tradition.

1) Rejecting a two-tiered theology of nature and grace and the ethic that goes with it does not mean that grace is everywhere in the same way.

The general trend of Catholic theology in the twentieth century was to seek a closer integration of nature and grace, rejecting the "dualist" account in which nature is a self-enclosed structure upon which grace builds a kind of superstructure and proposing instead that grace is the fulfillment of nature's intrinsic dynamism.[8] Along with this rejection goes a rejection of the similarly two-tiered approach to the Christian life, in which the laity are expected to fulfill the precepts of the natural law as a kind of foundation to which sacramental grace is superadded, while the lives of vowed religious are called to a higher standard embodied

8. For a brief, general account of the "dualist" approach and the more integrated approach that has replaced it, see Paul McPartlan, *Sacrament of Salvation: An Introduction to Eucharistic Ecclesiology* (Edinburgh: T&T Clark, 2000), 47–53.

in the evangelical counsels of poverty, chastity, and obedience. This theological shift is registered most clearly at the Second Vatican Council in the strong affirmation of a "universal call to holiness" for all Christians by virtue of their baptism.[9]

However, having said this one has not said a whole lot, because the vast majority of theologians in the second half of the twentieth century would say that they reject the dualist approach, that they believe that grace and nature are integrally related, and that they believe that holiness is not the special prerogative of the vowed religious. What matters is *how* one integrates nature and grace. Recognizing that I am risking parody via oversimplification, I would say that one can discern two different approaches to this integration while recognizing that any single person probably combines elements of both.

In one approach, the emphasis falls upon the always already graced character of the world. In such a view, the anthropological starting point for theology seems natural: when we do theology, we are articulating common human experience in a Christian way. This experience is already a graced experience, even if its graced character is as yet unthematized in Christian categories. Such things as sacraments or preaching are "causes" of grace principally in the way that they thematize, and thereby make available for conscious appropriation, the grace that is already present. As Karl Rahner put it, "Preaching is the awakening and making explicit what is already there in the depths of man, not by nature but by grace."[10] Some theologians, following in Rahner's wake (though perhaps in a way that he himself would not have endorsed), have drawn the conclusion that, as Elizabeth Dreyer puts it, "grace flows primarily from the world to the church and not the other way around." In this view, the world is the "primordial

---

9. See Vatican Council II, *Lumen Gentium* 5, in *Decrees of the Ecumenical Councils*, ed. Norman Tanner (Washington: Georgetown University Press, 1990), 2:880–84.

10. Karl Rahner, *Nature and Grace: Dilemmas in the Modern Church*, trans. Dinah Wharton (New York: Sheed & Ward, 1964), 134.

arena" in which we experience God's grace and the purpose of the Church and its sacraments is to "name, symbolize and celebrate the grace we encounter in the world."[11]

But this is not the only way in which grace and nature might be integrated. Rather than emphasizing the always already graced character of human existence, one might emphasize what the scholastics called the *potentia obedientialis* of human nature, understood not simply as human nature's passive "non-repugnance" toward grace but as a true *appetitus naturalis* for the vision of God, which is at the same time constitutive of human nature *and* something elicited by grace. Karl Rahner can be invoked in support of this view as well: "We can only fully understand man in his 'undefinable' essence if we see him as *potentia obedienialis* for the divine life; this is his *nature*. His nature is such that its *absolute* fulfillment comes through grace, and so nature *of itself* must reckon with the *meaningful* possibility of remaining without absolute fulfillment."[12] In this approach, no less than the first, there is no "pure nature" untouched by grace, yet here the touch of grace manifests itself in an elicited desire. In the concrete, historical order of things, human nature is characterized not so much by its possession of grace as by its restless yearning for fulfillment—a fulfillment that is in no way guaranteed but yet is trusted in through faith. In this approach, such activities as sacraments and preaching are efficient causes of grace. Yet, the grace they cause is encountered by the restless human spirit neither as something alien to it nor as something already possessed unthematically by it but as the arrival of the bridegroom whose presence has been anxiously awaited.

Regarding how these two different integrations of nature

11. Interview by Art Winter with Elizabeth Dreyer, "Spirituality more easily found in the world than in churches," *National Catholic Reporter* 33 no. 7 (December 13, 1996): 9–10.

12. Rahner, *Nature and Grace*, 140–41. As Hans Urs von Balthasar noted, "there are many Karl Rahners!" (*The Moment of Christian Witness*, 3rd ed., trans. Richard Beckley [San Francisco: Ignatius, 1994], 148).

and grace play out in one's understanding of the universal call to holiness, we might say that the first would take the form of an affirmation of the "secular" or "worldly" realms, while the second would take the form of a call to all Christians to let every sphere of their lives be shaped by narratives and practices of the Christian faith. In the first approach, the worldly occupations and activities of lay Christians are affirmed as just as much a path to holiness as the consecrated life. One can be a saint in a corporate boardroom or on a picket line, just as much as in a monastery. Indeed, some might argue that, in the modern world, holiness is more easily achieved *in* the world than apart from it.[13] The Church is less a school for holiness as it is the place in which the grace that has been bestowed in our worldly callings is named and celebrated. In the second approach, Christians are not affirmed in their worldly vocations but are called to discern what is godly in them and to transform or abandon what is not godly. Indeed, this second approach begins with a presumption that our worldly vocations are in some sort of fundamental need of transformation by grace so that they might more closely approximate—or even embody, although in a distinctively "lay" manner—the evangelical counsels.[14] Is sitting on the board of directors of a multinational corporation compatible with the counsel of poverty? Is participation in the entertainment industry compatible with chastity? Is climbing the corporate ladder compatible with obedience? The answer to any of these questions might well be "yes," but only if one lets the way in which one does these things be transformed by the pattern that we find in Christ and the saints.

In terms of Portier's thesis, what advocates of the first approach fail to realize is that what they take to be the workings of

13. See, for example, the correspondence between Thomas Merton and Rosemary Radford Ruether in *At Home in the World: The Letters of Thomas Merton & Rosemary Radford Ruether*, ed. Mary Tardiff (New York: Orbis, 1995).

14. One might say that the presumptions of this second approach are not unlike those found in Hippolytus and other early Christian writers regarding the "forbidden professions." See *Apostolic Tradition*, 16.9–25.

grace in the secular realm are often simply echoes of the rapidly dissipating Catholic subculture. Prior to the 1960s, Catholics in America were, in many cases, so formed by the Catholic culture in which they lived that they thought certain attitudes, dispositions, and values were simply part of human nature rather than something cultivated by teaching, preaching, and the grace of the sacraments. This kind of optimism about the concurrence of nature and grace persists in many quarters, though if Portier is correct the optimism wanes along with the subculture that engendered it. The Catholics whom he describes as "evangelical," on the other hand, evince a much keener awareness that holiness must be consciously cultivated and that the sacramental and other practices of the Church are the chief means by which the field of sanctity is sown.

2) An affirmation of the fundamental goodness of human nature should always be accompanied by a keen awareness of the paradoxical constitution of that nature and, consequently, of the limitations of natural reason and natural law.

The view of nature as *appetitus naturalis* for the beatific vision rather than always already graced lends itself to a chastened view of the capacities of that nature. Though one could hardly reject all notions of natural law and natural reason and still claim to stand within the Catholic tradition, an evangelical Catholic theology recognizes that, as Portier puts it, "the way forward is not to jettison natural law but to re-theologize it."[15] Consequently, such a theology emphasizes our need for divine revelation and the assistance of grace in order to know and do the good that accords with human fulfillment.

In part, this is simply a matter of taking seriously the effects of sin on our capacity to know and do the good. As Thomas

15. Portier, "Evangelical Catholics," 65.

Aquinas says, while human beings in the state of integrity, prior to the fall, were capable of doing "the good in proportion to nature," in the state of corrupted and fallen nature "human beings fall short of what is according to human nature, so that they are unable to fulfill it by their own natural powers." Thus, in our fallen state we can do some good actions—i.e., a carpenter does not need the intercession of St. Joseph to build a house that does not collapse—but we are, in Thomas's example, like "a sick person [who] can make some movements by himself, yet cannot move fully, like the movements of a healthy person, unless cured by the help of medicine."[16]

But this limitation of the human capacity to know and act is not simply a result of sin. It is constitutive of our nature as beings who are created and finite while at the same time called to share in the vision of God. Thus, Thomas notes that, both in the state of integrity and in the state of corruption, "human nature needs the help of God as first mover, to do or wish any good whatsoever." And beyond this general need for divine providence, human beings also need the special assistance of sanctifying grace in order "to do and wish supernatural good."[17]

Without, therefore, rejecting the Catholic affirmation of the fundamental goodness of human nature, we ought to foster, like Thomas, what might be called an "Augustinian sensibility" with regard to the human capacity for thought and action. While human reason can discern God's existence from creation, it seems more inclined to be led astray into idolatry; while human reason can discern the moral law, we more often use our intellects to search out self-justifications. In other words, without grace, human nature in the concrete order in which we find it is inadequate for leading a truly human life, much less leading the life by which we become partakers of the divine nature. One might

16. *Summa theologiae* 1-2.109.2.
17. *Summa theologiae* 1-2.109.2.

say that our nature reveals God to us not primarily through those things that reason can discern, but through the restlessness of a reason that is perpetually unsatisfied by what it knows and a will that is perpetually unsatisfied by what it desires.

Again speaking in terms of Portier's claims, an evangelical Catholicism would grant in principle the ability of unaided human reason to have some limited knowledge of God and the good but would emphasize that even in principle this knowledge is quite limited—as Thomas Aquinas says, "only for a few, and after a long time, and mixed in with many errors."[18] And in actual practice, human sin means that reason misses the mark more often than not. Thus we ought to be dubious about attempts at "public theology," suspecting that this is in fact nothing but a theology stripped of all substantive Christian convictions.[19] Even when speaking in terms of natural reason and natural law, an evangelical Catholicism will want a robustly theological version of these, seeing natural theology and law not as an apologetic tool, nor as a neutral place of dialogue, but as a way for Christians themselves to understand how it is that human beings without the aid of revelation can come to some sort of knowledge of God and the good. It is a theological claim about the goodness of God, not an instrument for influencing public policy.

Even if one shifts from natural theology and law to the anthropological approach favored since *Gaudium et Spes*, the same concerns and emphases apply. Theological anthropology has its proper place, but that place is not as the basis for dialogue if for no other reason than the thoroughly paradoxical character of human nature, which makes it an unstable and contested foundation.[20]

18. *Summa theologiae* 1.1.1.

19. See Michael J. Baxter, "'Blowing the Dynamite of the Church': Catholic Radicalism from a Catholic Radicalist Perspective," in *The Church as Counterculture*, ed. Michael L. Budde and Robert W. Brimlow (Albany, NY: SUNY, 2000), 195–212.

20. I do not mean to imply here simply that theological anthropology is an inadequate foundation for dialogue with the world, but rather that the very idea of needing some sort of foundation for dialogue at all is highly questionable. We speak by speaking, not by producing theories about how speech is possible.

We do not have a firm grasp on what it means to be human, since, as Pascal wrote, the human being is "equally incapable of seeing the nothingness from where he came, and the infinite in which he is covered."[21] We might go so far as to grant to Foucault his claims about the contingency of "man" and even to see the truth in the idea, again in the words of Pascal, "that nature is itself only a first custom, just as custom is a second nature."[22] Yet, against Foucault and nihilism in general, we must maintain the claim that the contingent events of history that produce what we take to be human nature are not simply random but have a providential pattern, discernable through the eyes of faith. So, one can affirm that there is something like "human nature"—indeed, the doctrine of the Incarnation requires it—without making it a category that is frozen in time or immediately accessible to our comprehension.

3) The practice of Jesus and the saints is the norm for Christian life and thought.

In order to discern this providential pattern that is human nature we must have recourse to Christ and his saints as the pattern of true humanity. This is simply another way of saying what I have already quoted from *Gaudium et Spes* 22: "it is only in the mystery of the Word incarnate that light is shed on the mystery of humankind." This is hardly a new insight; once again in the words of Pascal:

> Not only is it through Jesus Christ alone that we know God but it is only through Jesus Christ that we know ourselves. We know life and death only through Jesus Christ. Without Jesus

21. Blaise Pascal, *Pensées*, Sellier ed., §230, in *Pensées and Other Writings*, trans. Honor Levi, ed. Anthony Levi (Oxford: Oxford University Press, 1995), 67.
22. *Pensées*, §159 (39).

Christ we do not know what our life, nor our death, nor God, nor ourselves really are.[23]

Such a view runs against the grain both of the older dualist account of nature and grace as well as those attempts at integrating nature and grace that stress the always already graced character of human existence. As different as these two are, they agree on this: human nature has a kind of self-transparency such that it interprets itself, whether this is because it is purely natural and can be grasped by reason apart from the illumination of grace, or because our way of knowing is already, albeit unthematically, illuminated with grace. But if human nature is neither purely natural nor always already illuminated by grace but paradoxically characterized by an *appetitus naturalis* for the beatific vision that it can in no way satisfy on its own, then it is a mystery that awaits illumination. Christ, the light of the world, is that illumination.

This means that the truly human life is one that is lived in imitation of the concrete and particular pattern manifested in the life, death, and resurrection of Christ. As Thomas Aquinas said, "Christ's action is our instruction."[24] This is true not simply for some elite group of spiritual proficients—the vowed religious—but for all the baptized. The universal call to holiness is the call of Christ to follow him. When one is accepted into the order of catechumens in preparation for Baptism, she is signed with the cross on the forehead, with the words, "learn to know and follow him."[25] This bearing of the cross is how Christians live the Law of Christ, which takes precedence over any other law and all purely human notions of prudence.

Of course, if grace indeed "perfects and does not destroy nature,"[26] then there ought to be some continuity between the

23. *Pensées*, §36 (10).
24. *Summa theologiae* 3.40.1 ad 3.
25. *Rite of Christian Initiation of Adults* 55.
26. *Summa theologiae* 1.1.8 ad 2.

Law of Christ and the natural law; the path of Christ ought to follow in some sense the bent of our nature. The emphasis, however, ought perhaps to fall on the phrase "*in some sense.*" There is truth in Irenaeus's oft-quoted phrase, "the glory of God is the living man": God wills that our natures be fulfilled through grace. But the second half of what Irenaeus wrote is somewhat less-oft-quoted: "and the life of man is the vision of God."[27] And this vision, Irenaeus makes clear, is given to us in Christ the Word, the revealer of the Father. So, while the path of Christ does follow the bent of our nature, we must reckon with the paradoxical and fragmented character of that nature. We ought not assume that what first occurs to us when we think of human flourishing *is* in fact true human flourishing.

Though it is absolutely true that Christ came so that his followers might have life in abundance (John 10:10), the road to Calvary is not likely to fit easily into prevailing cultural notions of abundant life. Paul, therefore, calls upon Christians to "not be conformed to this world, but be transformed by the renewing of your minds" (Rom. 12:2), and this renewing takes the form of imitating the pattern of self-sacrificing love "that was in Christ Jesus" (Phil. 2:5). This pattern is the heart of Scripture as *norma normans non normata* by which we interpret both human wisdom and ecclesial doctrine. This is not, however, simply a matter of asking, "What would Jesus do?" In claiming the normativity of Jesus for Christian life and thought, I am not proposing that we can naively read doctrinal and moral instruction directly out of the New Testament. While I am more inclined than some theologians to think that the doctrine of the Trinity is at its heart a "scriptural" doctrine,[28] we must recognize that ecclesial teaching

27. Irenaeus, *Against Heresies* 4.20.7, trans. Robert M. Grant, in Robert M. Grant, *Irenaeus of Lyons* (London: Routledge, 1997), 153.

28. That is, I think it is a faithful articulation of the identity, as rendered in Scripture, of Jesus, the one he calls Father, and their Spirit. For a defense of this view, see David S. Yeago, "The New Testament and the Nicene Dogma: A Contribution to the Recovery of Theological

on such matters develops over time. Likewise, we must realize that we face moral questions today that were undreamt of by the human authors of Scripture. However, while recognizing the reality of development, the Church must never take its eyes off Christ or replace his normative role with a philosophical or scientific theory.

This is why we should stress the crucial role of the saints as what we might call "canonical extensions" of the pattern of thought and action we see in Jesus. Of course, any Catholic theology must assign some role for tradition as the medium through which we understand Jesus Christ. But within tradition, the saints should have preeminence because they offer us an image in motion of the ongoing work of the Spirit. Philosophical and scientific discourses have a place in the Church, but they must not displace the discourse that is the saints, for, unlike various philosophies and sciences, the saints engage us in an ongoing process that is at the same time *aggiornamento*, because they like us live in the last days that are the time of the Church, and *ressourcement*, because their holiness consists entirely in pointing us toward Jesus Christ.

4) The Church must think through the consequences of its identity as the pilgrim people of God.

If human nature is something historically *produced* and not something simply "there," then the Church serves the world precisely by producing a particular kind of humanity—one that takes Christ's humanity as its pattern. Christians believe that this humanity is the true humanity to which we are called, but this is a matter of faith, not knowledge (is there any reason to think that the true humanity of Christ is any more knowable by reason than

Exegesis," in *The Theological Interpretation of Scripture*, ed. Stephen E. Fowl (Oxford: Blackwell, 1997), 87–100.

his true divinity?). To be a Christian is to wager that the truth of the humanity of Christ will exert a force of attraction upon human beings if it is convincingly presented by being embodied in the preaching, sacraments, and saints of the Church and in the formation of the *plebs sancta Dei*—the common holy people of God. This task of the Church has become perhaps more apparent today.[29]

Here we engage most explicitly with Portier's central thesis: evangelical Catholicism is a response to the changed social situation of the Church. As he puts it, "In a completely voluntary situation where the only boundaries between Catholics and other Americans are the ones we make, the Church needs to be more clearly the Church." In other words, the Church is "in diaspora" and must live accordingly. And what it means to "live accordingly" is not to take up a stance of anonymous servility toward the world but rather to serve the world boldly by living Catholic Christianity in all its fullness. As Gerhard Lohfink memorably put it, "*Precisely because the church does not exist for itself, but completely and exclusively for the world, it is necessary that the church not become world, that it retain its own countenance.*"[30]

Portier's thesis might be extended beyond the borders of contemporary Catholicism in America. First, the Church has *always* lived in diaspora, whether it has recognized this or not. It has always been the case that "here we have no lasting city, but we are looking for the city that is to come" (Heb. 13:14). Like its Lord, the Church has no place to lay its head as it travels through history. The author of the *Epistle to Diognetus* knew it when he said of Christians that "they dwell in their own fatherlands, but as if sojourners in them; they share all things as citizens, and suffer

29. For an argument, plus more theses, about how we should think about formation and initiation today, see Frederick Christian Bauerschmidt, "Baptism in the Diaspora," in *On Baptism*, ed. Gerald W. Schlabach (Kitchener, ON: Pandora, 2004), 16–61.

30. Gerhard Lohfink, *Jesus and Community: The Social Dimension of Christian Faith*, trans. John P. Galvin (Philadelphia: Fortress, 1984), 146, emphasis in the original.

all things as strangers. Every foreign country is their fatherland and every fatherland is a foreign country."[31] Origen knew it when he wrote to the pagan Celsus, "we know of the existence in each city of another sort of country, created by the Logos of God."[32] Augustine knew it when he spoke of Christians as *"redempta familia domini Christi et peregrina ciuitas regis Christi* [the redeemed household servants of the Lord Christ and the pilgrim city of Christ the King]."[33] Thomas Aquinas knew it when he spoke of us as having the knowledge of "wayfarers" so long as we are in this life.[34] The Fathers of the Second Vatican Council knew it when they spoke of the Christians as "making our pilgrimage on earth . . . in tribulation and persecution."[35]

But if the pilgrim nature of the Church has been remembered in principle throughout its history, it has in practice been more often forgotten. Like Peter at the mount of Transfiguration, the Church has too often wanted to pitch camp on the site of glory rather than journey with Christ to Jerusalem and the cross. However, the Church's "homelessness" in the world has become increasingly difficult to ignore since the beginning of the nineteenth century. As the worldly power and prestige of the Church has declined, the contours of the line between the Church and the world have reappeared with glaring obviousness. Despite this obviousness, some have chosen to ignore this shift, whether by pretending that any day now confessional states will be reestablished or by stressing the worldly vocation of Christians as "men for others," fully immersed in the business of the world. Where the changed status of the Church has been recognized,

31. *Epistle to Diognetus* 5, in *The Apostolic Fathers*, trans. Kirsopp Lake (Cambridge, MA: Harvard University Press, 1950), 2:361.

32. Origen, *Contra Celsum* 8.75, trans. Henry Chadwick (Cambridge: Cambridge University Press, 1965), 510.

33. *De civitate Dei* 1.35.

34. See, e.g., *Summa theologiae* 2-2.8.7.

35. *Lumen Gentium* 7, in *Decrees of the Ecumenical Councils*, 2:853. The description of the Church as a "pilgrim" pervades the documents of Vatican II. See *Dei Verbum* 7; *Lumen Gentium* 48; *Dignitatis Humanae* 12; *Ad Gentes* 2.

the response has sometimes been a defensive retrenchment and a nostalgia for past glories. More often, however, I believe the response of the Church has been a positive desire of Catholics to rediscover our distinctive identity as a community called by God to be light for the world. We are discovering ourselves to be what we have always been: God's pilgrim people who live in the midst of the world for the sake of the world.

If the diaspora of the Church is not confined to our contemporary situation, neither is it confined to America. The Church in Europe, no less than the Church in North America, finds itself increasingly in a dispersed minority situation. Though the Church in Europe was not, in most places, a subculture but rather an integral part of the dominant culture, the current situation is essentially the same: Catholics no longer dwell in a cultural milieu that transmits and reinforces Catholic beliefs and practices. But because the patterns of church-state relations in Europe differ from those in the United States so that the Church and its institutions are often financially supported by the state, the Church in Europe has perhaps, on some levels at least, been slower to recognize this fact. There persists among some European Catholics a tendency to see the Church still as a branch of the state, like the Post Office, providing services like Baptism, First Holy Communion, Marriage, and Burial for those who desire them. At the same time, the cultural legacy of the aggressive secularism of the French Revolution has saved many European Catholics from the illusion that there is some natural fit between Catholicism and the "civil religion" of the state, an illusion to which many Catholics in the United States fall prey.

There is much that European and North American Catholics can learn from each other about how to live in the diaspora. Americans have the benefit of long experience of having had to run their churches without assistance from the state; they are not likely to confuse the Church with the Post Office. But they might confuse it with the UPS: a private enterprise that they opt into as individuals. European Catholicism, unlike Catholicism in the United States, has tended to respond to its diaspora with a proliferation of new ecclesial movements. Movements such as the Community of Sant'Egidio or Communion and Liberation reflect a more communal and perhaps less voluntarist understanding of being Catholic, from which Catholics in North America can learn.

5) The Christian understanding of history is apocalyptic rather than progressive.

In his encyclical *Evangelium Vitae*, John Paul II wrote that "*life is always at the center of a great struggle* between good and evil, between light and darkness."[36] This sort of apocalyptic language makes some uncomfortable, striking them as "Manichean" in its stark opposition of good and evil, light and darkness. But the loss of the apocalyptic perspective brings with it the loss of a proper understanding of human history and the Church's place within it.

First, the apocalyptic perspective does not mistakenly see humanity's pilgrimage through history as fundamentally one of "progress." We can, of course, speak of progress in a certain sense: human knowledge increases, and with technological advances, things become possible that were not possible before. And one should not slight such things. But the apocalyptic perspective asks whether an increase of knowledge is the same as an increase in wisdom. Do technological advances necessarily correlate with human flourishing? Most importantly, do these sorts of progress hasten the consummation of history? What we have here is something of a replay of the debate in the 1950s and '60s between the "incarnational" and the "eschatological" approaches to history,

36. Pope John Paul II, *The Gospel of Life* [*Evangelium Vitae*] (New York: Random House, 1995), 104, emphasis in the original.

debates that were important in the drafting of Schema 13.[37] Put no doubt oversimply, the question is whether the fulfillment of history develops gradually from within history via human activity or whether history's fulfillment comes crashing in upon it with the return of Christ in glory. The latter view does not deny that Christians must act to alleviate suffering by attending to both the sources and the effects of injustices, yet it maintains, as Louis Bouyer put it, "that all this work will, so far as we can judge from the hints of divine revelation, never be successful in the sense of establishing any lasting and universal Christian state of things."[38]

Second, the apocalyptic perspective reminds us that we are in the midst of a struggle between cosmic forces of good and evil. It is crucial, however, that such a claim be accompanied by a nonprogressive view of history, for we ought not to think that the evils of today are any greater or less that the evils of the past. John Paul's statement that life is *always* at the center of a struggle between good and evil serves as a salutary warning against those who would claim that our historical moment presents a unique opportunity and that we must act now to implement some scheme that would bring about a comprehensive elimination of evil. Evil is something that must be endured until it consumes itself. But at the same time, John Paul's emphasis on *struggle* indicates that the endurance of evil is not the same as passive acceptance. Indeed, the Letter to the Ephesians is at pains to remind us that it is *because* "our struggle is not against enemies of blood and flesh, but against the rulers, against the authorities, against the cosmic powers of this present darkness" that our proper means of combat is "to take up the whole armor of God," which consists

37. "The Incarnationalists, stressing the Person of Christ and His Mission and His Church, include among their ranks de Lubac, Teilhard de Chardin, and Père Paul Henry, SJ. The eschatologists, stressing the Parousia, the last days of Scripture in which the human race is now present, fix their gaze upon Christ who is to come. These latter number Père Feret, Louis Bouyer and, preeminently, Jean Danielou" (James M. Connolly, *The Voices of France: A Survey of Contemporary Theology in France* [New York: Macmillan, 1961], 149).

38. Louis Bouyer, *Liturgical Piety* (Notre Dame, IN: University of Notre Dame Press, 1955), 260.

not in swords or guns or five-year plans but in truth and right-eousness and whatever will make us ready "to proclaim the gospel of peace" (Eph. 6:12–15). As the book of Revelation makes clear, Christians are not called to success but to perseverance, and faithful Christian endurance in the time-between-times *is* resistance to evil.

No doubt these theses will one day seem as dated as the optimistic predictions about the fruit issuing from the Church's embrace of the modern world that were penned in the years following the Second Vatican Council. Portier points out well that evangelical Catholicism is a response to a particular set of historical circumstances and, as Foucault would no doubt wish to remind us, if the forces that produced evangelical Catholicism were to disappear, then it too would be erased, like a face drawn in the sand at the edge of the sea. However, inasmuch as it is an attempt to be faithful to the Gospel of Christ by fostering faith, hope, and love—that is, inasmuch as it is *truly* evangelical—then I believe that it has enduring value.

Catholics emerging from their ecclesiastical subculture rightly felt liberated from narrow intellectual, cultural, and social confines. But among some Catholics, particularly those who have known nothing but life outside the subculture, it is beginning to appear that we have simply exchanged one set of intellectual, cultural, and social confines for another—the confines of the postindustrial bourgeoisie. Some of us wonder if the real choice is not whether we should choose confinement or liberation, as if human life were not always lived under some form of discipline, but rather which form of discipleship will lead to true freedom, which form of life is truly a human one.

2

Aesthetics

The Theological Sublime

VERSIONS OF POSTMODERNITY

Readings of the postmodern are legion, and these legions seem locked in perpetual combat.[1] In this essay I will attempt to distinguish two among the many versions of the closure of modernity—postmodernity as the end of "metanarratives" and postmodernity as the end of "suspicion"—and sketch a theological version of the latter as a genuine path forward. Postmodernity is too easily identified with nihilistic accounts of truth, for such an association presumes an identification of modernity with truth and reason. In this essay I will gesture toward a theological account of truth—an account that belongs neither to modernity nor premodernity nor postmodernity—that can begin to acquire new force as the end of the reign of modern "clear and distinct ideas" comes into view. In this sense, postmodernity can be a propitious moment for theology. Still, postmodernity in no way constitutes the condition for the possibility of theology; the

---

* This essay was originally published as "Aesthetics: The Theological Sublime." In *Radical Orthodoxy: A New Theology*, ed. John Milbank, Catherine Pickstock, and Graham Ward (London: Routledge, 1999), 201–19.

1. For a partial catalogue of instances of the use of the term "postmodern" (or "post-modern") dating back to 1934, see Margaret A. Rose, *The Post-modern and the Post-industrial: A Critical Analysis* (Cambridge: Cambridge University Press, 1991), 171–75. For a genealogy and analysis of the postmodern in relation to theology (including the distinction between "postmodernity" and "postmodernism"), see Graham Ward, "Introduction, or, A Guide to Theological Thinking in Cyberspace," in *The Postmodern God: A Theological Reader*, ed. Graham Ward (Oxford: Blackwell, 1997).

possibility of speech about God can be founded on nothing less than God's own speaking.

In perhaps its most common usage, associated with Jean-François Lyotard's *The Postmodern Condition*, the "postmodern" marks the end of the master narratives of modernity, indeed, the end of *all* grand narratives. This, at its extreme, is the idea of postmodernity as the death of meaning and the triumph of wild and unregulated interpretation. In this reading postmodernity is a time in which strong poets assert their will to power without regard to such eternal values as truth, goodness, unity, or beauty, in which the deconstruction of signs negates all stable meanings from within, in which modernity's universal narrative of human reason is shattered into micro-narratives of race, class, and gender through which the previously suppressed Other is presented to us with a new force. A corollary of all this is the end of the modern subject, conceived as gnoseologically stable and morally self-possessed.[2] Lyotard writes: "A *self* does not amount to much, but no self is an island; each exists in a fabric of relations that is now more complex and mobile than ever before."[3] The self becomes a pastiche of fragments collected around nothing more than the remote control that connects it to the cable television with its 57 channels (and nothin' on).

But before we get too excited or worried, I would note that this seemingly apocalyptic version of postmodernity is in fact in substantial continuity with the modernity that preceded it. The modern turn to the subject has been intensified as the subject turns on itself so that what we have in this purported death of

2. According to Lyotard, the narrative form of knowledge is the most basic form, and even science has recourse to narrative for its legitimation. See *The Postmodern Condition: A Report on Knowledge*, trans. Geoff Bennington and Brian Massumi (Minneapolis, MN: University of Minnesota Press, 1984), 29. The modern master narratives by which knowledge was legitimated—which he describes as the speculative (Hegel) and the emancipatory (Kant, Marx)—have been fragmented into a multitude of language games that cannot be "unified or totalized in any metadiscourse" (36). What we are left with is *local* knowledge, fragmentary knowledge, knowledge of how to go on in this or that particular instance, but not of how to go on "in principle."

3. Lyotard, *Postmodern Condition*, 15.

grand narratives is actually the triumph of the modern narrative of emancipation. Traditionally for Christians, submission to the master narrative of Scripture, as Augustine knew so well, meant the surrender of our *free* will (our capacity to choose) so as to possess a *freed* will (our capacity to do the good). Part of the modern project—and perhaps its *defining* feature—has been the valorization of the contentless freedom of the will, the sheer capacity of human self-assertion against any external imposition.[4] Postmodernity, as the end of master narratives (which seem always to be construed as heteronomous), then simply becomes the intensification of modernity's quest for autonomy—freedom without terminus or telos. For the ultimate in contentless freedom is the negation of any stable, narratively given identity. This may be the apocalypse, or it may be more of the same.

In a later essay entitled "Answering the Question: What is Postmodernism?" Lyotard gives us a second, somewhat different account of the postmodern. In this account, postmodernity is marked by a particular mode of figuring the sublime. Following Kant, Lyotard understands the aesthetics of the sublime to be grounded in "the incommensurability of reality to concept" that occurs when "the imagination fails to present an object which might, if only in principle, come to match the concept."[5] In other words, the sentiment of the sublime arises from the gap between our ability to conceive of, for example, totality and our inability to imagine (to present ourselves or others with an image of) that totality. Thus, the imagination presents to itself not the unpresentable idea but the very unpresentability of the idea. Kant notes that this "can be nothing but a mere negative presentation, but which yet expands the soul."[6] Or, as Gilles Deleuze puts it,

4. See Hans Blumenburg, *The Legitimacy of the Modern Age*, trans. Robert M. Wallace (Cambridge, MA: MIT Press, 1983). Reading human self-assertion as the defining trait of modernity suggests how thinkers as different as Descartes and Nietzsche can both properly be called "modern."

5. Lyotard, *Postmodern Condition*, 78–79.

6. Kant, *Critique of Judgement* §29, trans. J.H. Bernard (New York: Hafner, 1951), 115.

"The feeling of the sublime is experienced when faced with the formless or the deformed (immensity or power). It is as if the imagination were confronted with its own limit, forced to strain to its utmost, experiencing a violence which stretches it to the extremity of its power."[7]

According to Lyotard, the modern aesthetic of the sublime is a "nostalgic" one, in which a unified form is used to present the missing content (Proust is his example). The postmodern aesthetic, on the other hand, is one that "denies itself the solace of good forms" and presents the unpresentable in the deformation of the signifier itself (Joyce is his example).[8] In other words, immensity and power are registered not simply as that which is absent from representation but as the very twisting and bending of beautiful forms into what are, by previous standards, hideous and grotesque forms. One might say that the modern and the postmodern mark two distinct modes of negation of form. And in postmodernity, this deformation of forms has no terminus but is an ongoing process driven by the ceaseless and insatiable desire to convey a sense of the unpresentable.

What is of particular interest for my purposes is Lyotard's way of distinguishing the modern from the postmodern and how this relates to what is perhaps the preeminent modern virtue: suspicion. Lyotard notes that modernity carried with it the destruction of belief and the discovery of the "lack of reality" of all representations of reality.[9] The Kantian problematic of the sublime is indicative not only of a suspicion of all received representations (and thus in continuity with Kant's reading of enlightenment) but also of a profound pessimism about our ability to produce *any* adequate image or account. Reality is the unpresentable, which can be put forth only as the "missing contents" of the form from

---

7. Gilles Deleuze, *Kant's Critical Philosophy*, trans. Hugh Tomlinson and Barbara Habberjam (Minneapolis, MN: University of Minnesota Press, 1993), 50.

8. See Lyotard, *Postmodern Condition*, 80–81.

9. Lyotard, 77.

which all superfluous ornamentation has been stripped away. Yet this aesthetic is still "nostalgic" for the real and thus seeks a kind of clarity and distinctness of form—one might think of the functionalism of the so-called "international style" of architecture or, for that matter, of Descartes's *Meditations*.

The postmodern shares with the modern a sense of the lack of reality of all representation, but it is no longer suspicious of received representations, for it realizes that a lack of reality only warrants suspicion if one presumes that there is a "real" to which one has some sort of (at least negative) access. Rather the postmodern "puts forward the unpresentable in presentation itself" by a proliferation of forms created out of those received representations.[10] The spareness and functionality engendered by modernist suspicion is replaced in postmodernity by a baroque superficiality. In modernism the corrosion of suspicion strips away all exterior decoration—whether in art or philosophy—to reveal the sublime as what cannot be indicated by the bare form, while in postmodernity the sublime *is* the ever-shifting figuration of the surface. This flux creates a fantastic space in which the unpresentability of the sublime may be presented.

In some ways Lyotard's second account of postmodernity is, like his first, still fundamentally grounded in a hypermodern master narrative of emancipation. The relationship of this second account to the first can be seen in its concluding clarion call: "Let us wage war on totality; let us be witnesses to the unpresentable."[11] There is the same questioning of any unified discourse or presentation of such sublime concepts as totality or simplicity. Having finally thrown off the dead hand of the past, the self need not fear nor be suspicious of that past; the self is freed to use whatever fragmented forms of the past that it wishes. Rather than being suspicious of those forms, the postmodern self is ironic about

10. Lyotard, 81.
11. Lyotard, 82.

them and thus no longer so threatened by them. Forms no longer possess us, but rather we them. A classical column here, a snatch of Gregorian chant there, and an image of Elvis thrown in for a smile all are assembled by the ironic subject into a pastiche. Thus in his ironic path beyond modern suspicion, Lyotard seems to retain at least enough of a centered subject to provide a locus for the ironic gaze, to act as a *bricoleur*.[12] Suddenly, ironic pastiche does not seem so "postmodern," for while it renounces suspicion, it partakes of an essentially modern view of the subject as a contentless freedom that constructs the world, a freedom into which the powerful tonic of irony has been infused, so that it is no longer threatened by (and therefore suspicious of) the forms of the past.

While Lyotard does not himself fully distinguish them, he still presents us with at least two distinguishable ways in which we might think about "postmodernity." On the one hand, we have the end of metanarratives, the end of all totalizing schemes, the decentering of meaning and the self. On the other hand, we have the end of suspicion through a refiguring of the sublime so that metaphors of depth are replaced with those of superficiality and unpresentability becomes a quality of figuration rather than something lurking behind figuration. The first, as I have argued, seems more an intensification of the modern project of emancipation than a surpassing of it. The second, particularly when tied to the first, can also be understood as a consequence of the emancipatory project, but it need not be.

The claim that all metanarratives have become incredible is, of course, simply an assertion, and one about which we might have well-founded suspicions, particularly given how the emancipatory metanarrative of modernity seems to be smuggled back in. We might well turn suspicion and even irony back upon themselves and ask, "Incredible to whom?" Whose interests are served

12. For the post-structuralist appropriation of Levi-Strauss' notion of *bricolage*, see Jacques Derrida, "Structure, Sign, and Play in the Discourse of the Human Sciences," in *Writing and Difference*, trans. Alan Bass (Chicago: University of Chicago Press, 1978), 278–93.

by the disembedding of the subject from any and all metadiscourses so as to bounce through cyberspace? If one questions both modern suspicion and the postmodern assertion of the end of master narratives, then one is presented with the possibility of a true (or real) metanarrative presentation (or presence) of the sublime. The self is decentered, not in the sense of being fragmented, but of being unlocked from its Cartesian isolation so as to discover truth in the concrete objects of the world.

The two versions of postmodernity that we find in Lyotard have their theological analogues. On the one hand, some theologians (or a/theologians), such as Mark Taylor, have taken up the idea that we are living at the end of all metanarratives and argued that in such a situation the very notion of God must be jettisoned.[13] Similarly, there are those who also conceive of the postmodern as the end of metanarratives but are not willing to go quite so far, arguing instead for a postmodern Christian theology that rejects the universal and totalizing pretensions of much traditional Christian theology in favor of some more modest version. The Christian story can no longer be understood or presented as the world's true story; it is at best simply the story that Christians tell about the world, and which they cannot impose upon the world or even preach to the world in the hope that the world might turn and be converted. Such theologians point to the contemporary awareness and tacit acceptance of religious pluralism as creating a new situation in which such notions as the necessity of Christ for salvation or the Church as the locus of grace are simply incredible and should be abandoned.[14] Indeed, they must

13. Or so it seems. In "Denegating God" (*Critical Inquiry* 20, no. 4 [1994]: 592–610), Taylor seems to want to retain "the sacred" as that which remains after the death of God, "a lack that leaves us wanting" (609). However, Taylor's account of the sacred strikes me as simply atheism in vestments.

14. In its accession to the givenness of the "situation" that determines what is and is not possible for theology, such a view resembles Rudolf Bultmann's famous statement, "We cannot use electric lights and radios and, in the event of illness, avail ourselves of modern medical and clinical means and at the same time believe in the spirit and wonder world of the New Testament" ("New Testament and Mythology: The Problem of Demythologizing the New Testament

be abandoned, for they inevitably wage war against the Other. Instead, we are given a Christianity that understands its mission as one of service to a world that has become increasingly secular, emancipated, and autonomous. In this version of postmodern theology, the Church's task is to bring the Reign of God, now glossed as the modern project of emancipation, to its completion.[15]

On the other hand, there is a way of conceiving a theological closure of modernity that corresponds to the understanding of postmodernity as the end of suspicion. In this understanding, modernity is characterized by the "ugly broad ditch" that Lessing saw stretched between the "accidental truths of history" and the "necessary truths of reason."[16] In modernity these necessary truths could never be represented in historically contingent facts. With the closure of modernity and the jettisoning of the modern account of "necessary truths of reason" understood as Cartesian "clear and distinct ideas," however, it once again becomes possible to put forward the notion of the sublime presented through the contingent and historical. It is to such an understanding of the task of theology after modernity and beyond suspicion that I will now turn.

BEYOND SUSPICION

Christianity, of course, has its own form of suspicion—a suspicion of representation inherited from Israel's strictures against idolatry. As is clear from the charges of "atheism" lodged against the early Christians by their pagan opponents, Christianity antedates modernity in its destruction of belief and the discovery of

Proclamation," in *New Testament and Mythology and Other Basic Writings*, ed. and trans. Schubert M. Ogden [Philadelphia: Fortress, 1984], 1–43, at 4).

15. For such a self-described "weak" postmodern position, see Paul Lakeland, *Postmodernity: Christian Identity in a Fragmented Age* (Philadelphia: Fortress, 1997). I will have recourse to Lakeland later as an example of one understanding of postmodernity, though of course there is a perhaps infinite variety of positions that might claim this name.

16. Gotthold Lessing, "On the Proof of the Spirit and of Power" in *Lessing's Theological Writings*, trans. Henry Chadwick (Stanford, CA: Stanford University Press, 1956), 51–56, at 53.

the "lack of reality" of all representations. And just as postmodernity moves beyond the suspicion characteristic of modernity in its ironic appropriation of representations through pastiche and bricolage, so too Christianity moves beyond suspicion in its proclamation of faith in Jesus Christ as God incarnate, the image of the invisible God (Col. 1:15).

In recent theology, it is Hans Urs von Balthasar's theological aesthetics that is best known for stressing the importance of the "form" (*Gestalt*) of revelation. Less well known is the historiographic scheme in which Balthasar locates his theological project.[17] According to Balthasar, the Gospel first took root in a world that was viewed by its inhabitants as fundamentally sacred. The approach of the early apologists (e.g., Justin Martyr and Clement of Alexandria) was not to preach God's Word to a godless world but to gather together into unity the fragmentary manifestations of the Word in the world (the *logoi spermatikoi*) through the proclamation of the personal incarnation of that Word in Jesus Christ. This provides an organizing and form-imparting center to the sacred cosmos of antiquity. As Balthasar writes:

> the ancient world's unifying principles—the Stoic's cosmic Logos, the Neoplatonic hierarchy of being that extends from matter to the superessential One, the abstract majesty of Rome's world-unifying power—are redeemable schematic prefigurations of the personal God-Logos, who has drawn close to the world through the history of Israel, a history that fulfills the cosmos and the various religions [*Ökumene*]. The world was created in this Logos, the true "place of the ideas," and can therefore be understood only in light of this Logos.[18]

17. This is most fully spelled out in *The Glory of the Lord: A Theological Aesthetics*, vol. 4, *The Realm of Metaphysics in Antiquity* and vol. 5, *The Realm of Metaphysics in the Modern Age*. However, a more succinct, and clearer, presentation of Balthasar's historiography can be found in the first three chapters of his little book *Love Alone is Credible*, trans. D.C. Schindler (San Francisco: Ignatius, 2004).

18. Balthasar, *Love Alone*, 17.

In such a scheme, the line between philosophy and theology, between faith and reason, could be extremely blurry or, indeed, nonexistent. This situation, and therefore this form of Christian theology, persists throughout the Middle Ages and into the Renaissance in such writings as Thomas More's *Utopia*, in which the "natural" religion of the inhabitants of Utopia is "the reduction of Christianity to its luminous fundamental truths."[19]

Yet in Renaissance humanism, the seeds are sown for a new worldview and therefore a new fundamental approach for theology. As Balthasar writes:

> in imperceptible steps, it replaced the ancient and Christian world-logos with "natural" religion, ethics, and philosophy, as they correspond to the nature common to all peoples and ages. According to its interpretation of Romans 1:18f., one part of the content of revelation was inherited by this natural religion, another part by the "positive" religions—Christianity and others. But these positive religions were being summoned before the judgment seat of mankind with increasing insistence, and with ever-greater charges to answer for.[20]

In other words, in a world disenchanted by human reason, it is the human being rather than the cosmos that becomes the backdrop against which revelation takes place. Thus, as Balthasar writes, "the locus of verification" was displaced "from the increasingly demythologized cosmos (which was becoming less of a rival to Christianity) to the human being, who recapitulated the entire world in himself."[21] Such a shift is implicit in the sixteenth century—e.g., in Luther's question, "how can I find a gracious God?"—but comes fully into view with the post-Kantian theology of Schleiermacher. Balthasar notes that, in Schleiermacher's

19. Balthasar, 24.
20. Balthasar, 25–26.
21. Balthasar, 31.

theology, Christology is subsumed under the consciousness of salvation as its precondition so that "dogmatic statements are genuinely scientific only insofar as they relate to this consciousness."[22] Theological propositions no longer find their intelligibility in the context of the cosmos but become descriptions of human self-consciousness. Consequently, their "reality" becomes questionable: is the source of the feeling of absolute dependence— the absolute subjectivity that stands in tension with our finite subjectivity—simply, à la Fichte, the formal and transcendental structure of the human person? Is it not the case, as Feuerbach argued, that talk about God is a fundamentally alienated and deceptive mode of speaking about human beings? What compelling reason can one give to move beyond the anthropological referent to some purported divine referent? Thus, even apart from any postmodern critique of the notion "man" as, in Foucault's famous words, "an invention of recent date" that is perhaps destined to "be erased, like a face drawn in sand at the edge of the sea,"[23] there are strong theological grounds for being wary of the attempt to ground theology in anthropology.

After the desacralization of the cosmos coincident with the modern turn to the subject, and after the modern subject's theological collapse upon itself, what is left? It is at this point that Balthasar puts forward what he calls "the third way of love," which can be approached from two different paths. The first is the path of "personalism"—the confrontation of the "I" with the irreducible otherness of a "thou"[24]—and the second is the path of aesthetics—the confrontation of the perceiver with the "inner, undemonstrable necessity" of the beautiful object.[25] Both of these modes of encounter indicate a kind of thinking, a *logos*, that

22. Balthasar, 38.
23. Michel Foucault, *The Order of Things: An Archeology of the Human Sciences*, trans. Alan Sheridan (New York: Random House, 1970), 387. See Essay 1, above.
24. Balthasar, *Love Alone*, 44–48.
25. Balthasar, 53.

neither simply reads truth off of the surface of the cosmos nor discovers it in the depths of the self but which dwells in a space of interlocution between self and other. Still, these modes of encounter are insufficient in themselves, for they "can serve at best as a sign of Christianity."[26] And that toward which they point us is the Word that God speaks to humanity, "the Son, who interprets the Father in the Holy Spirit as divine Love."[27]

Thus, the third alternative that Balthasar presents us with is a theological aesthetics in which the sublime unrepresentability of God is taken up with full seriousness. Though ancient and medieval writers are mined for insights that have been lost in modernity, no appeal is made to the premodern sacred cosmos that transparently radiates divine wisdom. Balthasar accepts, at least on a certain level, the brute opacity of modernity's mechanized and quantified universe, in which "all the evidence . . . seems to point to the absence of love in the world."[28] Balthasar seeks not a path backward, prior to suspicion, but a path forward, beyond suspicion, to a kind of Kierkegaardian "immediacy after reflection." It is simply facile to consign him, as David Tracy does, to the dustbin of "antimodernity."[29] The modern destruction of the ancient sacred cosmos is a *fait accompli* of intellectual history, and one that should be accepted on Christian grounds as giving a clarity previously lacking to the distinction between Creator and creation.

It is true, however, that the path forward that he seeks is not one that accepts as enduring achievements the speculative and emancipatory master narratives of modernity, for to proceed with these as baggage is to continue the self-defeating project of

26. Balthasar, 53.
27. Balthasar, 56.
28. Balthasar, 143.
29. See David Tracy, "On Naming the Present," in *On Naming the Present: Reflections on God, Hermeneutics, and Church* (Maryknoll, NY: Orbis, 1994), 3–24.

modern theology.[30] One might say that just as modern aesthetics sought to register the sublime by stripping away superfluous ornamentation in the pursuit of pure functionality, so too the modern theological project has been to seek the "essence" of "religion" by clearing the ground of dogmatic, ritual, and narrative accretions. And when this essence is found, it is found as a certain kind of experience, just as for Kant, the sublime is registered as a certain expansion of the soul. Once this essential experience is distilled, it may be left bare or the ornaments of doctrine, ritual, and narrative may be brought back in, but the basic impulse with which one starts is still the same as in modern aesthetics: a reduction to that which is essential. And granted that basic impulse, it is difficult not to treat doctrine, ritual, and narrative as mere ornamentation. This can be seen in the theology of Karl Rahner. He clearly stresses the importance of the categorical experience of God associated with doctrines, rituals, and narratives as "the necessary but historical and objectifying self-interpretation of the transcendental experience which constitutes the realization of man's essence."[31] However, when it comes to the *reductio in mysterium* of the Christian life, he writes that, while "a Christian does indeed live a tangible and ecclesial life, . . . the ultimately Christian thing about this life is identical with the mystery of human existence. . . . And to this extent to be a Christian is simply to be a human being, and one who also knows that this life which he is living, and which he is consciously living, can also be lived even by a person who is not a Christian explicitly and does not know in a reflexive way that he is a Christian."[32] It is difficult to see how one could avoid a certain ironic stance toward the

---

30. In this sense there clearly *is* a distinction between the postmodernity of Tracy or Lakeland, which has affinities with Habermas' call to "complete" modernity, and that of Balthasar, which takes more seriously the need to sublate "epic" (the speculative narrative) and "lyric" (the emancipatory narrative) into "drama."

31. Karl Rahner, *Foundations of the Christian Faith: An Introduction to the Idea of Christianity*, trans. William V. Dych (New York: Crossroad, 1987), 153.

32. Rahner, *Foundations*, 430.

contingent particularities of Christian story and practice once one has glimpsed the truth that the Christian life is ultimately the same thing as authentic human existence. Perhaps the best one could hope for would be to maintain a sentimental attachment to those particularities.[33]

Balthasar's theological aesthetic is fundamentally different, for he seeks the unrepresentable mystery of God not through abstraction from particular, categorically apprehended forms but precisely *in* those forms, viewed in light of the glory revealed in the Christ-form.[34] He writes, "The distinctive Christian factor is that here we not only 'start from' the corporeal and the sensory as from some religious material on which we can then perform the necessary abstractions; rather, we abide in the seeing, hearing, touching, the savoring and eating of this flesh and blood, which has borne and taken away the sins of the world."[35] One does not move beyond the particularities of the presentation to their essence. In this sense, a true theological aesthetic, like Lyotard's postmodern aesthetic, "puts forward the unpresentable in presentation itself" because it proclaims Christ as the filial image of the paternal *archè*, an image that is "equal" to that which it images. As Balthasar writes, "the form of revelation does not present itself as an independent image of God, standing over against what is imaged, but as a unique hypostatic union between archetype and image."[36] The sublime archetype is in the form; one might say that the form is the "real presence" of the archetype.

Further, one might say that for Balthasar, as for Lyotard, the

33. It is possible, however, to read Rahner's transcendental method as more of an *ad hoc* technique. See Fergus Kerr, *Immortal Longings: Versions of Transcending Humanity* (Notre Dame, IN: University of Notre Dame Press, 1997), 173–84.

34. For an admirably clear and balanced examination of the philosophical roots of the disagreement between Rahner and Balthasar, see Rowan Williams, "Balthasar and Rahner," in *The Analogy of Beauty: The Theology of Hans Urs von Balthasar*, John Riches, ed. (Edinburgh: T&T Clark, 1986), 11–34.

35. Hans Urs von Balthasar, *The Glory of the Lord: A Theological Aesthetics*, vol. 1, *Seeing the Form*, trans. Erasmo Leiva-Merikakis (San Francisco: Ignatius, 1982), 313–14.

36. Balthasar, *Seeing the Form*, 432.

sublime is put forward through the *shattering* of aesthetic form: "it is only through being fragmented that the beautiful really reveals the meaning of the eschatological promise it contains."[37] But before we effect a *rapprochement* between Balthasar and Lyotard, it is important to mark a crucial difference, one that in fact makes any reconciliation between the two impossible. As I said earlier, Lyotard's aesthetic remains one that is bound to an emancipatory narrative and therefore, I have argued, a fundamentally modern one. The sublime that is presented in presentation itself is, in fact, the rapturous tremors of the strong poet's will to power as it shatters and reassembles previous forms. For Balthasar, on the other hand, it is *one particular* fragmented form that reveals the eschatological promise of the beautiful: what he calls the Christ-form. One might put this in Lyotard's terms by saying that for Balthasar, there is, in fact, a master narrative that speaks the truth of the world. This is a fragmented, *crucified* narrative, but it is still *one* narrative, which presents the glory of the triune God's differentiated unity.

Balthasar notes that "Christ's mediating form is multiple . . . in its very exercise, and yet this multiplicity can ever give expression only to the one form."[38] In explaining this multiplicity, Balthasar appeals to the ancient notion of the *corpus triforme*, or the threefold body of Christ: his "natural" body that was born of the Virgin Mary and ascended into heaven, his ecclesial body, and his Eucharistic body (in which Balthasar also includes Christ's scriptural "body").[39] In what follows, I will not follow Balthasar's

37. Balthasar, 460.

38. Balthasar, 529.

39. Balthasar, 529–531. Balthasar's discussion of the *corpus triforme* is somewhat confusing, in part because he does not clearly delineate what the three bodies are (something that is not clarified by his combining the Eucharistic and scriptural bodies of Christ). No doubt this lack of clear delineation is in part a witness to the ultimate unity of Christ's body, though it may also testify to a conceptual unclarity on Balthasar's part. Also, the notion of the *corpus triforme* itself has a very complex historical development, and there are in fact several, not always compatible, versions of this threefold body of Christ, relating particularly to whether the term is used in connection with scriptural exegesis or liturgical commentary. My appropriation draws from the exegetical tradition. See Henri de Lubac, *Corpus Mysticum: L'Eucharistie et l'Église au Moyen-Age*, 2nd ed. (Paris: Aubier, 1948), passim.

specific discussion of the threefold body of Christ. Rather, I will take it as a pattern that can help us understand Jesus Christ as the sacrament of God, the Church as the sacrament of Christ, and the Eucharist as the sacrament that, in Henri de Lubac's phrase, "makes the Church." In presenting this threefold body, I will attempt to sound themes that I have alluded to earlier, which are sometimes thought of as distinctively "postmodern"—negation, bricolage, and alterity. The theological reading of these themes, however, can perhaps move us beyond suspicion toward a theological realism.

THE THREEFOLD *CORPUS CHRISTI*

a) Negation: The Body of Jesus

The primary referent of the phrase *Corpus Christi* is the human flesh of Jesus, his natural body, and by extension his human nature as a whole. This human nature is the "primordial sacrament" because it is the sign and instrumental cause of human salvation.[40] As St. Thomas says, the "flesh [*caro*]" of Christ "and the mysteries accomplished therein [*et mysteria in ea perpetrata*]" are both instrumental and exemplary causes of grace.[41] In what Jesus does and suffers in his human history, the intention-laden events of his flesh, we are presented with nothing less than the life of God, and through the instrumentality of the action and passion of that history, divine life is communicated to us.

This notion of Christ as the sacrament of God is the foundation of any Christian theological aesthetic that seeks to move beyond the modern aporia of the sublime. Jesus is the "effective" or "causal" sign of the saving presence of God. His death and resurrection are the "sign of Jonah," the only sign that is given (Matt.

40. See Edward Schillebeeckx, *Christ the Sacrament of the Encounter with God* (New York: Sheed & Ward, 1963), 15.
41. *Summa theologiae* 3.62.5 ad 1.

12:38–40), and they present us with the reality of God as triune love, and not simply a *re*presentation of that reality. This is not to collapse the distinction between visible sign and fundamentally invisible referent, for to do so would be to obliterate the gracious distance between God and creation (thus the distinction between the immanent and economic Trinity remains a relevant one). But it is to claim that the sign (the human nature of Christ) is "assumed" by the reality (the Word of God) into a personal union in which there is, in the words of Chalcedon, difference without division or separation. This distinction or "distance" between sign and referent is not a division only if it is, to borrow a phrase from Jean-Luc Marion, "saturated" by the referent, and this is in part what the Christian tradition has meant by "hypostatic union."[42]

As befits a visible presentation of that which is fundamentally beyond presentation, Christ is a sign of contradiction (Luke 2:34), the form (*morphē*) of God become the form of a slave (Phil. 2).[43] Jesus is a sign *sous rature*; his whole life is one of negation of himself so as to be a sign that is transparent to the will of the Father (John 4:34; 14:7). Thus, it is the cross and resurrection that have been the focal points for understanding the saving work of Jesus. It is in the fragmentation of his crucified body, and the unrecognizableness, apart from his self-revelation, of his resurrected body, that, from a human point of view, Jesus's human nature attains its perfection as the sacrament of the God who is beyond human representation. The cross, the tomb, the

42. Jean-Luc Marion, *God Without Being: Hors-Texte*, trans. Thomas A. Carlson (Chicago: University of Chicago Press, 1991), 46, 156. For a fuller development of the notion of "the saturated phenomenon" as a philosophical concept that opens out toward the possibility of divine revelation, see Jean-Luc Marion, "Le phénomène saturé" in *Phénoménologie et théologie*, ed. Jean-François Courtine (Paris: Criterion, 1993), 79–128. In this essay Marion sketches a phenomenology that overcomes the Cartesian and Kantian commitment to the paradigmatic status of phenomena that are "poor in intuition" in favor of those that are "saturated," in particular those of historical events and revelation.

43. Note that in Philippians Paul speaks of the *morphē* of God, not the *eidos*. While we should not try to get too much philosophical mileage out of this, we might simply note that Paul wishes to speak of a divine "shape" and not simply a divine "idea" (though the relationship between *morphē* and *eidosis* is a complicated one).

way to Emmaus are all places of negation, of vanishing. At the same time, the transparency of the sign does not make it, in all of its contingent particularities, nugatory. For it is this *particular* negation (cross and resurrection) of this *particular* sign (Jesus of Nazareth) that moves us beyond mere negation of meaning to an excess of meaning.

Of course, how we read this sign depends on the larger narrative in which we locate it. When placed within a master narrative of emancipation, even the shattering of the Christ-form could appear, as it did for Nietzsche, as a manifestation of the will to power. But when we start from the narrative of the cross, the narrative of power as the kenotic donation of being on those things that are not (Rom. 4:17), and we let this narrative shape our perception of the sign, then its negation is not will to power but love unto death. Balthasar writes:

> God's incomprehensibility is now no longer a mere deficiency in knowledge, but the positive manner in which God determines the knowledge of faith: this is the overwhelming inconceivability of the fact that God has loved us so much that he surrendered his only Son for us, the fact that the God of plenitude has poured himself out, not only into creation, but emptied himself into the modalities of an existence determined by sin, corrupted by death and alienated from God. This is the concealment that appears in his self-revelation; this is the ungraspability of God, which becomes graspable because it *is* grasped.[44]

44. Balthasar, *Seeing the Form*, 461.

The sublime is not the will to power but the outpouring in love of God's plenitude, even to the ultimate point of human sin and alienation.[45]

One might, of course, posit a different "postmodern" reading of Christ, one that takes its cue from the proclaimed end of meta-narratives. In this reading, the "decentering" of postmodernity makes the Christocentric account of God that I have sketched highly problematic. Jesus can be at best one of the plurality of manifestations of the divine; his self-negation includes his nega-tion as privileged sign. As Paul Lakeland puts it, "the particularity lies in the messenger, not the message."[46] In other words, Jesus is a particular messenger who bears a universal message, one borne by many others. From this perspective, claiming the identity of message and messenger, the hypostatic union of referent and sign, makes the human history of Jesus into a master narrative. Yet this putatively postmodern Christology sounds quite similar to the liberal theology of Harnack and others (the Gospel *of* Jesus, not the Gospel *about* Jesus), which might lead us to ask whether such an approach really takes us beyond the master narratives of modernity.[47] In particular, it retains the modern suspicion of rep-resentation, the sense that there is some obscured message lurking *behind* its various messengers, and that there is some standpoint from which we can discern the fact of such a message, if not its content.

But the event of the cross presents us with a path beyond suspicion. It is not the path of the strong poet's Nietzschean confidence in his ability to master any and all master narratives through irony. Rather it is the hope that is given paradoxical voice in Christ's cry of dereliction, the hope given birth by the cross

45. Hence the importance played in Balthasar's narrative by Holy Saturday. See Hans Urs von Balthasar, *Mysterium Paschale*, trans. Aidan Nichols, OP (Edinburgh: T&T Clark, 1990), 148–88.

46. Lakeland, *Postmodernity*, 112.

47. See Adolf von Harnack, *What is Christianity?*, trans. Thomas Bailey Saunders (Phila-delphia: Fortress, 1986),142–46.

seen as a Trinitarian event in which God's very being is extended to encompass even the ultimate alienation of hell and damnation, the hope beyond death that is awakened by Christ as he breaks bread with the disciples at Emmaus. We are no longer citizens of the ancient cosmos imbued with the divine; our experience of the world is an experience of godlessness. But in the cross we are presented with a God who is present even in godlessness, and in the Resurrection, we are promised that godlessness shall not have the last word.[48]

This provides a ground of critique by which we might distinguish false representations of God from true or, perhaps more precisely, by which we might distinguish "idols" (our representations of the divine) from "icons" (God's self-presentation in revelation).[49] The "cruciform" life of Jesus—and his life is cruciform in that it is lived in its entirety "toward" the cross—serves as the norm of holiness, and all other claims to righteousness must fall under its critique. The cross and Resurrection, in their very negativity and obscurity, become the icon by which God presents to us God's own unpresentable Trinitarian life, and we are called not to irony but to adoration and participation.

b) Bricolage: The Ecclesial Body

Yet we must take a further step. For the presentation of God in the negated sign of Jesus on the cross and in the resurrection—the shattering of the Christ-form by which it "reveals the meaning of the eschatological promise it contains"—is an event that cannot be confined to a single moment in time but is Eucharistically extended through history in the Church. In John's Gospel Christ's side is pierced to bring forth sacramental water and blood (John 19:34), a healing river flowing from the Lamb who reigns

48. One might compare Simone Weil's "The Love of God and Affliction," in *Waiting for God*, trans. Emma Craufurd (New York: Harper, 1951), 117–36.

49. See Marion, *God Without Being*, 7–24.

from the throne of the cross down through the middle of God's new city (Rev. 22:1–2). Just as the postmodern sublime is figured through both the fragmentation of form and the regathering of that form through pastiche or bricolage, so too the Christian sublime involves both the shattering of the Christ-form upon the cross and a regathering of that form through the Resurrection, a regathering that has as an intrinsic element the regathering of the scattered disciples into an *ekklesia*, which is fused by Pentecostal fire to become part of the form.[50] Balthasar writes, "the Christ-form attains to its plastic fullness only through the dimension of the Holy Spirit—and this means also through the Church."[51] Or, as Gregory of Nyssa put it even more boldly, "he who sees the Church looks directly at Christ—Christ building and increasing by the addition of the elect."[52]

Said differently, the Church is "the universal sacrament of salvation."[53] Though this notion of the Church as a sacrament has patristic roots, it owes its modern articulation not least to Henri de Lubac, who wrote in his 1938 book *Catholicism*: "If Christ is the sacrament of God, the Church is for us the sacrament of Christ; she represents him, in the full and ancient meaning of the term; she really makes him present."[54] The Church is the sacrament of Christ, according to the Dogmatic Constitution on the Church, in that it is "a sign and instrument" of salvation understood as both "union with God and . . . the unity of the whole human race."[55] Otto Semmelroth notes that "a sacrament

50. This is not to say that the Resurrection simply *is* the regathering of the community. On the relationship between the Resurrection and the regathering of the disciples, see Rowan Williams, *Resurrection: Interpreting the Easter Gospel* (Harrisburg, PA: Morehouse, 1994), esp. chs. 3–5.

51. Balthasar, *Seeing the Form*, 408.

52. Gregory of Nyssa, *Commentary on the Song of Songs*, Sermon 13, in *From Glory to Glory: Texts from Gregory of Nyssa's Mystical Writings*, selected and introduced by Jean Daniélou, SJ, trans. and ed. Herbert Musurillo, SJ (Crestwood, NY: St. Vladimir's Seminary, 1995), 272.

53. *Lumen Gentium* 48.

54. Henri de Lubac, *Catholicism: Christ and the Common Destiny of Man*, trans. Lancelot C. Sheppard and Sr. Elizabeth Englund, OCD (San Francisco: Ignatius, 1988), 76.

55. *Lumen Gentium* 1.

is something eschatological in the sense that the 'eschaton,' the heavenly salvation we are yet to reach, has already invaded this world in the sacramental sign."[56] It is an effective sign—not simply representing salvation but bringing it about. Again, the gap between sign and referent is saturated through the self-giving of the referent. Not in this case a hypostatic or personal union of two natures, but a union in love between head and members to form one communion in love. This union fills the gap that might call into question the veracity of the sign, so that, as John Zizioulas puts it, "Christ Himself becomes revealed as truth not *in* a community, but *as* a community."[57] It is the quality of life of those who are in Christ that manifests—or fails to manifest—the truth of Christ.

We might also put this in terms of the *totus Christus* of which Augustine wrote in his *Homilies on the First Epistle of John*. Because of the union of love between Christ and the Church, to speak of the whole Christ is to speak of both head and body.[58] Reflecting on the statements in 1 John that "God is love" (1 John 4:8) and that "no one has even seen God" (1 John 4:12), Augustine notes that the fundamentally invisible reality of God manifests itself not simply in Christ, the Word made flesh, laying down his life for us, but also through the manifold concrete acts of *caritas* enacted within the Body of Christ—gifts of alms and instruction, acts of adoration and attentiveness.[59] And acts of charity are not simply a way of showing forth the reality of God, but they are themselves acts of seeing God: "Love your brother; in loving your

---

56. *Commentary on the Documents of Vatican II*, ed. Herbert Vorgrimler (New York: Herder, 1967), 1:282.

57. John D. Zizioulas, *Being as Communion: Studies in Personhood and the Church* (Crestwood, NY: St. Vladimir's Seminary, 1985), 115.

58. Augustine, *Homilies on the First Epistle of John* 1.2, in *Augustine: Later Works*, ed. and trans. John Burnaby (Philadelphia: Westminster, 1955), 261. In what follows in this paragraph, I am indebted to Lewis Ayres' essay "Augustine on God as Love and Love as God," *Pro Ecclesia* 5, no. 4 (Fall 1996): 470–87.

59. See Augustine, *Homilies* 7.10.

brother whom you see, you will see God at the same time. For you will see charity itself, and there within is God dwelling."[60]

In the Church that is one yet spread over all the earth, the invisible God becomes visible in a multitude of acts of charity, not as some original that is imitated—even for those who do them there is no way of seeing the original apart from these acts—but as the sublime that is presented in that multitude. As Lewis Ayres puts it, to live in ecclesial charity is to "see" the Trinity; moreover, it is to become a mirror of the self-transcending *caritas* of Father, Son, and Spirit.[61] And this charity remains "christomorphic," judged and determined by Christ as the primal sacrament of God (and here one might speak properly of imitation). Thus, preeminent among those actions that manifest the invisible reality of God are acts of forgiveness, particularly forgiveness extended to our enemies, by which we see them as the brothers and sisters for whom Christ died. This, for Augustine, is perfect love, for it enacts and manifests the charity shown by Christ on the cross.[62]

Again, if one takes the end of master narratives as the key feature of postmodernity, then one might argue for a different account of the Church from the one I have sketched here. The myth of the *totus Christus* is simply one more example of a totalizing master narrative that, of its very nature, eradicates difference.[63] It makes the Church, if not the sole locus of salvation, at least the point out of which salvation flows into the world. And if one accepts a "polycentric" view of the world, then this is clearly unacceptable. A more truly postmodern role for the Church, on this reading, would be as the servant of the world. Rather than imposing its story on the world, or even proclaiming it to the world as the world's true story, the servant Church places itself at the world's disposal. Not,

60. Augustine, *Homilies* 5.7.
61. Ayres, "Augustine on God," 485–87. On the Trinity as *caritas* that transcends the mutual love of one for another, so as to engender a third, the *locus classicus* is Richard of St. Victor's *De Trinitate*, Book III.
62. Augustine, *Homilies* 1.9; 9.3.
63. For this claim about master narratives, see Lakeland, *Postmodernity*, 30–36.

of course, uncritically. The Church must retain its prophetic role, but that prophetic role cannot be the preaching of Christ crucified or any other such particularistic story. For the story by which the Church lives is, at its very core, a partial one and thus not in itself the source of the Church's critical judgments with regard to the world. What then can be the source of those judgments? It seems it would have to be some constellation of "thin" human values, such as autonomy and self-determination. Again, as Paul Lakeland puts it, "Prophecy today . . . is not a matter of presenting a substantive message to an uncomprehending multitude, but rather of demanding—through acting out—an uncompromising openness to the future revealed through unconstrained discourse."[64] And thus it seems that we have returned to the emancipatory master narrative of modernity.

In what I am proposing, in contrast, the Christian community is called to be "light to the world," to speak and enact the story of Christ so as to give back to the world the story it has lost through sin. One might go so far as to say that because of the unity of the *totus Christus*, the Church simply *is* that (Eucharistically) enacted story. This story is complete because perfectly enacted in the life of Christ and at the same time yet to be fulfilled, as the sinful and repentant Church of tears journeys toward its eschatological wedding with the Lamb. It is thus in one sense a "master narrative," yet it is one that is pneumatologically constituted (or "edified") by the sheer variety of the gifts of the Spirit (1 Cor. 12) and is fragmented into a multitude of Eucharistic enactments—the Church in its fullness being present in each Eucharistic community.[65] Similarly, the closure of the narrative awaits its eschatological consummation; final knowledge of who has in fact enacted that story and who will constitute the multitude gathered around the throne of the Lamb is deferred (Matt. 25:31–46; Rev. 7:9–17). It is for this reason that

64. Lakeland, 105. For Lakeland's "weak" postmodern account of the Church, see 101–7.

65. On the Eucharistic assembly as the fullness of the Church, see *Lumen Gentium* 26. On the Church as comprised of *charismata*, see Zizioulas, *Being as Communion*, 111.

Henri de Lubac says of the Church that it is "one living being" that is "vivified by the one Spirit," yet "its scope remains God's secret."[66]

Thus, rather than having recourse to facile (and fundamentally deceptive) claims about the "end of master narratives," we may look to the narrative of the *totus Christus*, the narrative of the particular historical figure of Jesus of Nazareth raised in power to God's right hand and of the body that claims that same Jesus as its head, the body animated by the Spirit with the diversity of gifts. This is the Spirit who, as Gerard Manley Hopkins put it, "delights in multitude," yet who is always the Spirit of Christ and thus conforms that multitude to him. Hopkins writes:

> as the breath is drawn from the boundless air into the lungs and from the lungs again is breathed out and melts into the boundless air so the Spirit of God was poured out from the infinite God upon Christ's human nature and by Christ, who said: Receive the Holy Ghost: as my Father sent me so I send you, was breathed into his Apostles and by degrees into the millions of his Church, till the new heavens and new earth will at last be filled with it.[67]

The Spirit is the ecclesial *bricoleur* that blows where it will, along whose errant path the *ekklesia* is gathered from the world into Christ's body, only to be impelled forth again by that same Spirit to dwell in peace among the nations.

c) Alterity: The Eucharistic Body

We must take one final step. If Christ is the sacrament of God, and the Church is the sacrament of Christ, then the Eucharist is the sacrament of the Church since it is the "sign and cause"

66. De Lubac, *Catholicism*, 47.

67. Gerard Manley Hopkins, *The Sermons and Devotional Writings of Gerard Manley Hopkins*, ed. Christopher Devlin, SJ (London: Oxford University Press, 1959), 98.

by which the Church is constituted in union with Christ its head. Again, to quote Henri de Lubac, "the Eucharist *makes* the Church."[68] A certain "eucharistic realism" is a corollary of an "ecclesial realism" that sees the Church as the *corpus verum*, the true Body of Christ.[69]

The Eucharist is thus not simply a reproduction, whether psychological or metaphysical, of a past reality, but it is a genuine production—an "edification" or building up—of the present and future reality of the Church.[70] Here again we have a complex play of depth and surface or, in scholastic language, of *res* and *sacramentum*. The reality (*res*) which is to be signified is the unity in love of the *totus Christus*—the unity of the members among themselves and with Christ as their head. But this reality is not, as it were, self-subsisting but is produced through the instrumentality of the sign (*sacramentum*) of bread and wine, through which the power of Christ's Eucharistic body, which is both reality and sign (*res et sacramentum*), is exercised.[71] This odd category of that which is both reality-and-sign seeks to articulate the co-inhabitation of depth and surface: it is through the Church's visible ritual action with bread and wine that the Church herself is produced as Body of Christ; the agent is produced as it "exteriorizes" itself in action. But this is only the case because something that is *neither* a mere sign *nor* bare reality intervenes—the reality-and-sign of the Eucharistic Christ. Only if Christ is present in the Eucharist as *res et sacramentum* can the skeptical gap between reality and signs be bridged. Again, the gap between sign and referent is "saturated" by that which is both sign *and* referent.

A similar point has been argued by Jean-Luc Marion in his defense of the traditional doctrine of transubstantiation in the

68. De Lubac, *Corpus Mysticum*, 104.

69. De Lubac, 283.

70. De Lubac, 79–80.

71. The historical development of this terminology, and consequently its use in any particular instance, is quite complex. See de Lubac, 189–209.

face of various attempts to reformulate it in "nonmetaphysical" terms, such as transignification. His fear is that attempts to articulate the Eucharistic event in terms of meaning will end up reducing the Eucharistic presence to a matter of the consciousness of the celebrating community.[72] Though he does not put it this way, one might say that he fears that transignification in the end capitulates to Feuerbach: the Eucharist is finally a matter of humanity's coming to consciousness of itself. In contrast, for Marion the doctrine of transubstantiation means that "the consecrated host imposes, or rather permits, . . . the irreducible exteriority of the present that Christ makes of himself in this thing that to him becomes sacramental body."[73] The irreducible exteriority of the doctrine of transubstantiation makes it possible to understand the Eucharist according to a "christic temporality," in which real presence is the present, understood not (metaphysically) as the stable given of the here-and-now but as the gift of the present, which is both a memorial (or, perhaps better, *anamnesis*) of the covenant pledged in the past and a stretching out in hope toward the eschatological future.[74]

Whether or not one agrees with Marion's argument that *only* the doctrine of transubstantiation secures the irreducible exteriority of the Eucharistic Other,[75] he makes a compelling case for the claim that only if the Other who is encountered in the Eucharist is not determined by human consciousness but rather determines human consciousness—*saturates* human

72. Marion writes: "The immediate consciousness of the collective self hence produces the first appearance of the presence of 'God' to the community. The (human and representational) present commands the future of divine presence" (*God Without Being*, 167).

73. Marion, 169.

74. Marion, 172–76.

75. See Gerard Loughlin, *Telling God's Story* (Cambridge: Cambridge University Press, 1996), 234–37, for a defense of what might be called transignification (or at least Herbert McCabe's version of it) against Marion's critique. It strikes me that the primary object of Marion's critique is not so much contemporary Catholic reformulations of transubstantiation (though these may fall more generally under that critique) as it is Hegel's remarks on the "externality" of Catholicism. See Hegel, *The Philosophy of History*, trans. J. Sibree (New York: Dover, 1956), 377–78.

consciousness—can the Eucharist be anything other than idolatry and the Eucharistic community anything other than one more human community. Of course, for those who would see postmodernity as the end of metanarrative, all that the Church *should* claim to be is, at best, one human response in faith to the experience of the divine or, at worst, a human mystification of the workings of power.[76] Similarly, to claim that Eucharistic worship is more than simply one human language game among others, to claim that it is an act of divine speech through the priest acting *in persona Christi*, which brings about a "substantial" change, seems thoroughly "metaphysical." But if Marion is correct, only a divine discourse that breaks into and breaks apart human speech can in fact rupture the totalizing discourse of metaphysics; it is only such a claim that can in fact confront us with a God who is truly other, without delivering that Other to us as an effect of our consciousness.[77]

Thus, perhaps oddly, Eucharistic discourse as master narrative does not obliterate otherness but in fact instantiates it as "irreducible exteriority." It recalls to us that the Church is not simply the Body of Christ but also the Bride who receives as gift the Body of her divine Spouse. Separated from "Eucharistic realism," "ecclesial realism" can domesticate the relationship between Christ and the Church into a kind of autoeroticism that makes the self-donation of one to the other impossible. The gap between Bride and Spouse must be saturated by the Spirit who only intensifies the Bride's longing for the return of her Bridegroom: "The Spirit and the bride say, 'Come.' And let everyone who hears say, 'Come.'" (Rev. 22:17).

76. The former view can be found in Lakeland's understanding of the Church as one form among others of "faithful sociality." See Lakeland, *Postmodernity*, 60.

77. One must keep in mind that Marion uses "metaphysics" in a highly specific way, referring to "the system of philosophy from Suarez to Kant, as a single science concerned both with what is universal in 'common being' (*l'étant commun*) and in 'essence' (or 'essences')" (Jean-Luc Marion, "Metaphysics and Phenomenology: A Summary for Theologians," in *The Postmodern God*, 279–96, at 281).

But the story does not end here. The union of Bride and Spouse is not simply an ecclesial romance but the occasion for a banquet to which countless particular human "others" are invited. The mutual hospitality of Bride and Spouse toward each other opens out to become coextensive with hospitality toward all who hunger or thirst or are naked or imprisoned (Matt. 25:34–40). The Bride's invitation to her Spouse overflows immediately into an invitation to all: "And let everyone who is thirsty come. Let anyone who wishes take the water of life as a gift" (Rev. 22:17).

CONCLUSION

If the claim to be living at the end of modernity means that modern confidence in human reason's capacity to tell the world's true story has come to an end and that we are thus at the end of all master narratives, of all attempts to articulate the *one* true story of the world, or even of the attempt to construe the world as *having* a single story, then theology must say "yes" and "no" at the same time. Inasmuch as modernity has been the attempt to ground human reason in itself and has sundered "necessary truths of reason" from "accidental truths of history," theology may welcome claims to its demise as opening a path beyond suspicion. And such characteristically postmodern notions as negation, *bricolage*, and alterity may prove tactically useful in preaching and understanding the Gospel. But theology cannot tie its fate to postmodernity, for modernity has also been an exercise in human self-assertion, and in this sense, much of so-called postmodernity is simply a nihilistic intensification of the modern project. The claim to be at the end of all master narratives may simply be a covert way of liberating the self from any claims upon it. Theology, however, is the language given to a community, the *ekklesia* that exists only insofar as it is called and claimed by God. It is this call and claim that beckons the

Bride on her pilgrimage to the banquet of the Lamb, passing from premodernity through modernity to postmodernity . . . to whatever lies beyond.

3

Doctrine

Knowing and Doing

I

I recall seeing, a number of years ago, a photograph taken in the late 1960s of a Mass concelebrated by Lutheran pastors and Catholic priests. Behind the concelebrants was a banner with the slogan "Doctrine divides; service unites."[1] For me, this image captures a moment in history. A moment of particularly groovy sideburns but also a moment of intense ecumenical optimism: an optimism rooted in the idea that the disputes of the sixteenth century that had divided the Church could, in the twentieth century, be set aside in light of the overwhelming consensus among Christians concerning the pressing issues of the day: civil rights, the elimination of poverty, and world peace. It is an image that expresses what Bernard Lonergan said, in a much more sophisticated way, when he wrote in 1972 that the division among Christians

resides mainly in the cognitive meaning of the Christian message. The constitutive meaning and the effective meaning

* This essay was originally published as "Doctrine: Knowing and Doing," in *The Morally Divided Body: Ethical Disagreement and the Disunity of the Church*, ed. Michael Root and James J. Buckley (Eugene, OR: Cascade, 2012), 25–42.
1. This is a dictum originally coined in 1922 by the German jurist and theologian Hermann Paul Kapler, according to Archbishop Nathan Söderblom in his 1930 Nobel Peace Prize lecture. See "The Role of the Church in Promoting Peace," in *Peace: 1926–1950*, Nobel Lectures: Including Presentation Speeches and Laureates' Biographies, vol. 2, ed. Frederick W Haberman (Singapore: World Scientific, 1999), 106.

are matters on which most Christians largely agree. Such agreement, however, needs expression and, while we await common cognitive agreement, the possible expression is collaboration in fulfilling the redemptive and constructive roles of the Christian church in human society.[2]

In other words: doctrine divides (at least for the moment); service unites.

It was an optimistic moment not simply in the dialogue among divided Christians but also, perhaps especially for Roman Catholics, in the dialogue between the Church and the modern world. It was a moment captured in the Second Vatican Council's Pastoral Constitution *Gaudium et Spes*, in which the Church, recognizing that it could never find common ground with modernity on the question of God, turned instead to the question of humanity. The Council Fathers introduced the Constitution by noting, "it is around humankind therefore, one and entire, body and soul, heart and conscience, mind and will, that our whole treatment will revolve."[3] They went on to say that the Council "offers the human race the sincere cooperation of the Church in working for that universal community of sisters and brothers which is the response to humanity's calling."[4] Even in dialogue with the modern world, where doctrine divides, service unites, and thus the Pastoral Constitution offered in its second half a series of reflections on the "urgent problems" of the world of today: "marriage and family, human culture, socio-economic and political life, union within the family of nations, and peace."[5] The Pastoral Constitution does not ignore the theological and, particularly, the Christological grounding of the Church's position

2. Bernard Lonergan, *Method in Theology* (Minneapolis, MN: Seabury, 1972), 368.

3. Vatican Council II, *Gaudium et Spes* 3 in *Decrees of the Ecumenical Councils*, ed. Norman Tanner (Washington, DC: Georgetown University Press, 1990), 2:1070

4. Vatican Council II, *Gaudium et Spes* 3, in Tanner, 2:1070.

5. *Gaudium et Spes* 46, in Tanner, 2:1100.

with regard to these urgent problems.[6] One might, however, be forgiven for thinking that, at least for the time being, the common ground between the Church and the world was not to be found in common profession of belief but rather in the common service that would address these urgent problems. Doctrine divides; service unites.

Such a view presumes, of course, a high degree of moral consensus among Christians and between Christians and non-Christians, a consensus that seemed particularly robust in the post–World War II era. I suspect in Europe that consensus was a result of residual Christian social values combined with the post-Shoah revulsion against totalitarianism that was shared by Christians of all stripes with non-Christians. In the United States, it was a result of a fairly robust civil religion that was, in fact, a form of deracinated Protestantism into which Catholics and Jews were being assimilated, a civic religiosity that was nicely summed up by President Eisenhower when he said, "our government has no sense unless it is founded in a deeply felt religious faith, and I don't care what it is."[7] Whatever the source of the consensus, it was clear well into the 1960s to people of differing religious confessions that certain things, like the civil rights movement, were good and that certain other things, like the war in Vietnam, were bad. Of course, the goodness and badness of these things are, at least in popular perception, much easier to judge in hindsight, for as much as Christians were united across doctrinal lines by these moral issues, they were also divided by them. What was significant at the time, however, on a symbolic level, was the sight

6. In particular the first half of *Gaudium et Spes* makes clear that the anthropological starting point must terminate in Christ. In the phrase much quoted by John Paul II, "it is only in the mystery of the Word incarnate that light is shed on the mystery of humankind" (*Gaudium et Spes* 22, in Tanner 2:1081). For more on the implications of this sort of theological anthropology, see Essay 1 of this volume, "Confessions of an Evangelical Catholic."

7. For a source-critical analysis of this Eisenhower *logion*, see Patrick Henry, "'And I Don't Care What It Is': The Tradition-History of a Civil Religion Proof-Text," *Journal of the American Academy of Religion* 49, no. 1 (Spring 1981): 35–49. Henry argues that, seen in context, Eisenhower's statement is not as vapid as it may at first seem.

of Catholic priests and nuns marching in Selma, Alabama, with Martin Luther King or the key roles played by Fr. Daniel Berrigan, the Rev. William Sloane Coffin, and Rabbi Abraham Joshua Heschel (not to mention Richard John Neuhaus) in the founding of Clergy and Laymen Concerned About Vietnam. Here could be seen vividly the way in which consensus on the great moral issues of the day could bridge the divide created by creeds.

Things look a bit different today. Indeed, to some it might seem, in light of theological agreements like the Roman Catholic and Lutheran *Joint Declaration on the Doctrine of Justification* or the World Council of Churches' document on *Baptism, Eucharist and Ministry*, on the one hand, and the divisions within Christian denominations along culture-war party lines, on the other, that it is now doctrine that unites and service—or at least ethics— that divides. The neuralgic questions dividing Christians seem no longer to be whether righteousness is forensic or intrinsic, or whether Christ is present in the Eucharist through transubstantiation, sacramental union, virtual presence, or simply our act of remembering. Rather, they are questions of the role of women in Church and society, of the moral status of embryos and how this should shape public policy, or of the acceptance of homosexuality as normal and healthy that have pitted Christians against one another.

I would like to suggest, however, that this shift from doctrine to morals—from knowing to doing—is more apparent than real. Specifically, it was true in the past and remains true today that knowing and doing are mutually implicating. So-called doctrinal disputes about belief are equally disputes about the shape of the lives of those who hold those beliefs, while so-called moral disagreements often imply differing systems of belief in which particular moral positions are embedded. As Charles Sanders Peirce put it, "to be deliberately and thoroughly prepared to shape one's conduct into conformity with a proposition is neither more nor less than the state of mind called Believing that proposition."[8] To believe a doctrine is to be prepared to act in a certain way; and our readiness to act in certain ways is attendant upon a network of beliefs.

II

Before looking at a specific example to illustrate this point, I should like to say a bit more about my own particular understanding of terms like "morals" and "ethics." Though I do not subscribe to the view that etymology is equivalent to definition, I do think it is instructive to ponder the roots of "moral" in the Latin *mos* and of "ethics" in the Greek *ēthos*, both of which mean "custom." It would be a mistake to draw from this the lesson that morals are simply a matter of custom or convention, but I do think it is true that our moral sense—our sense of whom to praise and whom to blame, our sense of which goods to pursue and which evils to avoid—derives from a complex web of specific beliefs, institutions, practices, social habits, and so forth that might be described as constituting a "moral ecology."[9] Moral norms can only be fully intelligible and convincing in the context of a "culture," which Clifford Geertz defined as "an historically transmitted pattern of meanings embodied in symbols, a system of inherited conceptions expressed in symbolic forms by means of which men can communicate, perpetuate, and develop

8. Charles Sanders Peirce, "A Neglected Argument for the Reality of God," in *Collected Papers of Charles Sanders Peirce*, ed. Charles Hartshorne and Paul Weiss (Cambridge, MA: Harvard University Press, 1935), 6:467.

9. On "moral ecology," see Allen Hertzke, "The Theory of Moral Ecology," *The Review of Politics* 60, no. 4 (1998): 629–60. Pope Benedict XVI speaks of a "human ecology" in his encyclical *Caritas in Veritate*, noting, "Just as human virtues are interrelated, such that the weakening of one places others at risk, so the ecological system is based on respect for a plan that affects both the health of society and its good relationship with nature. . . . The book of nature is one and indivisible: it takes in not only the environment but also life, sexuality, marriage, the family, social relations: in a word, integral human development" (51).

their knowledge about and attitudes toward life."[10] This rooting of morality in culture need not, as some have feared, commit one to "cultural relativism."[11] What it does commit one to, however, is abandoning any clear delineation between "moral" matters and all of the other elements that go into creating the culture or ecology in which questions of the goodness or badness of human actions find their intelligibility.[12] As with a natural ecosystem, a moral ecology cannot be engineered, with elements eliminated or introduced willy-nilly, though it may of course undergo incremental change.[13]

One ought not, therefore, separate too easily matters of belief from matters of behavior, matters of doctrine from matters of morality. Of course, one might protest that such a separation is precisely something that Christianity, and the Western

10. Clifford Geertz, *The Interpretation of Cultures* (New York: Basic, 1973), 89. Talal Asad has criticized this definition of culture as being focused too narrowly on "consciousness" and thus excluding the material conditions of such consciousness. When this definition is then applied to religion as a cultural system, it skews our understanding of religion in an individualist and interiorized direction and obscures the workings of power in the transition from discourse to action, from cognition to behavior. It seems to me that part of what is at work in Asad's criticisms is a Nietzschean/Foucauldian presupposition against any universal claim or definition and a fascination with "power" as the occluded *tertium quid* linking religious discourse and religious practice. Yet this appeal to "power" seems no less vague and no less universalizing than Geertz's appeal to "culture" or "religion." That being said, Asad offers a salutary reminder that the connection between knowing and doing, while intimate, is not entirely seamless, and that particular social configurations do have a role in "authorizing" both beliefs and behaviors. See Talal Asad, "Anthropological Conceptions of Religion: Reflections on Geertz," *Man*, New Series 18, no. 2 (Summer 1983): 237–59.

11. Geertz himself notes that "the notion that the essence of what it means to be human is most clearly revealed in those features of human culture that are universal rather than in those that are distinctive to this people or that is a prejudice we are not necessarily obliged to share. . . . [I]t may be in the cultural particularities of people—in their oddities—that some of the most instructive revelations of what it is to be generically human are to be found" (*The Interpretation of Cultures*, 43).

12. This view was argued, somewhat obliquely, in Elizabeth Anscombe's classic 1958 essay "Modern Moral Philosophy," in *The Collected Philosophical Papers of G. E. M. Anscombe*, vol. 3, *Ethics, Religion and Politics* (Oxford: Blackwell, 1981), 26–42. It has been robustly developed by Alasdair MacIntyre in, *inter alia, After Virtue*, 2nd ed. (Notre Dame, IN: University of Notre Dame Press, 1984); *Whose Justice? Which Rationality?* (Notre Dame, IN: University of Notre Dame Press, 1988); and *Three Rival Versions of Moral Inquiry* (Notre Dame, IN: University of Notre Dame Press, 1990).

13. Also, unlike a natural ecosystem, a moral ecology is almost wholly determined by human choices. Thus, the organic metaphor ought not to be taken as anything more than a metaphor, such that we forget that decisions about faith and morals are always matters of human agency, even if that agency is an instrument of the Holy Spirit.

intellectual tradition in general, has always done. For example, Aristotle and, following him, Thomas Aquinas distinguished between intellectual and moral virtues.[14] As Thomas makes clear, this distinction grows at least in part from the phenomenon, known to St. Paul no less than to Aristotle, of moral weakness, in which knowing the good does not always equal doing the good.[15] Conversely, this distinction can also explain how someone might be a good biologist or accountant—i.e., possess certain intellectual virtues—without being a good human being. Yet even within the tradition that distinguishes intellectual virtues from moral virtues, it is clear that there is a profound connection among all the virtues. For Thomas, perfect possession of any moral virtue requires the possession of all the other moral virtues, in particular prudence, which itself is something of a hybrid between a moral and an intellectual virtue.[16] And the moral virtues themselves are not truly and perfectly virtuous apart from the infused gift of charity, which in turn cannot exist apart from faith, which is a virtue perfecting the intellect.[17] Indeed, Thomas calls faith the first of the virtues and says that "there are no real virtues unless faith be presupposed."[18]

The unity of knowing and doing is perhaps best captured in Thomas's discussion of the gift of wisdom, which is the gift that corresponds to the virtue of charity, and therefore has its cause in the will, while having the intellect as its subject, thus being both speculative and practical.[19] It is precisely this unity of the speculative and the practical that finds expression in the unique structure that Thomas gives to the *Summa theologiae*, in which

14. Aristotle, *Nichomachean Ethics* 1.13 (1103a); Thomas Aquinas, *Summa theologiae* 1-2.58.2.

15. See Romans 7:14–20.

16. *Summa theologiae* 2-2.47.1.

17. See *Summa theologiae* 1.2.65 for one of Thomas's discussions of the connectivity of the virtues.

18. *Summa theologiae* 2-2.4.7.

19. *Summa theologiae*, 2-2.45.2–3.

the discussion of what would later be called "moral theology" is situated within doctrinal reflection: on the one side, discussion of the nature of God, one and triune, as well as creation, and, on the other side, Christology and eschatology. As Leonard Boyle pointed out a number of years ago, the *Summa* represents a pedagogical experiment on Thomas's part, in which he sought to present the instruction required for the training of Dominican friars in what was one of their most important tasks—the administering of the sacrament of Penance—within the context of their other most important task—the preaching of Christian doctrine. Thomas's identity as a Dominican led him to see doctrine and ethics as part of a single task or, to use the metaphor I employed a moment ago, as elements within a single ecosystem of knowing and doing. Boyle further notes that the frequency with which the *Pars Secunda Secundae*—the section of the *Summa* that deals with "practical" matters of virtue and vice—circulated separately from the rest of the *Summa* indicates that Thomas's confreres either didn't understand what he was trying to do or thought it misguided.[20]

This unity of knowing and doing, of doctrine and ethics, is by no means peculiar to Thomas or the Catholic tradition. The other obvious example of a unified treatment of doctrine and ethics is Karl Barth's *Church Dogmatics*. Barth's way of speaking about this connection is of course quite different from Thomas's. We find little talk of virtue and much of divine command and an explicit rejection of any appeal to natural law. In Barth the connection between knowing and doing is thought of in terms of the revelation of the God who commands. The action of human beings is always a response to God's action, and the fundamental act of God is self-revelation: "The Word of God does not need to be supplemented by an act. The Word of God is itself the act of

---

20. Leonard E. Boyle, OP, *The Setting of the* Summa theologiae *of St. Thomas* (Toronto: Pontifical Institute of Medieval Studies, 1982).

God."[21] Thus Barth is clear that "The one Word of God is both Gospel *and* Law. . . . It is the Gospel which contains and encloses the Law as the ark of the covenant the tables of Sinai."[22] Ethics is therefore a part of dogmatics and not a separate topic. Barth furthermore recognizes that Thomas, for all the (from Barth's perspective) shortcomings of his approach, is at one with him in locating ethics within theology.[23]

It does seem odd, however, to speak of a "moral ecology" (or any other sort of ecology, for that matter) in connection with Karl Barth. The claim that knowing and doing are co-implicated in a complex network of specific beliefs, institutions, practices, social habits, and so forth seems at odds with what might be called Barth's "occasionalism," the strong emphasis in his theology on the vertical relationship of obedience to the divine command that would seem to undercut any sense of moral growth or development and the need for an environment in which such growth takes place. The unified knowing-doing of the creature seems to exist suspended in mid-air, in a moment of existential decision, which itself hangs suspended from the free speech-act of the electing God. Yet perhaps the starkness of Barth's formulation of the unity of knowing and doing might be read as a corrective to any tendency to treat our discussion of moral ecology as something purely natural, as if the beliefs and practices that make up the ecosystem of Christian existence might be understood on a purely anthropological basis. It reminds us that the health of this ecology stands or falls on its rootedness in God's revelation in Christ and on its ongoing cultivation by the Spirit.

Thus, both Thomas and Barth, in rather different ways,

21. Karl Barth, *Church Dogmatics*, vol. 1.1, *The Doctrine of the Word of God*, trans. G.W. Bromiley, 2nd ed. (Edinburgh: T&T Clark, 1975), 143.

22. Karl Barth, *Church Dogmatics*, vol. 2.2, *The Doctrine of God*, trans. G.W. Bromiley et al. (Edinburgh: T&T Clark, 1957), 511.

23. Barth writes, "It is certainly remarkable that although Thomas' ethics refers unmistakably to an independent basis it is not presented independently of his dogmatics, but in a subordinate position within it" (*Church Dogmatics*, vol. 1.2, *The Doctrine of the Word of God*, trans. G.T. Thomson and Harold Knight [Edinburgh: T&T Clark, 1956], 783).

present the Christian life as a unity of knowing and doing, the speculative and the practical. Thomas has a perhaps more robust account of the "horizontal" dimension of the interwoven web of beliefs and practices that make up the fabric of the Christian life, whereas Barth offers a perhaps stronger rebuke to any temptation to forget that the Christian life is fundamentally a life of thankful response to God's prior act. But both of them present the knowing and doing of Christians in such an intricately interwoven way that it should forestall the invocation of slogans such as "doctrine divides; service unites," for to separate doctrine and service, faith and works, the speculative and the practical, is precisely to unravel the fabric of the Christian life, to fracture the ecology of Christian belief and practice.

III

To give a sense of how all of this might be in play in divisions among Christians, I would like to look at a historical example: the case of Augustine and the Donatists in the fourth and fifth centuries. This controversy is notoriously complex, particularly if one takes into account the analogous and historically related controversies involving Cyprian of Carthage and Stephen of Rome in the third century. Aside from historical questions of who did what when, and who took which side and for what reason, there are theological questions of how exactly the positions of the various parties hang together and relate to each other. By the Middle Ages, and continuing on into the Reformation era, a considerable simplification of the issues involved had taken place: Donatism was identified as a heresy—a deviation of belief—regarding the efficacy of sacraments administered by sinful clergy.[24] It was never entirely lost sight of, however, that the particular question of

---

24. See, e.g., Thomas Aquinas, *Summa theologiae* 3.64.9 *sed contra*; John Calvin, *Institutes of the Christian Religion*, 4.15.16; *Augsburg Confession* a. 8.

the sacraments was part of a larger debate over the nature of the Church, and modern historical investigations have once again brought to the fore the complexity of the issues involved.

The Donatist controversy arises from an argument in the North African Church over who would become the bishop of Carthage not long after the end of the Diocletian persecution in 305 AD.[25] To greatly simplify, we might speak of a spectrum of attitudes within the Church with regard to those who had collaborated with Roman authorities under persecution, particularly those Church leaders who had handed over the Scriptures rather than face martyrdom or imprisonment. At one end were the rigorists, who, even after the end of the persecution, saw their relationship with the authorities as an antagonistic one, and who also took a hard line with those who had compromised during the persecution, in particular the clergy, whom, they argued, should only be readmitted to the Church, if at all, as laymen. At the other end were those who had a less antagonistic attitude toward the Roman authorities and who sought an easier path back into the Church for those who had compromised. Mensurius, who tended toward the latter end of the spectrum, was bishop of Carthage in the immediate aftermath of persecution and managed to hold this divided community together. Upon his death, shortly before Constantine issued the Edict of Toleration, Caecilian, who shared Mensurius' general approach, was elected to be his successor in what appears to have been a hotly contested election. Among the many charges that the rigorists subsequently leveled against Caecilian was that one of the bishops who participated in his ordination had collaborated with the Roman authorities during the Diocletian persecution, and therefore the ordination itself was "tainted." They elected Majorinus as the true bishop of Carthage, and thus a schism was born. Majorinus' successor was Donatus,

25. For a concise account of Donatism, see Robert A. Markus, "Donatus, Donatism," in *Augustine Through the Ages: An Encyclopedia*, ed. Allan D. Fitzgerald, OSA, et al. (Grand Rapids, MI: Eerdmans, 1999), 284–87.

from whom we derive the name "Donatists." The followers of Caecilian called themselves "Catholics" because they saw themselves as representing the consensus of the Church outside of Africa. By the time of Augustine, the chief "doctrinal" issue between the two parties was the Donatist refusal to accept Catholic baptisms as true baptism, because of the "taint" of the ministers who administered them, and thus the requirement that converts from Catholicism submit to a second baptism; the Catholics, in contrast, did accept Donatist baptisms. But the issues went far beyond this particular doctrinal point.

The Donatists did not begin from the speculative premise that collaborator-bishops—or those guilty of any other sin, for that matter—were no longer capable of confecting "valid" sacraments. Rather, they were concerned about the purity of the Church, a purity that was at once a ritual purity and a moral purity. They saw themselves as the true heirs of the great North African martyr-bishop Cyprian, who in the mid-third century had led the Church of North Africa through an analogous conflict in the wake of the Decian persecution. Cyprian writes that "all are absolutely bound to the sin who have been contaminated by the sacrifice of a profane and unrighteous priest."[26] Again, Cyprian writes, "it is manifest that they who are not in the Church of Christ are reckoned among the dead; and another cannot be made alive by him who himself is not alive, since there is one Church which, having attained the grace of eternal life, both lives forever and quickens the people of God."[27] The question was not primarily one of the moral status of the individual minister of the sacraments, but whether or not those sacraments were administered within the ambit of the true Church. And for the Donatists, the true Church, the Church that was the true heir of Cyprian,

---

26. Cyprian, *Epistles* 67.3, in Ante-Nicene Fathers, vol. 5.
27. Cyprian, *Epistles* 70.1.

was the Church of the martyrs and confessors, who had resisted and continued to resist Roman authorities.

When Augustine became bishop of Hippo and began to address the Donatist problem, he realized that winning over the people of North Africa to the Catholic side depended upon being able to claim Cyprian, the venerated martyr-bishop, for his side. As the quotations above indicate, this was no small feat, for Cyprian was unambiguous that there could be no true Baptism outside the true Church. In what was either a brilliant insight or a rhetorical sleight of hand, Augustine argued that while Cyprian stood against the practice of accepting heretical and schismatic baptisms, his overriding concern was not the purity of the Church but its unity. He noted that Cyprian was less concerned with moral or doctrinal pollution than he was with the sin of schism—a concern manifested in his refusal to break communion with Pope Stephen over their disagreement concerning the baptism question.[28] It is true that Cyprian was mistaken on what, in his day, was an undecided issue concerning Baptism, but "his error was compensated by his remaining in catholic unity, and by the abundance of his charity."[29] While the Donatists might be Cyprian's descendants in sharing his error, they could lay no claim to his inheritance of unity and love. It was in the context of arguing this larger point that Augustine made his claim that "the baptism of Christ, consecrated by the words of the gospel, is necessarily holy, however polluted and unclean its ministers may be."[30]

IV

Though this is only a sketch of the controversy, it will have to suffice for my purpose, which is to ask, was the Donatist-Catholic schism

28. See Augustine, *On Baptism: Against the Donatists* 5.25.36, in Nicene and Post-Nicene Fathers, Series 1, vol. 4.

29. Augustine, *On Baptism*, 1.18.28.

30. Augustine, 3.10.14.

over doctrinal matters or moral matters? "Donatism," as the name of a heresy, as this name is used in later theological discussions, seems to be a doctrinal position concerning sacramental efficacy. But in Donatism as a historical phenomenon, this specific doctrinal position was a secondary and perhaps tertiary concern. The specific "doctrinal" question of sacramental efficacy was embedded in a host of other sorts of questions that might strike us as "moral" or "ethical" ones. For instance:

- Is it ever acceptable to simulate apostasy by obtaining, either by bribery or forgery, an official certificate testifying that one had sacrificed to the Roman gods? Is it acceptable to simulate apostasy by offering an animal or incense to the gods, if one is not making such an offering sincerely (what the Jesuit casuists of the seventeenth century would call "making a mental reservation")? These are questions that arose in Cyprian's day during the Decian persecution and shaped the later perspectives of both Donatists and Catholics.[31]
- Should there be, for certain grave crimes, a permanent exclusion from the Church, an excommunication without remit, a sort of spiritual capital punishment? Similarly, should Church leaders who have betrayed the Church, if they are readmitted, be permanently barred from all leadership and perpetually marked as *traditores*, perhaps the ecclesial equivalent of being placed on a public sex offender's list (an analogy that, sadly, is particularly striking today)? What, in short, are the limits to forgiveness, and is punishment meant to be a means of rehabilitation or retribution?
- Should violence ever be employed by Christians? In the case of the Donatists, are the insurgents known as

---

31. See the casuistry in which Cyprian engages in works such as *Epistle 51* or *On the Lapsed*.

circumcelliones warranted in their acts of violence against the state-supported Catholic Church? In the case of the Catholics, is the use of the power of the state warranted in defense against the Donatist insurgents? If allowable as a means of defense, is it also justified as a means of coercing the Donatists into the Catholic Church?

In light of these questions, we might be inclined to say that the North African schism was not over doctrinal issues at all but moral issues concerning truth-telling, retribution, or violence. These moral issues are certainly weighty and perhaps a blessed relief from the moral issues that currently seem to be dividing churches. But before we decide that the Church-dividing issues in fourth-century North Africa were moral ones, we ought to take a further step back and ask about the broader theological background of these particular issues.

For example, questions of the moral gravity of "simulated" apostasy can only be adjudicated against a background of common assumptions about how interior and exterior acts are related, and of how Christians are called to bear witness, and of what sort of privileged place martyrs have in the Christian imagination. Questions of exclusion and forgiveness are embedded in further questions of divine justice and mercy and of how the relationship between these two is imagined, as well as questions concerning grace and merit and the degree to which the Church is called to purify itself of all corrupt elements. They are also related to exegetical questions concerning, for example, Matthew 13:24–30, and whether the Church should be conceived of as the wheat among the tares (the Donatist reading), or as the field that contains *both* wheat *and* tares (Augustine's reading). Likewise, questions of Christians and violence, particularly the violence of the state, perhaps depend upon how one understands the relationship of the thirteenth chapter of Romans to the thirteenth chapter of Revelation, the relationship of salvation history to world history, or even the relationship of nature to grace.

In short, the long dispute that split the Church in North Africa involved questions about what Christians should do, all of which in turn were only answerable in terms of what the various parties thought that they knew about God and the world. How we act in the world as intentional agents—that is, our distinctively human mode of action—always depends upon how we see the world, upon the possibilities and parameters that present themselves to us. The Donatists, rooted in the North African experience of harsh persecution and the memory of the martyrs, saw a hostile world in which the Church was an enclave of purity that must police its borders in order to maintain itself in purity until the day when the Lord of the harvest would come to gather the Church into his kingdom. The Catholics, more closely connected to the center of the Empire, saw a somewhat more benign world in which the Church was a dynamic force, transforming the world gradually so that eventually God would be all in all. Augustine, who had a foot in North Africa and a foot in the wider world of the Roman Empire, might be seen as offering something of a synthesis of these two worldviews, combining the dynamic, transformative vision of Catholic Christianity with a mitigated form of Donatist dualism, such that the City of God, which is not entirely identifiable with the visible Church, is perpetually on the move, on pilgrimage through history, living cheek by jowl with the earthly city, even within the sacramental bonds of the Church.

It is between these differing visions that disagreements over moral issues have their place. Between Catholics and Donatists there was no significant disagreement over the morality of truth telling, but there was a difference over the degree to which the Church could accommodate within her bounds those who had failed to bear truthful witness. More striking are the differing attitudes toward Christian use of violent coercion. Some partisans for both sides were willing to countenance the use of violence for certain ends, whether the insurgent violence of the Donatist *circumcelliones* or the state-sanctioned violence employed by the Catholics.[32] The *sort* of violence that each side saw as allowable differed in part, no doubt, because of the coercive force that each had available to it: the Donatists had the widespread popular support that enables insurgent violence, while the Catholics had the Empire on their side. But it also fit within a particular view of how the Church related to the world. For the Catholics, the Church had the capacity to absorb the world, transform the Empire, and even turn its violence to holy ends. For the Donatists, the Church was to remain apart from the world, the ark of salvation sheltering God's chosen ones from the coming judgment, an ark defended by the blood of the martyrs, but also, perhaps, by insurgent counterviolence. Augustine, again, found himself somewhere in the middle. His understanding of the pilgrim nature of the City of God led him initially to reject the use of coercive state power against the Donatists, but eventually he acceded to a limited use of violence as a legitimate employment of the "peace" of the earthly city. These differences are not differences simply on the question of violence but rather of entire moral or, more generally, theological ecologies.

The conflict over Donatism is sometimes reduced by the sort of histories of doctrine inflicted on seminarians to a dispute over sacramental efficacy. I hope I have indicated how this sacramental question is embedded within a host of other questions, some of which we might characterize as "moral," such as the question of the legitimacy of the use of violence by Christians. These other

32. For a discussion of the variety of Donatist attitudes toward insurgent violence and the rhetorical strategies of their opponents, see Peter Iver Kaufman, "Donatism Revisited: Moderates and Militants in Late Antique North Africa," *Journal of Late Antiquity* 2, no. 1 (Spring 2009): 131–42.

questions, in turn, can only properly be understood when seen as part of a larger worldview, a theological "ecology" that shapes not only the answers to our doctrinal and moral questions, but also the very questions that we ask. For Catholics and Donatists, to reach a consensus on the question of sacramental efficacy or the moral question of the legitimacy of the use of violence by Christians would have involved a convergence of ecologies, requiring a common thinking through of such things as the meaning of martyrdom, the relation of Church and world, the economies of divine mercy and justice, the role of grace in human transformation, and even the nature of human history itself. In the end, the path of one side suppressing the other proved to be the easier alternative.

V

I think one could give a similar analysis of various other divisive issues in the history of the Church. To take what is probably the most obvious example, the doctrinal reformations of the sixteenth century—both Catholic and Protestant—were part of a wider transformation of the spiritual ecology of early modern Europe. A sense of the complex interplay of belief and practice, doctrine and morals, was pioneered by Max Weber, as articulated in the much-contested thesis of his *The Protestant Ethic and the Spirit of Capitalism*. One might have doubts about his views on the supplanting of ascetic medieval Catholicism by worldly Protestantism, but he was surely correct in trying to draw connections between theological conceptions and practical attitudes, between knowing and doing.[33] More recent revisionist social historians of the sixteenth century, such as John Bossy and Eamon Duffy, have followed Weber's general impulse, if not his specific conclusions,

33. See Max Weber, *The Protestant Ethic and the Spirit of Capitalism* (New York: Scribner's, 1976). For a further discussion of Weber, see Essay 8 of this volume, "The Politics of Disenchantment."

in offering a complex picture, rich in detail, of the transformation of knowing and doing in the early modern period.[34] One cannot grasp the full significance of the Reformers' teaching on justification unless one also attends to changing practices regarding liturgy, catechesis, pilgrimage, penance, clerical celibacy, the role of the secular state, usury, almsgiving, and so forth.[35] Nor can one fully appreciate the teaching of Trent on this same question unless one attends to the desire to retain and reform these same practices.[36] The change of one element—whether in the realm of knowing or doing—may well lead to changes within the ecology as a whole.

Thinking of the division of Christendom in the sixteenth century in terms of the development of distinct ecologies can account not just for confessional and moral differences but also for similarities, whether of continuing practices or new developments. The set of relationships within an ecosystem are so varied and complex that a change in one element might only gradually make its effect felt. Indeed, the very notion of an ecosystem should lead us to expect that we ought to think not in terms of revolutions but of evolutions. For example, despite Luther's grudging acceptance of the practice, attitudes toward divorce changed only gradually. At the same time that Catholicism and Protestantism

34. John Bossy, *Christianity in the West: 1400–1700* (Oxford: Oxford University Press, 1985); Eamon Duffy, *The Stripping of the Altars: Traditional Religion in England, 1400–1580* (New Haven: Yale University Press, 1992).

35. Steven Ozment offers a fairly exhaustive list: "Protestants proposed a revolution in religious concepts, practice, and institutions. Even in its modest forms the Reformation called for, and in most Protestant areas permanently achieved, an end to mandatory fasting; auricular confession; the worship of saints, relics, and images; indulgences; pilgrimages and shrines; vigils; weekly, monthly, and annual masses for the dead; the belief in purgatory; Latin worship services; the sacrifice of the Mass; numerous religious ceremonies, festivals and holidays; the canonical hours; extreme unction, confirmation, holy orders, and penance; clerical celibacy; clerical immunity from civil taxation and criminal jurisdiction; nonresident benefices; excommunication and interdict; canon law; episcopal and papal authority; and traditional scholastic education of the clergy" (*The Reformation in the Cities: The Appeal of Protestantism in Sixteenth-Century Germany* [New Haven: Yale University Press], 117–18).

36. David Power emphasizes in particular Trent's concern to articulate a doctrine of Eucharistic sacrifice that would secure the practice of offering Masses for particular intentions, as well as the distinctive role of the priest over against the worshipping community. See *The Sacrifice We Offer: The Tridentine Dogma and Its Reinterpretation* (New York: Crossroad, 1987).

slowly grew apart in some ways, they were often developing along analogous paths in other ways. John Bossy points out in particular the growth, albeit in different modes, of a more interiorized and individualized approach to Christianity in both Catholicism and Protestantism.[37] This is because the spiritual ecologies of Catholics and Protestants were not sharply divided from each other, nor were they clearly distinguished from the developing ecology of modernity. Despite their doctrinal disagreements, both Catholics and Protestants in the sixteenth and seventeenth centuries were equally subject to such forces as the rise of the nation-state and the development of print culture. Mary Midgely notes that if one thinks of cultures on the analogy of ecosystems then we should expect that different cultures would "shade into one another,"[38] not unlike the way a desert shades into a plain, which in turn shades into a forest. From the center of these ecosystems the differences might seem quite clear; along the borders the differences might seem so insignificant that one could pass from one to the other without noticing.

VI

So where does all this leave us with regard to doctrinal and moral divisions within the Body of Christ?

First, there ought to be no sharp delineation of the doctrinal and the moral. If, as Peirce said, the state of believing is "to be deliberately and thoroughly prepared to shape one's conduct into conformity with a proposition," then there is something arbitrary about deciding that the presence of Christ in the Eucharist is a doctrinal question while homosexuality is a moral one. Certainly, our beliefs about the Eucharist have implications for our actions,

---

37. Bossy, *Christianity in the West*, 126–40.
38. Mary Midgely, *Can't We Make Moral Judgments?* (New York: St. Martin's, 1991), 90.

not only in the liturgy but also in the realm of politics.[39] Likewise, our views on homosexuality imply and should be informed by our convictions concerning theological anthropology, the nature of the authority of Scripture, or whether we believe there is a natural law and how we understand it in relation to culture. The doctrinal and the moral are simply inseparable because what we believe to be true is but the flip side of how we believe we should act. This is not to say that people with differing beliefs cannot agree upon a common course of action—that is, where there are doctrinal divisions, people might still unite in common service. But it is to say that the accounts people give of the significance of their actions might vary widely, and may indeed be incommensurable, such that there is no real agreement in action without an agreement in conviction, at least not if we are to speak of a *moral* act.

Second, in light of the unity of knowing and doing, ecumenical dialogue and consensus seem a more daunting venture than we might have imagined in the past. This is true whether one prioritizes knowing or doing. If we take seriously the analogy of belief systems with ecosystems, then there is a real sense in which one cannot address a piece without addressing the whole. Have we reached consensus on justification if we continue to differ on what constitutes social justice? Can there be real agreement in theological anthropology so long as differences remain over the practice of marriage? Piecemeal agreements on specific doctrines, as well as piecemeal alliances made around specific moral issues, do not necessarily fit together to form a larger whole that we might call "Christian unity." They may, in fact, constitute nothing more than a heap of fragments that the slightest wind could blow apart.

Finally, and maybe more hopefully, as daunting as the task

---

39. See, e.g., William T. Cavanaugh, *Torture and Eucharist: Theology, Politics, and the Body of Christ* (Cambridge: Blackwell, 1998).

is, we might still believe that the ecumenical venture, even the venture to reach agreement on contentious moral issues, is not impossible. True, it is taken up piecemeal—now this doctrine, now that moral question—but this is true of everything in life. We live in a world in which knowing and doing are always going on at the same time, but we find our way through that world in a piecemeal fashion. So, there is no in-principle objection to taking up issues as they come and reaching consensus as best we can, as long as we recognize that such consensus will be provisional and that it may have to be revisited in light of a later issue that comes up for discussion. We must be open to the possibility that the agreement that we thought we had regarding theological anthropology might prove to be of insufficient depth when we come to discuss the practices of marriage. Likewise, we ought not to be surprised if our agreement on a matter of social justice begins to unravel once we examine the differing beliefs that undergird our practices. But just because the venture proves to be more complex than we imagined does not mean that it is impossible. Indeed, Christ's prayer for the unity of the Church ought to compel us to believe that it is possible.

4

The Trinity and Politics

There is something peculiarly "modern" in the question of the relationship between the doctrine of the Trinity and how one might think about politics. The explicit suggestion that there is a connection between how one thinks about political life and how one understands God as Father, Son, and Spirit is rare, if not entirely unknown, prior to the twentieth century. In this essay, I will focus on twentieth-century theologians who bring together "Trinity" and "politics" in an attempt to show what such a conjunction can and cannot do.

Before looking at specific theologians, however, we might ask why modern Christians would suddenly turn to the doctrine of the Trinity as a resource for thinking about politics. This can best be understood if we see it as part of a larger shift in philosophy and theology regarding how we understand the nature of talk about God. If I might take Immanuel Kant as a representative modern figure, one can see in his philosophy the transformation of God from something to be speculatively contemplated into a postulate of practical reason—something of which we can have no knowledge but which we must posit in order to undergird morality. As Kant puts the matter, "It concerns us not so much to know what God is in himself (his nature) as what he is for us as moral

*This essay was originally published as "The Trinity and Politics," in *The Oxford Handbook on the Trinity*, edited by Gilles Emery and Matthew Levering (Oxford: Oxford University Press, 2011), 531–43.

beings."[1] In the relocation of religion into the realm of practical reason, much Christian doctrine concerning God would seem to vanish, being irrelevant to us as moral beings. Thus, for Kant, once we are no longer concerned to know God *in se* but only *pro nobis*, we can abandon the doctrine of the Trinity, at least as something that says something true about God. He writes,

> the doctrine of the Trinity, taken literally, has no practical rel-
> evance at all, even if we think we understand it; and it is even
> more clearly irrelevant if we realize that it transcends all our
> concepts. Whether we are to worship three or ten persons in
> the Deity makes no difference.[2]

Because the Trinity both transcends all our concepts *and* has no practical moral relevance, it cannot even properly be called a "mystery" in the way that creation, atonement, or election can.[3] It is, it seems, simply sophistry.

If God in modernity must become a postulate of practical reason, then one possible way to acquit the doctrine of the Trinity of the charge of irrelevance would be to show that it is a valuable *practical* resource for human political and social life. Thus, the very topic "Trinity and politics" answers to a modern exigency, and we ought not to be surprised if theologians who deal explicitly with this connection are found almost exclusively in the modern period.

MODERN SCHEMATIC APPROACHES

Surveying the last hundred years, we find two approaches to the question of the Trinity and politics that might be characterized as

1. Immanuel Kant, *Religion within the Limits of Reason Alone*, trans. Theodore Greene and Hoyt Hudson (New York: Harper, 1960), 130.

2. Immanuel Kant, *The Conflict of the Faculties*, trans. Mary J. McGregor (Lincoln, NE: University of Nebraska Press, 1979), 67.

3. Kant, *Reason Alone*, 133–34.

"schematic," by which I mean that they take the Trinity as offering a pattern or paradigm that can be employed in reflection on human social life.[4] The first, which obeys Kant's strictures most faithfully, is the approach exemplified in the American Protestant theologian H. Richard Niebuhr. In this approach, the relevance of the doctrine of the Trinity has nothing to do with what it does or does not say about God; it is an entirely anthropological doctrine. According to Niebuhr, "Trinitarianism is by no means as speculative a position and as unimportant for conduct as is often maintained." Instead, it addresses the quite practical problem of "the relation of Jesus Christ to the Creator of nature and Governor of history as well as the Spirit immanent in creation and in the Christian community,"[5] which for Niebuhr is a problem of knowledge. That is, it is a meta-doctrine that coordinates three sources of religious knowledge: nature, history, and experience.

Niebuhr works this out most fully in a 1946 essay entitled "The Doctrine of the Trinity and the Unity of the Church."[6] In this essay, Niebuhr presents the Trinity as a way of holding together the three "Unitarianisms" that are the *de facto* religion of Christians: the Unitarianism of the Father, which focuses on creation, reason, and natural law; the Unitarianism of the Son, which focuses on salvation, revelation, and the Sermon on the Mount; and the Unitarianism of the Spirit, which focuses on contemporary experience, both individual and communal. One can say that for Niebuhr the doctrine of the Trinity has the pragmatic value of holding together reason, revelation, and experience and, in terms of ethics, of balancing natural law, the teachings of Christ, and conscience. The doctrine of the Trinity becomes a way of saying that in their practical lives Christians do not need just natural

4. I have discussed these two approaches also in Frederick Christian Bauerschmidt, "The Trinity," in *Gathered for the Journey: Moral Theology in Catholic Perspective*, ed. David Matzko McCarthy and M. Therese Lysaught (Grand Rapids, MI: Eerdmans, 2007), 68–87.

5. H. Richard Niebuhr, *Christ and Culture* (New York: Harper, 1951), 80–81.

6. Reprinted in H. Richard Niebuhr, *Theology, History, and Culture: Major Unpublished Writings*, ed. William Stacy Johnson (New Haven: Yale University Press, 1996).

law, which might lead to a staid conventionalism, but also the revealed teachings of Jesus; at the same time, the sometimes impractical teachings of Jesus need to be balanced with the demands of human nature; and both of these need to be in turn balanced with individual conscience and contemporary experience, which have the role of adjudicating conflicts between the demands of nature and the demands of the Gospel.

Niebuhr's concern, at least in part, is to counter the putative "Christomonism" of theologians like Karl Barth, who, by their strong focus on Christ and their criticisms of appeals to both nature and experience, would seem to restrict the ability of Christians to enter into public discourse with non-Christians. Niebuhr's positive point is that a fully Trinitarian faith—with its claim that God reveals himself in nature, history, and experience—allows Christians to enter into civic discourse in a religiously diverse society. Though a secular polity might not allow appeal to the historical revelation of truth in Jesus Christ, appeal can still be made to nature and conscience as a common ground shared by all people.

The problems with this approach are obvious. First, from a doctrinal point of view, the account of the Trinity Niebuhr offers is a modalist one at best: "Father," "Son," and "Spirit" are simply ways of naming the activity of God as eternal Creator, historical Redeemer, and personal Inspirer. Second, the distinctions between reason, history, and interiority seem to be worked out prior to their correlation with the names "Father," "Son," and "Spirit." Not only does the Trinity not reveal anything about God *in se*, it does not really reveal anything about God *pro nobis*; one can know quite well that God is Creator, Redeemer, and Inspirer—that God is known through reason, history, and interior reflection—without any knowledge of the Trinity. How is the Christian's "Trinitarian" account of nature, historical revelation, and experience any different from that of a Jew or Muslim? Third, as Niebuhr presents it, the doctrine of the Trinity tells us that an adequate Christian ethics must take account of nature, history, and experience but says nothing about *how* these three are to be related. Does nature always trump history, such that political positions based on the teachings of Christ (e.g., non-retaliation or the prohibition of divorce) have no place in the public realm? Is it the role of experience to interpret nature and history, or is experience shaped historically, or given naturally, or is it somehow both? Were Niebuhr more inclined toward Trinitarian speculation, he might have claimed that there is a *perichoresis* or "mutual indwelling" of nature, history, and experience, but even this claim does nothing to help sort out the priority given in concrete situations to these different sources of ethical reflection.

As Niebuhr uses it, the Trinity is at best a heuristic device for talking about something that we know on an entirely different basis; at worst, it is simply linguistic decoration. To be fair to Niebuhr, this is something he is well aware of. At the end of "The Doctrine of the Trinity and the Unity of the Church," he notes with sincere modesty that what he has said is "only one approach, and that not the most significant or promising."[7] At the same time, I would note that this is the *only* approach to the doctrine that Niebuhr himself took in his writing. James Gustafson notes, "through and through, his reflections about God were impregnated by his Kantian mentality and his Troeltschian learning, which led him to take statements about God very seriously, without taking them with the seriousness that assumed he or any other man was making literal statements about the One beyond the Many."[8] In the end, Niebuhr's appeals to the doctrine of the Trinity are less a defense of the doctrine than an occupation by a foreign power: God is driven entirely out of the doctrine, and its linguistic shell is transformed into a vehicle for anthropological statements.

7. Niebuhr, *Theology, History, and Culture*, 62.

8. James Gustafson, introduction to *The Responsible Self: An Essay in Christian Moral Philosophy*, by H. Richard Niebuhr (New York: Harper, 1963), 6–41, at 27.

The second approach, more common today than Niebuhr's approach, is to see in the communion of Father, Son, and Spirit a model of human community. This approach does make a genuine claim about the divine nature and has a respectable, if not lengthy, ecclesiastical pedigree. In *Gaudium et Spes*, we read that there is "a certain similarity between the union of the divine persons and the union of God's children in truth and love."[9] Numerous recent examples of this approach can be given. Catherine Mowry LaCugna claims that Gregory of Nyssa's "idea of a shared divine *arché* . . . contained the seeds of a radical social order."[10] Michael Novak sees in the Trinitarian "pluralism-in-unity" a "dark illumination" of democratic capitalism, which is "a political economy differentiated and yet one."[11] Leonardo Boff, in contrast, claims that within Trinitarian communion, "mutual acceptance of differences is the vehicle for the plural unity of the three divine Persons," and that "by their practice and theory, capitalist regimes contradict the challenges and invitations of Trinitarian communion."[12]

One could go on at some length multiplying examples of this approach, which is usually characterized as "social Trinitarianism." This approach does not employ Trinitarian doctrine in the purely pragmatic and heuristic way that H. Richard Niebuhr does. LaCugna, who in places seems very wary of talk about God as Trinitarian *in se*, clearly maintains that the Trinity truly is how God is *pro nobis*—the God revealed in the economy of salvation is the triune God. Many of these thinkers are also cognizant of possible objections. Miroslav Volf, for example, notes that "the

9. Vatican Council II, *Gaudium et Spes* 24, in *Decrees of the Ecumenical Councils*, ed. Norman Tanner (Washington, DC: Georgetown University Press, 1990), 2:1083.

10. Catherine Mowry LaCugna, "God in Communion with Us: The Trinity," in *Freeing Theology: The Essentials of Theology in Feminist Perspective*, ed. Catherine Mowry LaCugna (New York: HarperCollins, 1993), 83–114, at 87.

11. Michael Novak, *The Spirit of Democratic Capitalism* (New York: Simon, 1982), 338–39.

12. Leonardo Boff, *Trinity and Society*, trans. Paul Burns (Maryknoll, NY: Orbis, 1988), 150.

road from the doctrine of the Trinity to proposals about global or national social arrangements is long, torturous, and fraught with danger"[13] and points by way of example to the fact that Novak and Boff use the Trinity to underwrite quite different economic arrangements.[14] Still, Volf, with a host of others, maintains that it is in some sort of "social" account of the Trinity that the vital future of Trinitarian thought lies.

Amidst their differences, social Trinitarian approaches share some formal features beyond simply recommending the doctrine of the Trinity as a remedy for certain social and political ills. Primarily, they all emphasize the distinctness of the Trinitarian persons and are critical of Western theology's purported emphasis on the unity of the divine nature. Social Trinitarianism is "social" not simply in taking the Trinity as a model for human societies but also in seeing the Trinity itself as a kind of divine society in which the divine persons have priority over the unity of essence. This, of course, makes a certain sense; if the Trinity is supposed to offer us a model for human persons in communion, then the closer the analogy between divine and human persons, the more effective the Trinity is as a model. It is noteworthy that Catherine LaCugna appeals to Andrei Rublev's icon in which the Trinity appears as the three visitors who received the hospitality of Abraham at Mamre as key to understanding the Trinity. This icon depicts a community of which we can see ourselves as part.[15] We might say that social Trinitarianism encourages us to look at Rublev's icon and take our place at the table, or perhaps simply to arrange ourselves at our own tables in a similarly egalitarian manner.

Despite the hegemony of what Karen Kilby calls this "new orthodoxy" in Trinitarian theology, a few critical voices have begun to be raised. Kilby herself argues that what we find in social

13. Miroslav Volf, "'The Trinity is Our Social Program': The Doctrine of the Trinity and the Shape of Social Engagement," *Modern Theology* 14, no. 3 (Summer 1998): 403–23, at 406.

14. Volf, "The Trinity," 419.

15. LaCugna, "God in Communion with Us," 83–84.

Trinitarianism is a process by which theologians first identify *perichoresis* as the name of whatever it is that makes the Father, Son, and Spirit one. The meaning of *perichoresis* is then supplied by projecting onto God what we value most in our relations with other human beings (e.g., warmth, love, empathy, equality, etc.). Finally, the divine *perichoresis* is offered as the model for human interrelation. Kilby acknowledges that all our human talk about God inevitably involves some projection of human qualities and values onto God, but what she finds so problematic about the projection involved in this case is the way in which what we project onto God is immediately commended to us as what is most significant about the Trinity.[16]

Kathryn Tanner also raises several issues with regard to this approach. She points out first that appeal to *perichoresis* yields a very vague politics. As she puts it,

> unless one purports to know much more about relations among the trinitarian persons than is probably warranted, one is still left with very vague recommendations—about the social goods of equality, a diverse community, and mutual relationships of giving and receiving. All the hard, controversial work of figuring out exactly what any of that might mean … seems left up to the ingenuity of the theologian arguing on other grounds.[17]

Tanner further points out that much of what Trinitarian doctrine says about the persons of the Trinity simply cannot apply to human persons. In particular, human persons are not constituted by their relations, at least not in the same sense that Trinitarian

---

16. Karen Kilby, "Perichoresis and Projection: Problems with Social Doctrines of the Trinity," *New Blackfriars* 81, no. 957 (November 2000): 432–45; reprinted in Karen Kilby, *God, Evil and the Limits of Theology* (London: T&T Clark, 2020), 5–16.

17. Kathryn Tanner, "Trinity," in *The Blackwell Companion to Political Theology*, ed. Peter Scott and William T. Cavanaugh, 2nd ed. (Oxford: Blackwell, 2018), 363–75, at 368.

persons are. Further, human relatedness is marked by sin in a way that divine relatedness is not, and any moral theology or politics that ignores this can hardly be relevant. She notes, "To a world of violent, corrupt, and selfish people, the Trinity seems to offer only the feeble plaint, 'Why can't we all just get along?'"[18]

One might, of course, argue that the violence, corruption, and selfishness that we find in human political struggles have some sort of analogue in God. Thus, Thomas Parker writes that "The Trinitarian life of God as a *perichoresis* of the 'persons' embraces the struggle for community as well as the achievement of communion."[19] Yet the risks involved in such a strategy ought to give one pause. Are the persons of the Trinity really involved in a "struggle for community"? If so, with whom are they struggling? Each other? Would it not be saner to see the human struggle for community as a result of our fallen state, or even our creaturely finitude, and not as something that can be projected onto God? Otherwise, the Christian understanding of God lapses into mythology. This seems too high a price to pay for political relevance.

The critiques of both Kilby and Tanner focus on how the attempts of social Trinitarianism to make the Trinity relevant to practical concerns fail because they simply impose on the doctrine a set of ethical positions that are, in fact, held on other grounds. In this way, social Trinitarianism does not seem all that different from the more "modalist" approach of H. Richard Niebuhr. Both approaches risk simply applying a theological gloss to a predetermined set of political and ethical concerns and are really more about us than they are about God. Also, both of these approaches might be characterized as "schematic," in that the doctrine of the Trinity is emptied of its specific content so as to serve as a schema or blueprint for various commendable

18. Tanner, "Trinity," 370.

19. Thomas D. Parker, "The Political Meaning of the Doctrine of the Trinity: Some Theses," *The Journal of Religion* 60, no. 2 (April 1980): 165–84 at 179.

things—whether the avoidance of Christomonism or the ideal of a peaceful communion of persons. What seems lost is the Trinity itself: the Father, Son, and Holy Spirit. Both of these approaches fail to the extent that they present the doctrine of the Trinity as being about something other than the Father who sends the Son into the world for our redemption in the Spirit. Any political relevance of the Trinity must be found not in abstractions made from the doctrine but in the actual life of God as this is revealed to us in its threefold fullness.

READING THE FOURTH CENTURY

These schematic approaches are not the only modern attempts to think "Trinity and politics." A significantly different approach can be found in two twentieth-century interpretations of Trinitarian disputes of the fourth century: the work of the German Catholic patristics scholar Erik Peterson and the American Protestant church historian George Huntston Williams. Their works are significant not only as interpretations of the fourth century but also as creative contributions to political theology.

In "Der Monotheismus als politisches Problem," first published in 1935, Peterson argues that certain early Christian thinkers, most notably Eusebius of Caesarea, developed a "political theology" based on a dual premise: that the monarchy (*monarchia*) of God was mirrored on earth by the monarchy of the Roman emperor, and that the Roman Empire played a providential role in establishing the peace necessary for the spread of the Gospel. It is the former claim that concerns us here because it is precisely this claim that Peterson sees as destroyed by orthodox Trinitarian theology.[20] In the approach outlined by Peterson, the orthodox understanding of God as Trinity is a hedge against

20. The latter claim, according to Peterson, is destroyed by the eschatological reserve of thinkers like Augustine. See Erik Peterson, "Monotheismus als politsches Problem," in *Theologische Traktate* (Munich, DE: Kösel-Verlag, 1951), 49–147, at 103–4. Translations mine.

any attempt to sacralize politics by claiming its adherence to a divine pattern.

Peterson argues that this view develops in the world of Greek thought, which links divine monarchy with political monarchy. Peterson further argues that in Philo (the first to use the term *monarchia*) we have a fusion of the politically inflected philosophical monotheism of the Greeks with the biblical monotheism of Judaism. In this fusion, Philo purges the model of divine governance of its polytheistic overtones by an emphasis on a divine monarch who rules by law rather than through lesser gods.[21] Philo's association of monotheism and *monarchia* is taken up by early Christian apologists, such as Justin. Peterson also notes that it is used in attempting to formulate Christian Trinitarian faith by theologians such as Tertullian, who appeals to the idea of the Roman co-principate as a way of arguing against the modalism of Praxeas—that is, Father and Son share their *monarchia* the way rule can be shared by a king and his son.[22] After the Peace of the Church, this approach to thinking of God in terms of *monarchia* and its association with the Roman Empire becomes even more politically freighted. This is, according to Peterson, particularly the case with Eusebius of Caesarea, for whom "the *one* monarch on earth—and that is for Eusebius no one other than Constantine—corresponds to the *one* divine monarch in the heavens."[23] Peterson concludes his argument with some brief remarks indicating how the orthodox Trinitarian theology developed by the Cappadocians and other pro-Nicene theologians undercuts the possibility of using *monarchia* to develop a political theology. Semi-Arians like Eusebius continued to understand the divine monarchy by analogy with the monarchy of the Roman emperor, in which power derives from a single person (the Father) to the exclusion of all others. Understood in this

21. Peterson, "Monotheismus," 59–60.
22. Peterson, 70–71.
23. Peterson, 92–93.

way, "monotheism is a political requirement, a piece of Imperial politics." Peterson contrasts this with a passage from Gregory of Nazianzus's *Third Theological Oration*, in which Gregory, while still affirming the *monarchia* of God, associates it with all three persons of the Trinity, thereby distancing it from any earthly *monarchia*.[24] Gregory writes:

> monarchy is that which we hold in honor. It is, however, a monarchy that is not limited to one person, for it is possible for unity if it is at variance with itself to come into a condition of plurality; but one that is made of an equality of nature, and a union of minds, and an identity of motion, and of a convergence of its elements to unity—a thing which is impossible to the created nature.[25]

What is notable here is the distance Gregory places between the divine *monarchia* and any created *monarchia*. The shared *monarchia* of Father, Son, and Spirit in no way provides a model for earthly rulers and therefore provides no legitimation for them either. In this way, Peterson forestalls any "political theology" if one understands by this the claim that particular human political arrangements follow a divine pattern of rule.

Of course, this is not to say that orthodox Trinitarian theologians in the fourth and fifth centuries were never enthusiastic supporters of the Roman Empire and never indulged in the kind of rhetoric associated with Eusebius, for whom Constantine "provides an example of divine monarchic sovereignty."[26] Nor is it to say that semi-Arian Trinitarian theology, which was more

---

24. Peterson, 102–3.

25. Gregory of Nazianzus, *Third Theological Oration* 2, in *Christology of the Later Fathers*, ed. Edward H. Hardy (Philadelphia: Westminster, 1954), 161; cf. Peterson, "Monotheismus," 103 and 144 n. 164.

26. Eusebius of Caesarea, *Oration on the Thirtieth Anniversary of Constantine's Reign* 3, in *The Early Church and the State*, ed. and trans. Agnes Cunningham, SSCM (Philadelphia: Fortress, 1982), 45–62, at 51.

or less the traditional subordinationist theology of the third century, was embraced by Eusebius simply because of its utility as a political theology.[27] What Peterson suggests, rather, is that the "low" Christology of the semi-Arians, for whom the Logos essentially serves a mediatorial function between God and the world, is more easily at home with the idea of the emperor as the earthly correlate to the Logos. As Eusebius puts it, the Logos is "the light that transcends the universe and surrounds his Father, mediating and keeping the Eternal and Uncreated Form apart from all that is created" and is also the one by and through whom "the emperor, so favored by God, receives an image of the heavenly kingdom and, in imitation of the greater Master [that is, the Logos], pilots and guides the course of the ship of state."[28] Thus, on Peterson's reading, both the Arian emphasis on the sole *monarchia* of the Father, along with the view of the Logos as the quasi-divine mediator between the uncreated God and creatures, enabled a political theology in which the monarchy of the emperor was the earthly image of God's monarchy, and his ordering of the Empire was an imitation of the Logos ordering creation.

Peterson's suggestion regarding orthodox Trinitarian theology was taken up and developed with great vigor by George Huntston Williams in a lengthy 1951 essay, in which he argued that the high Christology of the pro-Nicene theologians, along with their correlatively high doctrines of the Eucharist and the Church, not only forestalled the political use of theology but actually pushed these theologians toward a conflictual relationship with the Empire. The root of this conflict was the assertion by pro-Nicene theologians of the authority of Christ over that of the emperor and the insistence that the Spirit-filled Church, rather

---

27. For a nuanced reappraisal of Eusebius's theological interests, focusing more on his providential reading of history than on his Trinitarian theology, see Michael Hollerich, "Religion and Politics in the Writings of Eusebius: Reassessing the First 'Court Theologian,'" *Church History* 59, no. 3 (September 1990): 309–25.

28. Eusebius, *Oration*, 1.

than the Empire, was the exemplary form of universal human community. As Williams sums up his conclusions:

> As a consequence of their high Christology, the Catholics could not so easily see in the emperor a kind of temporal savior, coordinate with Christ, nor could they yield to the God-ordained emperor as a source of authority in matters of faith and order superior to the earthly Christ. Caesar, merely for being a Christian, could not usurp the place of God. The primary loyalty of the Nicene Christian could be to no other than to the historic *and* eternal Christ, fully God, to the tradition embodied in his Church, and to the consubstantial Holy Spirit suffusing this Church with grace, peculiarly present in the apostolic bishops.[29]

Williams argues that the pro-Nicene party's conviction that the historical Christ was God, *homoousios* with the Father—and that Christ's laws and traditions therefore took precedence over the laws and traditions of the emperor—made them much less supine in the face of imperial interference with the Church. Likewise, Nicene convictions regarding the Spirit led them to assert the rights of the Church over and against the claims of the Empire: it is the Church and not the Empire that is the *oikoumene*, and the emperor is a member of and subject to the Church.

Williams admits that "the Arianizing view of the divine authority of the Christian emperor" is something that must be reconstructed "from the meager and disparate remains."[30] While Williams can cite an impressive array of texts to support his views, in the end there are many gaps that must be filled in with supposition and conjecture. We might wonder about the degree

---

29. George Huntston Williams, "Christology and Church-State Relations in the Fourth Century (Part II)," *Church History* 20, no. 4 (1951): 3–26, at 25.

30. George Huntston Williams, "Christology and Church-State Relations in the Fourth Century (Part I)," *Church History* 20, no. 3 (1951): 3–33, at 21–22.

to which those embroiled in the debates over the Trinity in the early Christian centuries were conscious of the political implications that Peterson and Williams find in their different positions. Perhaps, for example, Constantius's enthusiasm for Arian theology is purely coincidental, and had he been zealously orthodox it would have been the Arians, and not the orthodox, who resisted the claims of the state.

In assessing the work of both Peterson and Williams, it is important to bear in mind the context in which and the purposes for which they wrote. Peterson's target is clearly not fourth-century Arianism but the "political theology" of Carl Schmitt, who wrote in 1922 that "a continuous thread runs through the metaphysical, political, and sociological conceptions that postulate the sovereign as a personal unit and primeval creator."[31] Specifically, Schmitt understands the sovereign to be "he who decides on the exception"[32] meaning that sovereignty is "principally unlimited authority, which means the suspension of an entire existing order."[33] Schmitt later notes that "the exception in jurisprudence is analogous to the miracle in theology."[34] In another work, first published in 1932, Schmitt writes, "The juridic formulas of the omnipotence of the state are, in fact, only superficial secularizations of theological formulas of the omnipotence of God."[35] He criticizes liberal political orders for creating a social order without the sovereign exception, thus losing "the decisionistic and personalistic element in the concept of sovereignty."[36] Liberal democracy, by eliminating true sovereignty, the sovereign

31. Carl Schmitt, *Political Theology: Four Chapters on the Concept of Sovereignty*, trans. George Schwab (Cambridge, MA: MIT Press, 1985), 47. On Peterson and Schmitt, see György Geréby, "Political Theology versus Theological Politics: Erik Peterson and Carl Schmitt," *New German Critique* 35, no. 3 (Fall 2008): 7–33.

32. Schmitt, *Political Theology*, 5.

33. Schmitt, 12.

34. Schmitt, 36.

35. Carl Schmitt, *The Concept of the Political*, trans. George Schwab (Chicago: University of Chicago Press, 1996), 42.

36. Schmitt, *Political Theology*, 48.

power to make the exception, is the political mirror of deism or pantheism. Against these liberal political philosophies, Schmitt pits "Catholic political philosophers such as de Maistre, Bonald, and Donoso Cortés"[37] to whom the elimination of the exception "must have appeared . . . to be a strange pantheistic confusion."[38] In other words, liberalism was not simply an inadequate political philosophy; it was heresy, precisely because it denied the political equivalent of the miracle.

Peterson's opposition to Schmitt was not because he was a liberal stung by the charge of heresy, nor was it because he thought the profession of the Christian faith to be a purely private matter. Indeed, Peterson, a convert from Lutheranism, was quite traditional in his theological views, and in particular, he rejected what he took to be the liberal Protestant attempt to restrict Christianity to a realm of private interiority.[39] The problem with Schmitt's political theology was not its anti-liberal politics per se but its faulty theology. Nothing in Schmitt's account of "political theology" would ever lead one to think that God is triune: that the Father has sent the Son so that we might live in the Spirit. Indeed, Schmitt's God might be characterized as an extreme form of the depiction of God in certain late medieval nominalists: a hidden and capricious deity who at any moment might override the order established by God's ordained power (*potentia ordinata Dei*) through the exercise of the absolute power of God (*potentia absoluta Dei*). The power of God, as Schmitt conceives it, is that which flashes forth from outside the normal course of things, erupting from behind an opaque veil that is utterly impenetrable to reason. The mystery of sovereignty invoked by Schmitt is quite different from the "open mystery" of the triune God, in which

---

37. Schmitt, 53.

38. Schmitt, 61–62.

39. See Geréby, "Political Theology," 24, and Michael J. Hollerich, "Retrieving a Neglected Critique of Church, Theology, and Secularization in Weimar Germany," *Pro Ecclesia* 2, no. 3 (August 1993): 305–32.

human comprehension fails not because God is hidden but because God is so fully revealed.

Moreover, Schmitt rejects any political relevance to the teachings of Jesus, particularly his teaching with regard to love of enemies. For Schmitt, the concept of the political itself hangs from the distinction between friend and enemy.[40] Political identity is only secured by an "other" with whom "we"—those of us who are "friends"—have a relationship that is essentially conflictual. Christ's command to love our enemies does not, according to Schmitt, apply to the enemy in this political sense: "in the private sphere only does it make sense to love one's enemy. . . . It certainly does not mean that one should love and support the enemies of one's own people."[41] Neither does Schmitt take account of the New Testament notion of friendship with God, which John's Gospel places in an explicitly Trinitarian context: Jesus's disciples are no longer slaves but friends because he reveals to them *everything* that he has heard from his Father (John 15:15), and they will be confirmed in this friendship by the Spirit of truth, whom Christ sends from the Father to testify on his behalf (John 15:26). This friendship with God established in Christ and the Spirit is able to overcome even the "otherness" of sin, reconciling those who were formerly enemies of God (Rom. 5:10). The world that hates Jesus and his disciples (John 15:18–25) is precisely the enemy that God sent the Son to save and not to condemn (John 3:16–17). Thus, Peterson rejects Schmitt's political theology not because it is political but because it enshrines as normative a sub-Christian conception of God: a sovereignty and monarchy more suited to paganism than to the Church. It is this, rather than the theology of Eusebius or other semi-Arians, that is his true target.

Likewise, George Huntston Williams is more concerned about mid-twentieth-century mainline Christians in America

40. Schmitt, *The Concept of the Political*, 26.
41. Schmitt, 29.

who lie supine before the state than he is about similarly supine fourth-century Arians.[42] Williams' abiding interest in the question of church and state and his own opposition to McCarthyism, the Vietnam War, and legalized abortion testify to a life spent pushing Christians in a countercultural direction.[43] Though surely not intended as such, his account of the Trinitarianism of the pro-Nicene party of the fourth century might be read as a rejoinder to H. Richard Niebuhr's appeal to Trinitarianism as a cure for "Christomonism." As Williams sees it, and in this he is surely correct, the Nicene doctrine of the Trinity does not in any way mitigate the significance of Jesus Christ (history) by "balancing" him with the Father (nature) and the Spirit (experience). Rather, "the authentic Nicenes held tenaciously to the historic Christ who, by his unique and paradoxical act of divine self-sacrifice at once secured the eternal salvation of mankind *and established the ecclesiastical law to which even the Christian sovereign is subject.*"[44] In claiming that the historical figure Jesus of Nazareth is *homoousios* with the Father, the pro-Nicene party commits itself to, if not a Christomonism, certainly a Christological intensity that is not subjected to any balancing act. The subsequent affirmation of the divinity of the Spirit, and the identification of the apostolic and sacramental Church as the principal (albeit not exclusive) *locus* of the Spirit's activity, makes clear that it is this community, and not any empire, that can claim the status of being God's people.[45] The Christological and Pneumatological vigor of the pro-Nicene theologians gave them the theological resources necessary to maintain

42. In light of the strong claims he makes for the value of Nicene orthodoxy, it is interesting to note that Williams was, at least by ecclesiastical affiliation, a Unitarian—albeit a self-described "Trinitarian Unitarian."

43. Forrest Church, "George Huntston Williams: Historian of the Christian Church 1914–2000" in *Notable American Unitarians 1936–1961*, ed. Herbert Vetter (Cambridge, MA: Harvard Square Library, 2007), 245–47.

44. Williams, "Christology (Part I)," 16, emphasis in the original.

45. See Williams, "Christology (Part II)," 12.

the ancient Christian conviction that the Church is a distinctive people, set apart from the world for the sake of the world.

The Trinitarian reflections of Peterson and Williams are quite different from those of Niebuhr or of the social Trinitarians. Do they point to a different way of thinking about the connection between Trinitarian theology and politics? I think that they do. Peterson points out the danger of trying to place the doctrine of the Trinity—or any doctrine of God—into direct service undergirding a particular politics. The example of Carl Schmitt shows us how the Christian understanding of God can be warped when it is expected to answer to the exigencies of a particular political vision. On the other hand, Williams shows that Trinitarian theology, while not directly applicable to political questions, is still relevant in thinking of how the Church relates to various forms of worldly power. But it is not relevant because the divine life provides an image of human community, nor because it gives us a formula for balancing sources of ethical reflection. It is relevant because it tells us that Jesus of Nazareth is Emmanuel, God with us, and that his Holy Spirit gives life to an ecclesial community that has its own public, "political" identity. In other words, the doctrine of the Trinity is politically relevant precisely because it is neither more nor less than what Christians have always taken it to be: a way of understanding the claim that in Christ and the Spirit we encounter God directly.

David H. McIlroy, in a recent work that offers an example of a Trinitarian "political theology" that both avoids the dangers identified by Peterson and has the robust Christological and Pneumatological contours that Williams identifies, helpfully distinguishes between two different ways of thinking about the Trinity and politics. He writes:

On the one hand, there is the model of God standing on one side and human beings on the other. That which is to be found on one side of the divide is to be mirrored on the other side. On the other hand, significance may be drawn from the way in which the triune God invites human beings to participate in God's triune life. On this account, God the Holy Spirit seeks to transform human beings into the likeness of God the Son and to bring them into relationship with God the Father.[46]

McIlroy later goes on to note, "the deployment of the Trinity as a bare image is an inadequate and misplaced use of the doctrine."[47] Rather than a bare image, we need the full-blooded narrative of God's triune identity as revealed in the economy of salvation. Thus, if we wish to speak of a Trinitarian political theology, then we ought to eschew any attempt to make the Trinity into a schema or pattern that we are to imitate and instead speak of how God the Holy Spirit conforms us to Jesus Christ so that we can become sons and daughters of God the Father.

The political relevance of the doctrine of the Trinity only reveals itself as Christians attempt to live out their Spirit-given conformity to Christ. If they do so, they will not have to worry about Kantian concerns over the practical import of the doctrine of the Trinity. Those who rule over others with the power that grows from what Augustine called the *libido dominandi* will quickly recognize that the people who have been marked by Baptism in the triune name pose a threat to such power simply by showing the world that there is another way for human beings to live together, a way that Christ lived with his disciples and which the Spirit makes possible even today in the community of the Church. This is not to say, of course, that the Church as a whole always, or even often, lives in this way. Yet the political relevance of the doctrine

46. David H. McIlroy, *A Trinitarian Theology of Law* (Eugene, OR: Wipf and Stock, 2009), 14.

47. McIlroy, *Trinitarian Theology*, 208.

of the Trinity remains directly proportional to the faithfulness of the baptized, to their living out the distinctive way of Christ, the way of friendship with God through the Spirit. It is in such faithfulness that the disruptive insertion of the triune life into human history becomes visible.

Earlier I mentioned Rublev's icon of the Holy Trinity, noting how its three angelic figures seated around a table are sometimes taken to embody what, in social Trinitarianism, seems most important about the Trinity: the model of a community of equals that we humans can mirror. What I am suggesting, in contrast, is that we think instead of an image like Masaccio's fresco of the Trinity in Santa Maria Novella in Florence.[48] This painting takes the form of the traditional medieval representation of the Trinity known as the "mercy seat," in which the crucified Christ is supported by God the Father, with the Holy Spirit, in the form of a dove, flying between them. The figure of Christ is flanked by Mary and John, who are in turn flanked by the two kneeling donors of the painting. Through his innovative use of perspective, Masaccio is able to locate the Trinity in its own "space," which seems to lie in a chamber beyond the walls of the Church, preserving the Trinity as something true of God *in se*. Yet this same use of perspective allows him to depict the crucified one being projected into our space by the figure of the Spirit, so that the form of the crucified is impressed upon the viewer who contemplates this image. We are not invited to imitate the Trinity but rather to receive the image of the crucified, who receives his formative power from his place within the Trinitarian *taxis*. And this formative power is manifested in the saintly figures of the beloved disciple and the Blessed Mother who stand on either side of the cross as figures of the Church Triumphant but also in the images of the donors, who kneel on a visual plane between the saints and

48. For a fuller discussion of the theology of Masaccio's *Trinity*, see Essay 14 of this volume, "Masaccio's *Trinity*."

us as figures of the Church Suffering, for whom we are bidden to pray. And ultimately, this formative power is manifested in us, the viewers, who are the Church Militant on pilgrimage to the kingdom.

5

Christendom and the Marian Path of the Church

What does "social Catholicism" mean after the end of Christendom, the sociopolitical formation that the philosopher Chantal Delsol describes as "the civilization inspired, ordered, guided by the Church"[1]—a civilization that endured for sixteen centuries, beginning during the reign of Theodosius in the late fourth century, and that carried with it a host of presumptions about how Catholicism can and should be "social," but which lies now in its death throes? In what follows, I will begin by briefly suggesting how Christendom narrowed our understanding of the social nature of the Church. I will then turn to the analysis offered by Delsol of the rise and fall of Christendom. Finally, I will explore how locating the end of Christendom within a Marian-figural reading of the story of the Church can suggest what a post-Christendom social Catholicism might look like.

THE CHURCH AND/AS POLITICS

These days it is difficult, though not impossible, to find defenders of Christendom. For many Catholics, Christendom was the offspring of an unseemly power grab by the Church that brought

* A version of the second half of this previously unpublished essay was delivered as a lecture at the Academy of Catholic Theology, Washington, DC, 2008.

1. Chantal Delsol, *La fin de la Chrétienté* (Paris: Cerf, 2021), 9–10.

about immense human suffering in the name of religion and compromised the Church's witness to the Gospel of Jesus Christ by seeking to make his kingdom into a worldly one. There are, however, some historically nuanced interpretations of Christendom that, while recognizing that Christendom cannot be reconstituted, also recognize that Church leaders in the fourth and fifth centuries were simply responding to the novel exigencies of the times, particularly the collapse of Roman imperial structures, and that the sixteen hundred years of Christendom brought not simply human suffering and worldly compromise, but also a patrimony of arts, thought, and institutions.[2] One even finds some "integralists" who suggest that Christendom's day is not past and that it is, by virtue of its integration of the temporal and the spiritual and the subordination of the former to the latter, the only social order than can address modern ills.[3] But most Catholics accept that Christendom, if not entirely vanished, is today reduced to the fumes emanating from an empty bottle.

This does not mean, however, that Catholicism has become a purely private, apolitical affair, though some may wish it so. Of course, if one takes for granted that by politics we mean "statecraft"—elections and legislation and public policy decisions—it is difficult to think about the political nature of Catholicism outside of the construct of Christendom. But while the operation of states is certainly one of the activities that might fall under the category of the "political," the collapse of politics into statecraft

2. See, for example, Robert Louis Wilken, *The First Thousand Years: A Global History of Christianity* (New Haven: Yale University Press, 2012).

3. See the writings associated with the website *The Josias*, which sums up its "integralist" social vision as follows: "Catholic Integralism is a tradition of thought that, rejecting the liberal separation of politics from concern with the end of human life, holds that political rule must order man to his final goal. Since, however, man has both a temporal and an eternal end, integralism holds that there are two powers that rule him: a temporal power and a spiritual power. And since man's temporal end is subordinated to his eternal end, the temporal power must be subordinated to the spiritual power" (http://thejosias.com/2016/10/17/integralism-in-three-sentences/). See also the sermon preached in 1985 at the traditionalist Catholic Pentecost Pilgrimage to Chartres by Dom Gérard, Abbot of Le Barroux, "An Exhortation to the Restoration of Christendom," https://thejosias.com/2014/10/31/exhortation-to-the-restoration-of-christendom/.

is not the only way to think about the political. If we follow Aristotle in defining a political community as "a community . . . established with a view to some good,"[4] then our understanding of the political widens considerably, allowing us to see the "political" character of various forms of human association that are involved with the cultivation of the good for human beings. Indeed, it raises the possibility that we might think of the Church herself as a "political" community, instituted by God for the sake of obtaining the good that is participation in the divine life. This could help us to make sense of the use of political terminology in the New Testament: not only the term *ekklesia* itself, which referred to the public deliberative assembly of the Greek *polis*, but also Paul's statement that our true *politeuma* is in heaven (Phil. 3:20), or the description of the Church in 1 Peter as a holy *ethnos* (2:9), or indeed Jesus's own proclamation of God's *basileia*. It also can help us understand why early Christian writers, such as the author of the *Epistle to Diognetus*, speak of Christians as having their own distinctive *politeias*.[5]

Beginning with this broad understanding of the political as the shared pursuit of the common good, we can then proceed to make some important distinctions. Aristotle argues against those who would see the difference between various forms of human association as simply a matter of scale and not of kind.[6] Thus, for Aristotle, the household (*oikos*) is a different kind of association from the village (*kōmē*), and the village from the city (*polis*), and what distinguishes the *polis* from other forms of association is its end, for it aims at the highest good and thus subordinates to itself all those associations, such as households and villages, that only aim at partial goods. It is only the life of the *polis*—only political life—that is in a complete sense the good life for human beings.

And here we see why we cannot, according to the classical

4. Aristotle, *Politics* 1.1 (1252a), trans. Benjamin Jowett (Oxford: Clarendon, 1946).
5. *Epistle to Diognetus* 5.
6. *Politics* 1.1 (1252a).

understanding of politics, restrict Christianity to the realm of the private, and why the social nature of Christianity must be thought of in specifically "political" terms. For Christianity from the outset arrives on the scene as a rival to the earthly *polis*, inasmuch as it claims to be the community that aims at what is truly the highest good, the good to which the goods pursued by all other forms of human association, including the *polis*, must be subordinated (in the sense of "ordered beneath"). It is only in the *ekklesia* of God that one lives fully the good life for human beings, for it is only within the Body of Christ that human beings can attain the supreme good of participation in the divine life. In light of this supreme good, the goods of all human political communities are revealed to be as fragmentary as the goods pursued by households and villages.

Unlike households and villages, however, earthly political communities are constantly tempted to claim for themselves ultimate human loyalty and thus seek to heal their own fragmentariness with the *pharmakon* (remedy-poison) of prideful bluster. This is the thought to which Augustine gives exhaustive expression in *The City of God*. All the political communities of antiquity, in their inordinate self-exaltation, are for Augustine distorted shadows of the true city, which exists perfectly in the fellowship of the saints above, and which lives a life of pilgrimage within human history. Thus, for Christians to think politically is not simply to think about public policy or elections; primarily, it is to think about their common life in Christ's body and to think about how the Church, which claims to aim at the supreme good, ought, while in her *status viatoris*, to cultivate the civic virtues that befit citizens of the heavenly city and to understand the relationship of these citizens to the earthly cities in which they dwell while on pilgrimage.

It is understandable why Christians of the fourth and fifth centuries would draw from this view of the Church as a human association whose end is the highest good the conclusion that this truth should express itself in a civilization inspired, ordered, and guided by the Church—that is, Christendom. At the same time, there is a sense in which the political nature of the Church was occluded by the advent of Christendom. Or, perhaps more accurately, the variety of ways in which the Church as *polis* might interact with the earthly *polis* became constricted in the Christian imagination, reduced to the Christendom model of the Church having her hands upon the levers of worldly power, either directly or indirectly. But as Christendom faded from our world, if not from our imaginations, Catholics began to ponder how the Church might think anew about her public, political nature, her role as witness to the nations concerning the true nature of humanity's highest good, and how worldly goods might be ordered beneath spiritual goods. It is from this situation that the "social Catholicism" of Wilhelm von Kettler and Leo XIII was born.

What are we to make of this fading of Christendom? To help with our evaluation, I now turn to a recent work by Chantal Delsol (b. 1947), whose analysis of the situation of the Church in France, where de-Christianization is well advanced (around half the population identifies as Catholic, but only about 5% attend Mass), offers us a sketch of what the increasingly post-Christian West might look like. More than that, Delsol offers a narrative that suggests ways in which we might understand the immense social upheavals brough about by both the genesis and the demise of Christendom and also suggests ways the Church might understand her public character at the end of Christendom.

THE BIRTH AND DEATH OF CHRISTENDOM

Chantal Delsol is a thinker well known for her political philosophy, and her work *La fin de la Chrétienté* (The End of Christendom) continues a line of inquiry that is well developed in other works. Her approach is marked by a philosophical anthropology that acknowledges the social and historical construction of human identity without totally abandoning all notion of human nature. In this sense, her project is not unlike that of Alasdair MacIntyre and leads her to pay close attention to the play of historical contingencies in such notions as human dignity. Rather than a static identity, for her human nature is a dynamic, evolving reality—indeed, if anything is "essential" to our nature it is our ceaseless desire to exceed that nature. As she writes memorably of the human person in her book *Qu'est-ce que l'homme?* (What is a Human Being?): "Rooted, he wants to be emancipated from his roots. Put another way, he seeks an inaccessible dwelling place through a succession of temporary way stations."[7] The result is an Augustinian anthropology of the "restless heart" inflected by (post)modern historical consciousness. All of this informs her account of the fate of Christianity in the contemporary West.

Delsol begins by examining how a Church that so resolutely resisted modernity for two centuries in the name of Christian civilization came, since the 1960s, to embrace modern values such as religious freedom, values utterly at odds with Christendom. She also offers an analysis of early twentieth-century fascism and corporatism as integralist attempts to save Christendom that "proved to be worse than the disease."[8] Animated by a utopian nostalgia that proved to be merely the mirror image of modernity's utopian futurism, these sorts of movements fell prey to those, such as Charles Maurras, who wanted Christendom but really could care less about Christianity. In the end, these movements proved to be nothing but "the convulsions of a dying Christendom."[9]

---

7. Chantal Delsol, "Introduction to *Qu'est-ce que l'homme?*," in *Lucid Mind, Intrepid Spirit: Essays on the Thought of Chantal Delsol*, ed. Lauren Hall and Paul Seaton (Plymouth: Lexington, 2012), 9.

8. Chantal Delsol, "Conclusion to *Qu'est-ce que l'homme?*," in *Lucid Mind, Intrepid Spirit*, 16.

9. Delsol, *La fin*, 27. In France today, the embrace of Catholicism as a civilizational heritage, but not a living faith, is still a political force, sometimes referred to as "zombie Cathol-

Unlike thinkers like Jacques Maritain and, more recently, Jean-Luc Marion, Delsol is skeptical that old Christendom can be replaced by a "New Christendom" in which Christians cooperate with a benignly secular society in order to realize commonly held goods.[10] She is skeptical of this because she is generally skeptical that any society can, in fact, be benignly secular, or indeed secular at all. Secularity is a fantasy indulged in by intellectuals, but for ordinary people, "for whom common sense whispers that there are mysteries behind the door,"[11] religion of some sort is unavoidable. Our present moment is not one of secularization but of revolution, "in the strict sense of a cyclical return."[12] Ancient paganism is reborn, albeit in new forms marked by the sixteen centuries of Christendom. This revolution involves a kind of Nietzschean transvaluation both in morals ("the normative inversion") and in worldview ("the ontological inversion"). Though herself a committed Catholic, Delsol tries to retain a certain analytic detachment in describing these inversions of prior moral norms, seeking to cast herself as an observer of this moment of historical transition and not a partisan. What she does want to insist upon is the significance of this inversion, for the mores of a society form a kind of architecture of our existence, a structure more stable than codified laws, shaping not only our actions but our feelings and habits.

icism." See Pascal-Emmanuel Gobry, "Zombie Catholics vs. French Secularism," *America*, April 7, 2017, americamagazine.org.

10. For Maritain, after the demise of the old Christendom, the Church's public role is to provide the state with the values it needs to sustain what he called "the democratic secular faith," a faith that was, if not Christian, at least "Christianly inspired" and forms a people that "at least recognized the value and sensibleness of the Christian conception of freedom, social progress, and the political establishment" (see *Man and the State* [Chicago: University of Chicago Press, 1951], 109). Marion does not use the term "New Christendom," but seems confident that "Christians furnish society with its best citizens from the point of view even of the interests of the city of men, because their disinterestedness toward earthly power makes them honest workers who are efficient and reliable in community life" (*A Brief Apology for a Catholic Moment*, trans. Stephen E. Lewis [Chicago: University of Chicago Press, 2021], 57–58). Delsol explicitly rejects Maritain's New Christendom approach, calling it one of "the last illusions" of the post-war era (*La fin*, 155).

11. Delsol, *La fin*, 34.

12. Delsol, 36.

To shed light on our current situation, Delsol looks back to the birth of Christendom, the last great inversion of norms in the West. She insists upon what might seem at first contradictory claims: the advent of Christendom was both a radical break with the pagan past and also unthinkable without that past as a basis upon which it was built. Christians constructed their civilization utilizing elements of pagan culture, in particular Stoic morality, though now "democratized" and framed within a new system of beliefs that transformed what was appropriated. In contrast to the profoundly unified religious world of the Romans, in which the gods and humanity were fellow citizens of the cosmos, Christianity "introduced a dualism between the temporal and the spiritual, the here-and-now and the beyond, human beings and God."[13] The advent of Christendom also brings a sharp reversal of societal attitudes regarding divorce, abortion and infanticide, suicide, and homosexuality. Delsol evinces a keen sympathy for those pagan Romans, conservators of traditional values, who felt that, with the advent of Christendom, they had entered "an intellectual and spiritual world torn apart," and she shows genuine admiration for those who continued to battle in the face of what was clearly inevitable defeat.[14]

So too, in our own day, the partisans of Christendom—whether in its old form, in integralism, or the new form proposed by Maritain and others—fight in service of what is, particularly since the 1960s, a manifestly lost cause. Delsol points to shifts in both laws and popular attitudes toward divorce, abortion, and assisted reproduction. Though there are pockets of resistance to these developments (particularly, she notes, in the United States), the path of this arc is clear: "humanitarianism, the morality of today, is a morality entirely oriented toward the well-being of the individual, without any vision of the human person [*vision*

---

13. Delsol, 51.
14. Delsol, 51.

anthropologique]."[15] What we see is an "inversion of the inversion,"[16] an undoing of the revolution of the fourth century that made the ideals of Christianity socially enforced norms. This might be identified by enthusiasts for modernity as a result of our progressive realization of the inviolability of individual conscience with regard to ultimate questions, but Delsol resists any narrative of progress: "in each era, 'progress' consists simply in reconciling realities (laws, customs, mores) with diffuse and sometimes as-yet-unexpressed beliefs that evolve in silence."[17]

This suggests that human beings are not simply behavers but also believers. The moral norms of the ancient world changed because the beliefs of Christianity supplanted those of paganism, making long-accepted pagan practices appear odious. Delsol quotes Tacitus, whose remarks concerning Jewish monotheism applied no less to Christians: "They hold profane all that we hold as sacred and, on the other hand, permit all that we hold to be abominable."[18] In particular, Delsol ascribes to Judaism and Christianity a key role in desacralizing the world. The dualism of Christianity, with its transcendent God standing over and against the world, replaced the "cosmotheism" of antiquity, which saw the cosmos itself as saturated with divinity. Or, more precisely, monotheism was layered on top of cosmotheism, as a "secondary religion" covering over (but just barely) the "primary religion" of humanity, which "arises, so to speak, on its own, proliferates without fertilizer, and instantly occupies and reoccupies a place as soon as it is free."[19] Christianity has been replaced not by atheism and secularity, as the Enlightenment *philosophes* foretold, but by a religion "more primitive and more rustic."[20]

15. Delsol, 64.
16. Delsol, 65.
17. Delsol, 76.
18. Delsol, 84, citing Tacitus, *Histories* 5.4.
19. Delsol, *La fin*, 87.
20. Delsol, 90.

Delsol notes numerous writers who have described modernity as parasitic on Christianity, but she prefers to speak of modernity as a "palimpsest" written over the Christian text, in the same way that Christianity was written over the text of antiquity. This is always the way that human societies work: "using all the possible materials" from the past, "but depriving them of their meaning in order to reinvent them for the benefit of a new epoch."[21] Just as Christendom replaced paganism, a religion founded in mythos, with one that claimed foundation in truth and persecuted those who denied that truth and clung to their myths, so now, in our postmodern moment, "truth" has once again been eclipsed by mythos. Yet this new mythos is ineradicably marked by the Christian appeal to "truth," for it does not breed tolerance, as the myths of antiquity did, but retains the moral force of the universalism and absolutism of the Christendom that it has overwritten. For Delsol, those whom the French refer to as *les Woke* "have taken over the concept of dogmatic truth, and excluded their adversaries from public life, just as the Church had excommunicated in times past."[22] The fate of the West is neither nihilism nor ancient pagan religion but humanitarianism: "the evangelical virtues . . . recycled to become a kind of common morality."[23] We are left with what Delsol calls, invoking Flannery O'Connor's *Wise Blood*, "the Church without Christ."

Blame for this outcome can be laid at the feet of Christendom itself: "in its pretention to establish itself as a civilization, Christianity ended up producing a monstrous avatar that is at the same time its alter-ego and its mortal enemy."[24] But, Delsol reminds us, Christendom is not Christianity but simply one sociopolitical manifestation of Christianity, and the demise of the former is not the demise of the latter. Nor does she see much

21. Delsol, 115.
22. Delsol, 129.
23. Delsol, 133.
24. Delsol, 161.

point in lamenting the errors of Christendom. Even if we today rightly judge aspects of Christendom as distortions of the Gospel, Delsol's historicist sensibilities lead her to cast a jaundiced eye at excessive Christian breast-beating over the past, "which can resemble masochism,"[25] and she sees little point in condemning those in the past who did not have the benefit of our hindsight. Even Augustine, who expected very little from Christian emperors in terms of aiding people in their journey to the heavenly city, saw no reason for Christians not to try to make use of the peace of the earthly city. Today it seems obvious for us to ask, "who was making use of whom?" but this was not so obvious in the late fourth century. Delsol comes neither to praise nor condemn Christendom but to bury it.

She is, however, concerned that, in their fear of repeating the errors of Christendom, Christians will mute their distinctive voice: "To dialogue is not to dissolve oneself in the theses of the adversary, and one does not need to cease to exist in order to be tolerant—in fact, the opposite is the case."[26] But the call to Christian distinctiveness is not the integralist call for a return to Christendom. It is, as Delsol puts it, a call to "a spiritual revolution,"[27] which by worldly standards might issue in what looks like defeat. Christians must form their children "to carry themselves like Kierkegaard's knight of faith: resigned, but also able to walk toward the infinite."[28] Christians without Christendom must take up the role of witnesses rather than rulers and learn the virtues characteristic of a minority: "equanimity, patience, and perseverance."[29] Delsol does not see the social kingship of Christ as requiring his followers, in integralist fashion, to have their hands on the levers of temporal power. Yet, in rejecting integralism, she

25. Delsol, 148.
26. Delsol, 152.
27. Delsol, 154.
28. Delsol, 155.
29. Delsol, 163.

also seeks to avoid a progressivism that would dilute Christian witness into a vague spirituality. It is through robust witness, not through coercion, that the Church engages the world and seeks to change it.

THE MARIAN PATH OF THE CHURCH

Delsol's narrative of Christendom—its rise and flourishing and demise—helps us understand where we are and what the next step forward might be. In a sense, she is doing what Augustine did in *The City of God*: narrating the rise and fall of earthly cities as well as the story of God's pilgrim people in order to discern the workings of God's providence in the world and to gain some idea of the virtues that are required in order to participate in the good life of the heavenly city while on pilgrimage. Delsol differs from Augustine inasmuch as the story of Christendom's rise and fall is added to those of the empires of the pagans. This, in effect, relativizes Christendom, making it, in at least one sense, simply another instantiation of the earthly city. But is that really all that can be said of Christendom? Is it really nothing but the earthly city, as it were, dressed up in vestments?

Delsol's narrative also raises some discomfiting questions for social Catholicism, which often presumes a neutral public space in which the Church and other social actors cooperate. If the post-Christian world is not neutrally secular but is, in fact, a revived rustic cosmotheism inflected by the absolutist claim of the Christendom over which it has been written, then any account of social cooperation between the Church and the civilization of modernity will have to recognize an element of conflict in that relationship since the heavenly and earthly cities both seek to define the highest good for human beings. Indeed, this conflict seems manifest in the rejection, often in quite absolutist terms, by many today of the Church's position on such social questions as the beginning and ending of life, the nature of marriage, and the proper understanding of sexuality and gender. If Delsol is correct about the religious nature of modernity, does the conflict between competing accounts of the highest good get the last word?

To combine these two concerns, we might ask whether it is possible to narrate Christendom as a moment within the story of the heavenly city's earthly pilgrimage, a story that includes both conflict and cooperation between the two cities? Such a narration must move beyond the merely historical to a theological reading of history and the path of God's people. Pope St. John Paul II's 1987 encyclical *Redemptoris Mater* suggests that the life of the Virgin Mary can be seen as charting the path of the Church's pilgrimage. He writes:

> Strengthened by the presence of Christ (cf. Mt 28:20), the Church journeys through time toward the consummation of the ages and goes to meet the Lord who comes. But on this journey—and I wish to make this point straightaway—she proceeds along the path already trodden by the Virgin Mary.[30]

He reiterates later, "[Mary's] exceptional pilgrimage of faith represents a constant point of reference for the Church, for individuals and for communities, for peoples and nations, and in a sense for all humanity."[31] John Paul seems to suggest that we ought to look to the life of Mary in order to understand the pilgrim path of Christ's body through history. In other words, we ought to read the history of the Church "typologically" or "figurally" in such a way that Mary is the antitype for which the Church is the type.[32] This typological identification of the Church and Mary is possibly as old as the book of Revelation and has represented a

30. John Paul II, *Redemptoris Mater* 2, in *Mary: God's Yes to Man* (San Francisco: Ignatius, 1987).

31. John Paul II, *Redemptoris Mater* 6; cf. 37.

32. See John Paul II, *Redemptoris Mater* 42.

major trend in modern Marian theology at least since Matthias Scheeben in the nineteenth century.[33] What is relatively novel in John Paul's suggestion is that we are to see Mary not as a static image of the Church but rather as a figure in motion,[34] so that we see in the trajectory of Mary's life an image of the trajectory of the Church's path through history.

It is this suggestion—that the life and destiny of Church is seen in the living icon-in-motion of Mary—that I wish to develop in what follows. I am not suggesting that we can find some sort of precise one-to-one correspondence between the events of Mary's life and the past and future events of the Church's history. Such a use of Scripture has rightly been viewed with suspicion in the tradition of the Church. However, I do wish to explore how John Paul II's claim that the Church's path through history is the one already trod by the Virgin might provide the broad outline of an interpretive framework for the Church's understanding of its distinctive path within the course of world history. If Mary is iconically figured in the Church, and if we can discern in Mary's life a trajectory, then from her life, we ought to be able to gain some insight into the historical trajectory of the Church and in particular how we might locate Christendom within that trajectory and how conflicts between the Church and the world might be negotiated.

While we can see in Mary's Immaculate Conception and early life a kind of parallel with the election of Israel and the "pre-history" of the Church under the Old Law, it is with the Annunciation that the figural relationship between Mary and the Church comes

33. Matthias Scheeben, *Mariology*, trans. T.L.M.J. Geukers (St. Louis, MO: Herder, 1946), 1:211–18.

34. On Mary's distinctive relation to time, and the need for what we might call a "narrative Mariology," see René Laurentin, "The Blessed Virgin Mary," in *The Historical and Mystical Christ*, ed. A.-M. Henry, trans. Angeline Bouchard (Chicago: Fides, 1958), 266–69. Laurentin notes that the narrative of Mary's life is given an "impression of a necessity," albeit not a logical necessity; rather, it is "the type of necessity that occurs in the order of art and of love" (267). It is only narrative that can do adequate justice to God's election of Mary in grace and her free response.

clearly into view. Just as, at the Annunciation, Mary conceives God the Son in her womb by the power of the Spirit, so too at Pentecost, the ecclesial Body of Christ is conceived by the power of that same Spirit. As *Redemptoris Mater* notes:

> in the redemptive economy brought about by the action of the Holy Spirit, there is a unique correspondence between the moment of the Incarnation of the Word and the moment of the birth of the Church. The person who links these two moments is Mary: *Mary at Nazareth* and *Mary in the Upper Room at Jerusalem.*[35]

John Paul points to Mary's presence to the Spirit on these two occasions as key in establishing her as the one whose life reveals the Church's journey through history. He writes, "In the Upper Room Mary's journey meets the Church's journey of faith."[36]

But as we move beyond the Annunciation-Pentecost typology into the post-apostolic period, such a figural reading of the historical path of the Church must be put forward with great tentativeness. This is especially the case with the question, particularly relevant to political theology, that I wish to pose now: how can this Marian-figural reading help us address the question of the seeming collapse of Christianity as a social and cultural force in the modern West? Delsol offers a historical and sociological analysis of that collapse, but how can it be understood theologically? What accounts for what John Paul II called, in relation to Europe, this "silent apostasy"?[37]

We might be tempted to answer, curtly, "sin." But as with every case of hardening human hearts, we ought to probe deeper to ask how God's providence is being manifested in this story of the Western world's seeming enthusiastic embrace of Christianity

35. John Paul II, *Redemptoris Mater* 24.
36. *Redemptoris Mater* 26.
37. John Paul II, *Ecclesia in Europa* 9, June 28, 2003, vatican.va.

and then widespread rejection. How is it fulfilling God's will for the Church to endure this rejection, and how ought the Church to live her common life in the face of such rejection? What light can Mary's path shed on this experience of the Church?

Such a figural reading might proceed in something like the following manner. Just as Christ's natural body grew in secret in Mary's womb for nine months, so too the ecclesial Body of Christ grew in secret in the first three centuries. When, "in the fullness of time, God sent his Son, born of a woman" (Gal. 4:4), Christ was revealed not simply to Israel but was manifested to the nations, as embodied in the Magi. The Magi came to the Virgin Mother seeking the Son of God who was born from her womb; four centuries later the nations came to Mother Church seeking to be reborn with Christ in the womb of Baptism as sons and daughters of God. And just as the Magi came bearing gifts, so too the nations came to the Church bearing gifts: not gifts of gold, frankincense, and myrrh, but gifts of philosophy, art, music, literature, and law. The emergence of the Church as a public social and cultural force after the Peace of the Church was not, as some would have it, a simple betrayal of the Church's ethos as a "contrast society" and the emergence of a fundamentally unfaithful form of "Constantinian" Christianity.[38] The Church could no more have turned away the nations than Mary could have turned away the Magi; to do so would have been to fail in the mission of manifesting Christ as a light to the world.

Yet those who criticize Christianity's welcome of imperial Rome do have a point, for the story of the Magi is inextricably intertwined with a story of betrayal. The bloody slaughter of the innocents and the Holy Family's flight into exile followed upon, indeed in a certain sense was occasioned by, the joyous visit of the

---

38. See, e.g., Gerhard Lohfink, *Jesus and Community: The Social Dimension of Christian Faith* (Philadelphia, PA: Fortress, 1984), 181–85, and John Howard Yoder, "The Constantinian Sources of Western Social Ethics," in *The Priestly Kingdom: Social Ethics as Gospel* (Notre Dame, IN: University of Notre Dame Press, 1984), 135–47.

Magi. And it is at this point that our Marian-figural reading of Church history becomes particularly delicate. Part and parcel of the story of the Magi is the story of their inadvertent betrayal of Christ to Herod. Of course, there is no hint of ill will on the part of the Magi, though perhaps there is an element of naiveté that belies the epithet "wise men." For in their quest for Christ they brought in their train a king who did not see in Jesus one to be worshiped but rather a rival claimant to royal power. In Herod we see the figure of the earthly city, all those forms of earthly power that establish themselves upon violence and are ruled by their own lust for domination.[39] Herod sees in Christ the antithesis and overcoming of precisely the kind of power that he himself wields, and thus he sees in Christ one who must be eliminated. Yet he masks his true intention, presenting himself as one who wishes to join in worship.

We see in the intertwined history of the Magi and Herod a figure of the ambiguous nature of the project of Christendom, the project of creating a Christian civilization, and the enduring interplay of cooperation and conflict between the Church and the world. In welcoming the nations, the Church also welcomed those who, as Augustine said, belonged to the Church by virtue of the outward bond of the sacraments but who interiorly remained citizens of the earthly city.[40] The gifts brought by the nations were genuine gifts, but for all that the dangers were no less genuine. To recognize this is not to reject wholesale the sixteen hundred years of Christendom that followed upon the Peace of the Church. But it is to see that this period was one of both promise and peril to the Church and her mission, just as the homage paid by the Magi was both promise and peril to the Virgin and her child. It is to see that only a discerning heart can distinguish the gift from the threat. It is also to see that one must be prepared to go into exile,

39. See Augustine, *De civitate Dei*, preface 1.
40. Augustine, *De civitate Dei* 1.35.

to flee to Egypt, even if this requires abandoning certain of the less portable gifts.

But is it to the Holy Family fleeing into exile that we should look to understand the current situation of the Church in the West?[41] As much as Christians might feel misunderstood and marginalized by the modern developed world, I suspect it is a bit too dramatic to see the Church as actively threatened. Now that the Church, particularly in Europe, is seen by most people to be quaintly irrelevant, there seems no need to keep it in exile. Aggressive anti-clericalism and persecution of Christians seem, at least in the West, to decrease in direct proportion to the decrease in the perceived power and influence of the Church. Stripped of political and cultural power, Christianity and its cultural relics can occupy a minor, folkloric place in society.

At the same time, the remnants of Christendom cannot be ignored. As Delsol suggests with her image of the palimpsest, the post-Christian West is haunted by ghosts of the Gospel that hover just beneath the text of modernity. The gifts that the nations brought to Christianity under Christendom were given back to the nations to become part of the cultural patrimony of the West, even if the story of that origin is forgotten or repressed. Notions such as human dignity are rooted in Christianity, even if "dignity" is understood by the modern world in ways that diverge from the Church's understanding. Perhaps now seen only in the cloudy mirror of humanitarianism, the manifestation of the Gospel to the nations continues to mark the rustic neo-paganism of

41. Here I would underscore that my reading of the Church's current location along the "Marian trajectory" is meant to apply primarily to the industrialized West. One thing that should be kept in mind in any attempt to follow St. John Paul's suggestion that we see the Church as following a path through history that has already been trod by the Blessed Virgin is that all local churches do not always follow that path at the same rate. It seems, for example, that the Church in Africa has not (yet?) experienced its own form of Christendom (as much as it may have suffered from certain aspects of the Christendom of the West), and consequently has not had the same sort of peril posed to it, has not yet had its own "Herods." If one accepts John Paul's suggestion, one might have some confidence that all local churches within the one Catholic Church will in some way follow the Marian trajectory, but how this following will play out in detail cannot be determined in advance.

the putatively secular West and to find an echo there. Hardly exiled, the Church's faith has instead been pillaged and repurposed. Thus, something of a return from Egypt has occurred, and we might see the Church as living an ecclesial life that is figured in the "hidden life" of the Holy Family in Nazareth. This life is far from the glory and drama of the visit of the Magi but is rather a time in which the Church must seek to foster among the offspring of the ecclesial womb the same growth "in wisdom and in stature" (Luke 2:52) that Mary fostered in Jesus.

We ought not think that accepting a certain "hiddenness" to the Church's life means an accession to modernity's circumscription of Christianity to the realm of the private. Such circumscription must be resolutely resisted, for it presumes a delineation of public and private that Christianity from its outset has called into question.[42] As I noted above, Aristotle distinguished the household or *oikos* from the city-state or *polis*, not simply because of differences in scale but also because of differences in the kind of end that each form of association pursued. The *polis* is that form of association that deals with the highest, the most comprehensive, the most public good, while the *oikos* is the realm in which more restricted, private goods are pursued, goods that must be subordinated to the good of the *polis*. Indeed, in some ancient accounts, notably the one given by Plato in the *Republic* (or by Sophocles in *Antigone*), the goods pursued within the *oikos* are not simply subordinate but actually inimical to those pursued in the *polis*, such that among those who are the guardians of the *polis* the *oikos* must be abolished.[43] Even in accounts more appreciative of the *oikos*, such as Aristotle's, the *polis* cannot be seen simply as the *oikos* writ large but as different in kind.

Yet from its inception, Christianity has blurred the difference

---

42. The public-private distinction of antiquity—a division between *oikos* and *polis*—is not identical to the modern rendering of this same division, which is between the individual and the state.

43. Plato, *Republic* 423e, 457a-b, 462.

between the *oikos* and the *polis*. Jesus's proclamation of the kingdom of God is inseparable from Jesus's proclamation of God as
Father and Christians as sons and daughters adopted in him, the
unique Son of God, into God's household. Thus, the social body
of the Church could be described alternately in *polis*-terms or
in *oikos*-terms. In the Letter to the Ephesians, Christians are addressed both as "fellow citizens [*sympolitai*] with the saints" and as
"members of the household [*oikeioi*] of God" (2:19).[44] Christian
theology speaks not only of the heavenly city in which Christ the
Lamb reigns but also of the economy of salvation and of Christ as
the master of the house (*oikodespotes*) that is the Church.[45] What
the Letter to Diognetus calls "the wonderful and confessedly
strange character of the constitution of their own citizenship"[46]
found concrete expression in the first centuries in the domestic
setting in which the citizens of the pilgrim city gathered to celebrate the Eucharist as the *familia Dei*, an image that continues
to this day in the Eucharistic liturgy.[47] Perhaps the most striking
instance of the "household" character of the Church, however, is
seen in the unprecedented roles that women have had in Christianity. Excluded from citizenship in the public realm of the ancient *polis* and restricted to the private sphere of the *oikos*, women
found in the Church a kind of "public *oikos*" in which they were
valued fellow members without having to imitate the supposedly
masculine virtues of self-sufficiency that were seen as necessary
for political life.

Thus, in speaking of the Church entering into a "hidden

44. On the significance of this passage from Ephesians, as well as illuminating comments
on the *oikos/polis* distinction in antiquity and Christianity, see Reinhard Hütter, *Suffering Divine
Things: Theology as Church Practice* (Grand Rapids, MI: Eerdmans, 2000), 160–64.

45. See Ignatius of Antioch, *Ephesians* 6.1.

46. *Epistle to Diognetus* 5.

47. For example, the ancient Roman Canon (Eucharistic Prayer I) prays: *Hanc igitur
oblationem servitutis notrae, sed et cunctae familiae tuae, quaesumus, Domine, ut placatus accipias.*
Josef Jungmann notes, "God's people is here conceived of as a domestic group with God as
its *pater familias.*" See *The Mass of the Roman Rite*, trans. Francis Brunner (Christian Classics,
2012), 2:184, n. 22.

life," I do not at all mean to say that the Church is relegated to the sphere of the private. As I noted earlier, because the good that the Church pursues is the most common, the most comprehensive, of all goods—the good that is God, the Creator of all good gifts— the Church is always and everywhere the most public of human associations. Even in the upper room on the day of Pentecost, the Church was public and catholic in its pursuit of the highest good. Indeed, even in the home in Nazareth, the common life of the Holy Family was the supreme exemplar of the shared pursuit of the good. Thus, to identify the life of the Church today with the hidden life in Nazareth is not a sectarian call for retreat from public life but is rather to understand that the public task, the political task, of the Church is the "domestic" task of nurturing disciples through the cultivation of the virtues distinctive of the household of God. Those distinctive virtues are at the heart of the public witness of the Church before the watching world.

THE POLITICS OF THE MAGNIFICAT

When we in turn ask just what are those virtues that are distinctive of the household of God, we see another aspect of the "hiddenness" of the Church's life, and Mary's Magnificat appears as a scriptural witness of particular relevance. As I noted, when Jesus proclaimed God's kingdom, that proclamation was inseparable from his proclamation of God as Father. This is, of course, first and foremost the proclamation (*pace* Harnack) that God is *his* Father. But it also says something about the nature of God's kingdom; it is the proclamation that God exercises his kingship in the form of fatherly care for the poor, the defenseless, and the outcast. In this Jesus brings to perfection the prophetic proclamation of God's care for the *anawim*, the "little ones." In the household of God, according to the Letter of James, the pure and undefiled sacrifice (*threskeia*) is "to care for the widows and orphans in their distress" (James 1:27). But more than simply possessing the virtue of generosity toward those in need, the members of God's kingdom are to identify *themselves* with little children (Matt. 19:14; Mark 10:15; cf. John 13:33); they are to understand *themselves* as the "little flock" that receives the kingdom as a gift (Luke 12:32); they must see *themselves* as the foolish, the weak, the lowly (1 Cor. 1:26). Imitating the Lord who came not to be served but to serve (Mark 10:45), the politics of the household of God is based not on an economy of violence and coercion, the economy seen in a figure like Herod, but on one of self-giving through self-identification with those in need, a self-identification that is embodied in ascetical practices of self-dispossession. These practices cultivate a capacity to make the concerns of the *anawim* one's own, to subordinate self-love to the love of those little ones who are especially beloved of God as the concrete means by which we subordinate love of self to love of God. This, to use Delsol's terminology, is the true "inversion"—both normative and ontological—brought about within the Christian economy of salvation.

This economy is given iconic form in Mary and her Magnificat. In the Magnificat, Mary sings of what *Redemptoris Mater* calls God's "love of preference for the poor,"[48] a love that, more than any act of violence, disrupts the economy of power, casting down the mighty from their thrones and lifting up the lowly. Amid the rise and fall of earthly cities, and even of Christendom, this is the true revolution, the only true basis for a human community in which the supreme good is sought. Beyond all calculation of advantage or even effectiveness, Mary's identification with the poor bursts forth from her realization of the generosity that God has shown to her. And in accepting this generosity, Mary must identify herself as a "lowly servant." It is this generosity and identification that the Church is called to make its own, not as the basis of a program for ameliorating social ills—though undoubtedly

48. John Paul II, *Redemptoris Mater* 37.

in a society in which a large number of people understood the cause of the poor to be their own cause the poor would be less exposed to savage exploitation—but as a way of bearing witness to the God who has done great things for his people. Like Mary, the Church loves and identifies with the poor because this shows forth most truly what it means to be the bearer of Christ, the bearer of good news incarnate.

This preferential love is a key aspect of the paradoxical public hiddenness to which the Church is called and is the characteristic civic virtue of God's household. The life of the Church is not hidden in private realms of individual or sectarian faith. Rather, the life of the Church is hidden because it is a life that, like Mary's, is identified with the little ones who are overlooked by the Herods of the world. It is a kind of "hiding in plain sight" that takes advantage of coercive power's tendency to overlook that which seems small and weak. The Church, like Mary, makes the cause of these little ones her own cause: the poor, the unborn, the homeless, the stranger, the condemned, the dying. The life of the Church is hidden in the lives of those who do not count in the economy of violence and coercion, except as replaceable units of exploitation. As Chantal Delsol puts it, Christians must take as their model not the sixteenth-century Spanish philosopher and theologian Juan Ginés de Sepúlveda, who justified the conversion-by-conquest of the Americas, but the martyred Trappist monks of Tibhirine, who died because they would not abandon their Muslim neighbors.[49] If the Church faithfully lives out God's preferential love and identification with the poor, then the hiddenness of the Church is no failure but rather judgment upon the world.

We might have been tempted to think that the end of Christendom, the end of the period in which the world's rulers brought their gifts to lay at the feet of Mother Church, was the end of the Church's public role. But, in fact, it is simply the next step

49. Delsol, *La fin*, 169.

along the path that Mary has already trod. The "hidden life" of the Church in the West—her (at times unwilling) renunciation of worldly power—involves a deepening of the Church's Marian identity, as the Church, like Mary, learns to identify with the little ones of God rather than the mighty. Unlike Mary, the Church might have to repent for having at times been dazzled by displays of worldly power, for the type has not always conformed to the antitype. In the transition from epiphany to exile to hidden life, the Church has undoubtedly had to leave behind not only some gifts that were of genuine value but also some that were unfitting, in order, like Mary, to have its hands free to carry Christ.

In terms of the project of social Catholicism, discerning the Marian path of the Church requires that we reckon with the possibility of genuine conflict between competing accounts of the common good—in particular, those accounts that privilege the "little ones" versus those accounts, whether of the political "left" or the political "right," that see self-assertion and domination as the primary means for establishing a just social order. But we must also reckon with the possibility of genuine cooperation, the possibility that unexpected visitors from afar might arrive bearing gifts that will enrich our conception of the good. And to reckon with both of these possibilities requires an exercise of prudence that can distinguish the Herods of our day from the Magi.

Finally, we must bear in mind that if the trajectory of the Church's pilgrimage does in fact follow the trajectory of the Virgin's life, then the most significant events of that life are yet to unfold. The first miracle at Cana, the teaching of multitudes, the casting out of demons—the entire public ministry of Jesus—which the Church, like Mary, will be privileged to witness, lie ahead of us. And so, too, does the great conflict figured in Mary's vicarious sharing in Christ's Passion and in the woman clothed with the sun. And so, too, does our being raised to eternal life in heavenly glory.

Politics: Liberty and Its Discontents

6

Order, Freedom, and "Kindness"

Julian of Norwich on the Edge of Modernity

What is it about a fourteenth-century English anchoress that is so appealing to people living at the beginning of the second millennium?[1] Every time I turn my mind to Julian of Norwich, I note, with unabated astonishment, her immense current popularity. The torrent of both popular and scholarly books about her, as well as new translations of her work, far outstrips that of any other religious or, with the exception of Chaucer, secular writer from the fourteenth century. Though there are different possible ways of accounting for this popularity, in the end I must say that I do not know why Julian is so popular; I cannot say why people read her. But I will say why Christians today *should* read her. They should read her because, like us, Julian lived at the edge of modernity. As a fellow boundary-dweller, she offers an invaluable resource for thinking about how to live on that edge.

Let me clearly state that the attempt to locate both Julian and us on the edge of modernity is not an exercise in nostalgia or repristinating the past, in which Julian becomes a cipher for the wisdom of the premodern era. I am inclined to agree with

---

* This essay was originally published as "Order, Freedom and 'Kindness': Julian of Norwich at the Edge of Modernity," *Theology Today* 60, no. 1 (April 2003): 63–81.

1. For an examination of possible answers to this question that are different from—though not necessarily incompatible with—my own analysis, see Sheila Upjohn, *Why Julian Now? A Voyage of Discovery* (Grand Rapids, MI: Eerdmans, 1997).

Louis Dupré's claim that "the cultural revolution of the modern age was an event of ontological significance" and therefore there is no way to put the genie of modernity back into the bottle.[2] Rather, I shall argue that Julian's relevance derives from how her thinking belongs neither to modernity nor to premodernity but presents a distinctive, if not unique, articulation of Christian belief that is both at home in, and alien to, any era or location. In what follows, I will characterize modernity and premodernity by adopting a pair of truisms that, I believe, just happen to be true. The first truism is that the premodern world conceived of the universe as, in some sense, an organic whole or, in other words, a "cosmos." The second truism is that the modern world is born out of the dissolution of the premodern cosmos (under the pressure of intellectual shifts, scientific discoveries, technological innovations, and indeed of the Christian faith itself) and the enthroning of freedom in the place once occupied by order. Let me briefly elaborate on these two characterizations.

ORDER

Obviously, the very term "premodern" defines those various cultures in terms of their deficient—or at best incipient—modernity. Similarly, the notion of *the* premodern is misleading since it obliterates the specificity and variety of thought and practice in various times and places. While acknowledging these difficulties, I believe that it is still possible to show how premodern or "traditional" cultures conceived of the world as an ordered whole in a way that distinguishes them from modern cultures. Let us begin with the notion of the universe as *cosmos*. Louis Dupré has argued that the ancient Greek term *cosmos*, which originally meant "order," is a comprehensive term that includes not simply the order

2. Louis Dupré, *Passage to Modernity: An Essay in the Hermeneutics of Nature and Culture* (New Haven: Yale University Press, 1993), 7.

of the physical universe but also "the *ethos* of personal conduct and social structures, the *nomos* of normative custom and law, and the *logos*, the rational foundation that normatively rules all aspects of the cosmic development."[3] Dupré goes on: "If there is one belief Greek thinkers shared, it must be the conviction that both the essence of the real and our knowledge of it consists ultimately of *form*. Basically this means that it belongs to the essence of the real to *appear*, rather than to hide, and to appear in an orderly way."[4] Christianity had to make some modifications to this notion of *cosmos*, particularly since the Greeks conceived of the gods as located *within* the cosmos, while Christians (like Jews and, later, Muslims) believed in a God who created and therefore *transcends* the cosmos. But late ancient and medieval Christians, like their pagan forebears, still saw this creation as a manifestly ordered place from which human beings could take guidance for the ordering of self and society.

Let us pursue this notion of *cosmos* by looking at the ordering of society. Medieval Europe conceptualized the ordering of society chiefly in terms of three "orders" or "estates": clergy, nobility, and peasantry.[5] The estate into which one was born was thought to be a divinely determined manifestation of the ordering of the cosmos. As the twelfth-century abbot Philip of Harvengt wrote to a French count, "whatever station in life you have been awarded is determined by Fortune, as the pagans would have it, or by the grace of God, which is what Christian authors teach."[6] The estates were conceived of as mutually dependent so that the well-being of society as a whole depended on one performing the duty appropriate to one's estate: The peasant and noble depended on the

3. Dupré, *Passage to Modernity*, 17.

4. Dupré, 18.

5. This tripartite division seems to have roots deep in Indo-European culture and is perhaps related to the Hindu division of Brahmin, warrior, and peasant castes.

6. Philip of Harvengt, "Letter to Henry, Count of Champagne," in *Medieval Political Theory—A Reader: The Quest for the Body Politic, 1100–1400*, ed. Cary J. Nederman and Kate Langdon Forhan (New York: Routledge, 1993), 66.

prayers of the cleric; the noble and cleric depended on the food grown by the peasant; and the cleric and peasant depended on the military prowess and protection of the noble. John of Salisbury, writing in the twelfth century, says:

> For the creative Trinity, the one and true God, has so ordered the parts of the universe for the sake of a more firmly joined connection and protective charity that each one requires the assistance of the others and a defect in one is repaired by the others, insofar as each individual part is like a member of the other individual parts. All things are, therefore, incomplete if they are disconnected from one another, but otherwise they are perfected if they are associated, because everything stands in a firm relation of reciprocal aid.[7]

For the cleric or peasant to aspire to glory on the field of battle, for example, was not simply a threat to the ruling class but to the divine ordering and unity of society and, ultimately, of the cosmos.

While it is important to note the mutuality of aid among the three estates, it is equally important to note that social ordering, like the ordering of the cosmos as a whole, was firmly hierarchical. The spiritual power of the clergy was superior to the secular power of the nobles, and both were superior to the powerless peasants. Within the three estates, there were further subdivisions of rank, not unlike the ranks of angels in the cosmic hierarchy. There might have been disputes between clerics and nobles over exactly how the divine authorization of secular power was mediated, but no one questioned the basically hierarchical constitution of cosmos and society. Superior should rule inferior, and the lower ranks should defer to the higher.

Even acknowledging the tremendous variety in premodern

---

7. John of Salisbury, *Metalogicon* 1.1, in *Medieval Political Theory*, 28.

societies, this profound sense of the world as a cohesively ordered cosmos appears with remarkable consistency. While we must recognize the potentially—perhaps inherently—oppressive nature of a worldview in which every person and thing has a fixed, immutable place within a hierarchy of dignity and power, we should at the same time acknowledge that such a worldview also gave people a profound sense of unity and coherence. The cosmos was a meaningful place and living in that cosmos was a common project in which all the various ranks of society jointly participated.

FREEDOM

If we think of so-called premodern cultures as characterized by this sense of the world as a *cosmos*, then we might define modernity negatively as marked by the general loss of the view of the world as *cosmos*.[8] This demarcation was certainly advocated by Max Weber, who contrasted "the ethical postulate that the world is a God-ordained, and hence somehow *meaningfully* and ethically oriented, cosmos" with modernity's "empirical" and "mathematically oriented view of the world," which "develops refutations of every intellectual approach which in any way asks for a 'meaning' of inner-worldly occurrences."[9] Modernity is, according to Weber, the world drained of any inherent order or meaning. With the increasing rationalization of life, "the world's processes become disenchanted, lose their magical significance, and henceforth simply 'are' and 'happen' but no longer signify

8. I willingly acknowledge the difficulty of locating the beginning and end of modernity. My presumption is that modernity began at some point between the Gregorian Reform and Immanuel Kant and ended at some point between Hegel and the day after tomorrow.

9. Max Weber, "Religious Rejections of the World and Their Directions," in *From Max Weber: Essays in Sociology*, ed. H. H. Gerth and C. Wright Mills (New York: Oxford University Press, 1946), 351.

anything.'"[10] If the ancient cosmic unity of *ethos*, *nomos*, and *logos* is broken, what takes its place?

The answer is complex, and any statement must be provisional since we are still sufficiently close to modernity that it is difficult to gain an accurate perspective on it. Stephen Toulmin has argued persuasively that the "hidden agenda" of mid-seventeenth-century modernity was restoration of the ordered world following the religious and political chaos of the sixteenth and early seventeenth centuries. Thinkers like Descartes and Newton sought to restore a "cosmopolis," an "overall harmony between the order of the heavens and the order of society."[11] But if this is the case, then how does this modern social order differ from the ancient and medieval unity of *ethos*, *nomos*, and *logos?*

The key difference lies in the modern conception of human beings as essentially characterized by "freedom." The modern cosmopolis reflects the order of "Laws of Nature," an order so absolute, so mechanical, that it leaves no room within it for free beings. Thus, human freedom must be located outside of the cosmo-political order, whether in the matter/mind dualism of Descartes, or the phenomenal/noumenal distinction of Kant. Located in this space, human freedom becomes radicalized as absolute spontaneity. This radicalized notion of freedom, not the project of constructing a cosmopolis, determined modernity.

This is not to say that premodern societies had no concept of freedom, nor that modernity has a single conception of freedom: Luther, Descartes, Kant, and Hegel hardly speak with one voice on the question of human freedom. Rather, my claim is that freedom, understood as the autonomous spontaneity of the will, becomes modernity's reigning obsession, whether we are dealing

10. Max Weber, *Economy and Society: An Outline of Interpretive Sociology*, ed. Guenther Roth and Claus Wittich (Berkeley: University of California Press, 1978), 506.

11. Stephen Toulmin, *Cosmopolis: The Hidden Agenda of Modernity* (Chicago: University of Chicago Press, 1990), 67.

with philosophers trying to reconcile human freedom with a mechanistic universe or politicians trying to reconcile individual freedom with the needs of the state. As the world is drained of inherent, ordered meaning, the free human subject becomes the sole source of self-created meaning, with a freedom that is quite different from the freedom that Paul identifies with the Spirit of the Lord.

The roots of this shift from cosmos to freedom are not to be found in the seventeenth century, with scientific advances, the consolidation of nation-states, and thinkers such as Descartes and Newton. Rather, the beginning of the shift starts earlier. The fourteenth century, during which Julian lived, was a crucial turning point between the worldview dominated by cosmic order and the worldview dominated by spontaneous human freedom for a number of reasons. On a material level, we have tremendous political and economic transitions—particularly the demographic depression brought about by the Black Death—that deal a series of fatal blows to the old order of clergy, nobles, and peasants. New classes arise, and greater social mobility becomes possible. The well-being of the social body comes to be seen to depend less on adherence to a static, divinely given order and more on the dynamic initiative of individuals. Similarly, the Great Western Schism breaks the unity of Christendom, and France and England each declare the Hundred Years War a holy crusade by appealing to rival popes. At the same time, in the intellectual realm, we have the rise of nominalism in philosophy and theology, introducing new and radicalized notions of individuality and freedom. It is this intellectual shift on which I wish to focus.

Modern attempts to pin down the nature of late-medieval nominalism have proved to be somewhat frustrating. The usual villain, the early-fourteenth-century theologian and philosopher William of Ockham, is perpetually being exonerated of the more exotic charges leveled against him. But at the risk of stumbling by running too quickly over this rocky terrain, let me focus on two features usually associated with nominalism: (1) the view that only individuals have positive ontological status (thus denying such status to universals such as "human being" and to relations such as "paternity") and (2) the distinction between the absolute and ordained powers of God (what God *can* do and what God in fact *does* do). The relationship between these two features of nominalism is not immediately apparent—and indeed some deny that there *is* any relationship—but I will venture to establish a connection and to try to relate it to the modern radicalization of human freedom.

First, "nominalism" itself is the view that in the statements "John is a human being" and "Mary is a human being," the term "human being" refers not to some really existing thing possessed by both John and Mary but to a concept that can refer to diverse things (John and Mary), a concept that exists only and entirely in the mind of the one making the statement. Correlatively, in a statement such as "John is the father of Mary," the phrase "the father of" does not refer to some really existing thing in John (or in Mary) but solely to a concept. This view was undeniably held by Ockham and numerous other late medieval thinkers. Ockham writes: "the universal is one particular content of the mind itself, of such a nature as to be predicated of several things."[12] And regarding the ontological status of relations, he says, "if we leave aside all authority and follow [just] natural reason, then it can be proved evidently that every created thing is absolute and that among creatures there are no relations outside the soul distinct from absolute things."[13] Behind both of these denials stands the view that only singular, particular things are real, and universals

12. William of Ockham, *Summa logicae* 1.14, in *Philosophical Writings*, ed. Philotheus Boehner (Indianapolis: Hackett, 1990), 34.

13. William of Ockham, *Quodlibet* 6.15, in *Quodlibetal Questions*, trans. Alfred Freddoso (New Haven: Yale University Press, 1991). The caveat that he offers in the first part of this quotation refers to his acceptance of the Church's teaching that the persons of the Trinity are constituted by their relations.

and relations are "beings of reason." So, we find in nominalism a kind of radical metaphysical individualism. John and Mary are real; "humanity" and "paternity" exist only in the mind.[14]

More recent work on nominalism has stressed not its philosophical views on language and ontology but its understanding of the theological distinction between God's "absolute power" (what it is possible for God to do) and God's "ordained power" (what God has in fact chosen to do). The issues here are extremely complex and it is possible to overstress the novelty of the views of Ockham and other nominalists on this question.[15] However, while we find earlier figures such as Thomas Aquinas using this distinction,[16] Ockham and later nominalists employ the distinction much more widely, using it to resolve a whole host of theological questions, such as whether a human being can be saved without created charity, whether God must save someone who has the gift of created grace, and, conversely, whether God can save someone who *does not* have the gift of created grace.[17] In each of these cases, Ockham argues that, while certain things are possible for God in an absolute sense, God has bound himself to a particular order of things, so that, for example, one can be saved only if one has the gift of created grace. But this order of things has no intrinsic necessity and exists only because God

14. We should be clear about exactly what Ockham is and is not saying: He is not saying that Mary and John are not *really* human beings, nor that John is not *really* the father of Mary, but rather that "humanity" and "paternity" are not "things" but only "beings of reason" or "concepts." These concepts should not be confused with Kantian categories; they are not the knower's imposition upon reality but arise from commonalities between John and Mary that exist independently of the knower. So, for example, if John is a human being but Mary is in fact a porpoise, then no matter how much we might wish to apply the concepts "human being" to both of them, we would be wrong to do so. It is not because John has something called "humanity" that Mary does not, but because John has feet while Mary has flippers, and our concept of "human being" includes feet but does not include flippers. In other words, concepts signify "naturally" and not by "convention."

15. The best discussion of how Ockham's views fit into prior discussions is found in William Courtenay, *Capacity and Volition: A History of the Distinction of Absolute and Ordained Power* (Bergamo, IT: Pierluigi Lubrina, 1990). Courtenay presents Ockham as a fairly traditional and moderate figure on this question.

16. See *Summa theologiae* 1.25.5.

17. See Ockham, *Quodlibetal Questions* 6.1, 6.2, and 6.4.

has willed it to be as it is; God could presumably have willed it to be otherwise. Perhaps most famously, Ockham argues that God could, according to his absolute power, command someone to hate him, so that hatred of God would be a duty.[18] Later nominalists, such as Gabriel Biel, went further than Ockham to claim not only that God *could* have willed a different order to the world, but that God can and does, through the exercise of his absolute power, suspend the world's actual ordering.[19] Increasingly, God's will appears capricious.

The important point to see here is that, in a universe consisting solely of individual things existing independently of other individual things, their ordering lacks any intrinsic necessity and depends entirely on God's will. Ockham says, "every absolute thing that is distinct in place and subject from another absolute thing can by God's power exist when that other absolute thing is destroyed."[20] In later nominalist thinkers like Biel, divine power can intervene to overturn the normal causal order of the universe because that order depends entirely upon the divine will. What has been lost is, as Dupré puts it, "the conviction that both the essence of the real and our knowledge of it consists ultimately of *form*."[21] For nominalism, "form" is simply a being of reason, not the essence of the real. What we have here is a radicalization of the concept of freedom as applied to God, along with a destruction of the sense of the world as an intelligible *cosmos*. To use Weber's terms, we still have a notion of the world's processes as "God-ordained," but these processes are robbed of any intrinsic meaningfulness and "simply 'are' and 'happen' but no longer signify anything." Because God's power is absolute, human reason is blinded with regard to God's inscrutable will.

18. Ockham, *Sentences* 4.16.

19. On Biel's understanding of this distinction, see Heiko Oberman, *The Harvest of Medieval Theology: Gabriel Biel and Late Medieval Nominalism* (Durham, NC: Labyrinth, 1983), 30–56.

20. Ockham, *Quodlibetal Questions* 6.6.

21. Dupré, *Passage to Modernity*, 18.

Ironically, this radicalization of God's freedom makes God irrelevant to the world. As Hans Blumenberg has argued, it is but a short step from the inscrutability of God's will to the elimination of God entirely: "The modern age began, not indeed as the epoch of the death of God, but as the epoch of the hidden God, the *deus absconditus*—and a hidden God is *pragmatically* as good as dead."[22] Incapable of discerning the *logos* of God, human reason turns itself upon the world, accepting its given order and investigating it as a contingent conglomeration of individual entities. No longer woven into the fabric of a coherent *cosmos*, the human will begins to take on the lineaments of the absolute will of the now-hidden God, and the modern world is born. The actual contingent order of the world may constrain our *acting* upon our will, but in the spontaneous act of *willing itself*, human beings are radically free. As the ancient sacred *cosmos* collapses into modernity, human beings find themselves strangely liberated.

If the network of mutual obligations that modern scholars call "feudalism" is a social correlate of the world conceived as cosmos, we might see in modern liberal democracy a correlate of the human person understood as radically autonomous and free. While recognizing the constraints established by the ordaining sovereign power (now "The People" rather than God), liberal democracy seeks to ensure the maximum freedom of individuals. The chief purpose of political power is not to ensure an order that manifests the order of the cosmos but to ensure the individual's freedom to exercise his own will—so long as it does not infringe on another's freedom to exercise *her* own will. Even the forms of association that we collectively designate "civil society" exist primarily as vehicles for the pursuit of individual goals. The Left-Handed Theologian's Association

22. Hans Blumenberg, *The Legitimacy of the Modern Age* (Cambridge, MA: MIT Press, 1983), 346.

exists to protect *my* rights as a left-handed theologian. Even the Church exists not as a body manifesting the ordered communion of beings but as a means by which I pursue and express *my* "spirituality."

THE END OF MODERNITY?

Having argued that Julian lived on the leading edge of modernity, represented by the nominalist positing of radical freedom, I will now make a few remarks about why we might think of ourselves as living on the trailing edge of modernity. The end of modernity and the arrival of so-called postmodernity—what Foucault called "this perilous imminence whose promise we fear today, whose danger we welcome"—is surely news to no one.[23] On the whole, I tend to cast a rather jaundiced eye upon such pronouncements. Yet, it does appear true that the radicalization of freedom that we find beginning in the fourteenth century is exhausting itself, and the picture of the autonomous human subject that has developed over the last six hundred years is beginning to collapse.

What I wish to claim here is simply that Julian found herself in an uncertain space between the passing world of the premodern *cosmos* and the emerging modern world of radical individual freedom of will; therefore, she was able to think in a way that was, to a certain extent, freed from the order of the past but not yet enslaved to the freedom of the future. And similarly, we, on the other side of modernity, find ourselves also in an uncertain space where we can perhaps think in a new, or at least a different, way. Freedom, order, power, language, God, the self . . . all seem to be reconfiguring themselves. However, what will

23. Michel Foucault, *The Order of Things: An Archeology of the Human Sciences*, trans. Alan Sheridan (New York: Vintage, 1973), 385.

emerge from this reconfiguration is by no means clear; there is, as yet, no anointed heir to modernity.

Several contenders for the throne present themselves. One version of postmodernity—what we might call the "nihilistic" option—hands humanity over to the grim reaper of "discourse," proclaiming the death of the subject at the hands of the forces that construct it. In this account of things, freedom is simply an illusion, an epiphenomenon of language. This version of post-modernity has had only passing appeal, appearing in the early Foucault and today found mainly among black-clad graduate students who do not seem to have heard about the dangers of smoking. Another version of postmodernity is simply a further radicalization of modernity's emancipatory project, in a spectrum tending at one end toward the sunny Americanized Nietzschean pragmatism of Richard Rorty and at the other toward the deadly serious social theory of Jürgen Habermas. However, this is not so much postmodernity as upgraded modernity—"Modernity 2.0"—and it is unclear that the upgrade has fixed the bugs found in the original. Yet another postmodernity seeks to take "discourse" seriously yet still retains a chastened notion of human agency, one that operates within the boundaries of linguistic and cultural traditions. This, too, comes in subvarieties, including the analysis of everyday practices that we find in Michel de Certeau and the tradition-constituted rationality of Alasdair MacIntyre.

While I incline toward some variety of this last version of postmodernity, I am not going to make a case for its merits here.[24] Instead, I will turn to what Julian has to say about such things as order, freedom, and divine and human nature in order to see what she offers to those of us for whom the modern notion of freedom as radical spontaneity has become irreversibly

24. See Essay 2 of this volume, "Aesthetics: The Theological Sublime."

problematic, yet who do not think that one can simply return to the ancient sacred *cosmos*.

"KINDNESS"

Julian has been popularly known as a "mystic" or a "spiritual writer." She has less often been thought of as a writer with serious theological, not to say philosophical, interests. There are several reasons for this oversight. The form that her only book takes—meditations on a visionary experience in which a crucifix bleeds—hardly seems the stuff of sober theological reflection, much less philosophy. She has been both praised and dismissed as a writer willing to throw reason aside in the pursuit of her own unique spiritual vision.

Such a picture of Julian, however, runs counter to what Julian herself says. True, she begins her thinking from the sixteen visions she received while lying on her sickbed. But these visions are brought into a mutually critical conversation with both her reason and the teachings of the Church. She writes that in this life there are three things by which God is worshiped and we are helped: "The first is use of man's natural reason; the second is the common teaching of holy church; the third is the inward gracious working of the Holy Spirit; and these three all come from one God. God is the ground of our natural reason; and God, the teaching of holy church; and God is the Holy Spirit."[25] Here we not only see Julian giving equal place in this life to reason and tradition alongside the inner workings of the Spirit, but we also see her using a Trinitarian allusion to indicate how reason, tradition, and experience mutually coinhere, testifying to her intellectual sophistication. If we read Julian as someone who thinks critically about both the traditions of the Church and her own visionary

25. Julian of Norwich, *A Revelation of Love*, ed. Marion Glasscoe, 3rd rev. ed. (Exeter, GB: University of Exeter Press, 1993), ch. 80. The modernization of the text is mine.

experience, then we are less likely to dismiss her as a sort of medieval Pollyanna and more likely to appreciate the theological and philosophical depth of what she says.

The central problem Julian addresses is divine wrath. How is it that wrath does not mar God's perfection? If God is eternal and unchanging, why is his wrath not also eternal? I am not sure she ever comes up with a solution to this problem, though she wrestles with it at length. However, Julian also asks the question in a more pastoral mode, reflecting on how our fear of God's wrath restrains us from giving ourselves unreservedly to God in faith. She again uses a Trinitarian figure (power, wisdom, and goodness as appropriated to Father, Son, and Spirit) to make her point: "some of us believe that God is almighty and may do all, and that he is all wisdom and can do all, but that he is all love and will do all—there we are held back."[26]

Julian asks if we know whether God wants our salvation and not our annihilation. Such a question might have felt particularly pressing in the world coming apart of the late fourteenth century. Certainly, events like the Black Death—indiscriminately killing as much as half the population of Europe—might make one doubt the benevolence of God. Ruptures in Christendom might indicate that God has abandoned the Church. And perhaps even the picture of God reflected by nominalism, a God of absolute will and power who could command hatred of God, also undermined people's sense that God could be trusted. In light of all this, Julian found it difficult to believe what has become, thanks to T.S. Eliot, the most famous of her revelations: "all shall be well, and all shall be well, and all manner of thing shall be well."[27] We might have no trouble believing in God's power to make all things well and even that, in his inscrutable wisdom, he can make all things well, but how can we know that God *wants* to make

26. Julian, *Revelation*, ch. 73.
27. Julian, ch. 27.

all things well? To this very practical question, Julian provides a speculative answer: If we properly understand God's nature and God's action in history, then we will no longer be held back by fear, because God's nature is, as she puts it, "kindness": "God is kind in his being."[28]

To say that God is by nature "kindness" can sound like another example of what Clifton Wolters called Julian's "consistently optimistic and sunny" outlook.[29] But in Middle English, the word "kindness" has a very complex set of meanings that today are largely lost to us: it indicates the *benevolence* we mean today when we speak of someone as "kind"; it also indicates the *nature* of a thing, what "kind" of thing it is, as when we speak of "humankind"; and somewhere between benevolence and nature, it indicates the *relationship* between those who share a common nature—thus the words "kin" and "kindred." In any particular instance, the word "kind" may well carry all of these meanings. To say that someone treated you "kindly" would be to say that she acted in a benevolent way (kindly), as if you were her relative (kindred), and in a way that is only natural to someone like her (her kind). Julian's use of this term encompasses all of these meanings. Thus, when she says that "God is kind in his being," she is making a claim not only about God's benevolence but also about God's relationship to us, as well as naming God not as a created nature (*natura naturata*) but as nature's Creator (*natura naturans*), and thus making a claim about the nature of reality as a whole.

In the later fourteenth century, punning on these multiple meanings of "kind" was not uncommon.[30] To take but one example, in the ninth passus of the B-version of William Langland's

---

28. Julian, ch. 62.

29. Clifton Wolters, introduction to Julian of Norwich, *Revelations of Divine Love* (Harmondsworth, GB: Penguin, 1966), 32.

30. See Andrew Galloway, "The Making of a Social Ethic in Late-Medieval England: From *Gratitudo* to 'Kyndenesse,'" *Journal of the History of Ideas* 55, no. 3 (1994): 365–83.

Piers Plowman, the dreamer Will asks the allegorical character Wit, "What kind of thing is Kind?" to which Wit replies that Kind "is the creator of all kinds of beasts, / Father and former, the first of all things, / And that is the great God that had beginning never, / Lord of life and of light, of relief and of pain."[31] Wit goes on to explain that, of all the natures created by God, humanity "is most like him in mien and in shape,"[32] particularly in the possession of "Inwit,"[33] which seems to be the capacity to act consciously and responsibly. He then goes on to denounce those who misuse Inwit, including "gluttons" and "guzzlers,"[34] but most especially those who act "unkindly" by not coming to the aid of their fellow Christians. These include godparents who do not provide spiritual aid to their godchildren[35] and prelates who ignore the material needs of the poor at their gate.[36] Wit asks, "Why are we Christians not as kind with Christ's goods?"[37] Precisely because it runs against the grain of the world as created by God, unkindness will have negative repercussions for society as a whole: "It will cost the commons dear for their unkindness, I fear."[38] As one author puts it, "Immediately after describing God ('Kynde') and the innate ('kynde') attributes of human beings, Wit defines 'unkyndnesse' as a failure to fulfill the natural unity of the Christian community by economic means."[39]

So, in speaking of "kindness," Julian is drawing upon its commonly accepted meanings. But in her discussion of God's

---

31. William Langland, *Piers Plowman: An Alliterative Verse Translation*, trans. E. Talbot Donaldson (New York: Norton, 1990), passus 9, lines 25–29. Subsequent citations shall be by passus (i.e., chapter) and line number.

32. Langland, *Piers Plowman*, passus 9, line 31.

33. Langland, passus 9, line 58.

34. Langland, passus 9, line 62.

35. Langland, passus 9, line 77.

36. Langland, passus 9, lines 82–83. Notice that the "kin" toward whom these people are "unkind" are not blood relatives, but those to whom they are bound by sacramental bonds.

37. Langland, passus 9, line 89.

38. Langland, passus 9, line 91.

39. Galloway, "Social Ethic," 380.

nature, Julian gives a distinctly Neoplatonic cast to God's "kindness." God is the ground from which creation comes forth and to which it shall return: "God is kind in his being: that is to say, that goodness that is kind, it is God. He is the ground, he is the substance, he is the same thing that is kindness, and he is very father and very mother of kind. And all kinds that he has made to flow out of him to work his will, shall be restored and brought again into him by the salvation of man through the working of grace."[40] As Julian sees it, God's very nature is self-communicating goodness, an overflowing fountain of "kindness" that engenders the diversity of natures in creation, and the supremely attractive good that lures all natures back through the workings of grace.

To put this another way, Julian refuses the nominalist implication that God's will is a contentless capacity for spontaneous action, which seems to place a gulf between God's will and God's hidden nature. For Julian, in contrast, God's will is always in accord with God's nature, God's kindness. Thus, the root problem she addresses—our lack of faith that God "is all love and will do all"—can be overcome by reintegrating our understanding of divine will and divine nature. God's freedom is not the freedom of modern spontaneity; God is free precisely and only to be who God is as Father, Son, and Spirit—a communion of love. To quote Karl Barth, "It is not that God first lives and then also loves. But God loves, and in this act lives."[41]

In all this, Julian does not deny that creation is an act of divine will, nor claim that God's nature *requires* that God create. Her vision of God's creation as "a little thing, the quantity of a hazelnut in the palm of my hand" that "lasts and ever shall because God loves it"[42] makes the contingency of creation clear. But Julian's emphasis falls equally upon the claim that the diversity of kinds that flow forth from God participate and find their ground

40. Julian, *Revelation*, ch. 62.
41. Karl Barth, *Church Dogmatics* 2.2 (Edinburgh, GB: T&T Clark, 1957), 321.
42. Julian, *Revelation*, ch. 5.

in God's own kindness. Julian's theology of God as uncreated nature in which all created natures participate gives a highly "realist" cast to her thought; things most truly are what their natures are because those created kinds participate in kindness itself.

This insight illuminates a striking difference between Julian's thought and the typical nominalist understanding of sin. On the whole, nominalists saw sin as a violation of divine legislation— the laws ordained by God. There is no intrinsic necessity to these laws, and God could conceivably have ordained different laws. What makes an act sinful is nothing in the nature of the act itself but simply the fact that God has forbidden it. Thus, Ockham's notorious claim that God could, in theory, make hatred of God right rather than wrong. This is related to Ockham's claim that God could, again in theory, save someone without their possessing the *habitus* of charity. God's justification of the sinner requires only the exercise of God's will in accepting the sinner; it does not require any change in the sinner. While Ockham thinks that God has ordained that no one can be saved without the *habitus* of charity, this is only because of God's contingent decree and not because of any intrinsic necessity. Marilyn McCord Adams' description of Ockham's position hints at the way in which a secularized version of nominalist theology manifests itself today:

> [R]efusing to identify worthiness with any such natural property or privation, [Ockham] insists that the divine acts themselves confer the property of worthiness on a person or act, just as the act of a king or government confers commercial value on coins or paper, and just as linguistic conventions confer semantic properties on spoken and written words. And just as the property of commercial value is logically independent of the natural value of the coins or paper, and the property of conventional signification of any natural properties and similarities belonging to a sound or mark, so worthiness of eternal

life or eternal punishment is logically independent of any created thing, whether naturally or supernaturally.[43]

In contrast to this, Julian maintains that sin is wrong not because
God forbids it but because it is *bad* for us, and that is why God
forbids it. Julian writes: "sin is far more vile and painful than hell,
without comparison; for it is contrary to our fair kind; for as truly
as sin is unclean, as truly is it unkind."[44] Sin is wrong by its very
nature, which is contrary to our nature. Against any tendency to
naturalize evil, Julian sees evil as profoundly unnatural, *unkind*.
What is most natural to us is to love God. Unlike Ockham, Julian
bases her hope for salvation not on God's decree, but on the fact
that our nature—by virtue both of our creation and our redemption in Christ—participates in God's own nature, and thus God's
love toward us is the "kind love" of motherhood.[45] Julian asks the
same question as Isaiah: "Can a woman forget her nursing child,
or show no compassion for the child of her womb?" (Isa. 49:15)
God's promise that *all* shall be well is credible precisely because of
the universal participation of creation in God's "kind."[46]

Should we, then, see Julian simply as a holdover from the
premodern sacred *cosmos*? Certainly, she comes close to the view
that Dupré claimed characterizes antiquity: "the essence of the
real and our knowledge of it consists ultimately of *form*."[47] However, Julian speaks of "kind" rather than "form," and this shift
is significant, because Julian does *not* conceive of "kindness" as
an immutable, eternal form that manifests itself in social bonds.
"Kindness" is a relational term that evokes the bonds established

43. Marilyn McCord Adams, *William Ockham* (Notre Dame: University of Notre Dame
Press, 1987), 1287.

44. Julian, *Revelation*, ch. 63.

45. Julian, ch. 60.

46. Thus, I must disagree with Nicholas Watson, who sees Julian's putative universalism
based in something like the nominalist distinction between God's *potentia absoluta* and *potentia
ordinata*. See "Visions of Inclusion: Universal Salvation and Vernacular Theology in Pre-Reformation England," *Journal of Medieval and Early Modern Studies* 27, no. 2 (1997): 167–68.

47. Dupré, *Passage to Modernity*, 18.

by the activity of social charity. Yet this could still lend itself to a reading in which charity is exercised by each according to his or her "kind": peasants growing food, nobles fighting battles, the clergy praying. But Julian does not take her account of "kindness" from the social *status quo*; with the exception of the mother's kind love for her child, she never treats the worldly ordering of kinds as a manifestation of a sacred order. Her emphasis, rather, is on the revelation of "kindness" in the cross of Jesus Christ.

Julian sees creation as grounded in Christ, the second person—or, as she says, the "mid-person"—of the Trinity:

> By the endless assent of the full accord of all the Trinity, the mid-person would be ground and head of this fair kind, out of whom we are all come, in whom we are all enclosed, into whom we shall all go; in him finding our full heaven in everlasting joy by the foreseeing purpose of all the blessed Trinity from without beginning; for before he made us he loved us; and when we were made we loved him; and this is a love made of the kindly substantial goodness of the Holy Spirit, mighty because of the might of the Father, and wise in mind of the wisdom of the Son; and thus is man's soul made by God and in the same point knit to God.[48]

What Julian is saying in this rather complicated passage is that humanity is eternally enfolded in God's love because the creation of humankind is, through Christ the eternal exemplar of creatures, grounded in God's own triune life. The love with which we love God is a participation in the "kindly substantial goodness of the Holy Spirit," the eternal love shared between the Father and the Son. And the revelation of this love in history is the cross.

After she sees, in a vision, the crucifix before her start bleeding, Julian says, "in the same showing, suddenly the Trinity filled

48. Julian, *Revelation*, ch. 53.

my heart most full of joy," and she explains that "where Jesus appears the blessed Trinity is understood, as to my sight."[49] As Herbert McCabe puts it, "The cross and resurrection are the eternal dialogue of Father and Son as projected on to the screen of history, what it looks like in history. If you want to know what the Trinity looks like, be filled with the Holy Spirit and look at the cross."[50] The meaning of "kindness" cannot be read off of fallen nature (which has become "unkind"), but must be a reading of the incarnate, crucified, and risen Word.

Such a reading must highly qualify, if not disallow, any notion of a sacred cosmos. While Julian would agree that, as Dupré puts it, "it belongs to the essence of the real to *appear*, rather than to hide, and to appear in an orderly way," she would also want to say that its clearest appearance is not in nature and culture but in cross and resurrection, which force us to reassess our notions of what is "orderly." The tumultuous upheaval of the sacred *cosmos* in Julian's day once again makes thinkable, as it was in the early days of the Church, the prospect that the true order of things is manifest in a wisdom that to the world appears as foolishness. In Julian's vision, power is revealed in weakness, passion is compassion, faults are happy, lords exalt servants, and the privation of the cross becomes the plenty of salvation. In recovering a vision of the cosmos as "created kind" grounded in the "uncreated Kind" of God revealed in Christ, Julian overturns static notions of order while at the same time resisting the nominalist grounding of all order in will.

HOW DOES ONE LIVE AT THE EDGE OF MODERNITY?

Julian gives us a picture of how the world is—one that differs from both the premodern picture of a world ordered by eternal

49. Julian, ch. 4.
50. Herbert McCabe, *God Matters* (London: Geoffrey Chapman, 1987), 100.

forms that present themselves to reason and the modern picture of a world ordered by a will, whether divine or human, that is freed from all constraints. But what implication does this picture have for us Christians at the trailing edge of modernity? What difference does it make? Even if one is convinced by Julian's picture, how does one make that notoriously difficult passage from "is" to "ought"?

Julian herself recognized this problem, albeit obliquely. At the beginning of her final chapter, she writes, "This book is begun by God's gift and grace, but it is not yet performed, as to my sight."[51] The statement is obscure. Why, at the end of the book, does Julian declare it "begun"? Julian implies that the theology she is attempting to write is one that only *is* in being *performed*, much as a play or a symphony; what she has written is a script or a score that requires performance. One might go so far as to say that the picture of the world that she offers can really be seen only by those who perform it. The passage from "is" to "ought" cannot be mapped; rather, it is made by following Christ on his pilgrimage through history: "[H]e is here with us, leading us, and shall be until he has brought us all to his bliss in heaven."[52]

I conclude by offering six tentative suggestions, informed by Julian's theology, about what it means for Christians to perform the kindness of God here, on the far edge of modernity.

1. We must not succumb to nostalgia for the sacred cosmos.

It would be a mistake to think that Christians have a stake in the restoration of an order of self and society based on the notion of immutable essences read off nature. While the Christian tradition has been able to borrow from the cosmological vision of the ancients, such a vision remains essentially pagan and can

---

51. Julian, *Revelation*, ch. 86.
52. Julian, ch. 81.

only uneasily incorporate the Jewish and Christian belief that, as Julian puts it, "all things have their being by the love of God."[53] Therefore, calls for a return to organic conceptions of the world and society are rightly viewed with the suspicion that they mask a desire to contain disorder at all costs. In a sometimes chaotic world, the siren song of order can become irresistible. However, it can all too easily be transposed into the pagan ideology of blood and soil.

2. We must not succumb to the allure of the modern conception of freedom.

In some ways, the modern picture of freedom as unconstrained spontaneity is so ingrained in us that it is almost impossible to think ourselves out of it. We inevitably think of freedom as the capacity for unconstrained choice. But ultimately, such a conception of freedom is nihilistic because, at its limit, such freedom's only recourse is to will its own annihilation. But perhaps we are beginning to be freed from the grasp of modern freedom, and while Julian offers no particular theory of freedom, she does offer a couple of instructive hints about how else we might conceive of freedom. First is her notion of the "godly will . . . which . . . is so good that it may never will evil, but ever good."[54] To our modern way of looking at things, such a will cannot be free because it is not free to will evil. But, for Julian, the godly will is that part of the self that is truly free precisely because it is *not* enslaved to sin and blindness. Second, Julian's theology of prayer does not presume that prayer is some sort of confrontation between two spontaneous wills, in which I try to bend God's will to my will. Rather, prayer is the means by which I bring my will into accord with God's: "Prayer unites the soul to God...[P]rayer [is] a witness that the soul wills

53. Julian, ch. 5.
54. Julian, ch. 37.

as God wills."[55] Perhaps the place to begin thinking anew about our freedom is in the context of prayer.

3. We must not succumb to despair.

This is perhaps Julian's central theme, and it seems as relevant on our side of modernity as on hers. In speaking of hope, Julian was a truly apocalyptic thinker. I do not, of course, mean by this that she offered a detailed script of future events. Rather, like the seer John in the book of Revelation, Julian unveils the truth that all of history is in God's hands: that God not only may and can make all things well, but that God will make all things well. And like John's message of endurance to the seven churches, Julian's message of hope is quite austere: "He said not 'You shall not be tempested, you shall not be travailed, you shall not be dis-eased', but he said: 'You shall not be overcome.'"[56] Part of the legacy of the modern understanding of freedom is the temptation to see ourselves as responsible for making history turn out right. But Julian speaks of "the great deed ordained by our Lord God from without begin-ning, treasured and hid in his blessed [blissid] breast, only known to himself, by which deed he shall make all things well; for just as the blissful Trinity made all things from nought, just so the same blessed Trinity shall make well all that is not well."[57] Our goal is not to secure the triumph of God's will—as if God somehow needed our help—but to endure faithfully the inevitable trials that life brings, in the sure hope that God will make all things well.

4. We must cleave to Christ as the key to the true order of the world.

In rejecting both pagan notions of order and modern conceptions of freedom, we must turn to Christ as the exemplar and ordering

55. Julian, ch. 43.
56. Julian, ch. 68.
57. Julian, ch. 32.

principle of creation. In particular, we must learn to see the universe as a place ordered by the logic of kindness, revealed in the cross and resurrection of Jesus. Christians must resist the modern version of "realism" (accepted by all too much of so-called post-modernism) that sees the world as, at its root, ruled by violence. Rather, we must learn with Julian the difficult lesson that sin "has no manner of substance nor part of being"[58] and "that everything that is done is well done, for our Lord God does everything."[59] This is not a denial of the real effects of sin in the world; it is simply a refusal to grant any ontological ultimacy to evil, and it is to hold fast to faith in God's providence, to the faith that the world is moved not by violence but by, as Dante put it, "the Love that moves the sun and the other stars."[60] The love that Julian sees displayed in the cross overcomes evil because what is most natural is most "kind." She writes that "Adam's sin was the most harm that was ever done, or ever shall be," but the redemption wrought by Christ "is more pleasing to God and more worshipful for man's salvation, without comparison, than ever was the sin of Adam harmful."[61]

5. We must find a place in which to dwell.

Where do we go to live out a theology like Julian's? One of the few things we know historically about Julian is that in her own day, unlike ours, her book was not popular. There are no medieval manuscripts of the complete long text of her work, and we do not know if any copies were made at all. This should not surprise us since Julian's book is something of an "untimely meditation," poised between times infatuated by order and by

---

58. Julian, ch. 27.

59. Julian, ch. 11.

60. Dante Alighieri, *The Divine Comedy: Paradiso*, 33.145 in *The Portable Dante*, ed. and trans. Mark Musa (New York: Penguin, 1995), 585.

61. Julian, *Revelation*, ch. 29.

freedom, holding a strikingly different account of the nature of things before us. In light of this, her choice to live enclosed as an anchoress, alone in a room beside a church, seems to fit the loneliness of her thinking. An anchorite is a liminal figure who lives at the boundary, the edge. And perhaps at the edge of modernity, a boundary is the most appropriate place to dwell. We must take more seriously than we have hitherto the passing of Christendom and face up to the need to construct conceptual and material spaces in which it is possible to think "order" and "freedom" in a genuinely Christian way. Of course, since Christians believe that the order of cross and resurrection is the true order of the universe, such "enclosure" can be seen only as a temporary expedient; the boundary of this enclosure must always be a frontier opening out toward God's world.

6. We must embody Christ's compassion.

Despite her enclosure, Julian speaks constantly of her fellow Christians—her "even Christians" as she calls them—and sees her revelation as expressly for *them*: "all this teaching of true comfort is general to all my even Christians . . . , and this is God's will."[62] One might say that, despite the lonely, untimely nature of Julian's thinking, she seeks a community that can embody what God has already revealed. For in the Church's performance of the compassion first revealed in Christ's passion, Christ is enfleshed anew in our world: "each kind compassion that man has on his even Christian with charity, it is Christ in him."[63] It is precisely because compassion is "kind," the true nature of things, that it is the key to true order and true freedom.

There are dangers peculiar to the edges. The Welsh poet and artist David Jones writes: "it is easy to miss Him / at the turn of

62. Julian, ch. 68.
63. Julian, ch. 28.

a civilization."[64] In order not to miss Him, Christians today, as always, must hold fast to the appearing of divine love in the flesh of Jesus Christ. Perhaps, at the turn—the edge—of modernity, our sister Julian can teach us how to do this.

64. David Jones, "A, a, a, Domine Deus," in *The Sleeping Lord and Other Fragments* (London: Faber, 1974), 9.

7

Making Religion
Safe for Democracy

William James and the Monotony of Religious Experience

* This essay was originally published as "Making Religion Safe for Democracy: William James and the Monotony of Religious Experience," in *Divinising Experience: Essays in the History of Religious Experience from Origen to Ricœur*, ed. Lieven Boeve and Laurence Hemming (Leuven, BE: Peeters, 2004), 113–31.

SITUATING WILLIAM JAMES AND
THE VARIETIES OF RELIGIOUS EXPERIENCE

William James's 1900–1902 Gifford Lectures, given at the University of Edinburgh and published as *The Varieties of Religious Experience*, are one of the great works of modern religious studies. They are beautifully and engagingly written, crammed with the brilliant insights of a truly creative thinker, and highly sympathetic to their subject matter. They are also, I will eventually suggest, dead wrong in their approach to religious experience and ultimately pernicious in their effect. But before we get to this critique, I want to briefly sketch their context and try to account for their enduring appeal.

1. The context of the Varieties

The Gifford Lectures were established by Lord Adam Gifford in his will as a series of lectures given at the ancient Scottish universities of Edinburgh, Aberdeen, St. Andrews, and Glasgow to "promote and diffuse the study of Natural Theology in the widest sense of the term—in other words, the knowledge of God." Since the first lectures given in 1888, the Gifford Lectures have constituted a veritable who's who of modern theology, philosophy, and religious studies, including series of lectures by Henri Bergson, James Frazer, Alfred North Whitehead, Étienne Gilson, Albert Schweitzer, Reinhold Niebuhr, Rudolf Bultmann, Karl Barth, Paul Tillich, Niels Bohr, Iris Murdoch, Paul Ricoeur, Alasdair MacIntyre, Stanley Hauerwas, and David Tracy. Being asked to deliver a series of Gifford Lectures is, in the world of religion, analogous to winning a Nobel Prize. Indeed, the Gifford Lectures have become so important in recent years that some Gifford Lecturers feel compelled to spend much of their lectures talking about past Gifford Lectures.[1]

While the Gifford Lectures had not yet achieved this status in 1900 when James began his lectures, he still took time to note that his invitation to give the lectures was something of a sign that American thought had "arrived" or that its arrival was at least on the horizon. Having spent his life learning from Europeans, *he* was now asked to teach *them*. As he says at the beginning of his first lecture, "the current . . . has begun to run from west to east." He also expresses the hope that, as British and American thinkers begin to mutually influence one another, "the peculiar philosophic temperament, as well as the peculiar political temperament, that goes with our English speech may more and more pervade and influence the world."[2] We will have occasion to return to this peculiar pair of temperaments.

1. For a general account of the Gifford Lectures, see Stanley L. Jaki, *Lord Gifford and His Lectures: A Centenary Retrospect* (Macon, GA: Mercer University Press, 1987). For a critical account of the ideology underlying the Giffords, see Alasdair MacIntyre's own Gifford Lectures, published as *Three Rival Versions of Moral Inquiry: Encyclopaedia, Genealogy, and Tradition* (Notre Dame, IN: University of Notre Dame Press, 1991).

2. William James, *The Varieties of Religious Experience: A Study in Human Nature* (New York: Longmans, 1902), 2.

It is also worth noting how James fit with the idea behind the Gifford Lectures. William James (1842–1910) was a physician (his first academic position was teaching anatomy and physiology at Harvard Medical School), a pioneer in the field of psychology (the opening lecture in the *Varieties* is entitled "Religion and Neurology"), and one of the founders, along with C.S. Peirce, of the pragmatist school of philosophy. Of all the things that he was, note that he was not, nor did he claim to be, a theologian. He begins at the outset noting that his will be a *psychological* inquiry into religion; in other words, it will be scientific. It will not be "Natural Theology" in the sense of beginning from principles available to unaided human reason and proceeding to argue for God's existence but in the sense of treating religion as a "natural" phenomenon to be subjected to scientific inquiry. It is no accident that when James publishes *The Varieties of Religious Experience*, he will subtitle them "A Study in Human Nature." His focus is on the human experience of God, not on God. He hopes that virtually all of what he says about the psychology of religious experience will be as (but not more) acceptable to the atheist as to the theist. In taking this approach, James sees himself as contributing to the formation of a "Science of Religion."[3]

It is important to note, however, what sort of "psychologist" James was; in his day, "psychology" was quite a different discipline than it is today. Though James himself contributed greatly to developing the experimental—and therefore "scientific"—character of psychology, it was for James still primarily a science of the soul. Rather than our modern management of mental illness through pharmaceuticals or psychotherapy, James's psychology was a deep reflection on what it meant to be human, to know and act as a human, to think and experience as a human. So today, he is remembered more as a philosopher than a psychologist (though some might argue that he was a better psychologist than a philosopher).

3. James, *Varieties*, 433.

It is also important to note what sort of philosopher James was. "Pragmatism" is a philosophical approach that James himself traces to Charles Sanders Peirce (1839–1914).[4] However, James was its first great advocate (Peirce published little, and what he published was not nearly as readable as James's writings). Because James took up Peirce's notion of pragmatism and put it to his own use, in the end producing something quite different from Peirce, we can turn directly, and briefly, to James himself in order to understand what *he* meant by pragmatism.[5]

In a 1907 series of lectures, later published as *Pragmatism*, James offers an account of what he means by "the pragmatic method":

The pragmatic method is primarily a method of settling metaphysical disputes that might otherwise be interminable. Is the world one or many?—fated or free?—material or spiritual?—here are notions either of which may or may not hold good of the world; and disputes over such notions are unending. The pragmatic method in such cases is to try to interpret each notion by tracing its respective practical consequences. What difference would it practically make to any one if this notion rather than that notion were true? If no practical difference whatever can be traced, then the alternatives mean practically the same thing, and all dispute is idle. Whenever a dispute is serious, we ought to be able to show some practical difference that must follow from one side or the other's being right.[6]

---

4. See James, 444–45. The essay by Peirce that James points to is "How to Make Our Ideas Clear," *Popular Science Monthly* 12 (January 1878): 286–302.

5. For one account of the differences between Peirce and James, see Christopher Hookway, "Logical Principles and Philosophical Attitudes: Peirce's Response to James' Pragmatism," in *The Cambridge Companion to William James*, ed. Ruth Anna Putnam (Cambridge: Cambridge University Press, 1997), 145–65.

6. William James, *Pragmatism* (Buffalo, NY: Prometheus, 1991), 23.

In other words, the meaning of a concept is the practical difference that it makes: a difference that makes no difference *is* no difference. As he puts it in *The Varieties of Religious Experience*, "beliefs, in short, are rules for action."[7] So, for example, when confronted with a term like "substance," the pragmatic philosopher will ask not whether or not such a thing as a "substance" exists, but rather how the concept "substance" functions. What real difference does it make if we hold (following, say, Berkeley) that the qualities of the thing adhere in each other rather than (following, say, Aristotle) in something called a "substance"? James's answer is that it makes *no* difference whatsoever.[8]

James's "pragmatic method" is important for his treatment of religious experience. What he attempts to do in *The Varieties of Religious Experience* is to ask, "what practical difference do religious experiences make?" As he rather crassly puts it, what is the "cash-value" of such experiences?[9] Again and again in dealing with religious experiences and beliefs, James asks, what difference do these experiences and beliefs make? What actions do they engender? Are these actions commendable or condemnable? Such questions, he believes, can be answered scientifically, by a sympathetic but external scientific gaze. Once again, the Natural Theology of which Lord Gifford spoke becomes what James calls "the Science of Religion," a science that might "eventually command as general a public adhesion as is commanded by a physical science."[10]

I think that, in attempting to contextualize *The Varieties of Religious Experience*, we should see it as part of a shift from the Natural Theology over which Lord Gifford somewhat naively

7. James, *Varieties*, 444.
8. See James, *Pragmatism*, 39–41. The one exception James makes is what he no doubt considers the curious case of the scholastic doctrine of transubstantiation. In this case, the idea of substance *does* affect what we do: i.e., how we treat the Eucharistic elements.
9. James, *Varieties*, 443. James's crassness might well have been intentional, so as to deflate certain puffed-up accounts of "belief."
10. James, 456.

enthused to the Science of Religion that James saw as the future of "public" discourse about religion. As such, the *Varieties* are of crucial interest to us today because we still live in a world in which the Science of Religion (or, as we call it today, Religious Studies) is the dominant public discourse for speaking of religion. Part of the reason why *The Varieties of Religious Experience* has remained an appealing and vital work for a century now is because it operates within the paradigm of Religious Studies, a paradigm that still functions in the academic world today.

2. The Appeal of the Varieties

But the appeal of the *Varieties* goes beyond the familiar paradigm within which it operates. James was a scientist and a philosopher, but more than this, he was a great man of letters, as anyone who has read *The Varieties of Religious Experience* can attest. As much as his novelist brother Henry, William James is a master stylist who tosses off memorable lines with aplomb, as when he notes that the lamentations of Nietzsche and Schopenhauer "remind one, half the time, of the sick shriekings of two dying rats."[11] No doubt part of the success of the *Varieties* is due to the sheer pleasure they bring to the reader. It probably does not hurt that the sizzle of James's prose is accentuated by its contrast with the long and often tedious firsthand accounts of religious experiences with which the *Varieties* are filled. After reading several pages of Henry Alline's account of his religious conversion, one returns with relief to James's way with a turn of phrase.

Another aspect of their appeal is that the beauty of the language is often at the service of greatness of insight. James is often faulted for a certain fuzziness in his thinking, for inconsistency and self-contradiction. To take but one well-known example, James never seemed entirely clear on what he meant by "truth."

11. James, 38.

In some places (the places neo-pragmatists such as Richard Rorty like), James seems to identify truth with "what works" in practice, what you can convince others of. In other places, perhaps reflecting the influence of Peirce, he adopts a more "realist" stance. In a footnote in the final lecture in the *Varieties*, he notes, "The word 'truth' is here taken to mean something additional to bare value for life, although the natural propensity of man is to believe that whatever has great value for life is thereby certified as true."[12] We see here some of what drives philosophers crazy about James. What is this "something additional" to which he appeals? Why can he not distinguish more clearly between "truth" as a property of statements and "truth" as utility?

Yet part of James's greatness as a thinker lies precisely in this fuzziness, this unresolved plurality. It reflects the unresolved plurality that is the human person. As the philosopher Owen Flanagan puts it, "the attraction of James the philosopher is that he is to me the best example I know of *a person doing philosophy*; there is no hiding the person behind the work, no way of discussing the work without the person, no way to make believe that there is a way of doing philosophy that is not personal."[13] It is this refusal to be impersonal that makes James so insightful.

Perhaps the most appealing thing about the *Varieties*, at least for religious readers, is the great sympathy with which James approaches the topic of "religious experience." In a way analogous to Max Weber's *Protestant Ethic and the Spirit of Capitalism* but located in the realm of psychology rather than sociology, James wants to give a nonreductive account of religion by showing that there is something called "religious experience" that is not reducible to something else. And, again like Weber, he wants to argue that religious beliefs and experiences make an actual, empirical *difference* in the world and that, therefore, according to James's

12. James, 509.
13. Owen Flanagan, "Consciousness as a Pragmatist Views It," in *The Cambridge Companion to William James*, 47.

pragmatic definition of truth, we can speak of those beliefs and experiences as "true." James is convinced that even if one accounts for religious experiences psychologically—or biologically, or sociologically—one has in no sense "disproved" them, because, for a pragmatist like James, origins are only half, indeed, somewhat less than half, of the story. As he says, adapting the words of Christ, "by their fruits ye shall know them, not by their roots."[14] Though frank about his own difficulties with traditional Christianity, James is not dismissive of traditional beliefs when looked at from the perspective of their pragmatic effects. As Carol Zaleski has put it, "Never at home in the Christianity of his ancestors, James nonetheless manages in the *Varieties* to keep the door open for orthodoxy, for supernaturalism, for moral conviction, and for the kinds of religious engagement that make a real difference in the public square."[15]

So, James offers us what appears to be a defense of religious experience that is well written and insightful. I want to suggest, however, that we ought to resist the allure of *The Varieties of Religious Experience*. To make this case, I want first to explore what James means by "religion" and "experience" and then try to show why he conceives of religious experience the way he does. Then, in good pragmatist fashion, I will try to sketch some consequences of such a conception of religious experience.

"RELIGIOUS EXPERIENCE" ACCORDING TO JAMES

1. James on "religion"

14. James, *Varieties*, 20.
15. Carol Zaleski, "William James, *The Varieties of Religious Experience* (1902)," *First Things* 101 (March 2000): 61.

William James was one of the first people to use "religious experience" as a technical category.[16] James has rather interesting and original ideas about the nature of "experience," which I will come to in a moment, but first I would like to focus on the term "religion." What exactly do we mean when we describe an experience as "religious"? How are religious experiences different from other experiences? Is an experience designated as "religious" because of the object of the experience (e.g., a religious experience is an experience of God), or because of some subjective quality of the experience itself (e.g., a religious experience is one that unifies one's worldview), or does the designation "religious" depend on both subject and object? James is aware of these sorts of questions and the deeper issues that give rise to them. So, in his second lecture, he offers a "circumscription of the topic," in which he attempts to spell out what *he* means, at least in the Gifford Lectures, by "religious experience."

He says, quite wisely, that "the word 'religion' cannot stand for any single principle or essence, but is rather a collective name."[17] Abstract definitions of religion are not only unlikely to be helpful, but they may be positively misleading. Therefore, James says, his "lectures must be limited to a fraction of the subject."[18] James then goes on to note that there is "one great partition which divides the religious field"; on one side of this partition lies "institutional" religion, and on the other, "personal" religion.[19] Institutional religion is a matter of structures and rituals and creeds, which perhaps an anthropologist or sociologist or even a theologian might well treat, whereas what he calls "personal

---

16. See John E. Smith, "William James's Account of Mysticism: A Critical Appraisal," in *Mysticism and Religious Traditions*, ed. Steven T. Katz (Oxford: Oxford University Press, 1983), 277.

17. James, *Varieties*, 26.

18. James, 28.

19. James, 28–29.

religion pure and simple" is a matter of "inner dispositions,"[20] which makes it the obvious choice for James the psychologist.

But James's choice is guided by more than his own particular area of expertise. In opting for the personal over the institutional, he believes himself to be getting closer to the heart of religious experience. Though it is obviously not the whole of religion, James believes it is "more fundamental" than institutional religion. At the very beginning of his first lecture, James speaks somewhat disdainfully of the "ordinary religious believer . . . [whose] religion has been made for him by others, communicated to him by tradition, determined to fixed form by imitation, and retained by habit."[21] In his second lecture he writes:

> Churches, when once established, live at second-hand upon tradition; but the founders of every church owed their power originally to the fact of their direct personal communion with the divine. Not only the superhuman founders, the Christ, the Buddha, Mahomet, but all the originators of Christian sects have been in this case;—so personal religion should still seem the primordial thing, even to those who continue to esteem it incomplete.[22]

Returning to this topic in a later lecture, James notes that those who live firsthand upon experience gather followers to themselves, and that these followers build structures and institutions, and then "the spirit of politics and the lust of dogmatic rule are . . . apt to enter and to contaminate the originally innocent thing."[23] But this loss of innocence—what Weber called the "routinization of charisma"—is an alienation from religion in

20. James, 29.
21. James, 6.
22. James, 30.
23. James, 335.

its primordial, personal form.[24] So James's circumscription of his topic is not simply a practical delimiting of his field but rather a narrowing that, in fact, allows us to discern religion more clearly.

But what is it that we find in this pure and simple personal religion? James writes, "Religion . . . shall mean for us the feelings, acts, and experiences of individual men in their solitude, so far as they apprehend themselves to stand in relation to whatever they may consider the divine."[25] This description is borne out by the many examples James presents during the course of his twenty lectures.

First, his concern is almost exclusively with the emotional and volitional side of religion rather than the intellectual. The various theologies and doctrines that provided the vocabularies with which his examples speak are described by James as "over-beliefs, buildings-out performed by the intellect into directions of which feeling originally supplied the hint."[26] James acknowledges that over-beliefs can be interesting and important, particularly to the person who holds them,[27] but they are very much outside his core definition of religion. This can be seen by a look at how, in trying to give some order to his description of religious experience, James focuses not on differences of belief but on differences of mood and action. Thus, he distinguishes between the once-born soul's religion of healthy mindedness and the twice-born soul's—the "sick soul's"—religion of redemption (Lectures 4–7). He looks at the event of conversion (Lectures 9–10), the activity of saintliness (Lectures 11–15), and the experience of mysticism (Lectures 16–17) but is totally uninterested in the theology of conversion,

---

24. The one place where "ecclesiastical" religion seems to touch some primordial religious impulse is in the realm of the aesthetic (James, 458–59). James's remarks on this topic, brief though they are, are typically insightful. However, I would venture to say that he could not take the aesthetic very seriously as a religious category, for to do so would call his "great partition" between the personal and the institutional into question.

25. James, 31.

26. James, 433.

27. James, 515.

sanctity, or mystical union. Even when the examples he gives speak scriptural or doctrinal language, James almost never comments on that language but rather treats it as the clothing in which (for the sake of modesty?) feeling must be dressed.

Second, as we have already seen, religion is essentially a private and individual matter. James seems to gravitate toward examples of figures, such as George Fox or Leo Tolstoy, who were alienated from the religious and secular cultures of their days. Religion, particularly in the extreme case of the religious genius, is a lonely matter:

> The religious experience which we are studying is that which lives itself out within the private breast. First-hand individual experience of this kind has always appeared as a heretical sort of innovation to those who witnessed its birth. Naked comes it into the world and lonely; and it has always, for a time at least, driven him who had it into the wilderness, often into the literal wilderness out of doors, where the Buddha, Jesus, Mohammed, St. Francis, George Fox, and so many others had to go.[28]

This isolation is of a piece with James's emphasis on religion as mood and action. Because religion is essentially nonrational, and therefore prior to thought and language, it cannot be communicated to others without loss, without becoming "second-hand." And, in the case of the religious genius, when the individual's powerful religious experience is forced into the ossified vocabulary of prior orthodoxies, it cannot help but take the form of heterodoxy.

Third, while various experiences may involve the mood and action of individuals, it is essential to *religious* experience that it has to do with the individual's experience of whatever he or she may consider divine. The formulation in James's definition—they

28. James, 335.

apprehend themselves to stand in relation to whatever they may *consider* divine—is important. In speaking of the *object* of religious experience, James exhibits great circumspection. As the mentioning together of Buddha, Jesus, and Mohammed above indicates, James is very aware of the issue of religious pluralism, and he is also aware that not all religions share the Christian, Jewish, or Islamic understanding of God. Buddhism might be the most obvious case, but James also includes Emersonian transcendentalism as an essentially "religious" standpoint. In light of such examples, James says, "we must interpret the term 'divine' very broadly, as denoting any object that is god*like*, whether it be a concrete deity or not."[29] Yet he is not really satisfied with such vagueness, so he further specifies that godlike objects "overarch and envelope, and from them there is no escape"; they have to do with one's "total reaction upon life."[30] Even more specifically, one's attitude toward a godlike object must be "serious" but not "grumbling."[31] Note that what makes an object godlike has nothing to do with its intrinsic properties, such as eternity or omnipotence. Indeed, James has some uncharacteristically unkind words for those who speculate about divine attributes, saying that they offer a "metaphysical monster . . . to our worship."[32] What makes an object godlike is our stance toward it; how we apprehend ourselves in relation to it.

James is not afraid to draw certain logical conclusions from this view. For "us Christians" it is natural to "call this higher part of the universe by the name of God,"[33] but James realizes that from a pragmatic point of view all one need possess is "the belief that beyond each man and in a fashion continuous with him

29. James, 34.
30. James, 34.
31. James, 37–38.
32. James, 447.
33. James, 516. The fact that James thinks of "God" as part of the universe indicates the elasticity of the category "us Christians" for him.

there exists a larger power which is friendly to him and to his ideals."[34] All we need of our gods is that they be more powerful than we are, just powerful enough to draw us forward, beyond ourselves. He frankly acknowledges that this "larger power" could simply be "a larger and more Godlike self." He notes that if this were the case, we would have a radical religious pluralism, indeed, a sort of polytheism, with each person possessing his or her own god. James does not shy away from such a conclusion since it follows clearly from the emotional and individualist understanding with which he begins.

Yet what is particularly striking is that for all his celebration of pluralism and diversity, James ends up having a fairly low opinion of the religious particularities that constitute pluralism. They are "over-beliefs," and while James says that "the most interesting and valuable thing about a man are usually his over-beliefs,"[35] he does not himself, as I have noted, show much interest in them. He is like a number of other nineteenth-century intellectuals (the young Schleiermacher comes to mind) who are very interested in Religion, but not very interested in any particular religion.[36] Despite the title of his Gifford Lectures, there is not a lot of variety in religious experience as James presents it. It is true that he offers us the testimonies of Catholics and Calvinists, Buddhists and Baptists, Methodists and Muslims, and that these testimonies are themselves rich in the highly particular language of highly particular communal traditions, but what he draws from these testimonies, in the end, amounts to a fairly interchangeable set of moods and emotions that he calls "personal religion pure and simple."

34. James, 525.

35. James, 515.

36. There is some evidence that James was familiar with Schleiermacher's work, but none that Schleiermacher exerted any great influence on him. It seems more likely that the similarities between them are a result of similar cultural milieus (though separated by an ocean and nearly 100 years) and intellectual influences. For some brief comments on the Schleiermacher-James connection, see Stanley Hauerwas, *With the Grain of the Universe: The Church's Witness and Natural Theology* (London: SCM, 2002), 62.

2. James on "experience"

I will deal more briefly with James's account of "experience," not because what he says about experience is less interesting and important than what he says about religion, but because what he says on the topic is so interesting and rich that I am not even tempted to give anything like a comprehensive account. I will simply mention three points.

First, James thinks of experience in terms of consciousness. In his *Principles of Psychology* (1890), he describes experience as the "impress" of something "foreign" upon us.[37] To have an experience is to be affected by something external to us, something that changes our mind or brain so that our consciousness is (to borrow a scholastic term) conformed to it. More specifically, in experience our consciousness is not simply determined by an external agent, but we are *aware* of that agent as determining. This distinguishes experience from other, non-experiential determinations of consciousness. I may be depressed because of a chemical imbalance in my brain, but I do not *experience* that chemical imbalance because it does not itself enter into my consciousness. However, when I see a tree because of the "impress" of the tree upon my senses, I do, in fact, experience the tree. So, James normally restricts "experience" to those modifications of consciousness that enter through "the front door, the door of the five senses."[38]

Second, James's understanding of "consciousness" is highly nuanced. In particular, he opposes any reification of consciousness, any notion that consciousness is a "thing." In *The Principles of Psychology* he writes, "No one ever had a simple sensation by itself. Consciousness, from our natal day, is of a teeming multiplicity of objects and relations, and what we call simple sensations are results of discriminative attention, pushed often to a very high degree."[39] Though he describes his view as "empiricism"—indeed

37. William James, *The Principles of Psychology* (New York: Henry Holt, 1890), 2:619.
38. James, *Principles of Psychology*, 2:628.
39. James, 1:224.

as "radical empiricism"—his is not the empiricism of John Locke, with its discrete ideas jostling around in the mind. Rather, for James, consciousness is a "stream" or a "flow"[40] from which distinct objects of experience are, as it were, carved out. This, of course, is reminiscent of Kant's transcendental idealism, but with this difference: for James, the tools with which we carve out the objects of our experience are not universal categories of reason but rather are the accumulated "habits," both of the individual and the human race.[41] Yet these objects of experience are still not the discrete "ideas" of Locke and Hume; rather they are "waves" or "fields" of consciousness, which "contain sensations of our bodies and of the objects around us, memories of past experiences and thoughts of distant things, feelings of satisfaction and dissatisfaction, desires and aversions, and other emotional conditions, together with determinations of the will, in every variety of permutation and combination."[42] James particularly emphasizes how fields of consciousness have fuzzy, ill-defined boundaries so that shifts between one field of consciousness and another are often gradual, even unnoticed.

These brief indications should be enough to show the nuance with which James approaches "experience" and "consciousness." In particular, I hope they show that, for James, "experience" is always shaped by a variety of forces: our embodied existence, our education (and therefore the traditions in which we have been educated), the language we speak, our goals and aspirations and moods and what we had for lunch . . . the list could go on indefinitely. We know the world not because it is successfully mediated

40. James, 1:239.

41. On the similarities and differences between James and Kant, see Thomas Carlson, "James and the Kantian Tradition," *The Cambridge Companion to William James*, 363–83. According to Carlson, on the issue of experience, the chief difference between James and Kant was that "the influence of Darwin had shifted James's attention from an abstract and universal Reason to the concrete reasoning individual in the natural order" (371).

42. William James, *Talks to Teachers on Psychology and to Students on Some of Life's Ideals* (New York: Dover, 2001), 28. For James's discussion of "fields of consciousness" in *The Varieties of Religious Experience*, see 234–36.

to us by sense impressions or ideas, but because we are *in* the world that we know, acting and reacting.[43]

Third, James's account of experience seems to take a sharp turn when we come to *The Varieties of Religious Experience*. Here, experience is not shaped by the multitude of forces that normally shape our experiences; rather, religious experiences seem oddly isolated from the normal sorts of forces that operate within a field of experience.[44] Indeed, in the *Varieties*, James's account of "experience" becomes, at times, almost solipsistic. His emphasis on "personal religion" has already pointed to this. However, it becomes particularly evident in his discussion of mystical states of consciousness, which he calls the "root and centre" of all "personal religious experience."[45]

James lists four characteristics of mystical states of consciousness. These four characteristics that have achieved almost canonical status in the English-speaking world of the philosophy of religion. These are:

1. *Ineffability:* mystical experience "defies expression, no adequate report of it can be given in words."[46]
2. *Noetic Quality:* mystical states of consciousness *seem*, to those who have them, to be "states of insight into depths of truth unplumbed by the discursive intellect" and they "carry with them a curious sense of authority for after-time."[47]
3. *Transiency:* mystical states are of brief duration (usually half an hour, at most an hour or two).

43. As Hilary Putnam says, James "was the first modern philosopher successfully to reject the idea that our impressions are located in a private mental theater (and thus constitute an interface between ourselves and 'the external world')" ("James's Theory of Truth," in *The Cambridge Companion to William James*, 181–82).

44. The separation of religious experience from everyday experience is a major element in Nicholas Lash's critique of James in *Easter in Ordinary: Reflections on Human Experience and the Knowledge of God* (London: SCM, 1988).

45. James, *Varieties*, 379.

46. James, 380.

47. James, 380–81.

4. *Passivity:* as James puts it, "the mystic feels as if his own will were in abeyance."[48]

Let me make a few brief remarks about these characteristics, designed to draw out how this account of mystical experience diverges from James's account of everyday experience. Keeping in mind James's preferred metaphor of "fields of consciousness," we ought to note how James, with amazing and uncharacteristic consistency, refers to "*states* of consciousness" when speaking of mystical experience. Without making too much of the metaphors of "field" and "state," one gets the distinct impression that mystical states have tightly policed borders. No one enters or leaves a mystical state casually and unknowingly; the guards are there, and you had better have your papers in order. This is a territory where the language is different (ineffability) and information is doled out (noetic quality). It is so distinct from our ordinary field of consciousness that we cannot stay there long (transiency), and the actions that shape our normal consciousness must be left at the border (passivity).

Defenders of James might claim that it is a mistake to take what James says about mystical states as applying to *all* religious experience.[49] However, it is clear that James's account of religious experience culminates in his account of mystical states of consciousness; as he puts it, "such states of consciousness ought to form the vital chapter from which the other chapters get their light."[50] This would seem to imply that the earlier discussions of religious experience ought to be read in light of his discussion of mystical experience. So what we see in James's treatment of mysticism is simply an intensification of what he has already presented regarding religious experience. Though he begins his lectures by saying: "Things are more or less divine, states of mind are more or

48. James, 381.
49. See, for example, Smith, "William James's Account of Mysticism," 248–49.
50. James, *Varieties*, 379.

less religious, reactions are more or less total, but the boundaries are always misty, and it is everywhere a question of amount and degree,"[51] by the time we are finished with the lecture on mysticism, the boundaries between the religious and the everyday are clearly marked.

THE POLITICS OF "RELIGIOUS EXPERIENCE"

Why does James's account of religious experience not have the embodied, communal, linguistic character that his account of everyday experience does? Is it simply the case that religious experience just *is* drastically different from ordinary experience, a fact that James is faithfully recording? Or might we ask what interests are served by segregating religious experience from other sorts of experience? In the rest of this essay, I will argue that James's account of religious experience is determinatively shaped by his commitment to the American form of democracy. More specifically, it seeks to segregate religious experience from ordinary experience to create a pluralistic public space.

It is striking how the category of "religion" is transformed in the modern era. In the ancient and medieval worlds, *religio* referred to public acts of piety that served to "re-bind" (*re-ligere*) the members of the body politic; and this meaning was still operative in Thomas Aquinas' discussion of the virtue of religion, which he treated as a part of justice.[52] Religion was, by its very definition, a public matter, indeed, a political matter. It was analogous to Americans saying the Pledge of Allegiance or French people singing the "Marseillaise." Of course, it was at the same time more than that; as Aquinas put it, "it denotes properly a relation to God." It is by their common worship of God or the gods that the members of a body politic are bound into one. And, as Augustine

51. James, 39.
52. *Summa theologiae* 2-2.81.1.

argued in *The City of God*, the character of the god you worship determines the character of your political community.

All of this begins to change, of course, in the modern era. Exactly how this change happens has been a matter of some dispute in recent years.[53] The way in which the story has traditionally been told is that with the breakup of Christendom in the sixteenth century, and the Wars of Religion in the sixteenth and seventeenth centuries, the modern secular state arose as a response to religious violence. Religion had not only failed to serve as the ligaments binding together the body politic but actually had become the source of violence and disunity. Thus, religion had to be relegated to the private sphere, while the public sphere would be religiously neutral. This movement toward the privatization of religion culminates in the United States of America, with its separation of church and state and its religious pluralism.[54]

This is what we might call the "standard account" of religion and the modern state. In recent years a "revisionist" account has been offered that rejects the view of state as "savior" from religious violence. This revisionist account points out, first, that from a historical point of view, the chronology is wrong. Well before Luther, to say nothing of Philip II, thinkers like Marsilius of Padua and John Wycliffe had argued that only the secular powers had a right to the use of coercive force. Also, the era of violence that would evolve into the so-called Wars of Religion was not initially motivated by religion at all. Charles V and Philip II were far more

53. For what follows, both the "standard account" and the "revisionist account," see William Cavanaugh, *Eucharistie et mondialisation: La liturgie comme acte politique* (Geneva, SW: Éditions Ad Solem, 2001), esp. 33–58. See also William Cavanaugh, *The Myth of Religious Violence: Secular Ideology and the Roots of Modern Conflict* (Oxford: Oxford University Press, 2009).

54. Judith Shklar's version of this story is as follows: "liberalism . . . was born out of the cruelties of the religious civil wars, which forever rendered the claims of Christian charity a rebuke to all religious institutions and parties. If the faith was to survive at all, it would do so privately. The alternative then set, and still before us, is not one between classical virtue and liberal self-indulgence, but between cruel military and moral repression and violence, and a self-restraining tolerance that fences in the powerful to protect the freedom and safety of every citizen" (Judith Shklar, *Ordinary Vices* [Cambridge, MA: Harvard University Press, 1984], 5, quoted in Cavanaugh, *Religious Violence*, 34).

interested in the fortunes of the Habsburg Empire than they were in the beliefs of their subjects, and when one actually looks at the combatants in the various conflicts it is difficult to assign confessional allegiance based on who was fighting whom.

In this revisionist account, the point is not simply that rulers were cynically using the religious enthusiasms of their subjects to manipulate them. If this were the case, then the liberal state would still be the "savior" of society from religious violence, only in this case religion would be simply the dangerous weapon that must be taken away from those who would use it for their own purposes. Rather, the claim is that the violence of the sixteenth and seventeenth centuries was the "birthpangs" of the modern state, and that part of that birth was replacing the Church with the state as the bearer of those bonds by which the body politic was united. By the end of the sixteenth century, as John Figgis argues, "for many minds the religion of the State has replaced the religion of the Church, or, to be more correct, that religion is becoming individual while the civil power is recognised as having the paramount claims of an organized society upon the allegiance of its members."[55] The liberal state actually fulfills one of the goals of the warring princes of the fifteenth and sixteenth centuries: religion becomes a private matter, leaving the public realm free to be managed by the state. As Alexis de Tocqueville wrote, "If it be of the highest importance to man, as an individual, that his religion should be true, it is not so to society. Society has no future life to hope for or to fear; and provided the citizen profess a religion, the particular tenets of that religion are of little importance to its interests."[56]

What does this debate over the interpretation of the Wars of Religion have to do with William James? Well, for one thing it helps us understand how James's individualist, privatized account

55. John Neville Figgis, *From Gerson to Grotius, 1414–1625* (New York: Harper, 1960), 124, quoted in Cavanaugh, *Religious Violence*, 49–50.

56. Alexis de Tocqueville, *Democracy in America* (New York: Knopf, 1972), 1:303.

of religion is part of his commitment to democracy. Religion must be contained within its own individual, private sphere in order to ensure the secular neutrality of the democratic public space. James's strongly individualist account of religion and his near-solipsistic account of religious experience are ways of effecting such a containment.

While James is not known primarily as a political writer, his strong commitment to democracy manifests itself in a number of his works. It was perhaps only a bit of runaway rhetoric when he told one audience, "Democracy is a kind of religion."[57] However, even when speaking more soberly, he does seem to think that the advent of democracy has fundamentally shifted our way of thinking, not least about matters of religion. So, in the *Varieties*, after recounting some of the "absurd and puerile" things that St. Gertrude reports Christ saying to her, James goes on to say:

> What with science, idealism, and democracy, our own imagi-
> nation has grown to need a God of an entirely different tem-
> perament from that Being interested exclusively in dealing out
> personal favors, with whom our ancestors were so contented.
> Smitten as we are with the vision of social righteousness, a
> God indifferent to everything but adulation, and full of parti-
> ality for his individual favorites, lacks an essential element of
> largeness; and even the best professional sainthood of former
> centuries, pent in as it is to such a conception, seems to us
> curiously shallow and unedifying.[58]

And in a later series of lectures, he states, "the vaster vistas which scientific evolutionism has opened, and the rising tide of social

57. William James, "The Social Value of the College-Bred," in *The Moral Equivalent of War and Other Essays*, ed. John Roth (New York: Harper, 1971), 21.
58. James, *Varieties*, 346.

democratic ideals, have changed the type of our imagination, and the older monarchial theism is obsolete or obsolescent."[59]

Such remarks not only show that, in James's estimation, growing democratic consciousness undermines traditional Christian claims, they also make clear the low esteem in which James held traditional Christianity. In his own recent Gifford Lectures, Stanley Hauerwas has charged that "what is wrong with Christianity for James was not that it failed to be pragmatic but that it failed to be democratic."[60] In other words, Christianity is a threat to democracy. But why is this the case? Perhaps some light is shed by the kind of god (or "superhuman consciousness") James proposed to replace "older monarchial theism." In his 1909 Hibbert Lectures at Oxford University, James concluded by proposing that we "be frankly pluralistic and assume that the superhuman consciousness, however vast it may be, has itself an external environment, and consequently is finite."[61] Human beings should embrace a god, or what James called in the *Varieties* the "more," that "is finite, either in power or in knowledge, or in both at once."[62] Such a finite god is entirely able to fulfill the requirements for an object of religious experience laid out in *The Varieties of Religious Experience* and, in James's eyes, is infinitely preferable to the old God of Christianity.

The problem with traditional Christianity is that it insists on a God who is both infinite and other, indeed, a God who is not contained in any genus at all. As James puts it, such a God has a connection to us that "appears as unilateral and not reciprocal . . . our relation, in short, is not a strictly social relation."[63] Of course what James means by "social" is in fact "democratic"

59. William James, *A Pluralistic Universe* (Lincoln, NE: University of Nebraska Press, 1996), 30.

60. Hauerwas, *With the Grain of the Universe*, 85.

61. James, *A Pluralistic Universe*, 310–11.

62. James, 311.

63. James, 26–27.

(the only serious option for society). What is so offensive about traditional Christian notions of God is that such a God cannot be a fellow citizen with us in our pluralistic universe. Such a God is under no obligation to try to persuade us to his point of view, to engage in the give-and-take of democratic discourse, to compromise his own will in order to achieve social peace, or to run the risk of common suffering that all other citizens of the universe share; rather, he is the one who commands, and it is done. Such a God, unleashed in the public realm, undermines the pragmatic, pluralistic democracy that James so valued.

It would, of course, be undemocratic to eliminate Christianity, given democratic commitments to freedom of religion. But it *can* be contained, trivialized, made into the metaphysical equivalent of a hobby, and thereby disarmed. James writes in the *Varieties*, "over-beliefs in various directions are absolutely indispensable, and . . . we should treat them with tenderness and tolerance so long as they are not intolerant themselves."[64] But what does it mean to be "tolerant"? Is it sufficient for the Catholic who believes in transubstantiation to refrain from cleaving the skull of his Lutheran neighbor who believes in consubstantiation? There are hints in James's writings that he is asking for more, that anything short of a purely individualist and pragmatic version of religious belief fails the test. In particular, religious belief must give up any claim to any sort of public authority, any authority that extends beyond the range of the individual's private life. Richard Rorty, in his characteristic fashion, makes the same point more bluntly, noting that a pragmatist can be a theist, but

> pragmatist theists . . . do have to get along without personal immortality, providential intervention, the efficacy of the sacraments, the virgin birth, the risen Christ, the covenant with Abraham, the authority of the Koran, and a lot of other things

64. James, *Varieties*, 515.

which many theists are loath to do without. Or, if they want
them, they will have to interpret them "symbolically" . . . for
they must prevent them from providing premises for practical reasoning . . . . Demythologizing amounts to saying that,
whatever theism is good for, it is not a device for predicting or
controlling our environment.[65]

In other words, religious belief is fine, so long as it is treated as
something the truth of which is trivial for determining public
behavior. One may believe in the Resurrection of Christ so long
as one believes it purely as a matter of private opinion and does
not let it shape one's political life, which ought to be governed
by the principles of pragmatic compromise. Maybe this is what
James meant at the outset of his lectures, when he spoke of "the
peculiar philosophic temperament, as well as the peculiar political temperament, that goes with our English speech," the temperaments that he hoped would "more and more pervade and
influence the world."

Perhaps we ought to take James's remark that "Democracy
is a kind of religion" a bit more seriously. If we return to the
"revisionist" account of the Wars of Religion and the rise of the
state, we ought to entertain the possibility that James's segrega-
tion of the Christian God in the private realm of "religious experience" is simply the continuation of the campaign waged by the
absolutist monarchs of the sixteenth and seventeenth centuries,
in which the state replaced the Church as the true *religio* of the
body politic. Certainly, his relentless religious individualism and
his effective dismissal of "ecclesiasticism" and "over-beliefs" point
in such a direction. And if the democratic and pragmatic temperament of the English-speaking peoples does, in fact, come to
pervade the world, what place does this leave for a Christianity

65. Richard Rorty, "Religious Faith, Intellectual Responsibility, and Romance," in *The
Cambridge Companion to William James*, 92.

that refuses to be a species of "pure personal religion," but rather claims to be the Body of Christ, a visible and historical sign of God's redemption of the world? What place does this leave for the pilgrim city, whose belief in the risen Christ marks it out as a distinctive people in the midst of the nations? Because it prompts such questions, much is to be learned from *The Varieties of Religious Experience*, though what is learned may not be what James wanted to teach.

8

The Politics of
Disenchantment

What is it that makes us "modern"? When we think of ourselves
as "modern people," and thus distinguish ourselves from medieval, ancient, or primitive peoples, what are we in fact saying about
ourselves? Max Weber suggests that an important element in our
being denizens of modernity is the "disenchantment" of our
world. In what follows, I want to explore some of the connections
between Weber's notion of disenchantment and his understanding of mysticism as a response to this disenchantment to argue
that the relegation of religion to "the mystical" is not so much a
response to disenchantment as it is the condition for the very
possibility of disenchantment. In Weber's sociology, mysticism
becomes the irrational "other" of the rational, bureaucratic use of
coercive force that we, in our disenchanted world, call "politics."
In his work, we can clearly see a process whereby the categories of
the mystical and the political mutually create each other in such
a way that mysticism—a private and irrational religious experience—becomes the only viable future for religion, and politics—
the rational administration of territory through violence—becomes statecraft. In this respect, Weber is a paradigmatic modern
interpreter of religion and politics whose interpretive categories
continue to shape our discourse. Finally, I will argue that the

* This essay was originally published as "The Politics of Disenchantment," *New Blackfriars* 82, no. 965/966 (July 2001): 313–34.

power of Weber's story of disenchantment can be seen in current political and liberation theologies, even when they explicitly seek to reunite the "mystical" and the "political."

I beg the important question of whether it is helpful to speak of "modernity" at all. Certainly, Weber presents us with no consistent theory of modernity and uses the term "modern" in a variety of ways.[1] Thus I will not address the question of "mysticism and modernity" but rather the narrower question of the relation of mysticism and disenchantment, while at the same time presuming that "disenchantment" is a powerful description of whatever this thing is that we call "modernity."[2]

BEING MODERN, BEING DISENCHANTED

Weber claims that human history, at least in the West, has been the story of the progressive rationalization of life. Yet exactly what this claim amounts to is unclear since rationalization itself is a complex notion in Weber, divided as it is into value-rationality, which is concerned with ends, and instrumental-rationality, which is concerned with means.[3] Value-rationalization might encompass the supplanting of custom or mores (*Sittlichkeit*) by rationally derived ethical values (*Moralität*), as in the moral philosophy of Kant. But it might also include something like Plato's positing of the realm of the forms, for, according to Weber, value-rationalization involves "an increasing theoretical mastery of reality by means of increasingly precise and abstract concepts."[4] On the other hand, instrumental-rationality has to do with

1. See Charles Turner, *Modernity and Politics in the Work of Max Weber* (London: Routledge, 1992).

2. On "modernity" and "disenchantment," see Leszek Kolakowski, "Modernity on Endless Trial," in *Modernity on Endless Trial* (Chicago: The University of Chicago Press, 1990), 3–13.

3. See Max Weber, *Economy and Society: An Outline of Interpretive Sociology*, ed. Guenther Roth and Claus Wittich (Berkeley: University of California Press, 1978), 24–25.

4. Max Weber, "The Social Psychology of the World Religions," in *From Max Weber: Essays in Sociology*, ed. and trans. H.H. Gerth and C. Wright Mills (New York: Oxford University Press, 1946), 293.

developing methodical procedures for obtaining a goal and thus can encompass everything from magical spells to utilitarian moral calculus to strategic business (or military) planning.[5] For instrumental-rationality, what counts is not the end that is sought but "the methodological attainment of a definitely given and practical end by means of an increasingly precise calculation of adequate means."[6]

Weber believes that rationalization has not always been opposed to religious belief and, in the case of instrumental-rationality, has in fact been advanced through religious asceticism. As he first spells out in *The Protestant Ethic and the Spirit of Capitalism*, the reason that the West attained a rational form of capitalism was through the "inner-worldly asceticism" of certain forms of Protestantism, notably Calvinism. Protestantism inherited from medieval Catholicism a suspicion of the world yet rejected the asceticism of the monastery. With the Calvinist emphasis on the visible difference of the lives of the elect, a new form of asceticism arose that sought the methodical, godly ordering of one's everyday, worldly existence. In Weber's words, Christian asceticism "strode into the market-place of life, slammed the door of the monastery behind it, and undertook to penetrate . . . [the] daily routine of life with its methodicalness, to fashion it into a life in the world, but neither of nor for this world."[7] Capital was no longer acquired for the sensuous delights that could be obtained with it but as a sign of the methodical holiness and soberness of one's life. Thus freed from being squandered on sensual pleasures, capital could be reinvested, resulting in modern, rational capitalism.

Weber's "Protestant-ethic thesis" has been much contested, both on the empirical grounds that it is not borne out by the

5. On the rationality of magic, see Weber, *Economy and Society*, 400.

6. Weber, "Social Psychology," 293.

7. Max Weber, *The Protestant Ethic and the Spirit of Capitalism*, trans. Talcott Parsons (New York: Scribner's, 1976), 154.

evidence, and on the theoretical grounds that it posits what Alasdair MacIntyre calls a "facile interactionism" between beliefs and actions.[8] One might defend Weber by pointing out that he himself denied that he was claiming that "capitalism as an economic system is a creation of the Reformation."[9] But without, I hope, being too facile myself, I would prefer to say that whatever its empirical or theoretical merits, what is interesting in Weber's discussion of ascetic Protestantism is how it displays the dynamics of disenchantment in the thought of a paradigmatic modern thinker. In other words, whether Weber was right or not about Calvinism and capitalism, what is most interesting is what he shows us about how we think about religious belief in the modern world. There is an incredible irony that accompanies Weber's account of rationalization in *The Protestant Ethic and the Spirit of Capitalism*. This is because, as Weber points out, from the perspective of instrumental-rationality, "value-rationality is always irrational."[10] Thus these two forms of rationality tend to pull apart. What Puritanism provided was an instrumental-rationality—one of means rather than ends—that could be applied regardless of the end for which it was used. Indeed, the proper functioning of instrumental rationality can seem to become an end in itself. In Weber's analysis, ascetic Protestantism created the modern Western world, characterized by rational capitalism and the bureaucratic state, which has become severed from its spiritual roots (or, perhaps better, from its supernatural end); the worldly care that the Puritan ascetic took up with a sense of vocation has become a prison—in Weber's famous image, an iron cage in which the modern subject is trapped:

8. Cited in Bryan Turner, *Max Weber: From History to Modernity* (London: Routledge, 1992), 42.

9. Weber, *Protestant Ethic*, 91. For a fuller discussion of this issue, see Turner, *Max Weber*, 41–47.

10. Weber, *Protestant Ethic*, 181.

The Puritan wanted to work in a calling; we are forced to do so. For when asceticism was carried out of the monastic cells into everyday life, and began to dominate worldly morality, it did its part in building the tremendous cosmos of modern economic order. The order is now bound to the technical and economic conditions of machine production which today determine the lives of all the individuals who are born into this mechanism, not only those directly concerned with economic acquisition, with irresistible force. Perhaps it will so determine them until the last ton of fossilized coal is burnt. In [Puritan Richard] Baxter's view the care for external goods should only lie on the shoulders of the "saint like a light cloak, which can be thrown aside at any moment." But fate decreed that the cloak should become an iron cage.

Weber goes on to say that "today the spirit of religious asceticism—whether finally, who knows?—has escaped from the cage."[11] The rational world no longer needs a religious foundation; it has become an autonomous mechanism of coercion, a spirit-bereft prison for the modern soul.

Rationalization, being a progressive and evolutionary process, has therefore gradually extended itself to the point where the world has become "disenchanted" in such a way that all things become subject to abstraction and calculability. By bracketing the question of ends and focusing on means, instrumental-rationality issues in "a morally sceptical type of rationality, at the expense of any belief in absolute values."[12] We might say that instrumental-rationality erodes value-rationality.

Another way of describing this change is as a loss of metaphysical vision. What religious belief provides, and what the modern world has lost, is "a unified view of the world derived

11. Weber, 181.
12. Weber, 30.

from a consciously integrated meaningful attitude toward life."[13] The desire of reason to see the world as a "cosmos" is undercut by reason's own rationalization of the world. Disenchantment means that "there are no incalculable forces that come into play, but rather one can, in principle, master all things by calculation."[14] However, the key feature of a disenchanted world is not simply the absence of gods and demons, but the loss of the world as "cosmos"—the loss of meaning. As instrumental reason progressively strips the world's processes of their magical qualities in order to more methodically manage them, these processes "henceforth simply 'are' and 'happen' but no longer signify anything."[15]

POLITICS AS VIOLENCE AND THE REFUGE OF THE SPIRIT

The exemplary inhabitant of this disenchanted world of means without meaning is the bureaucrat who fulfills his function competently and efficiently without inquiry into the ultimate meaning or purpose of his role. Weber writes that in the modern world,

> the *homo politicus*, as well as the *homo oeconomicus*, performs his duty best when he acts without regard to the person in question, *sine ira et studio*, without hate and without love, without personal predilection and therefore without grace, but sheerly in accordance with the impersonal duty imposed by his calling, and not as a result of any concrete personal relationship. He discharges his responsibility best if he acts as closely as possible in accordance with the rational regulations of the modern power system.[16]

13. Weber, *Economy and Society*, 450.
14. Weber, "Science as a Vocation," in *From Max Weber*, 139.
15. Weber, *Economy and Society*, 506.
16. Weber, 600.

Or, as Weber says in his essay on "Politics as a Vocation":

> The honor of the civil servant is vested in his ability to execute conscientiously the order of the superior authorities, exactly as if the order agreed with his own convictions. This holds even if the order appears wrong to him and if, despite the civil servant's remonstrances, the authority insists on the order. Without this moral discipline and self-denial, in the highest sense, the whole apparatus falls apart.[17]

The bureaucrat is one who occupies himself with the rational efficiency of means, not the question of ends. Or rather, the bureaucrat is one who has segregated his manipulation of means and his concern for ends into separate "life spheres."[18] In his personal relations he may be vitally concerned for the moral significance of his actions, but his public role (and the salary he receives for fulfilling that role) requires that he be concerned not with significance but with efficiency, not with ends but means.

What is the arena, the "life sphere," in which the bureaucrat enacts his role? It is the state or the market. Though Weber equivocates on this point, the general tenor of his image of the iron cage implies that the modern bureaucratic state and the culture of rational capitalism have consumed the agora so that one who takes up a public role must do this in the space defined by modern politics and economics. This is important because, for Weber, both the state and the market are defined not by their ends (i.e., it is not the pursuit of a particular goal that makes a state a state or a market a market) but by their means. For my purposes, I will bracket the important question of the market and its relationship to the state (i.e., of economy to society) and focus on the state.

17. Weber, "Politics as a Vocation," in *From Max Weber*, 95.
18. Weber, 123.

What then, we must ask, is the distinctive means that defines the state? For Weber the answer is clear and simple: violence. In the definitions of basic sociological terms at the outset of *Economy and Society*, Weber says that "a 'ruling organization' will be called 'political' insofar as its existence and order is continuously safeguarded within a given territorial area by the threat and application of physical force on the part of the administrative staff."[19] More pointedly, in "Politics as a Vocation," Weber says that "the state is a relation of men dominating men, a relation supported by means of legitimate (i.e. considered to be legitimate) violence."[20] It is the state's monopoly on physical force as a legitimate means that defines it. The bars of the iron cage turn out to be the threat of violence, or perhaps the allure of being the one who administers that violence.[21] The bureaucrat, the new minister of the public realm, is the one who rationally—*sine ira et studio*—carries out this task. No wonder the world seems disenchanted.

But where has the spirit fled? It has not simply been eradicated because Weber's narration of the process of rationalization turns out to be a dialectical one, in which the history of the rational is chiefly registered as the overcoming of its antithesis through the "routinization of charisma."[22] By "charisma," Weber means "a certain quality of an individual personality by virtue of which he is considered extraordinary and treated as endowed with

19. Weber, *Economy and Society*, 54.
20. Weber, "Politics," 78.
21. Here is a place where the separation, for purpose of discussion, of economy from "society" raises some difficulties. Most bureaucrats do their jobs not because they lust after the administration of violence, but because they have a mortgage and a car payment.
22. In making this claim that rationalization is a dialectical process of overcoming, I am aware that rational authority and charismatic authority do not stand in a simple relationship of thesis and antithesis, since they are supplemented by a third type of authority, "traditional authority" (see Weber, *Economy and Society*, 215). However, it seems to me that traditional authority is in fact a mediating type in which rational procedures ("routinization") are developed on an irrationally founded authority. In Weber's terms, traditional authority represents technical rationalization without theoretical rationalization, and thus simply is an incomplete moment in the dialectic of disenchantment.

supernatural, superhuman, or at least specifically exceptional power or qualities." Charisma is "specifically irrational in the sense of being foreign to all rules." This means that it exists only *in statu nascendi*; the teaching of a charismatic figure is not sustainable beyond his or her immediate, personal presence and thus always requires for its perpetuation subsequent rational regulation.[23] Thus one might say that the transmission of charismatic teaching is parasitic upon rational routinization. On the other hand, there is a sense in which rationality is parasitic upon charisma, in that it finds its genesis in the overcoming of charisma through routinization. Charisma functions for Weber as a kind of safety valve: a permanent possibility that sustains the hope that the bureaucratic state will not attain complete hegemony and that history will be constantly renewed through new infusions of charisma.

Thus, Weber presents a vision in which the modern world has increasingly rid itself of the traces of its charismatic source in sectarian Protestantism and as a result has become spiritless and impersonal: *Gesellschaft* has replaced *Gemeinschaft*, the state has replaced the *polis*. In the face of this, "religion has been shifted into the realm of the irrational"[24] and thus into the realm of the apolitical. In the modern world, "[h]e who seeks the salvation of the soul, of his own and of others, should not seek it along the avenue of politics, for the quite different tasks of politics can only be solved by violence."[25] The public realm is now construed as the realm of constraint by violence, and religion has retreated to its origin in charismatic individuality.

Mysticism is the example par excellence of charismatic individualism that can exist at a total remove from the "pragma of violence which no political action can escape."[26] Weber writes:

23. Weber, *Economy and Society*, 241, 244, 246.
24. Weber, "Social Psychology," 281.
25. Weber, "Politics," 126.
26. Weber, "Religious Rejections of the World and Their Directions," in *From Max Weber*, 336.

The unity of the primitive image of the world, in which everything was concrete magic, has tended to split into rationalistic cognition and mastery of nature, on the one hand, and into "mystic" experiences, on the other. The inexpressible contents of such experiences remain the only possible "beyond," added to the mechanism of a world robbed of gods. Where this conclusion has been drawn without any residue, the individual can pursue his quest for salvation only as an individual.[27]

Similarly, in *Economy and Society*, Weber identifies "mysticism and an acosmistic ethic of absolute goodness" as one of the chief forms of an "increased tendency toward flight into the irrationalities of apolitical emotionalism."[28] Mysticism is safe from the kind of transformation that ascetic Protestantism underwent, and, in fact, Weber sees mysticism and asceticism as fundamentally opposed (ideal) types of religion.[29] Weber takes mysticism to be a distinctive type of experience: "that subjective condition which may be enjoyed as the possession of, or mystical union (*unio mystica*) with, the divine."[30] Whereas the inner-worldly asceticism of Calvinism is rational in its essence, "[t]he religious experience as such is of course irrational, like every experience."[31] Weber recognizes that mysticism is often associated with certain ascetical practices, but while true asceticism values the rational ordering of life as a godly end in itself, in mysticism "rationalization is only an instrument for attaining the goal of contemplation and is of an essentially negative type, consisting in the avoidance of

27. Weber, "Social Psychology," 282.

28. Weber, *Economy and Society*, 601.

29. Weber first develops this dichotomy in *The Protestant Ethic and the Spirit of Capitalism*, but there it is largely subordinated to the distinction between inner-worldly and other-worldly. It is only later, under the influence of his friend Ernst Troeltsch, that the ascetic/mystic distinction assumes an important place in Weber's sociology of religion.

30. Weber, *Economy and Society*, 545.

31. Weber, *Protestant Ethic*, 233.

interruptions caused by nature and the social milieu."[32] With its negative valuation of rational order, mysticism seems to provide an invulnerable refuge for the spirit.

It is important to understand here what Weber is saying about disenchantment. He is *not* saying that individuals have ceased to believe in God. What he is saying is that religious faith has become a private (and irrational) set of beliefs held by individuals. The former capacity of religion to organize social life has withered, being replaced by the instrumental rationality of the bureaucrat. In the early 1960s, Alasdair MacIntyre commented on "the combination of atheism in the practice of the life of the vast majority [of the English population], with the profession of either superstition or theism by that same majority."[33] Even in a country like the United States, where such indicators of religious commitment as church attendance remain relatively high in comparison with Europe, it is widely taken as axiomatic that one should not bring religion into politics. To do so is to practice a "politics of division," and religious beliefs are divisive precisely because they can be authoritative only for individuals. So even if everyone in the United States professed belief in God, this would not mean that they did not live in a disenchanted world.[34]

Roland Robertson has noted that this relegation of the

32. Weber, 233. See a similar comment by Friedrich Heiler: "Mysticism does not value moral action as a thing good in itself, an absolute aim, that is, as the realization of values in personal and social life, but as a means to deaden the senses and suppress the emotions" (*Prayer: A Study in the History and Psychology of Religion*, trans. S. McComb [London: Oxford University Press, 1932], 157–58).

33. Alasdair MacIntyre, "God and the Theologians," in *Against the Self-Images of the Age: Essays on Ideology and Philosophy* (London: Duckworth, 1971), 26.

34. One might argue that in a liberal polity like the US, religion has not been relegated to the inwardness of private belief but has simply been excluded from the realm of the state. Religious belief is free to organize forms of social existence in that middle realm between the state and the individual: civil society. Thus, civil society is the proper place for religious societies such as churches. This claim deserves more serious attention than I can give it here, but let me note briefly that political liberalism has tended to foster increasingly individualistic notions of religious belief, even among traditions, such as Roman Catholicism, which are thought to place a great emphasis on authority and community. Most US Roman Catholics are indistinguishable from their Protestant or Jewish or agnostic neighbors in terms of their views on the role of religion in society. One might recall Hilaire Belloc's comment that American Roman Catholics were Protestants who went to Mass on Sunday.

religious to an inward and private realm shows Weber's indebt-
edness to what Robertson calls "a Lutheran epistemology and ontology," by which he presumably means Luther's sharp distinction
between the "inner man" and the "outer man" as delineated in,
for example, *On the Freedom of a Christian*. Robertson goes on to
quote Marcuse: "German culture is inseparable from its origin
in Protestantism. There arose a realm of beauty, freedom, and
morality, which was not to be shaken by external realities and
struggles; it was detached from the miserable social world and an-
chored in the 'soul' of the individual."[35] While this is perhaps a bit
much to lay at Luther's feet—it is a viewpoint hardly restricted to
Germans—it does alert us to the presence in Weber (and indeed
in modernity) of what we might call "two kingdoms." Contained
in the inwardness of "mystical experience," the religious virtuoso
attains a kind of autonomy that renders him immune to the vi-
cissitudes of the vocation of politics and free to pursue the private
project of salvation and of universal, acosmistic love. Likewise,
the world of politics also becomes autonomous, so as to be freed
from the irrational moral constraints that religious beliefs might
impose upon the rational use of violence. "Mysticism" arrives on
the scene at the same time as disenchantment.

EAST OF EDEN

Another way of thinking about how "mysticism" relates to the
disenchanted politics of modernity is provided by Edward Said's
influential analysis of "Orientalism." In the late nineteenth and
early twentieth centuries, writers on mysticism sought to expand

35. Roland Robertson, "On the Analysis of Mysticism: Pre-Weberian, Weberian and
Post-Weberian Perspectives," *Sociological Analysis* 36, no. 3 (Autumn 1975): 245–48. The Marcuse quotation is from *Reason and Revolution: Hegel and the Rise of Social Theory*. Robertson also
notes that this "Lutheran epistemology" has in turn been transmitted through Weber to much
American sociology of religion. Robertson writes, "The easy, undialectical acceptance among
many American sociologists of the idea that religiosity is primarily a private, internal matter,
a stance strongly facilitated by methodologies which commit the individualist fallacy, testifies
further to the amorphous impact of traditional Lutheranism."

the horizons of "mysticism" (which hitherto had by and large been taken to be specifically Christian) to include the religions of the Orient; in fact, the East came to be seen as the source of mysticism in its purest form. This, of course, was not completely new. The East, perhaps because it was the direction of the rising sun, had long been seen as the direction from which would come spiritual renewal. Bernard of Clairvaux's friend and contemporary William of St. Thierry had spoken of the Carthusians of Mont-Dieu as introducing "to our Western darkness and French cold the light of the East and the ancient fervor of Egypt for religious observance."[36] Later, spiritual writers of the sixteenth and seventeenth centuries appealed to Dionysius the Areopagite as an Eastern source who was at the same time exotic and of unimpeachable authority.[37] Nor were all identifications of mysticism with the East positive. While the early Jesuit missionaries to Japan were not quick to identify the Zen Buddhist monks as mystics,[38] the Anglican bishop Edward Stillingfleet noted the similarity between the "Mystical Unions and Raptures" of "the Gentiles of Indoostan" and those of the Roman Catholic "fanatics" who espoused mystical theology.[39] Thus despite the long-standing appeal of the East, the non-pejorative identification of Christian and non-Christian mystics, especially by Christians, was largely an innovation of the nineteenth and twentieth centuries. But very quickly, for good or for ill, "mysticism" was possessed of an Oriental animus.[40]

"Orientalism," as described by Said, is both an academic

36. William of St. Thierry, *The Golden Epistle* 1.1, trans. Theodore Berkeley, OCSO (Kalamazoo, MI: Cistercian, 1980), 9.

37. Michel de Certeau, *The Mystic Fable*, trans. Michael B. Smith (Chicago: The University of Chicago Press, 1992), 1:102.

38. See Heinrich Dumoulin, SJ, *A History of Zen Buddhism*, trans. Paul Preachy (New York: Pantheon, 1963), 204–10.

39. Edward Stillingfleet, *An Answer to Mr. Cressy's Epistle Apologetical* (London, 1675), 81–83.

40. For the History of Religions school, mysticism was commonly taken to be Oriental in its essence: an importation from Greek mystery cults or from Neoplatonic philosophy and

discipline with roots stretching back to the Middle Ages, as well as a metaphor for a larger phenomenon by which Europe, the Occident, defines its identity through the imaginative construction of the Orient as its "other." Discourses about "the Orient" are less about the lands and peoples of Asia and the Middle East than they are about Europe: "the Orient and Islam are always represented as outsiders having a special role to play inside Europe."[41] In particular, the Orient functions as a way of circumscribing a site in which "mysterious" and "irrational" forces hold sway. As Said puts it:

The Oriental is irrational, depraved (fallen), childlike, "different"; thus the European is rational, virtuous, mature, "normal." But the way of enlivening the relationship was everywhere to stress the fact that the Oriental lived in a different but thoroughly organized world of his own, a world with its own national, cultural, and epistemological boundaries and principles of internal coherence. Yet what gave the Oriental's world its intelligibility and identity was not the result of his own efforts but rather the whole complex series of knowledgeable manipulations by which the Orient was identified by the West.[42]

We might expand the metaphorical boundaries of Orientalism so as to speak of the "Orientalizing" of mysticism: the process in

ultimately rooted in Indian religion. This often played into the apologetical interests of Protestant scholars who wished to see in Christian mysticism an alien "hellenization" and corruption of pure biblical faith. For example, Adolph von Harnack presents mysticism as the wholesale importation of Neoplatonism into Christian thought, primarily through its influence on Augustine and Pseudo-Dionysius (*History of Dogma*, trans. Neil Buchanan [New York: Dover, 1961], 1:360–61. See also *History of Dogma*, 6:97–108). One finds this same view expressed a generation later by Friedrich Heiler, for whom mysticism could be traced from Pseudo-Dionysius back through Plotinus and Plato, to Orphic-Dionysiac mysteries. These in turn could, in his view, probably be connected with a strand of Indian mysticism stretching back to the Upanishads (Heiler, *Prayer*, 116–17). For both Heiler and Harnack, this essentially Oriental mysticism was set in stark contrast with prophetic, biblical religion which was active and vigorous and masculine. Mysticism was a kind of passive, feminine corruption within Christianity which could be isolated, if not excised. For the characterization of mysticism as feminine, see Heiler, 146.

41. Edward Said, *Orientalism* (New York: Pantheon, 1978), 71.
42. Said, *Orientalism*, 38–40.

which the Orient functions as a code that, when applied to mysticism, delineates it as an autonomous sphere of religious experience that nonetheless can only be brought to articulation by the rational discourses that are exterior to it. This simultaneously guarantees a realm of private religious experience—mysticism—and a realm of public, utilitarian rationalism—politics.

The Orientalism that pervades the modern discourse on mysticism can be seen in a relatively benign form in the British and American infatuation with the mystical poetry of the Bengali poet Rabindranath Tagore (1861–1941). Tagore was from an elite family, and his education included broad exposure to English literature and philosophy. In the years immediately before the First World War, he presented those in the West interested in mysticism with a vision of the mystic East that was eminently palatable—so much so that he was given the Nobel Prize for literature in 1913 and knighted by George V in 1915. His serene appearance and long beard and robes fed English anxiety that, as one author put it, "India knew something that England did not know and ought, for her own good, to learn."[43] Fortunately for England, however, this secret mystic knowledge was not of much use in running a country; the Indians still needed the British for that. This Eastern wisdom was delivered in a form (lyric poetry) that testified simultaneously to its sublimity and its impracticality. The Oriental mind, mystical and mysterious, was suited for poetry but not for politics; the European mind, rational and logical, was alas inferior in its spiritual sensibilities but was ideal for organizing such things as colonial empires.[44]

Given Said's analysis of the logic of Orientalism, it is not surprising that Weber often casts the contrast between rationalism

43. Mary M. Lago, introduction to *Imperfect Encounter: Letters of William Rothenstein and Rabindranath Tagore, 1911–1941* (Cambridge, MA: Harvard University Press, 1972), 19.

44. Regarding the relationship between Orientalism and colonialism, one should note Said's comment: "To say simply that Orientalism was a rationalization of colonial rule is to ignore the extent to which colonial rule was justified in advance by Orientalism, rather than after the fact" (Said, *Orientalism*, 39).

and irrationalism in terms of the opposition between Occident and Orient. In Weber's general introduction to his *Gesammelte Aufsätze zur Religionssoziologie*, he repeatedly identifies the Orient with irrationality in the process of asserting that only in the West has a rational state and a rational capitalism arisen.[45] In *The Protestant Ethic*, Weber speaks of the "Oriental eroticism" of the Song of Songs that gave rise to Bernardine piety,[46] as well as of the "Oriental quietism" of some verses from the Psalms and Proverbs.[47] More explicitly, in *Economy and Society*, he says,

> The decisive historical difference between the predominantly oriental and Asiatic types of salvation religion and those found primarily in the Occident is that the former usually culminate in contemplation and the latter in asceticism.[48]

The Oriental mystic functioned for Weber as an "ideal type" (perhaps rooted in genetic structure[49]) against which the ideal type of the rational, inner-worldly ascetic could be defined. As is typical of Orientalist rhetoric, the invocation of the Orient signals an irrational element that is subject to regulation and ultimately exploitation by its "other"—the rational, secular Occident—but also an irrational element that the Occident somehow needs for its own identity.

Weber's attitude toward mysticism is fundamentally ambiguous, but in a way that is entirely fitting for the "Orientalist" role he assigns it. On the one hand, he admires the ideal of mysticism as engendering a loosely structured brotherhood of acosmistic

---

45. Translated as the introduction in Weber, *Protestant Ethic*, 13–31.
46. Weber, 238.
47. Weber, 164.
48. Weber, *Economy and Society*, 551.
49. Weber expressed some hesitation on this point. See his general introduction to his *Gesammelte Aufsätze zur Religionssoziologie*, translated in *Protestant Ethic*, 30.

love.[50] Indeed, in the record of a conversation between him and his wife, Marianne, he indicates that he at times thought of himself as a mystic:

Max: Tell me, can you think of yourself as a mystic?

Marianne: That would certainly be the last thing I could think of. Can you conceive of it for yourself?

Max: It could even be that I am one. Just as I have "dreamt" more in my life than one really ought to be allowed, I am also not really quite securely at home anywhere. It is as though I could (and wanted) to pull myself back from everything, and completely.[51]

On the other hand, as indicated above, Weber most often saw mysticism as simply a reaction to the disenchantment of modern life—a retreat into the "irrationalities of apolitical emotionalism"—and thus not a viable option for those whose vocation was to the intellectual integrity demanded by the modern world. It was more a pathology of modernity than any kind of realistic alternative for one's life. However, it was a pathology with which both society and the individual could live, provided it was managed with the right therapies. One might well be a mystic and a politician, so long as each identity was kept within its proper sphere. In Weber's own life, whatever tendencies toward mysticism and acosmistic brotherhood that he might have had were

---

50. See particularly his remarks about Russian mysticism quoted in Ferdinand Toennies et al., "Max Weber on Church, Sect and Mysticism," *Sociological Analysis* 34, no. 2 (Summer 1973): 140–49.

51. Recounted by Eduard Baumgarten, *Max Weber, Werk und Person* (Tübingen, GE: J.C.B. Mohr, 1964), 677, and quoted in Arthur Mitzman, *The Iron Cage: An Historical Interpretation of Max Weber* (New York: Knopf, 1969), 218.

kept firmly in the private sphere; his own politics were conservative and nationalistic.[52]

In the end, Weber's presentation of "mysticism"—understood as a radically apolitical faith grounded in the charismatic individual's private experience—as the only viable religious option in the face of the world's disenchantment serves to define its antithesis—politics—as the sphere of coercion through the rational administration of violence. Just as the Orientalist images of the East tell us more about Europe than they do about Asia, so Weber's understanding of mysticism tells us more about his understanding of politics than they do anything else. The construction of mysticism as the "other" of politics shows us the simultaneous construction of politics as the spiritless management of force.

MYSTICAL-POLITICAL THEOLOGIES: THE CASE OF EDWARD SCHILLEBEECKX

The tendency to construe religion as a "mystical" realm of inwardness that abandons any relation to the disenchanted world of politics, which we see exemplified in Weber, has not gone unresisted. Various political and liberation theologies have attempted to argue that Christian faith necessarily implies political engagement and thus cannot be seen simply as a private matter. Some theologians have construed the task of relating "faith" to "politics" as one of constructing "mystical-political" or "mystical-prophetic" theologies.[53] I cannot but applaud such attempts to maintain the

52. For a discussion of Weber's personal attitude toward mysticism, see Mitzman, *Iron Cage*, 190–230; Robertson, "Analysis of Mysticism," 248–53; and William R. Garrett, "Maligned Mysticism: The Maledicted Career of Troeltsch's Third Type," *Sociological Analysis* 36, no. 3 (Autumn 1975): 209.

53. See, for example, Claude Geffré and Gustavo Gutiérrez, eds., *The Mystical and Political Dimensions of the Christian Faith*, Concilium 96 (New York: Herder, 1974); Johannes B. Metz, *Followers of Christ: The Religious Life and the Church*, trans. Thomas Linton (New York: Paulist, 1978); and David Tracy, *Dialogue with the Other: The Inter-Religious Dialogue* (Grand Rapids, MI: Eerdmans, 1990). These authors have all obviously been influenced by each other in their choice of this formulation.

political character of Christianity. However, as one might suspect from the invocation of the category "mystical," the best intentions of these attempts are thwarted by an account of religious belief that is still only extrinsically or, at best, consequentially political and an understanding of politics as governed by the "real" (i.e., violent) workings of power. In many of these theologies, religion still finds its ultimate ground in an interior realm of experience and thus is not in itself political, historical, and communal but can only have "consequences" in those realms. Such a construal replicates Weber's conviction that the relationship of the "ideal" realm of religious faith to the "real" realm of politics is necessarily one of compromise at best and irrelevance at worst.

As in so much modern thought, the use of the word "mystical" in liberation and political theologies is vague. "Mysticism" is a cipher that signals the "purest" or most essential aspect of religion, to which it is impossible to attach any positive content. However, its hyphenated linkage with the word "political" seems to indicate a dialectical relationship between the two, thus implying that whatever mysticism is, it is the antithesis of politics. In this dialectic each term has its role. "Mysticism" usually functions to ensure that Jesus is seen as more than "just a political reformer," while "politics" counters the privatizing and ahistorical tendency inherent in mysticism.[54] 1 do not claim that all the theologians who invoke the phrase "mystical-political" explicitly intend such an antithesis; indeed, their overwhelming desire is to overcome a privatized and apolitical account of Christianity. However, their choice of this formulation registers the force of the very impulse

---

54. Thus, David Tracy writes, "Without the prophetic core, the struggle for justice and freedom in the historical-political world can too soon be lost in mere privacy. Without the mystical insistence on love, the spiritual power of the righteous struggle is always in danger of lapsing into mere self-righteousness and spiritual exhaustion" (*Dialogue*, 118). It is interesting to see in this particular quotation the mystical-political dialectic read through Reinhold Niebuhr's love-justice dialectic. See Reinhold Niebuhr, *An Interpretation of Christian Ethics* (New York: Harper, 1935).

towards a disenchantment of the public realms and the privatizing of religious faith that they seek to overcome.

One writer who increasingly invoked the dialectic of mysticism and politics is Edward Schillebeeckx (1914–2009). His
work can serve as an example of the way that the desire to construct a political theology can be vitiated by the dual movement
in which religion/faith/mysticism is interiorized and essentialized
as "experience" and politics is construed as management by the
state through the (threatened) use of violence. Such an interiorization of religious experience is counter to Schillebeeckx's stated
intentions to stress the mediated, and thus political, character of
religious experience.[55] Indeed at times he makes contradictory
statements that seem to reflect his desire both to develop a political theology as well as to endorse the modern secularization
of ethics and politics. I would argue that such contradictions are
built into his very understanding of the concepts "mystical" and
"political."

More than some others who invoke some version of the
"mystical-prophetic" dialectic, Schillebeeckx made an effort to
define what he meant by "mysticism." His use of the term seems
to vacillate between two understandings of mysticism. On the
one hand, the Dominican Schillebeeckx rejects what he calls "a
primarily Jesuit" understanding of spirituality, which stresses the
extraordinary character of mysticism, and identifies himself with
the "Thomistic-Carmelite" perspective, which sees mysticism in
continuity with the ordinary life of faith and the theological virtues of faith, hope, and love.[56] Thus Schillebeeckx in places identifies "the mystical" with "the religious" and "the théologal" (sic)
as "everything in Christian life that has God himself as an explicit

55. See, for example, *Christ: The Experience of Jesus as Lord*, trans. John Bowden (New
York: Crossroad, 1983): "It is precisely this break with an 'immediate' relationship with God in
faith which has opened the doors of our churches to political theology, to the origin of critical
communities and to a better, and above all a happy, world" (809).

56. Edward Schillebeeckx, *Church: The Human Story of God*, trans. John Bowden (New
York: Crossroad, 1990), 68–69.

object."[57] In this view, the mystical is simply explicit religious experience. On the other hand, while mystical experience does not differ in kind from the experience of the ordinary believer, Schillebeeckx speaks of it in places as a particularly "intense" form of that experience. Just as all Christian experience is mediated by concrete, historical objects and structures, [58] so too mysticism must be characterized as "mediated immediacy." However, unlike normal religious experience, it is a form of prayer "in which an attempt is made to transcend the elements of belief which are also mediated through politics, ethics and concepts, in order to place just oneself in the immediate presence of God."[59] Because of the mediated nature of experience, however, any such attempt is bound to fail and thus God is experienced by the mystic as a "dark night." In this way, mysticism might be seen as a "limit situation"—something extraordinary. Thus, Schillebeeckx's usage of the term "mysticism" seems to shift between two meanings: 1) the mystical as simply any explicit religious experience, and 2) the mystical as a particularly intense form of explicit religious experience that struggles against the mediations of politics and reason.

When found in opposition to the term "political," it seems to have the more general meaning of the explicitly religious, though with overtones of the "intensity" of the more specialized meaning. Schillebeeckx, noting that "[t]erms like mysticism and political are both ambiguous, even suspect," offers the following definition:

> I use the term mysticism here to denote an intensive form of experience of God or love of God, and politics to denote an intensive form of social commitment (and thus not the political

57. Schillebeeckx, *Church*, 90.
58. Schillebeeckx, 40–45.
59. Schillebeeckx, 70.

activity of professional politicians per se), a commitment accessible to all people.[60]

While these definitions do not exactly clear up the ambiguity, they do reveal the fundamental tension that runs through Schillebeeckx's work. As William Portier has noted, for Schillebeeckx "mysticism and politics" is a "conflictual theme."[61] He seeks to overcome a sharp distinction between the two by relating them dialectically; however, they still remain basic poles in his interpretation and thus continue to reproduce the very antinomies between sacred religion and disenchanted politics that he wishes to overcome. The antinomy of mysticism and politics is related to two more basic antinomies found in Schillebeeckx's theology: interiority versus exteriority and love of God versus love of neighbor.

In his book *Church*, Schillebeeckx explicitly criticizes the "modern liberal distinction between interiority (the private sphere) and externality (the public sphere)," which he identifies (correctly) with Weber's sociology. According to Schillebeeckx, this distinction "distorts the problems surrounding belief in God."[62] However, while he criticizes Weber's particular construal of the relationship between the two, he retains inner and outer—"individual" and "social"—as the antinomies that define the problem. He writes:

I myself in no way want to reduce the individual to a sum of social relationships, far less reduce society to the total of individual actions. The critical question is whether this sharp dividing line between an inside and an outside in human beings

60. Edward Schillebeeckx, *On Christian Faith: The Spiritual, Ethical, and Political Dimensions*, trans. John Bowden (New York: Crossroad, 1987), 71–72.

61. William Portier, "Mysticism and Politics and Integral Salvation: Two Approaches to Theology in a Suffering World," in *Pluralism and Oppression: Theology in World Perspective*, ed. Paul F. Knitter (New York: University Press of America, 1988), 268.

62. Schillebeeckx, *Church*, 46.

is justified, and whether it does not saddle us with the wrong picture of what it is to be human.[63]

Schillebeeckx wants to blur the line between individual (interior) and social (exterior), but he still has a stake in the terms of the distinction. It is, as he sees it, the sharp line between "inner" and "outer" that is the problem, not the distinction itself. Hence one finds him repeatedly speaking in terms that seem to posit an original religious experience that suffers a subsequent "fall" into communal expression.

This can be seen clearly in how Schillebeeckx utilizes Weber's routinization thesis in his ecclesiology. Belief in God is inevitably institutionalized, and this is "a sociological and also a religious necessity, and . . . at the same time it results in a degree of alienation from the original religious experience." Thus, while institutionalization of religious faith is not only inevitable, but even "necessary for the good of this faith," it is simultaneously a process of alienation from an original and pure (though unbearably intense) realm of experience.[64] Schillebeeckx is careful to maintain that this original experience is always one of "mediated immediacy" in which we encounter God through concrete, historical people and events. He even goes so far as to say, "everything about a person, including his or her inwardness, is social."[65] Yet the experience of mediated immediacy seems to acquire a kind of ineffable purity within the interior of the individual, so that its subsequent expression and institutional mediation becomes a "taming of the overwhelming power of this experience."[66] It is difficult to see

63. Schillebeeckx, 47.

64. Schillebeeckx, 59–60. In some ways, such a view can be seen to underlie his whole project in the books *Jesus* and *Christ*, whereby, in the former, historical-critical scholarship is used to reconstruct the original Abba experience of the charismatic figure Jesus and, in the latter, the story is recounted of how this original experience came to be routinized by the early Church.

65. Schillebeeckx, *Church*, 48.

66. Schillibeeckx, 59. It is tempting to give a biographical explanation of this tension between interior experience and exterior institution, given that Schillebeeckx was a theologian who suffered much at the hands of "the institutional Church" (see in particular his remarks in

how this differs from the Weberian sociology that Schillebeeckx criticizes.

The "tension in unity" of mysticism and politics is also related to the tension between love of God and love of neighbor.[67] Again, Schillebeeckx wants to hold the two together, to maintain with the First Letter of John that one cannot love God without loving one's neighbor (1 John 4:20–21) and positing the love of neighbor as an implicit form of the love of God (Matthew 25). At the same time, he wants to ascribe autonomy to the love of neighbor in its political form. For Schillebeeckx, one of the great achievements of modernity (of which he sees Thomas Aquinas as the herald)[68] is the creation of an autonomous ethic in which human beings live not by divine mandates but by self-imposed norms. Christian faith adds nothing to this autonomous ethic.[69] As a result of this autonomous ethic, human beings have a purely immanent notion of the human good, which means that the question of human salvation—of human flourishing—is no longer an exclusively religious question but a human question.[70] One can know what it means to love one's neighbor (and thus wish for the neighbor's "salvation") without loving God, at least not explicitly. This "autonomy of political reason" is not simply a fact to be accepted by Christians but something to be actively affirmed as a part of the Gospel. As Schillebeeckx writes: "the Christian message has freed us for freedom, rationality and morality; it has disarmed any attitude

---

Church, xiii–xv). His positive remarks in *Christ* about the "community-centered" approach of Latin American liberation theology, in which theology becomes "the theory of living church communities" (759) indicate that his assessment of the institutionalization of belief might be different given different institutions. Even granting all this, however, one must still see how Schillebeeckx's work reflects a fundamental theme of modernity: the opposition of subjective interior and objective exterior.

67. Schillebeeckx, *On Christian Faith*, 71.
68. Schillebeeckx, *Christ*, 655.
69. Schillebeeckx, *Church*, 30–31.
70. Schillebeeckx, *Christ*, 790–91; cf. Schillebeeckx, *Church*, 232.

which is dictated by anxiety and unreason."[71] In other words, disenchantment is Good News.

What place then for the love of God in this disenchanted world? In Schillebeeckx's view, secularization has freed God from being a "god of the gaps," a necessary postulate. Once the world is autonomously intelligible, belief in God once again becomes gratuitous.[72] This gratuity of belief is the reverse side of God's freedom and, as such, manifests itself politically in the form of an "eschatological proviso" that prevents the identification of God's liberating activity with any particular political program and thus "desacralizes" politics. Schillebeeckx does not believe that this makes love of God irrelevant in any positive sense to love of neighbor. He strongly rejects a purely formalized eschatological proviso that simply condemns all political activity in the face of God's judgment. Rather, he argues that God's proviso has been given a positive content in the life, death, and resurrection of Jesus of Nazareth.[73] At the same time, however, he is worried that too specific a positive content will lead to a return to the "classical political theologies" of the past.[74] Thus his unwillingness to identify God "with any particular historical liberation event" extends not only to current political events but also to Israel's exodus from Egypt and even to "the redemptive appearance of Jesus."[75] Despite his own warnings about a formalized eschatological proviso, Schillebeeckx consistently speaks of the love of God as simply providing an "orientation," "direction," or "inspiration" to political activity.

This results in a gap between how Schillebeeckx theorizes the relationship between "faith" and "politics" and his actual theological reflections on specific issues. For example, during the days

71. Schillebeeckx, *On Christian Faith*, 82.
72. Schillebeeckx, *Church*, 99–101.
73. Schillebeeckx, *Christ*, 776–79.
74. Schillebeeckx, *Church*, 100.
75. Schillebeeckx, 10.

of the Cold War, he went so far as to write that a "risky trust in unilateral disarmament seems to me to provide an extreme possibility, but at the same time it would appear to be the only concrete possibility for anyone who really believes in Jesus as the Lord of history."[76] Certainly, to claim that unilateral disarmament is the only choice for Christians seems to move beyond a simple "orientation" or "inspiration." And to base that choice on Jesus's lordship over history would seem to violate the autonomy of secular history, for Schillebeeckx must surely realize that unilateral disarmament based on the lordship of Christ does not fall within the reason of *realpolitik* but is rather rooted in "the mysticism of Christian surrender."[77] However, to follow out the implications of Schillebeeckx's claim here would seem to consign Christians to a theological ghetto in which the position demanded by faithfulness to its crucified Lord prevents the Church from making "realistic" policy recommendations to the state.

Schillebeeckx's dialectic of the "mystical" and the "political" reflects his desire to have it both ways: he wants to have a politically engaged and relevant Christianity while at the same time respecting Lessing's "broad, ugly ditch" between the necessary truths of reason and contingent historical events.[78] The actual content of the political praxis of Christians cannot be grounded in historical particulars such as Israel or Jesus if it is to provide universally valid ethical norms. It must be secularized and disenchanted to become available to all people, at all times and in all places. Thus, the very secularization that Schillebeeckx celebrates is predicated on the interiorization and depoliticization of Christianity; as with Weber, religion must become "mysticism" so that politics might become autonomous and rational. Religion, in the

---

76. Edward Schillebeeckx, "Eager to Spread the Gospel of Peace," trans. David Smith, in *Church and Peace*, Concilium 164 (New York: Seabury, 1983), 80.

77. Schillebeeckx, "Gospel of Peace," 80.

78. See G.E. Lessing, "On the Proof of the Spirit and of Power," in *Lessing's Theological Writings*, trans. Henry Chadwick (Stanford, CA: Stanford University Press, 1956), 54–55.

form of "experience of God," can "ensoul" politics but it cannot embody politics.[79]

Schillebeeckx's desire for a mystical-political theology is not only marked by modernity's desire for secular liberation; it is also marked by theology's desire to be "spiritual" in such a way as to transcend politics. Thus, for Schillebeeckx, "mysticism" functions as a remainder outside of the walls of the *polis* that serves to preserve the transcendent character of theology and keeps Christian discipleship from being mere politics. His underlying concern in the construct "politics and mysticism" is not simply to secularize politics but also to keep theology from being reduced to political activism. This is a valid, and even vital, concern if one assumes (as Schillebeeckx seems to) that politics must take the form of the coercive use of power by nation-states. However, if one thinks of politics in the more classical understanding of the formation of communities that make possible the shared pursuit of the good, then not only is it not wrong, but it is vitally important to see theology and theological discourse as "nothing more"—or, better, nothing less—than politics.

RE-ENCHANTING THE WORLD

What I have tried to do thus far is to show that Weber's construal of the politics of modernity depends on his construal of the paradigmatic form of the religion of modernity as one of mystical inwardness and to show how this Weberian scheme continues to inform attempts to construct mystical-political theologies. Such attempts are doomed to fail because, if I may put it somewhat combatively, the modernity game is rigged. In the vicious circle of modernity, religion must take the form of mystical inwardness because the public realm is disenchanted, and the public realm is disenchanted precisely because religion has become mystical

79. See Schillebeeckx, *On Christian Faith*, 74.

inwardness. In Weber's rule book for modernity, the one thing you cannot do is to bring the ethics of the Sermon on the Mount into the public realm. Despite the seriousness with which Weber takes that ethic, it is politically irrelevant. Indeed, *because* of the seriousness with which he takes it, it is politically irrelevant. He writes,

> By the Sermon on the Mount, we mean the absolute ethic of the gospel, which is a more serious matter than those who are fond of quoting these commandments today believe. This ethic is no joking matter. The same holds of this ethic as has been said of causality in science: it is not a cab, which one can have stopped at one's pleasure; it is all or nothing.[80]

But because the ethic of the Gospel is at absolute variance with the means proper to politics—violence—it can have no political relevance. If one wishes to play by the rules of modernity, religion can only be a matter of mystical inwardness; it can only be an ethic for the saint as an individual. Thus, Schillebeeckx's appeal for unilateral disarmament on the basis of the mysticism of Christian surrender is from the outset rendered apolitical by the standards of Weber.

Weber has in fact proved to be a very prescient prophet of our world. It is difficult not to see in the current rage for "spirituality" exactly the kind of retreat into inwardness that allows the everyday workings of state and market to continue as usual. Such a retreat is sounded, perhaps inadvertently, in the introduction to an anthology of medieval English mystics edited by the popular writer on religion Karen Armstrong. She writes:

> Today we have less confidence than before in the power of more external, socially oriented ideologies to change the

80. Weber, "Politics," 119.

world. We have watched the demise of enthusiasms like nationalism, Marxism, and Thatcherism, which promised a salvation of sorts. Many people feel that a deeper solution is necessary and seek the interior transformation of psychotherapy
or counseling. In the late twentieth century, therefore, people
may find the mystical experiment, which also urges the adept
to look within himself for the truth and warns against the
danger of simplistic ideas and projections about God, to be a
more attractive form of religion than the more conventional
and dogmatic types of faith.[81]

Clearly, Armstrong wants to say that "the mystical experiment"
has greater transformative potential than nationalism or Marxism
or Thatcherism, but note where this transformation takes place:
inside. But what happens outside? Can we presume that there
will be an inevitable movement from the inner to the outer, or
should we rather accept the analysis of Weber that disenchanted
modernity has a load-bearing wall of separation between inner
and outer?

I have no desire to deny the importance of inner transformation, nor do I wish to banish the writings of Teresa of Avila and
John of the Cross for pernicious complicity in the violence of the
nation-state. However, I do wish to say that much contemporary
talk about "inner transformation," "spirituality," and "mysticism"
does serve the interest of politics as usual. It is what allows us to
go to our jobs on Wall Street or at the Pentagon while practicing
yoga on the weekends to relieve our stress. While a thinker like
Schillebeeckx clearly wishes to challenge such perversions of the
Gospel, the very use of the language of "mysticism and politics"
continues to play by the Weberian rule book.

I wish to challenge the rules of the game as Weber sets them

81. Karen Armstrong, *Visions of God: Four Medieval Mystics and Their Writings* (New York:
Bantam, 1994), xxv.

out. What if, for example, we do not see in the Sermon on the Mount an ethic for individual saints, but the law by which a community lives? What if we try to take it seriously as a "politics"? I would argue that several things result. First, the notion of politics is "deterritorialized," because the community to which Jesus addresses the Sermon on the Mount is not a "state" defined by control of territory but rather the community of those who follow the Son of Man who "has nowhere to lay his head" (Matt. 8:20). He speaks to those who are to provide the world with an exemplary form of human community, yet who have no stake in any particular location, who are citizens of no particular city but who "are looking for the city that is to come" (Heb. 13:14). This deterritorialization of the *polis* severs the connection between politics and violence because, without territory to defend or manage, the followers of Jesus are not bound to the means of violence. In fact, there may well be an intrinsic connection between such deterritorialization and our ability to take seriously the command to turn the other cheek or to give to those who ask.

One might contend that this is not "realistic" politics. However, it is only the Weberian rule book that says that a city without territory is not a true *polis*. Whether one wishes to use the word "politics" or not, what is crucial is that lives shaped by the Gospel—and lived in continued repentance for our failures to let them be so shaped—are just as "public" as the life of the bureaucrat. The public markers of the *polis* of the Gospel, however, are somewhat different. Rather than monuments and institutions, it possesses "a house not made with hands" (2 Cor. 5:1), that is, "the household of God, built upon the foundation of the apostles and prophets, with Christ Jesus himself as the cornerstone" (Eph. 2:19–20). Rather than the rationalized procedures of bureaucrats, it possesses the foolishness of the cross (1 Cor. 1:18–25), by which love transforms all our calculations and turns social programs into works of mercy. Rather than a rationalized economy, it possesses an economy of Eucharistic gift. All of these things serve as markers that are just as "real" and "public" as the markers of modernity.

Such a politics can never be theoretically relevant to the state because the state has its own theory. Schillebeeckx writes that "[t]he task for us (for me, now, as a Christian theologian) is to combine the spirit of the gospel with political wisdom and thus to honor the truth in the intuition of both views."[82] However, such a view fails to realize that the "spirit" of the Gospel is itself a political wisdom and thus operates, as it were, within the same conceptual space as any secular wisdom. It fails to see the degree to which a theology is already a politics, and a politics is already a theology. The distinction between secularism (ideological) and secularization (nonideological) is specious. The state conceives itself as (*pace* John Courtney Murray) omnicompetent, and its laws do not simply manage the interaction between individuals and groups but serve a pedagogic function to form us into certain kinds of people. As Antonio Gramsci wrote: "In reality the State must be seen as an 'educator,' in that it aims precisely to create a new type and level of civilization."[83] Schillebeeckx and other political theologians do not appreciate the degree to which "political wisdom" in the modern, secular nation-state—precisely because it is not desacralized—comes into conflict with the spirit of the Gospel. By restricting Christianity's role to one of providing "inspiration" or "direction," the mystical-political model hands over the actual material existence of Christians to the pedagogic shaping of the state.[84]

By showing the world a way of life without violence that is not simply an ideal for exceptional individuals but the common

82. Schillebeeckx, *On Christian Faith*, 76.

83. Antonio Gramsci, "The Modern Prince," in *The Modern Prince and Other Writings*, trans. Louis Mar (New York: International, 1957), 187.

84. William Cavanaugh powerfully argues this point using the example of the Catholic Church in Chile prior to and during the Pinochet regime in *Torture and Eucharist: Theology, Politics, and the Body of Christ* (Oxford: Blackwell, 1998).

life of a historically embodied community, the followers of Jesus trace a path of re-enchantment through our world. Theology must find a way to make peace with Christianity's "others" that is different from one of state-regulated coexistence as interest groups within a pluralistic civil society. For such a peace is a false peace, secured through violence, and builds only a false city, some version of the city founded by Cain. Yet to seek another sort of city, another sort of politics, will require Christians to rediscover a theological imagination that can think beyond the antinomy of mysticism and politics. In our modern, disenchanted world perhaps the most pressing task of this politics of the Gospel is to break out of the mystical confinement in which it has been placed, so as to re-enchant the world, to restore the world's status as cosmos, to found a pilgrim city.

9

"All Things Counter, Original, Spare, Strange"

Liberal Society and Pluralism

The question of how to secure a society that allows for a genuine pluralism of religious and other comprehensive worldviews is not, for the most part, an explicit concern of *Dignitatis Humanae*, Vatican II's "Declaration on Religious Freedom." The fact of religious pluralism is reflected in the references to "religious communities" in the plural and in the acknowledgement of their freedom with regard to "conducting their affairs in their own way."[1] There is even something like an endorsement of such pluralism in the declaration's injunction that "the principle of full freedom is to be preserved in society according to which people are given the maximum of liberty, and only restrained when and in so far as necessary."[2] But the question of the limits of pluralism—questions of how far a society can go to accommodate the religious views of its citizens—is addressed simply by the injunction that liberty is tied to responsibility and the claim that it is the role of the civil authorities to make sure that claims to religious liberty do not

*This essay was originally published as "'All Things Counter, Original, Spare, Strange': Liberal Society and Pluralism," *Communio: International Catholic Review* 40, no. 2 (Summer–Fall 2013): 1–17.

1. Vatican Council II, *Dignitatis Humanae* 4, in *Decrees of the Ecumenical Councils*, ed. Norman Tanner (Washington: Georgetown University Press, 1990), 2:1004.

2. *Dignitatis Humanae* 7, in Tanner, 2:1006.

endanger "public morality."[3] Unquestioned is the presumption that there would be a consensus as to what constitutes public morality or that debates over this consensus would not be anything other than completely free and rational.

Matters look somewhat different several decades after the Council. Practical questions concerning the limits of the exercise of religious freedom (e.g., can citizens be required to pay for things that some find objectionable on religious grounds? can employees conscientiously refuse to perform certain duties normally required by their employers? etc.) have caused many to wonder whether societies that are "liberal" in the classical sense of giving a high priority to personal freedom are not in fact more constraining than they purport to be. Moreover, philosophers, social theorists, and theologians have, in recent decades, been asking whether the liberal ideal of unconstrained agreement is either true in theory or possible in practice. A growing number of voices argue that liberalism is not a neutral field upon which a thousand flowers can bloom but is actually a highly particular tradition that allows for, at best, a very limited sort of pluralism. Are these critiques cogent? If so, is there an alternative to liberalism that would be more genuinely pluralistic?

According to the influential account offered by Alasdair MacIntyre, the problem of liberalism and pluralism goes something like this: liberalism is

the project of founding a form of social order in which individuals could emancipate themselves from the contingency and particularity of tradition by appealing to genuinely universal, tradition-independent norms . . . [which] would enable those who espouse widely different and incompatible conceptions of the good life for human beings to live together peaceably

3. *Dignitatis Humanae* 7, in Tanner, 2:1006.

within the same society, enjoying the same political status and engaging in the same economic relations. [4]

In other words, liberalism brackets the question of the highest good on a societal level in order to create a society in which those with competing accounts of the ultimate end of the good life can coexist by agreeing on the less-than-ultimate good of getting along together in an atmosphere of, at best, mutual respect or, at least, mutual toleration. In other words, liberalism posits a society that can function effectively despite the presence within it of a pluralism of competing accounts of the ultimate good.

The problem arises, however, when these accounts of the good try to move from the realm of private or semiprivate opinion to the realm of public policy. MacIntyre continues:

> Every individual is to be equally free to propose and to live by whatever conception of the good he or she pleases, derived from whatever theory or tradition he or she may adhere to, unless that conception of the good involves reshaping the life of the rest of the community in accordance with it. [5]

In other words, while liberal society can admit a plurality of conceptions of the highest good, it must exclude those conceptions that feature, as an intrinsic element, the expectation that society as a whole ought to conform to that highest good. One is tempted to say that one's conception of the highest good can be admitted only so long as one is not so committed to its truth that one would impose it on others. As Auguste Comte put it, "Systematic

---

4. Alasdair MacIntyre, *Whose Justice? Which Rationality?* (Notre Dame, IN: University of Notre Dame Press, 1988), 335.

5. MacIntyre, *Whose Justice?*, 336.

toleration cannot exist and really never has existed, except with regard to opinions regarded as unimportant or doubtful."[6]

Yet not all conceptions of the ultimate good must be kept private; public arguments in terms of ends like "liberty" or "utility" as society-shaping conceptions of the highest good are admissible because such ends are, it is claimed, sufficiently broad as to be inclusive of all citizens, in contrast to ends like eternal happiness with God or the cultivation of virtuous persons, which are particularistic. The limits of pluralism in a liberal society are such that ends may have a society-shaping force only if they are something to which all rational people can assent, whatever their historical or cultural or religious or economic or social situatedness. The problem, from MacIntyre's perspective, is that no such abstract, universal reason exists; all rationality is situated in particular contexts and is therefore tradition-constituted. The shared rationality that is the basis of liberal democracy is not tradition neutral but is itself a tradition, with its own conception of the good that is in competition with the conceptions of the good found in other traditions.

The thinking of the political philosopher John Rawls might serve as a prime example in MacIntyre's case against liberalism.[7] What MacIntyre calls a "tradition" is what Rawls calls a "comprehensive doctrine," and what MacIntyre calls "universal, tradition-independent norms" Rawls calls "the political conception." About the relationship between comprehensive doctrines and political conceptions, Rawls writes,

> I assume all citizens affirm a comprehensive doctrine to which the political conception they accept is in some way related. But a distinguishing feature of a political conception is that it

6. Quoted in Emile Perreau-Saussine, *Catholicism and Democracy* (Princeton: Princeton University Press, 2012), 84.

7. See MacIntyre's discussion of Rawls in *After Virtue*, 2nd ed. (Notre Dame, IN: University of Notre Dame Press, 1984), 244–55.

is presented as freestanding and expounded without reference to any such wide background. To use a current phrase, the political conception is a module, an essential constituent part, that fits into and can be supported by various reasonable comprehensive doctrines that endure in the society regulated by it.[8]

For Rawls, these comprehensive doctrines—which he typically classifies as religious, philosophical, and moral—belong to what he calls "the 'background culture' of civil society," and therefore to "the social, not the political."[9] They are, within a democratic society, irreducibly plural because there is, for Rawls, no public way of adjudicating their differences.[10] This is because of what he calls "the burdens of judgment," which include the complexity of conflicting evidence, the difficulty of determining the weight and relevance of the evidence, the inherent vagueness of many of our concepts, the uniqueness of individual experience, and therefore the irreducible diversity of such experiences.[11] These epistemological limitations make it impossible to say that one's comprehensive doctrine is the *only* reasonable one.

Yet it is still possible to distinguish between those sets of comprehensive doctrines that are reasonable, and thus capable of having a public role, and those that are not. Rawls writes, "Reasonable persons see that the burdens of judgment set limits on what can be reasonably justified to others, and so they endorse some form of liberty of conscience and freedom of thought."[12] In other words, one's comprehensive doctrine is reasonable to the degree that it allows for the existence of other reasonable comprehensive doctrines, even if one does not judge those other doctrines to be

8. Rawls, *Political Liberalism* (New York: Columbia University Press, 2005), 12.
9. Rawls, *Political Liberalism*, 14.
10. Rawls, 36: "The diversity of reasonable comprehensive religious, philosophical, and moral doctrines found in modern democratic societies is not a mere historical condition that may soon pass away; it is a permanent feature of public culture in democracy."
11. Rawls, 54–58.
12. Rawls, 61.

rationally justified. What matters, politically speaking, is that the holders of these different comprehensive doctrines share a commitment to tolerance, fairness, and equality—the political conception of liberalism—not the background beliefs that undergird that commitment. This commitment is, in Rawls terms, a "module" that can be fitted into a variety of different comprehensive doctrines from which it can draw its power.

A second relevant aspect of Rawls' thought is his understanding of the "original position," which he describes as "a purely hypothetical situation" in which "no one knows his place in society, his class position or social status, nor does anyone know his fortune in the distribution of natural assets and abilities, his intelligence, strength, and the like." Moreover, those in the original position "do not know their conceptions of the good or their special psychological propensities." It is from behind this "veil of ignorance," Rawls says, that the principles of justice are chosen, and the social contract is formed, because it is only from this original position that one can choose social arrangements that are characterized by fairness.[13] Here we would seem to have a self, albeit a hypothetical one, that is, in MacIntyre's terms, emancipated from the contingency and particularity of tradition, emancipated even, it seems, from any awareness of one's own conception of the good.

From the perspective of someone like MacIntyre, the sleight of hand in which Rawls is engaged is to present what he calls "the political conception" of liberalism as something that is not embedded within its own distinct "comprehensive doctrine." The "module" of political liberalism, MacIntyre would maintain, is in fact a custom-built part that really only works when fitted into a comprehensive doctrine that is amenable to its secular, atomistic, and voluntarist presuppositions, which we see embodied in the notion of the person who stands in the original position.

13. Rawls, *A Theory of Justice* (Cambridge, MA: Belknap, 1971), 12.

Rawls is aware of this kind of charge, and he is resolute in rejecting the claim that his account of political liberalism presumes any particular comprehensive doctrine or metaphysical picture of the human person. For example, the "original position" of the human person behind the veil of ignorance is, he insists, not a metaphysics but what he calls a "representation" (one might say a thought experiment) for the specific purpose of forming a political conception of justice.[14] Still, one might yet wonder how free of metaphysics Rawls' political conception, in fact, is, particularly when he says things like this: "values of the political are very great values and hence not easily overridden: these values govern the basic framework of social life—the very groundwork of our existence—and specify the fundamental terms of political and social cooperation."[15] It is difficult to hear a phrase like "the very groundwork of our existence" as being entirely free of metaphysical entanglements.

Perhaps unfairly to Rawls, I would like to exploit this opening to raise the metaphysical stakes in the critique. I will do this by describing two different metaphysical accounts, both from the Middle Ages, of how we might think about the plurality that we find in the world: the account found in medieval Christian theology, as exemplified in Thomas Aquinas (1225–1274), and the account found in the orthodox Ash'arite theology of Islam, as presented by Abu Hamid Al-Ghazālī (1058–1111). These accounts are rooted in the soil of philosophical reflection, stretching back into antiquity, on the question of the one and the many.

From as far back as human beings have engaged in philosophical reflection, they have been aware that they find themselves living in a world with many different kinds of beings: inanimate and animate, animal and vegetable, irrational and rational, female and male, butchers and bakers and candlestick makers.

14. Rawls, *Political Liberalism*, 27.
15. Rawls, 139. The phrase "the very groundwork of our existence" is taken from Mill.

Moreover, within these diverse kinds, we find an even more radical plurality: this rock is not that rock, this woman has red hair and that woman has blond, this butcher is highly skilled and that one is missing several fingers. Yet at the same time, this world of diversity in some sense constitutes a single thing: a universe or a cosmos. Monotheistic theology raises the stakes even further by adding to the ancient question of the one and the many the further question of how the one Creator God relates to the unity-in-plurality of the cosmos and how that pluralistic cosmos glorifies its one Creator.

Thomas Aquinas' account of created plurality approaches the issue from the question of why it is that a cosmos marked by plurality reflects the glory of God better than one marked by uniformity. Could God's glory not be reflected in a creation containing just one kind of thing—say, hydrogen—or indeed containing a single individual—say, one most excellent hydrogen atom? For Thomas, the reason for a plurality of creatures and kinds is because the perfection of the infinite Creator is best imaged in a finite creation by a diversity of creatures, since as Thomas writes in the *Compendium theologiae*, "it was impossible that one thing perfectly represent the divine goodness because of the remoteness of each creature from God. Therefore, it was necessary that many things represent him, so that one thing supplied what another lacks."[16] For Thomas, the many is not, as it was for most ancients, a falling away from the One; he views it positively as the most fitting way God is reflected in creation.

Thomas' account of the diversity of creation, however, does not simply affirm a plurality of creatures and kinds but also requires that this plurality be an *ordered* one. That is to say, these many creatures must be differentiated across a hierarchically ordered series in which those beings that are more fully actual have a causal role in relation to those being that are less actual, acting

16. *Compendium theologiae* 1.102.

as secondary but genuine causes. For Thomas, to deny the ordered relationship of cause and effect between created beings is "to deprive them of their best possession, for individual things are good in themselves, but all things together are best because of the order of the whole." This "order of the whole" can only be a result of relationships of cause and effect, "for, in regard to things that are different in their natures, there can be no gathering together into a unity of order unless by the fact that some of them act and others undergo action."[17] Thus for Thomas, the reconciliation of the one and the many—how it is that the world God makes can be a unity in diversity—is dependent upon creatures being hierarchically differentiated by their relationships of cause and effect among themselves—relations that grow from properties intrinsic to the creatures entering into those relationships.

Thomas' understanding of the unity and plurality of the universe can be contrasted with what he at least took to be the view held by orthodox Muslim thinkers, a view sometimes described as "occasionalism." From Maimonides, he is aware of the Islamic *Kalam* theologians of the Ash'arite school who deny the genuine causal efficacy of creatures.[18] Al-Ghazālī, in his *The Incoherence of the Philosophers*, offers the famous example of fire burning cotton: "what proof is there that [the fire] is the agent? They have no proof other than observing the occurrence of the burning at the juncture of contact with the fire. . . . [Something's] existence *with* a thing does not prove that it exists *by* [that thing]."[19] In contrast to Thomas' view, Ash'arite theologians hold that there is no causal relationship between fire and the cotton that burns, at least not outside the mind of those who observe the phenomenon

17. *Contra Gentiles* 3.69.17.

18. *Contra Gentiles* 3.65, 3.97; *De potentia* 3.7.

19. Al-Ghazālī, *Tahâfut al-falâsifa*, Discussion 17.5–6, in *The Incoherence of the Philosophers*, trans. Michael E. Marmura (Provo, UT: Brigham Young University Press, 2000). Frank Griffel sees Al-Ghazālī as fundamentally ambiguous regarding his own views on the efficacy of created powers, and so not fully committed to the occasionalist position (*Al-Ghazālī's Philosophical Theology* [Oxford: Oxford University Press, 2009], 284–85). For my purposes, it suffices that he gives an accurate presentation of Ash'arite metaphysics.

of combustion. The specific concern among these Muslim theologians was to ensure that all agency not be reduced to necessary causality (the way that, in an Aristotelian view, fire necessarily burns cotton), which would, in their view, entail a denial of the possibility of miracles. A broader concern was to underscore the contingency of all occurrences and their radical dependence on God's will. Fire "burns" cotton in each and every instance only in the sense that God wills that it serve as the occasion for God's burning of the cotton.

This long-established "orthodoxy" among Muslim thinkers was undergirded by a metaphysics in which all creation consists solely of indistinguishable atoms and their accidental configurations, the former having no properties apart from the latter, which are perpetually perishing and are renewed in existence solely by God. This atomism rejects the view that creatures have stable natures by which they act; rather, it holds that created beings are contingent arrangements of atoms that are destroyed the instant after they come into existence, only to be replaced by new arrangements from moment to moment that may or may not be the same as the arrangements of the prior moments. Cotton does not burn because of fire, but because God rearranges the atoms in the cotton. Al-Ghazālī recounts, in *The Incoherence of the Philosophers*, how critics point out that on this view, someone who leaves a book in his house might return to find that it has turned into "a beardless slave boy—intelligent, busy with his tasks—or into an animal . . . that has defiled the library with its urine and its dung."[20] Al-Ghazālī responds to this criticism by saying that "God created for us the knowledge that he did not enact these possibilities," even though they remain genuine possibilities. In a way that seems to anticipate David Hume's later arguments, he says that what appear to us as stable natures and causal efficacy

20. Al-Ghazālī, Discussion 17.13.

are, in fact, simply the effect of "the continuous habit of their occurrence repeatedly, one time after another."[21]

What does Thomas have to say about this alternative account of the one and the many? While it might, at first glance, seem to enhance God's creative power, Thomas argues that a denial of causal efficacy to creatures "would imply a lack of power in the Creator: for it is due to the power of the cause that it bestows active power on its effects."[22] In the *Contra Gentiles*, Thomas offers a series of arguments against the occasionalist view that have a cumulative force. A diversity of causes better accounts for the diversity of effects and fits better with what we know through our senses: different created causes are associated with different effects. Further, if God causes everything directly, what purpose is there to the useless charade of what looks like created causation? Again, if things act to the degree that they are actual, and if things are actual to the degree that God has communicated to them the likeness of himself as *actus purus*, then the likeness of God in things is their capacity to act. And, yet again, "the perfection of the effect demonstrates the perfection of the cause. . . . So to detract from the perfection of creatures is to detract from the perfection of the divine power."[23] Thomas draws out the implications of the occasionalist position in such a way as to show that what this position seeks to secure—the singular power and glory of God—is precisely what it ends up undermining.

What do these debates among medieval thinkers have to do with liberalism and the question of pluralism? The account of the nature of created diversity that we find in Thomas and other medieval Christian thinkers seems to relate to how we imagine not only the cosmos but also the political order. This can be seen in the late Emile Perreau-Saussine's description of the social structure of pre-revolutionary France:

21. Al-Ghazālī, Discussion 17.15.
22. *Summa theologiae* 1.105.5.
23. See *Contra Gentiles* 3.69.12–20.

The society of the Ancien Regime was a complex web of privileges and corporations. Aristocratic by nature, it was a theory organized around a vertical chain of command that ran from top to bottom of the social scale with manifold ramifications.[24]

While we tend to think of aristocratic societies as being characterized primarily by the fixity of social status, what Perreau-Saussine draws our attention to is the plurality of the distribution of social power within such societies. This "aristocratic" pluralism was based on the ideal of every member of society having by nature a distinctive set of rights and obligations—we might say "effects and causes"—that bound them together within a hierarchically structured social system, a kind of political cosmos. In the first half of the nineteenth century Alexis de Tocqueville had written:

> As in aristocratic communities all the citizens occupy fixed positions, one above the other, the result is that each of them always sees a man above himself whose patronage is necessary to him, and below himself another man whose co-operation he may claim. . . . Aristocracy had made a chain of all the members of the community, from the peasant to the king: democracy breaks that chain and severs every link of it."[25]

Perreau-Saussine draws out this contrast between traditional aristocratic societies and democratic liberalism:

> Aristocratic regimes are intrinsically hierarchical. They are pluralist in that they recognize different levels of authority and power. . . . Democratic systems, in contrast, repudiate the heterogeneous nature of the hierarchical worldview. They do not

24. Perreau-Saussine, *Catholicism and Democracy*, 8.
25. Alexis de Tocqueville, *Democracy in America* (New York: Knopf, 1972), 2:99.

divide society up into "orders." This egalitarian denial of all hierarchy has a powerful leveling effect, setting all ways of life on one and the same plane.[26]

Thus, in contrast to an aristocratic political cosmos, the democratic political cosmos, at least in its ideal form, presumes not the plurality of social roles based on status and tradition but the interchangeable identities of its citizens. As John Rawls notes, "given the principles of justice, the state must be understood as the association consisting of equal citizens."[27] A principle as fundamental as "one person, one vote," which seems entirely intuitive to us citizens of liberal democracies, enshrines a view of society quite different from the aristocratic pluralism of the pre-modern world.[28] For the purpose of the most significant act of the citizens of a liberal democracy—the act of voting—the citizens are fundamentally identical; the veil of the voting booth stands as a symbol of the veil of ignorance. And, if Rawls is correct, the fundamental elements from which the political cosmos is created via social contract are these indistinguishable individuals behind the veil of ignorance, in the original position. In this description of things, it is not difficult to hear an echo of the atoms that are configured by the divine will in occasionalist metaphysics.

Of course, the difference is that the atomized citizens in a democratic political cosmos are not thought to be configured by the transcendent divine will but to immanently configure *themselves* into a body politic. The atoms of the democratic political cosmos are purportedly both radically equal and radically free. But how ought we conceive of the agency of an atom that is bereft of any nature by which it acts? It makes sense to think that I can

26. Perreau-Saussine, *Catholicism and Democracy*, 148.

27. Rawls, *Theory of Justice*, 212.

28. Thomas Gilby writes of Thomas, "One man one vote, that he never advocated—he had too strong a sense of graded responsibilities" (*The Political Thought of Thomas Aquinas* [Chicago: The University of Chicago Press, 1958], 294).

act in certain ways—speaking, classifying, walking bipedally—because I possess a human nature and not, say, an equine one. But how could a natureless atom act freely? Is there a conflict between claims for radical equality and radical freedom, both of which seem to be features of the democratic political cosmos?

In this regard, de Tocqueville observed that when the democratic values of freedom and equality come into conflict, equality seems to win out. As he put it, the people of democratic nations have "a natural taste for freedom. . . . But for equality their passion is ardent, insatiable, incessant, invincible; they call for equality in freedom: and if they cannot obtain that, they still call for equality in slavery."[29] In other words, democratic societies, with their insistence on equality, are open to totalitarian exploitation in a way that aristocratic societies, with their plurality of grades of citizens and their corresponding plurality of rights and obligations, are not. As de Tocqueville notes, "A man may be the equal of all his countrymen save one, who is the master of all without distinction and who selects equally from among them all the agents of his power."[30] In a cosmos of radical equality that is unable to sustain itself without some external agent to give shape to the body politic, the commanding God of the occasionalist cosmos reappears as the commanding despot of totalitarian egalitarianism.

Here, then, is the charge: an "aristocratic" vision of the world and society in which people by nature fall into a hierarchical order is one that is inherently pluralistic and resistant to totalitarian absolutism, while a liberal vision of the world and society in which all of the members of society are, as citizens, fundamentally equal units is constantly in danger of succumbing to a totalitarianism that obliterates all true plurality. Even short of out-and-out totalitarianism, liberalism still militates against true

29. De Tocqueville, *Democracy in America*, 2:97.
30. De Tocqueville, 95.

difference inasmuch as it requires citizens to leave behind the particularities of their identities when they enter into the public sphere. Democracy works best when it is constructed by social contractors occupying the original position, ignorant of race, class, gender, and even their own conception of the good.

How convincing is this charge against liberal society?

There certainly are accounts of liberalism that militate against a true pluralism. John Rawls would seem to claim not only that one must enter the sphere of politics properly speaking stripped of the particularities of one's religious or moral tradition, but also that this denuded self is in some sense ontologically prior to the self that is traditioned. Thus Rawls writes in his 1971 *A Theory of Justice*, "It is from the position of equal citizenship that persons join the various religious associations, and it is from this position that they should conduct their discussions with one another."[31] And in his 1993 work, *Political Liberalism*, which seeks to give a more positive role to "comprehensive doctrines," we still find the claim, "it is normally desirable that the comprehensive philosophical and moral views we are wont to use in debating fundamental political issues should give way in public life."[32] The self that contracts the basic framework of social life, which is "the very groundwork of our existence," is a self that has no comprehensive doctrine, a self that stands within no tradition, a self that stands rather in the "original position," behind the "veil of ignorance," a self that is by design identical to every other self so situated. And, as I have said, such a self bears a disturbing resemblance to the atoms that make up the occasionalist cosmos, subject to the despotic power of the divine ruler.

Rawls at least wants to claim that this self is more of a thought experiment—a "representation"—than a reality. Jeffrey Stout has noted that, given the actual social position of most of the students

31. Rawls, *Theory of Justice*, 219.
32. Rawls, *Political Liberalism*, 10.

who would read Rawls, "It is good for them and good for the rest of us that they have at least once had to ask themselves what sort of social ground rules they would select if they did not know they were about to occupy positions of power and wealth."[33] But even if we take the self of the original position as simply a representation and not a reality, we must still reckon with the fact that it sets the terms of political engagement; it is what determines the norm of tolerance, and it is tolerance that qualifies a comprehensive doctrine as "reasonable" and therefore itself a candidate for toleration. In other words, in order to be tolerated, a comprehensive doctrine must be compatible with the self behind the veil of ignorance and therefore willing and able to accept into itself the "module" of political liberalism.

All of this is troubling, yet I am not quite ready to give up on aspects of liberal society for positive and negative reasons. Positively, it seems clear to me that having tradition-grounded reasons for holding a particular view does not prevent one from giving reasons that might be acceptable to those who do not share one's tradition. We can see this in *Dignitatis Humanae* itself, which affirms that the dignity of human beings "is known from the revealed word of God and from reason itself."[34] While convictions held on the basis of a comprehensive doctrine might not be translatable without loss into another discourse, rough and ready communication is still possible, though not, of course, guaranteed. The demand of liberal society that we seek to make arguments that will be at least potentially convincing to the citizens holding different comprehensive doctrines is not in itself an unreasonable request, even though one might bristle at Rawls' rather narrow construal of what counts as reasonable. If we view the making of arguments in the political realm as an ad hoc enterprise, then entering into such arguments does not require that one accept

33. Jeffrey Stout, *Democracy and Tradition* (Princeton: Princeton University Press, 2004), 294.

34. *Dignitatis Humanae* 2.

the truth of the liberal account of the atomistic self. Moreover, the idea that one can give reasons with some hope of success even to those who do not share our conception of a final end seems compatible with the Catholic understanding of faith and reason.

Negatively, I am not sure that anyone really is anxious to live in a society that is simply a transposition of the aristocratic metaphysics that we find in Thomas Aquinas. Even if one thinks, as I do, that we can think of the universe as an ordered whole of agents and patients that by its differentiated order gives glory to God, one might well be less than enthusiastic about aristocracy as the societal correlate of that metaphysical vision. Even acknowledging the totalitarian uses to which democracy can be put, the idea of a sphere of public life in which people can meet as equal citizens seems on the whole less subject to abuse than an aristocracy, particularly if one rejects any of the possible metaphysical entailments of the atomistic self. Indeed, while all human beings might well have some set of metaphysical commitments that inform their politics, we should be particularly wary of anyone who would claim to directly translate such commitments into political commitments.

There is something fundamentally correct about what Rawls says about the burdens of judgment, particularly if we think of it as something akin to what Thomas says about law as a dictate of practical and not speculative reason.[35] While Thomas does not think that judgments about the truth of "comprehensive doctrines" are as uncertain as Rawls does, the implications of those doctrinal judgments for our political or moral judgments is often not readily apparent. Human law in particular deals with vast uncertainties and its details cannot simply be read off a metaphysical program.[36] In other words, there is a certain "looseness of fit" between our metaphysics and our politics: aristocracy is no

35. *Summa theologiae* 1-2.90.1 ad 2.
36. *Summa theologiae* 1-2.94.4.

guarantee against despotism and liberalism does not always bring it in its wake. Indeed, historically speaking, the opposite has often been the case, perhaps because, as Jeffrey Stout notes, thought experiments like the original position can engender tolerance and even sympathy for the comprehensive doctrines of others, which in a pluralistic society can serve a valuable purpose. It does not, however, serve *all* human purposes, and in particular does not serve the most important human purposes.

A non-Christian friend of mine once described voting as being like a sacrament. This is clearly false. But just because it is not a sacrament does not mean that it is nothing. Given the bloody handprints that often adorn the doors of power, things like an absence of state-sponsored religious violence or the peaceful transfer of governmental control are not to be regarded too lightly, and inasmuch as a profound sense of the burdens of judgment in political matters can foster such things, we should value it.

In the end, however, I suspect that liberalism is not enough. I suspect that something like Thomas Aquinas' account of the role of a hierarchically structured pluralistic cosmos that gives glory to its Creator might be necessary, not as a blueprint for society, but to found a deep appreciation of the intrinsic diversity of the world that not only gives us a true account of how things are but also serves as a hedge against both the totalitarian potential of egalitarian liberalism as well as the corrosive indifference toward ultimate questions that seems to propagate so readily in the environment of liberal societies. Ironically, this aristocratic metaphysics might be exactly what is needed for a liberal society to be truly pluralistic—not as a pattern for structuring political arrangements, but as a means of fostering in citizens the ability to see divine glory reflected in, to use Gerard Manley Hopkins' phrase, "all things counter, original, spare, strange." This is perhaps the distinctive political vocation of Christians who find themselves living in liberal societies. Emile Perreau-Saussine concludes his book *Catholicism and Democracy* with the following suggestion:

In a democratic world that works ceaselessly to eliminate otherness, even (perhaps especially) when it proclaims its commitment to pluralism, believers have an eye to something beyond the society of the here and now, and thus have an escape route from conformism. They form a breakwater against the tide of conformity. They are, par excellence, a sign of contradiction.[37]

37. Perreau-Saussine, *Catholicism and Democracy*, 152.

Culture: Other Cities

10

Walking in the Pilgrim City

Therefore Jesus also suffered outside the city gate in order to
sanctify the people by his own blood. Let us then go to him
outside the camp and bear the abuse he endured. For here we
have no lasting city, but we are looking for the city that is to
come (Heb. 13:12–14).

I

Blessed and cursed by a peculiar homelessness, Christians claim
fellowship with Christ who suffered outside the city gate and
are called to follow him into that wilderness beyond the camp,
that region other than the earthly *civitas*, from which we might
discern another city. This other city shows that the structures of
this world, which seem so solid and real, are afflicted with an
ephemeral quality, a kind of unreality, that makes them a source
of anxiety rather than a resting place for our restless hearts (Luke
12:12–34). And so, we exist in a state of perpetual pilgrimage to
our true *patria*, following "Jesus the pioneer and perfecter of our
faith, who for the sake of the joy that was set before him endured
the cross, disregarding its shame, and has taken his seat at the
right hand of the throne of God" (Heb. 12:2).

Dwelling "outside the camp" need not entail a removal to a
place apart. From its earliest days, Christianity was a predomi-
nantly urban phenomenon, enacting its peculiarly homeless form

* This essay was originally published as "Walking in the Pilgrim City," *New Blackfriars* 77,
no. 909 (November 1996): 504–18.

of existence within the institutional confines of the late ancient city.[1] Though there have been within Christianity from early on "monastic" elements that withdrew to uninhabited places, for the vast majority of Christians in the first four centuries, physical withdrawal from the city was not an option, nor was it held up as an ideal. Living "outside the camp" is clearly something that could be done in the midst of the city. At the same time, the Gospel call to homelessness is not a purely internalized indifference to this life nor an invisible kind of pious detachment. When Paul speaks of those "who walk not according to the flesh but according to the Spirit" (Rom. 8:4), he is not contrasting a "spiritualized" Gospel, which asks only for faith, to a "carnal" Law, which demands specific, visible actions. No less than the Law, the Gospel requires actions, gestures, and rituals (e.g., the collection for the poor in Jerusalem, Baptism, faithful participation in the Eucharist).[2] What is called for are actual, concrete social practices by which the community of the Church is manifested as "a chosen race, a royal priesthood, a holy nation, God's own people." That which marks out the Church as a distinctive community of people, a "nation," must be visible so it may "proclaim the mighty acts of him who called you out of darkness into his marvelous light" (1 Pet. 2:9).

1. As Wayne Meeks notes, "Within a decade of the crucifixion of Jesus, the village culture of Palestine had been left behind, and the Greco-Roman city became the dominant environment of the Christian movement. So it remained, from the dispersion of the Hellenists from Jerusalem until well after the time of Constantine" (*The First Urban Christians: The Social World of the Apostle Paul* [New Haven: Yale University Press, 1983], 11).

2. For a fascinating reading of Paul that sees him as arguing for an internalized (and therefore universally available) "faith" as the basis for participation in the people of God and opposing the "carnal" and historically particular basis of ethnicity and obedience to the Law, see Daniel Boyarin, *A Radical Jew: Paul and the Politics of Identity* (Berkeley: University of California Press, 1994). Boyarin's interpretation identifies a persistent Christian tendency to "spiritualize" and "universalize" so as to obliterate difference, but it is highly questionable whether Paul is in fact, as Boyarin claims, the "fountainhead" of such a "western universalism" (229). For a critique of Boyarin on this point, see Stephen Fowl's review in *Modern Theology* 12, no. 1 (January 1996): 131–33.

II

How this homelessness could be something other than physical withdrawal or internalized otherworldliness is illuminated by Michel de Certeau's analysis in *The Practice of Everyday Life* of the logic of oppositional practices and, in particular, of how "places" (*lieux*)—territories as defined by official boundaries and discourses—are "practiced" by their inhabitants so as to have overlaid upon them a multitude of "spaces" (*espaces*). "A space exists when one takes into consideration vectors of direction, velocities, and time variables. . . . In short, space is a practiced place. Thus the street geometrically defined by urban planning is transformed into a space by walkers."[3] Every place is in fact a palimpsest of spaces, which are no less real, no less visible, than the place upon which they are enacted. Such a conception of the relationship of space and place can help us see how the Church can be a distinct, visible community (a genuine space) without having to stake a claim to a particular territory, whether this be a theocratic state or a "sectarian" enclave. At the same time, we must recognize that the distinction between place and space should not be reified in the attempt to describe the Church entirely in terms of space, as an "event" without enduring institutions or structures of authority. The Church's homelessness is always enacted as the ambivalence of place and space.

III

One can see some of this ambivalence in the attitude of Jesus and the early Christians toward the temple in Jerusalem.[4] Jesus is "greater" than the temple (Matt. 12:6) and warns his disciples not to be impressed with its buildings, foretelling their destruction

3. Michel de Certeau, *The Practice of Everyday Life*, trans. Steven Rendall (Berkeley: University of California Press, 1984), 117.

4. One should note that this ambivalence is already present in Israel, manifested in the tension between the ideals of the tent of presence and the temple.

(Matt. 24:2). Speaking to the Samaritan woman, he relativizes the historic dispute between Jews and Samaritans by announcing the presence of that day "when you will worship the Father neither on this mountain nor in Jerusalem . . . [but] the true worshippers will worship the Father in spirit and truth" (John 4:20–24). At the same time, he pays the temple tax (Matt. 17:25) and speaks of the temple as God's house, which is defiled by the presence within it of money changers and which Jesus "cleanses" (Matt. 21:12–13; John 2:14–17). The Acts of the Apostles depicts the disciples continuing to worship in the Jerusalem temple even after the resurrection of Jesus (Acts 2:46), yet Stephen seemingly denounces the temple (Acts 7:47–50), and, in the narrative of the book of Acts as a whole, Jerusalem and its temple serve primarily as a point of dispersion—not a place in which to dwell but a place to leave so as to witness to the Gospel. It is the community of disciples that is to be God's temple (1 Cor. 3:16; 2 Cor. 6:16; Eph. 2:21–22), a dwelling place for God as visible as the temple in Jerusalem, but nomadic, on pilgrimage (1 Pet. 2:11). And the final vision of John the Divine is of a heavenly city that contains no temple but simply the multitude who worship before the Lamb that was slain yet lives (Rev. 21:22).

It is tempting to see Jesus and his followers as having abandoned entirely the "strategic" Jewish symbolic world—with its clearly delineated and painfully longed-for land, its ethnically defined people, its laws that precisely defined pure and impure, inside and outside, and its temple containing the Divine Presence and located at the center of the cosmos[5]—in favor of a new, "tactical" sense of peoplehood. Just as Abraham, Isaac, and Jacob, in the reading of the Letter to the Hebrews, "were strangers and foreigners on the earth" who were "seeking a homeland" and who desired "a better country, that is, a heavenly one" (Heb. 11:

5. On the four factors of Temple, Land, Torah, and ethnicity as definitive of the Jewish symbolic world, see N.T. Wright, *The New Testament and the People of God* (Minneapolis, MN: Fortress, 1992), 224–32.

13–16), so too the new people of God are a people on perpetual pilgrimage to the heavenly *patria*. Any sense of a Christian "place," in Certeau's sense, is "decentered" by this appeal to an eternal homeland, making impossible any clear delineation of sacred and profane places. The holiness of the new people of God can no longer be understood as a ritual purity defined by such dichotomies as circumcised versus uncircumcised. In the new community of Jews and Gentiles, God's holiness is manifest in the mixture of pure and impure, inside and outside.

And yet, the sacred geography of Israel is not simply left behind but continues to serve Christians both as a source of images and metaphors and as a set of specific historical and geographical points that provide the stage upon which the Christian drama is enacted. The permanent place of "carnal" Israel in God's economy, which Paul argues for in Romans 9–11, guarantees the abiding significance of Law and Land. And their significance is not simply negative. They are not simply "types" of spiritual realities but concrete markers that are necessary for telling the story of Jesus. Among the varied early Christian responses to the *realia* of Temple, Land, Torah, and ethnicity, we find not only a negative function (the "old" against which the "new" is defined) nor simply a spiritualization (e.g., the Letter to the Hebrews, in which the "sanctuary made by human hands" is "a mere copy of the true one" [9:24], that is, heaven) but also a positive concern for the *realia* in all their material particularity. This concern grew from the necessity of narrating the life of a historical individual, Jesus of Nazareth.[6] The story of Jesus is irrevocably tied to the "soil" of the land of promise and therefore to the people of the promise.

At the same time, the story of Jesus maps a new sacred geography onto the land of Canaan, and onto the world as a whole, which is no longer determined by the temple in Jerusalem but by

6. W.D. Davies, *The Gospel and the Land: Early Christianity and Jewish Territorial Doctrine* (Berkeley, CA: University of California Press, 1974), 366–67.

the nomadic tent of presence that is his body—both his human body (the temple that shall be raised in three days [John 2:21]) and his ecclesial body (the spiritual dwelling of living stones [1 Pet. 2:5]). The person of Christ, not the land, is the fulfillment of the promise to Abraham, and, as W.D. Davies notes, this "personalization of the fulfilment of the promise 'in Christ' demanded the deterritorialization of the promise."[7] The Spirit-filled community, dispersed throughout the world, enacting again the story of Jesus in a multitude of places, telling his story in alien tongues, creates sacred "spaces" in which the land of promise appears not as "this soil" but as "this people." As W. Janzen puts it, "A certain static land theology has been broken open in such a way as to designate all places on the map as potentially holy, contingent on God's election through the Spirit."[8]

IV

The eschatological character of Jesus's proclamation of the kingdom of God is not primarily found in its "future-oriented" prediction of "the end of the world" (in the sense of the end of time and space) but in its bringing to an end a particular "world order."[9] In declaring himself lord of the Sabbath (Matt. 12:8, Luke 6:5), in his freedom with regard to purity codes (Mark 1:23), in his willingness to come into contact with the defiled and the defiling (Luke 8:43–48) and those persons excluded from the people of Israel (Matt. 15:22–28, John 4:5–42), Jesus undermines an entire symbolic order of purity and defilement that constitutes the "world" of first-century Judaism. This symbolic world order,

7. Davies, *Gospel and the Land*, 179.

8. W. Janzen, "Land," *The Anchor Bible Dictionary*, ed. David Noel Freedman et al. (New York: Doubleday, 1992), 4:153. Cf. Wright, *New Testament*, 366: "Jesus and the church together are the New Temple; the world, I suggest, is the new Land." One should note that, after the destruction of the temple, Judaism too "deterritorialized" the promise. See Boyarin, *Radical Jew*, 251–59, on the rabbinic "displacement of loyalty from place to memory of place" (256).

9. On the nature of early Christian hope, and in particular its continuity with Jewish eschatology, see Wright, *New Testament*, 332–34, 401, 459–64.

formed by the matrix of Temple, Land, Torah, and ethnicity, is called into question by Jesus's proclamation of the immediacy of God's rule in his person and the manifestation of that reality in his preaching, his healings, his power over demons and nature, his forgiving of sins, and his table fellowship with outcasts. For the earliest Christian communities, Jesus's death and resurrection, along with the giving of the Spirit and the establishment of a new community of Jews and Gentiles, constitute the eschatological overturning of the world defined by Temple, Land, Torah, and ethnicity.

This is not, however, to deny the temporal dimension of this eschatological overturning, for the dimension of time is crucial to the articulation of the Church's movement, its pilgrimage, and in this sense, it is "future-oriented." One might use Certeau's image of the "trajectory" to capture a movement that is both spatial and temporal, noting his warning that this image can mislead since a trajectory can be plotted and taken in at a glance.[10] The trajectory plotted by Christian eschatological language, however, can never be captured by such a gaze because it is always directed toward an end point and an end time that is "other." The heavenly Jerusalem does not exist in some place that can be plotted on a map; the eschaton does not arrive as the final moment in a succession of moments. Christian eschatology signals the overturning of any privileged place or time, for the heavenly Jerusalem and the eternal Sabbath are already given as gift at the outset; it is a trajectory in which every place is haunted by the presence of the kingdom and every moment is the *parousia*. Moving in such a trajectory, yearning is fulfillment and homelessness is arrival, folly is wisdom, and the word of the cross is the word of life. The world is always ending because God's future has colonized the present.

10. Certeau, *Practice*, 35.

V

In this eschatological overturning, a new world is enacted within the old through the instantiation of a new set of social relations, a new narrative (and a new reading of an old narrative), and a new set of ritual gestures. When Paul writes that "if anyone is in Christ, there is a new creation: everything old has passed away; see, everything has become new!" (2 Cor. 5:17), he indicates the radical change that is effected by initiation into the Christian community. To be "in Christ" is to live within this particular set of relations, to pass through these rituals, to hear and tell these stories so as to live in a new world.[11] As Gregory of Nyssa put it, "The establishment of the Church is a re-creation of the world."[12] Yet it is a creation that, in terms of human activity, takes the form not of a making but of a using. It is through a particular mode of use or "consumption" of the world that the Church produces a new world. This is a genuine *poiesis*, but one that does not operate within its own place.[13] This is why the new *aeon* does not follow upon the completion of the old but is performed concurrently with it. Christians are already set free "from the present evil age" (Gal. 1:4) and "have tasted the goodness of the word of God and the powers of the age to come" (Heb. 6:5). Spoken as a wisdom that is "not a wisdom of this age or of the rulers of this age" (1 Cor. 2:6), the Gospel of Jesus, the crucified Messiah, opens the space of the new *aeon* within the interstices of the old, like a wound inflicted upon the wisdom of the world, an alien intrusion in the midst of normalcy.

This new *aeon* is not simply a permanent possibility within human history but has its moment of historical genesis in Jesus's proclamation of the kingdom. He effects what Certeau calls the

11. See Gerhard Lohfink, *Jesus and Community: The Social Dimension of Christian Faith*, trans. John Galvin (Philadelphia: Fortress, 1984), 126–28.

12. Gregory of Nyssa, *Commentary on the Canticle*, Sermon 13, in *From Glory to Glory: Texts from Gregory of Nyssa's Mystical Writings*, selected and introduced by Jean Daniélou, SJ, trans. and ed. Herbert Musurillo, SJ (Crestwood, NY: St. Vladimir's Seminary, 1995), 273.

13. See Certeau, *Practice*, xii, 30–34.

"founding rupture," which initiates a new social practice.[14] The new *aeon* is not simply a higher, "spiritual" reality that hovers above the old *aeon*. Instead, it intrudes at a particular moment, a *kairos*, to transform the old *aeon*. In sketching the logic of a tactical diversion, Certeau presents a sequence of events in which, "given a visible establishment of forces (I) and an invisible fund of memories (II), a punctual act of memory (III) produces visible effects in the established order (IV)." He then notes that "The goal of the series is thus an operation that transforms the visible organization. But this change requires the invisible resources of a time that obeys other laws and which, taking it by surprise, steals something from the distribution owning the space."[15] Using this very formal (perhaps too formal) schema to think about Jesus and the Church, we might say that Jesus is that "punctual act of memory" that forms the hinge between the *aeons*, gathering up the story of Israel in his person to transform it through cross and tomb and pentecostal fire into a new story, the story of the "Israel of God," that "new creation" that is the community of Jew and Gentile (Gal. 6:15–16), a "visible effect in the established order." And in the Eucharistic *anamnesis*, this community re-presents to God the story of God's people, transformed in the *kairos* of Christ's suffering, death, and resurrection. By this ecclesial re-presentation, God effects a visible change in the established order through the act of Eucharistic "consumption." The elements of bread and wine are no longer what the established order says they are— commodities to be given or withheld—but through the Eucharistic *poiesis* they become God's gift of the new *aeon* inaugurated in the person of Christ and his offering of himself.

14. Michel de Certeau, "La rupture instauratrice," in *La faiblesse de croire* (Paris: Editions du Seuil, 1987), 183–226, esp. 209–12.

15. Certeau, *Practice*, 84–85.

VI

The Church is founded by a divine speech-act. The very word *ekklesia* finds its root in *kaleo*, "to call." Through this act of calling, new circuits of passage are opened up within the place of the world. Just as God's speech calls forth the first creation from nothingness, so the Word made flesh utters the new creation in giving birth on the cross to the redeemed community and what Gerhard Lohfink calls its distinctive "praxis of 'togetherness.'"[16] Tracing the trajectory established by Christ, the Church opens passages through the wall separating Jew and Gentile (Eph. 2:14), and boundaries between social classes become frontiers of encounter through the Eucharistic-economic sharing at the Lord's table.[17] Virgins and consecrated widows blur the line between *oikos* and *polis*, creating new and ambiguous female spaces of sacred power.[18] The graves of the martyrs are no longer the graves of transgressors—defiled places for the excluded dead—but are venerated as holy sites. For Christians, this new sacred geography, brought about by the Word uttered by the Father, is the city to which they owe their allegiance, their true *patria* for which they long and in which they already dwell in hope.

Responding to the pagan writer Celsus's criticism of Christians for their refusal to serve in public office for the good of the city, Origen wrote, "But we know of the existence in each city of another sort of country, created by the Logos of God."[19] This "other country" is not defined by walls or ethnic identity or social contract but by the unruly Logos of God, who gives to

16. Lohfink, *Jesus and Community*, 99–106.
17. On the weekly Eucharist as the occasion for the distribution of goods from the rich to the poor, see Justin Martyr, *First Apology* 67.
18. See Peter Brown, "'A Promiscuous Brotherhood and Sisterhood': Men and Women in The Early Churches," in *The Body and Society* (New York: Columbia University Press, 1988), 140–59. On the Christian deconstruction of the antique distinction between *oikos* and *polis*, see Bernd Wannenwetsch, "The Political Worship of the Church: A Critical and Empowering Practice," *Modern Theology* 12, no. 3 (July 1996): 269–99.
19. *Contra Celsum* 8.75, in *Origen: Contra Celsum*, trans. Henry Chadwick (Cambridge: Cambridge University Press, 1965), 510.

his disciples a heavenly *politeuma* (Phil. 3:20) that both qualifies their loyalty to any earthly order and calls forth eccentric acts of hospitality so that "every foreign country is their fatherland and every fatherland is a foreign country."[20] By its very quality as utterance, "the word of God is not chained" (2 Tim. 2:9); it is not bound by the logic of place. Indeed, it is "living and active, sharper than any two-edged sword, piercing until it divides soul from spirit, joints from marrow" (Heb. 4:12). It effects a "cut" in proprietary systems;[21] it ushers in the moment of *kairos*.

VII

The profoundly subversive character of the Logos can be seen in the accusations of sedition lodged against early Christians. This subversion is already seen in the threat posed to the purity of Israel by this "Israel of God," which had hopelessly polluted itself through its table fellowship with the uncircumcised. But it becomes no less subversive as Christianity moves out of its original Jewish setting and into the pagan world of the empire. Celsus characterized Jesus's saying "It is impossible for the same man to serve several masters" as "a rebellious utterance"[22] because it drew people away from the acts of piety towards the gods that were the *religio* that bound the city together. Such charges, often put in terms of Christian *odium humani generis*, can be found in numerous pagan writers.[23] These writers recognized that the city is not so much a collection of buildings as it is an ideological project; it is a complex matrix of signification that forms the world of its inhabitants. The ancient concern for civic piety was an

20. *Epistle to Diognetus* 5, in *The Apostolic Fathers*, trans. Kirsopp Lake (Cambridge, MA: Harvard University Press, 1950), 2:361.

21. See Certeau, "La rupture instauratrice," 112.

22. Cited in Origen, *Contra Celsum* 8.2. Cf. *Contra Celsum* 8.49 where Celsus characterizes Christians as "suffering from the disease of sedition."

23. See Robert Wilken, *The Christians as the Romans Saw Them* (New Haven: Yale University Press, 1984), 117–25.

attempt to guarantee the well-being of the city as an institution of meaning, and in this sense, it was as much "religious" as it was "political."[24] The unruly secondary production of the Christians' "consumption" of the city, their stubborn insistence on "using" the earthly city but not "enjoying" it,[25] posed a threat to the official production of the matrix of meaning.

The policing of such a matrix of meaning is not and can never be total. Certeau notes, "Things extra and other (details and excesses coming from elsewhere) insert themselves into the accepted framework, the imposed order. One thus has the very relationship between spatial practices and the constructed order. The surface of this order is everywhere punched and torn open by ellipses, drifts, and leaks of meaning: it is a sieve-order."[26] In other words, the world can be contested not simply by seeking to replace it with another world order but by exploiting the fissures within it, by seeking not control but faithful perseverance, by practicing within the pagan city an other city, in which the holy sites are not the temples of the gods but the graves of martyrs. A distinctive Christian practice carves out within the place of the city a new space.

Such contestation of space need not be dramatic. The *Epistle to Diognetus* notes that "the distinction between Christians and other men is neither in country nor in language nor in customs. For they do not dwell in cities in some place of their own, nor do they use any strange variety of dialect, nor practice an extraordinary kind of life." Yet the author goes on to note that while Christians follow local customs in such things as dress and food, they also display the distinctive characteristics of "the

24. "The whole structure of the Empire was indivisibly 'political' and 'religious.' The main purpose of the Imperial rule was usually defined as 'Philanthropy,' and often even as 'Salvation.' Accordingly, the Emperors were described as 'Saviours'" (Georges Florovsky, "Empire and Desert: Antinomies of Christian History," *The Greek Orthodox Theological Review* 3, no. 2 [1957]: 133–59, at 135).

25. On the distinction between "use" (*uti*) and "enjoyment" (*frui*), see Augustine, *De doctrina Christiana*, 1.22–35.

26. Certeau, *Practice*, 107.

constitution of their own citizenship [*politeias*]." The Christians do the same kinds of things as their neighbors, but differently: they marry and bear children, but they do not practice infanticide; they share their meals, but not their wives.[27] Through the practice of such deviations, the Christians do not simply establish and preserve their own enclave of purity, but they disperse themselves throughout the body politic so as to animate it with a new spirit.[28]

In this dispersion, this diaspora, the Church is, like its founder, without any place to lay its head. It walks. And, as Certeau notes, "the long poem of walking manipulates spatial organizations, no matter how panoptic they may be: it is neither foreign to them (it can take place only within them) nor in conformity with them (it does not receive its identity from them). It creates shadows and ambiguities within them."[29] Being "in Christ," membership in the *ekklesia*, is participation in his long poem of walking. As Hans Urs von Balthasar writes,

> Christ himself was "in motion": he was not at home anywhere on earth, he was a wandering rabbi without a home, without the den of the foxes or the nest of the bird, without a cushion to rest his head, without ever having the prospect of returning to his own home. Nor was his food a solid, supratemporal truth-system, but the will of the Father at each instant. . . . There exists no other form of "abiding" here than that of walking: "Anyone who says that he abides in him, must himself walk in the way that he walked" (1 John 2:6).[30]

---

27. *Epistle to Diognetus* 5.
28. *Epistle to Diognetus* 6.
29. Certeau, *Practice*, 101.
30. Hans Urs von Balthasar, *Razing the Bastions: On the Church in This Age*, trans. Brian McNeil, CRV, (San Francisco: Ignatius, 1993), 80–81.

VIII

But is this true? Does the Church in fact "walk," or has it become itself a "place," defined not by a practice effected within the place of the other but by buildings and structures and institutions? Has there been a "fall" of the Church from its early "tactical" mode of life into the "strategic" mode of Christendom? Have Christians lost their sense of homelessness?

To a certain extent, one must answer "yes" to all of these questions. At the twilight of the ancient world, Christianity was at first legalized and then made the official religion of the empire. Bishops came to take on the trappings of imperial officials; basilicas, formerly places of law and commerce, became places of ecclesiastical pageantry; Sunday became an official holiday, no longer a moment of time "poached" from the pagan work week. Christians came to be at home in the world. And even with the gradual undoing of the world of Christendom, that sense of being at home persists. There is no need to resist the city, for it is *our* city, its values are *our* values, its peace is *our* peace.

To this affirmation, however, one must add a series of qualifications. What takes place in the fourth century is not an absolute shift; a sense of homelessness persists down through the centuries. One can find in the fourth century a figure like Eusebius, who was a kind of cheerleader for imperial Christianity, but one also finds a figure like Augustine, one of the most profoundly "homeless" Christians of all time. One also finds a burgeoning of monasticism: "the desert was made a city by monks, who left their own people and registered themselves for citizenship in the heavens."[31] Though the roots of monasticism are extremely complex, and it was not simply a reaction against a Church too at home in the world, there is clearly an element of truth in Georges Florovsky's claim that "as in the pagan Empire the Church herself

31. Athanasius, *The Life and Affairs of Our Holy Father Antony* 14, in *Athanasius: The Life of Antony and the Letter to Marcellinus*, trans. Robert Gregg (New York: Paulist, 1980), 42–43.

was a kind of 'Resistance Movement,' *Monasticism was a permanent 'Resistance Movement' in the Christian Society.*"[32] Particularly
in the fourth and fifth centuries, monasticism provided a kind of
"wild" element in the Church, effecting tactical deviations within
what was increasingly becoming an ecclesiastical "place."

The fact that this was accomplished through an actual physical withdrawal into the wilderness and the creation of monastic institutions should make us cautious about reifying what was
said above about distinctions between place and space. Certeau's
attempt to sketch the logic of everyday practices is immensely
useful for showing how acts of resistance to the dominant order
do not depend on taking control of that order for their success.
And, as I have tried to show, it is very helpful in trying to understand certain aspects of Christian eschatological existence and the
perpetual homelessness of Christians. But, perhaps unintention-
ally, Certeau so valorizes tactical practices that any attempt by a
people to actually gain a place of their own, an island of relative
stability and security, can seem almost a betrayal. But perhaps
there is a need—at least in certain situations—for Christian places: institutions and structures that have a kind of permanence
and order, which occupy a place that is in some sense their own.
Christians need places precisely for the sake of resistance.

Johann Baptist Metz asked whether, in comparison with Judaism, the tendency toward interiorization and spiritualization
that Christianity has displayed, at least from the time of Paul,
has caused it to "manifest historically a shattering deficit of political resistance, and an extreme historical surplus of political accommodation and obedience?" Is it merely a historical accident
that the history of Judaism has more consistently been one of
persecution than that of Christianity, or does it have something
to do with the resistance offered to the proprietary powers by

---

32. Florovsky, "Empire and Desert," 150. Emphasis in the original.

the resolute particularity of Judaism: *this* law, *this* land?[33] Perhaps a danger of too "tactical" an account of Christianity is the presumption that the Gospel can flourish (and not simply endure) under *any* regime, in *any* land. Perhaps the Church needs to recognize that sometimes it must "withdraw to deserted places and pray" (Luke 5:16), that one must sometimes heed the call "Come out of her, my people" (Rev. 18:14; cf. 2 Cor. 6:17), that sometimes the very structures that define a place must be changed, or else that place must be abandoned. Likewise, a sacred place—a cathedral, a shrine, a monastery, a hospice, a homeless shelter, a soup kitchen, even a Vatican embassy—can be a locus of resistance to those forces that oppose the Gospel.

IX

In the sixteenth and seventeenth centuries, the Jesuit missionaries in the Province of Paraguay and the Guaraní people with whom they worked undertook a remarkable experiment in establishing a Christian place: the so-called "Jesuit Reductions." These were towns and cities into which the Jesuits had gathered the semi-nomadic Guaraní, both to make the task of evangelization easier and to protect them from the *Paulistas*, slave traders from São Paulo, and the *encomenderos*, the colonials in charge of day labor who treated the Indians as virtual slaves. The Reductions, at their height, were known as the Guaraní Republic and consisted of thirty cities, which numbered between two and four thousand Guaraní inhabitants, under the direction of two or three Jesuits. In the face of considerable pressure from colonial expansion, the Reductions persisted, and at times even flourished, for 160 years.

33. Johann Baptist Metz, "Christians and Jews After Auschwitz: Being a Meditation also on the End of Bourgeois Religion," in *The Emergent Church*, trans. Peter Mann (New York: Crossroad, 1986), 26. Cf. the comment of Boyarin: "The insistence on the value of bodily connection and embodied practice emblematic of Judaism since Paul thus has significant critical force over against the isolating and disembodying direction of western idealist philosophies" (*A Radical Jew*, 232).

Their economic base was a system of communal farming that, by all reports, was highly successful, and the cities became centers of culture and education. The death knell for the Reductions was sounded in 1750 by a treaty between Spain and Portugal that gave some of the land on which the cities stood to Portugal and required the Jesuits and the Guaraní to move to Spanish territory. The final blow came in 1767, when the Jesuit order was expelled from Spain and her colonies. The Reductions did not last long without their Jesuit protectors.[34]

In many ways the Reductions conform to what Certeau describes as the logic of place. The Guaraní, a semi-nomadic people whose lives had previously been made up largely of hunting and fishing, were gathered together, placed in a highly structured environment in which they were called to prayer and to work by a bell, taught trades and crafts, and instructed in the European religion of the Jesuits. Even the layout of the towns themselves was uniform and regimented, built around a plaza, at the head of which was the church—the only building in the city more than one story high—and the other official buildings of the city (the Jesuits' residence, classrooms, offices, storehouses, etc.). Around the other three sides of the plaza were the houses of the Guaraní, lined up in neat blocks. The Reductions seem highly artificial, not cities that grew out of the life of the people, but carefully planned "places." As one of the early Jesuit missionaries, Father Ruiz de Montoya (1585–1652), said, "the Indians, who in their old way of life once lived in open or hilly country, or in forests, and in clusters of up to five or six dwellings, have now by our efforts been brought into large settlements and, through the constant preaching of the gospel, transformed from country-dwellers to

---

34. For a brief account of the reductions, along with a record of their artistic achievements, see C.J. McNaspy, SJ, *Lost Cities of Paraguay: Art and Architecture of the Jesuit Reductions, 1607–1767* (Chicago: Loyola University Press, 1982).

Christian citizens."[35] The Reductions were a panopticon that Bentham might envy; they transformed an unruly band of nomads into a well-regulated and highly productive cadre of ersatz Europeans.

And yet, such a description is only part of the story. For the Reductions were designed not simply as a way to regulate the Guaraní but also to protect them from enslavement. This establishment of what seems so clearly a "place" by the proprietary power of the Jesuits is also an act of resistance against other proprietary powers: the *Paulistas* and *encomenderos*. One cannot presume, simply because the Jesuits who oversaw the Reductions and the slave traders who were the vanguard of colonial expansion can both be described as embodying the logic of place, that the places that they set up were therefore significantly the same. Perhaps there is more than one logic of place. Perhaps there are places, disciplines, laws, and sacred sites where human beings can flourish and live in harmony with each other and with God. Does Certeau too unreflectively adopt the modern presumption that structure and order and even supervision always inhibit freedom and can never enable it?

For there are places where it simply is not true that "sly as a fox and twice as quick: there are countless ways of 'making do'"[36]—places where, no matter how sly or quick, one simply cannot "make do," places that one must leave or die. And in this sense the Guaraní Republic was also a pilgrim city. Beginning with the "exodus" of 1631, in which Ruiz de Montoya led twelve thousand Guaraní on a thousand-mile journey to escape the advancing *Paulistas*, the Reductions were constantly relocating themselves. Yet this movement transported a "place," an ordered world, so as to preserve it. The Reductions could not simply "play

---

35. Antonio Ruiz de Montoya, SJ, *The Spiritual Conquest Accomplished by the Religious of the Society of Jesus in the Provinces of Paraguay, Paraná, Uruguay, and Tape*, trans. C.J. McNaspy, SJ, et al. (St. Louis, MO: The Institute of Jesuit Sources, 1993), 30.

36. Certeau, *Practice*, 29.

on and with a terrain imposed and organized by the law of a foreign power."[37] For when that foreign power took away their land and took away their Jesuit protectors, the Reductions could not endure. In this way, they proved as ephemeral as any tactic.

x

The homelessness of the Church is both a blessing and a curse. It is a curse if it allows Christianity a kind of adaptability that can too easily become accommodation. Rather than being the radical following of the messianic Son of Man who has no place to lay his head, Christianity has, in many cases, simply become a kind of otherworldliness that hands *this* world over to the governing powers of the prevailing regime, and such a handing over can be nothing but a betrayal of the Gospel. As Henri de Lubac warned, "There is a danger that an exaggerated or misdirected critique of what is freely labelled 'Constantinian Christianity'. . . may tend to restrict, and restrict dangerously, the Church's sphere of action."[38] If Christians abide by walking (1 John 2:6), then sometimes they must walk by abiding. In the culture of modernity, which seeks to "disembed" us from all traditions,[39] which turns us into portable units of consumption, it may be that sinking roots deep into the earth, cultivating a sense of place, refusing nomadic existence . . . these are the most profound forms of resistance.

Yet homelessness can also be a blessing, for it grows out of Jesus's proclamation of the gracious immediacy of God's presence. It is a blessing because it relieves the Church of any absolute need to defend a particular territory or structure, giving the Church a freedom to live the Gospel of peace. This peace is not, of course,

---

37. Certeau, 37.

38. Henri de Lubac, *The Splendour of the Church*, trans. Michael Mason (New York: Sheed & Ward, 1956), 125.

39. See Anthony Giddens, *The Consequences of Modernity* (Stanford, CA: Stanford University Press, 1990), 21–29.

simply an absence of conflict. Rather, it is a contestation of the earthly city, which measures itself by a different standard of effectiveness and yearns for the Sabbath rest of the eighth day. Homelessness is a blessing because it can give the Church hope in affliction, for the homeless presence of God is never tied to a specific place or condition but is with the Church even in exile. Indeed, it transforms exile into pilgrimage.

11

The Catholic
Intellectual Tradition

Medieval Lessons

Whatever else a tradition is, it is something that connects us to a past, and not simply to a past fondly remembered, but one that continues to inform our present. So, it seems not implausible that we might look to the past in order to gain insight into what it means to be engaged in the Catholic intellectual tradition today. And because Catholicism seems, for good or for ill, to have a particular connection to the Middle Ages—the "Age of Faith"—we might look to that particular past to see what lessons we can learn about what we mean when we speak of a Catholic intellectual tradition, about what challenges are posed to and posed by this tradition, and about how we foster and further this tradition. I will proceed by first making and exploring a distinction and then proposing some points for consideration.

Medieval scholastic thought proceeded largely by making distinctions. Thus it would warm the heart of our scholastic forbears if we begin with a distinction. I suggest we might distinguish between what we mean materially by the Catholic intellectual tradition, and what we mean formally. In other words, when

*This essay was originally published as "The Catholic Intellectual Tradition: Medieval Lessons," in *The Catholic Intellectual Tradition: Scholarship, Faith, and Higher Education*, ed. John J. O'Keefe, Gina Merys, and Bridget Keegan, Journal of Religion & Society Supplement Series 6 (2011), 10–21.

we speak "materially" about the Catholic intellectual tradition, we mean those texts, works of art, figures, concepts, and so forth that are indispensable in the preservation, transmission, and extension of that tradition. When we speak "formally" about the Catholic intellectual tradition, we mean not so much the content of the tradition but rather what we might call "the rules of engagement." It is not simply what we talk and think about that constitutes the Catholic intellectual tradition, but also how we talk and think about that content. Taking both of these aspects of tradition seriously means that tradition is not, as Edmund Burke would have had it, "wisdom without reflection,"[1] but rather an ongoing conversation that involves a self-reflective appropriation of the tradition.

THE CATHOLIC INTELLECTUAL TRADITION, MATERIALLY CONSIDERED

One way the conversation that is tradition differs from what we typically mean by "conversation" is its extension across time and inclusion of the voices of the past as well as the present. As G.K. Chesterton famously said, "Tradition means giving a vote to the most obscure of all classes, our ancestors. It is the democracy of the dead. Tradition refuses to submit to the small and arrogant oligarchy of those who merely happen to be walking about."[2] And in actual practice, particular traditions are about listening to particular voices from the past, not to the complete exclusion of others, but with a particular intensity. Put differently, every tradition has certain "canonical" figures, texts, and cultural monuments. I will admit to having a certain trepidation about even raising this issue, recalling as I do the "canon wars" of the 1980s and '90s, in which multiculturalists wielding volumes by Zora Neale Hurston

1. Edmund Burke, *Reflections on the Revolution in France* (Harmondsworth, GB: Penguin, 1982), 129.
2. G.K. Chesterton, *Orthodoxy* (New York: Doubleday, 2001), 45.

clashed with neo- and paleoconservatives shielding themselves with copies of Alan Bloom's *The Closing of the American Mind*. But it seems to me manifestly dishonest to deny the crucial role of some sort of canon in every intellectual tradition, and if we are going to have a Catholic intellectual tradition—that is, an ongoing conversation about truth that is identifiably Catholic—then we will need to have certain touchstones to which we can refer, certain indispensable voices from the past that will be a part of that conversation.

During the High Middle Ages—for our purposes the twelfth and thirteenth centuries—there was a rather restricted range of canonical texts that were employed in schools. Pretty much everywhere students studying the liberal arts would read Priscian and Donatus for grammar; Cicero, Aristotle, and Boethius for rhetoric; Aristotle's *Organon* for logic; Boethius' adaptation of Nicomachus of Gerasa for arithmetic; Euclid's *Elements* for geometry; Ptolemy's *Almagest* for astronomy; and Boethius' *Musica* for music; as well as, eventually, the *Ethics*, *Physics*, *Metaphysics*, and other works of Aristotle.[3] In the higher faculties, Gratian was read for canon law, the *Digest* of Justinian for civil law, Galen for medicine, and Peter Lombard as well as, of course, Sacred Scripture for theology. In addition to the texts studied in the curriculum, there were a host of other authoritative texts that were universally consulted within certain disciplines, particularly the works of Avicenna in medicine, a variety of Arabic commentators on Aristotle in the natural sciences and philosophy, and Augustine and Dionysius the Areopagite, among others, in theology.

This canon of authoritative texts was central to the entire intellectual enterprise of the High Middle Ages. It served as a shared foundation from which conversation could proceed and which would provide guideposts along the way. The invocation

---

3. See James A. Weisheipl, "The Structure of the Arts Faculty in the Medieval University," *British Journal of Educational Studies* 19, no. 3 (1971): 263–71.

of authorities was common in medieval forms of argumentation; indeed, almost all advanced studies proceeded by means of the presentation of authoritative texts, either in the form of texts that were lectured upon by masters or texts employed in the presentation of conflicts between authorities, about which masters and students joined in public disputations that attempted to reconcile or decide between those conflicting authorities. Many will be familiar with the use of authorities in theological and philosophical disputations, but this was no less common in the faculties of law and even medicine.[4] To our modern way of thinking, the disputing of authorities might seem to make sense in the context of legal education—indeed, the law school moot court of today is a unique survival of something like the medieval disputation—but it seems most peculiar, even pernicious, in the context of medical education. Should not the study of medicine, indeed of any natural science, be purely empirical? Was it not the argument from authority that had to be thrown off before we could have the advent of modern science? Do not the modern natural sciences, with their restless questioning of received wisdom, demonstrate to us precisely the dangers of a canon endowed with too much authority?

I think there is a certain truth to such criticisms of medieval scholastic thinking, and not only in the field of medicine. Indeed, it was only when the social barriers between the scholastic master with his logical acumen and the artisan or craftsman with his ad hoc empiricism and experimentalism—that is, the barrier between the liberal and the mechanical arts—began to be broken down that something like modern natural science could emerge.[5] At the same time, we ought not to view the scholastic thinkers

4. See G.R. Evans, *Law and Theology in the Middle Ages* (London: Routledge, 2002), chs. 10–11; Roger Kenneth French, *Medicine Before Science: The Rational and Learned Doctor From the Middle Ages to the Enlightenment* (Cambridge: Cambridge University Press, 2003), ch. 4.

5. See Edgar Zilsel, "The Sociological Roots of Science." *The American Journal of Sociology* 47, no. 4 (January 1942): 544–62.

of the Middle Ages as somehow naive in their use of authorities. Not only were they aware that arguments based on authority were the weakest sort of arguments, yielding mere probability and not true knowledge (*scientia*), but they also found in the disagreements among these authorities grist for the intellectual mills that were the universities.[6] In other words, it was in part the conflicts within the canon of authorities that made the tradition a living and self-reflective conversation. Though every age has its share of academic hacks who seek in canonical sources "wisdom without reflection," no one who has attended carefully to the subtlety with which the best scholastic thinkers make use of their canonical authorities would ever think that the Catholic intellectual tradition coming out of the Middle Ages was simply a matter of parroting prepackaged authorities.

Likewise, we ought not simply assume that modern science does not have its own authorities. Certainly, no scientist proves every claim by means of his or her own empirical investigation. Rather, there are people and institutions, particularly the scientific journal, that "authorize" what counts as trustworthy scientific knowledge. It is the nature of human knowledge in general that most of what we speak of as "knowing" we in fact take on trust. I see no reason, *prima facie*, to think that this is not also true in the natural sciences. Medieval discussion had the advantage of at least being explicit about the role played by authorities.

In the thirteenth century, a great deal of intellectual effort was spent not only on adjudicating conflicts within the canon of authorities but also on the question of the shape of the canon itself, particularly the question of to what degree, if at all, the works of Aristotle ought to be included in that canon. To many, Aristotle's works were far too "naturalistic" in their perspective, too disruptive of the Catholic Christian conversation that had been

6. E.g., Thomas Aquinas, *Summa theologiae* 1.1.8; for a discussion of Thomas's understanding and use of "authorities," see M.-D. Chenu, OP, *Toward Understanding Saint Thomas*, trans. A.-M. Landry, OP, and D. Hughes, OP (Chicago: Henry Regnery, 1964), 126–55.

proceeding for centuries with a rather large measure of success. To others, Aristotle presented valuable resources for thought, resources that were worth the intellectual effort required to resolve the difficulties raised for the Christian tradition. Indeed, we might see in the thirteenth century's struggle to assimilate the works of Aristotle a model of the attitude that a tradition might take toward the disturbing voice of an "outsider" and how that tradition is able to engage in a discerning way with that voice. It shows us how a tradition can be reshaped while still remaining recognizably the same tradition.[7]

The medieval struggle over the inclusion of Aristotle indicates that a "canon" need not be a rigidly fixed body of texts. Today only a few of the canonical texts of the medieval university would be considered required reading at most Catholic universities. We also have far more texts available to us, both texts from the past and newly produced texts. The Catholic intellectual tradition today is a living thing, and part of what makes it live is the ongoing conversation about its canon of authorities, a conversation concerning which touchstones of that tradition are necessary for the conversation to continue in such a way as to allow Catholics and others to draw upon the riches of that tradition without becoming mere "traditionalists," mired in the past, imbibing "wisdom without reflection."

What should be included in the canonical works of the Catholic intellectual tradition today? Certainly, this would include works by Catholic authors, both "classic" and contemporary: Augustine, Dante, Newman, Bonaventure, Thérèse of Lisieux, Galileo, Hopkins, Aquinas, Waugh, Mendel, Catherine of Siena, Dawson, Greene, Pascal, Rahner, Lemaître, O'Connor, and so forth. There is a sense in which the Catholic intellectual tradition is something that is, as they say, "caught" more than

---

7. See Alasdair MacIntyre, *Three Rival Versions of Moral Enquiry: Encyclopaedia, Genealogy, Tradition* (Notre Dame: University of Notre Dame Press, 1990), especially chs. 5–6.

"taught," and there is no better way to catch this than to read Catholic intellectuals. At the same time, if we take the Middle Ages as a starting point, it is apparent that there is no reason why the canonical texts need be Christian. Indeed, in the medieval arts curriculum, Boethius seems to be the only Christian author who has a significant presence. If we transpose this into our contemporary context, it would seem that the fostering of the Catholic intellectual tradition not only allows for, but even requires, truth to be sought wherever it might be found, in authors who hold the Christian faith, or another faith, or perhaps no faith at all. Medieval debates over the inclusion of Aristotle show us that the inclusion of disturbing voices, voices not easily—or perhaps ever—assimilated, is itself an element in the Catholic intellectual tradition. The question of how, if at all, Aristotle's "naturalism" (about which I shall say more below) could be reconciled with the Christian faith should find its echo today in questions of what Christians have to learn from Marx or Darwin or—dare I say it?—even Nietzsche. As important as those texts that nurture and support the Catholic faith are those that challenge and provoke it. The relevant question to ask about the text is not, "Is the author Catholic?" but rather, "Is this text of sufficient quality and influence that engagement with it will further our shared pursuit of the truth?"

THE CATHOLIC INTELLECTUAL TRADITION, FORMALLY CONSIDERED

The challenge posed by the texts of Aristotle to the medieval Christian tradition provides us an opportunity to think not only about the question of the material constitution of the Catholic intellectual tradition but also about its formal constitution. We might say that, in the thirteenth century, a major preoccupation was not simply whether to read Aristotle but how to read Aristotle.

The incorporation of any figure or text or cultural monument into an intellectual tradition is never so simple as its inclusion on a syllabus. And in the case of Aristotle in the Middle Ages, even inclusion on the syllabus was at times a perilous enterprise.

At the beginning of the twelfth century, the Latin West knew only two works by Aristotle, the *Categories* and *De Interpretatione*, in sixth-century translations by Boethius. By the middle of the century, Aristotle's other logical works had surfaced in translation. By the end of the century Latin translations of most of Aristotle's works were available, though intensive study of them did not really begin until the thirteenth century.[8] Thus in a relatively short span of time, a new comprehensive view of the world was introduced into the Latin West, a view of the world in some ways strikingly at odds with what is typically characterized as the "Augustinian" synthesis of Christianity and Platonism. As the texts of Aristotle began to be studied, often alongside Arabic commentaries on those texts, worries arose. In 1210 the teaching of Aristotle's works was forbidden at the University of Paris. This ban was reiterated five years later, with an exception made for the optional teaching of Aristotle's works on logic and his *Ethics*. In particular, Aristotle's *Metaphysics* and his works of natural philosophy were banned. Around the middle of the century the ban on lecturing on Aristotle at Paris began to be ignored, and in 1255 the Arts Faculty (what we today would call the undergraduate division of the university) proclaimed a new syllabus that required the teaching of all of Aristotle's works.[9] But even with the inclusion of Aristotle in the syllabus, the hard questions of *how* he was to be read within a Catholic intellectual tradition remained to be addressed.

As I have mentioned, the chief difficulty posed by Aristotle was what might be called the resolute "naturalism" of his

---

8. Bernard G. Dod, "Aristoteles latinus," in *The Cambridge History of Later Medieval Philosophy*, ed. Norman Kretzmann et al. (Cambridge: Cambridge University Press, 1982), 46–48.

9. Dod, "Aristoteles latinus," 70–72; Fernand van Steenberghen, *The Philosophical Movement in the Thirteenth Century* (New York: Thomas Nelson, 1955), 34–35.

philosophy. To Christian intellectuals who had long since expunged, or at least reined in, the heterodox emanationist elements in Neoplatonic metaphysics and transformed the forms of Plato into ideas existing in the mind of God, the works of Aristotle must have been jarring . . . and exhilarating. Rather than a descending coming-forth of beings from the One, Aristotle offered a God who was a "prime mover," eternally bringing things from potentiality to actuality. Rather than forms in a transcendent realm, Aristotle saw forms in things, tied up with, and in a sense perishing with, concrete material substances. His writings raised fundamental questions about the cogency of such central Christian doctrines as the creation of the world in time and the immortality of the soul. Moreover, Aristotle presented a strikingly different account of human knowing. Whereas Christianized Neoplatonism saw a certain connaturality between the human mind and God, such that things were known by means of a divine "illumination" of the mind, for Aristotle the natural object of the human mind was the *quidditas* (the "whatness") of material things. In place of the "wisdom" of Christian Neoplatonism, a wisdom that is a real reflection of Christ the Wisdom of God, Aristotle offered a "science" of material things, known purely through the natural light of reason.

This should give some idea of the sort of intellectual challenges posed by Aristotle to the Catholic intellectual tradition during the thirteenth century. All who took up these challenges sought to find a way to appropriate what was true and good in Aristotle into the Christian worldview while maintaining the integrity of that worldview. How this was done varied. At Paris, the Arts Faculty had several luminaries who are today sometimes referred to as the "Latin Averroists" (because of their tendency to read Aristotle through his Arabic interpreter Averroes) or "Radical Aristotelians." They dedicated themselves to understanding the text of Aristotle and his Arabic commentators without any reference to Christian revelation, while at the same time affirming the truth of Christian doctrine, even when it contradicted what Aristotle had demonstrated. This emphasis on the autonomy of philosophical inquiry led critics to accuse them of holding a "double truth" theory, by which something could be true philosophically and false theologically and vice versa. Most scholars today think that the term "double truth" is misleading, implying either dishonesty or a violation of the principle of noncontradiction yielding radical incoherence. Neither of these seems to be the case with those Radical Aristotelians whose texts have survived. But it does seem to be that case that thinkers such as Siger of Brabant and Boethius of Dacia held that something might be demonstratively proven according to the principles of Aristotelian natural philosophy and yet disproved by divine revelation, which trumps natural philosophy. In this scheme, philosophy is autonomous, even though its most securely demonstrated conclusions might be undercut by theology.[10]

On the other hand, the Franciscan theologian Bonaventure seemed quite unconcerned about the autonomy of philosophy. Indeed, philosophy, and all of the arts, both liberal and mechanical, can be "reduced" or "traced back" to theology by means of a Trinitarian exegesis of the natural world as a "text" for which Sacred Scripture is the interpretive key.[11] Bonaventure is happy to pillage Aristotle's works for whatever useful ideas are ready to hand, but the framework into which he fits them is the

10. John Wippel notes of Siger and Boethius, "their efforts to reconcile faith and reason, and at the same time, to protect the intrinsic integrity and autonomy of purely philosophical inquiry, end by paying a considerable price, i.e., by placing the certainty of purely philosophical inquiry at risk or in question when dealing with certain issues" (John Wippel, *Medieval Reactions to the Encounter Between Faith and Reason* [Milwaukee: Marquette University Press, 1995], 70). If Wippel's interpretation is correct, then the so-called Latin Averroists are not, as typically thought, rationalists but rather radical fideists.

11. See Bonaventure, *De reductione artium ad theologiam,* translated as "On Retracing the Arts to Theology," in The Works of Bonaventure, vol. 3, *Opuscula: Second Series,* trans. José de Vinck (Patterson: St. Anthony Guild, 1966), and *Itinerarium mentis in Deum,* translated as *The Journey of the Mind to God,* trans. Philotheus Boehner, OFM, with notes by Stephen F. Brown (Indianapolis: Hackett, 1993).

Augustinian framework of divine ideas, exemplary causality, and illumination. Thus, Joseph Ratzinger argued that while Bonaventure's thought, considered materially, is "eclectic Aristotelianism," considered formally it is Augustinian.[12] In this way, Bonaventure made much use of the content of Aristotle's philosophy, while denying that philosophy any autonomy, thereby subordinating it to divine revelation.

Thomas Aquinas took a somewhat different approach. Contrary to some popular views of Thomas, he, no less than Bonaventure, subordinated philosophical knowledge to divine revelation.[13] However, within this subordination, he sought as much as possible to give a real autonomy to philosophical thought by not simply using Aristotle as an ad hoc conceptual resource, in the way that Bonaventure did, but by adopting the way of thinking that he found in Aristotle's texts. As Alasdair MacIntyre puts it, Thomas became "a native speaker of two first languages, each with its own distinctive conceptual idiom," the one being the inherited Augustinian synthesis and the other being Aristotelianism.[14] In the case of Thomas, rather than a "retracing" of all mundane knowledge back to theology, he proposed an approach in which "grace does not destroy nature but perfects it."[15] Natural reason, which Thomas takes Aristotle's philosophy to be a good, though not perfect, exemplar of, can tell us certain truths about the natural world and even about God. However, it is ultimately inadequate for human fulfillment, which is only found in the vision of God's essence.[16] Even in this life (*in via*, as Thomas puts it), the truth we can know through our natural reason and the good we can do through our natural powers are partial and fragmentary.[17] And

12. Joseph Ratzinger, *The Theology of History in St. Bonaventure* (Chicago: Franciscan Herald, 1971), 129.
13. Van Steenberghen, *Philosophical Movement*, 73.
14. MacIntyre, *Three Rival Versions*, 114.
15. *Summa theologiae* 1.1.8.
16. *Summa theologiae* 1-2.3.8.
17. See *Summa theologiae* 1.12.12; 1-2.109.2.

yet, we can know truth and can do good. Though grace brings us to a more perfect realization of truth and goodness, it does not contradict the truth of our natural reason nor the goodness of our natural inclinations, at least to the degree that reason and will are not warped by sin. Grace perfects the powers that are latent in nature: the capacity to respond to grace and be perfected in transcending the limits of nature.

Thus, we can discern in the Middle Ages at least three possible approaches to how one thinks about the figures, texts, and cultural monuments that are the "matter" of the Catholic intellectual tradition. For the Radical Aristotelians, nontheological disciplines are strictly autonomous, operating by their own methods and reaching their own conclusions in a sphere separate from theological concerns. To use a modern term, for thinkers like Siger and Boethius of Dacia, the arts are characterized by "methodological atheism," or at least a methodology that needs no God but the God of the philosophers. For Bonaventure, one cannot really understand the subject matter of the Arts at all until one has located them within their theological framework. Particularly in our fallen human state, nature is a strange hieroglyph that remains opaque to understanding until one discovers the Rosetta Stone of Scripture. For Thomas Aquinas, unaided human reason, even in its fallen state, can discern some degree of truth, and thus the arts can proceed according to their own inherent intelligibility. But at the same time, reason must recognize its own limitations, acknowledging that the wisdom that is received through grace can not only show us a truth that transcends this world but can show us this world's truth with a perfected clarity.[18]

18. My delineation of these three approaches is perhaps best thought of along the lines of sociological "ideal types" rather than actual historical descriptions. While I believe them to give an accurate account of the general tendencies of thought in the figures to which they are attached, close attention to the texts of Boethius, Siger, Bonaventure, and Thomas will, of course, reveal far more complexity and nuance than I have represented here. Often, particularly in the case of Bonaventure and Thomas, the differences are more matters of an intellectual "style" than of doctrine. Thus, though to my knowledge he does not use the phrase itself, Bonaventure can plausibly be construed as affirming that grace perfects nature; similarly, Thomas holds, no less

SOME FURTHER POINTS FOR CONSIDERATION

Whether due to historical contingency or, as some would claim, its innate superiority, the approach of Thomas Aquinas has been favored by the Catholic intellectual tradition at least since the mid-nineteenth century.[19] In part, he has been lauded for his seemingly unique ability to defeat modern errors that were eroding not only faith but also the foundations of civil society. As Pope Leo XIII wrote in his 1879 encyclical *Aeterni Patris*, which commended Thomas as a philosophical resource for the Church confronting modernity, "single-handed, he victoriously combated the errors of former times, and supplied invincible arms to put those to rout which might in after-times spring up." But in addition to this more combative use of Thomas, Leo XIII also commends him for the harmonious relationship that he establishes between faith and reason: "clearly distinguishing, as is fitting, reason from faith, while happily associating the one with the other, he both preserved the rights and had regard for the dignity of each; so much so, indeed, that reason, borne on the wings of Thomas to its human height, can scarcely rise higher, while faith could scarcely expect more or stronger aids from reason than those which she has already obtained through Thomas."[20] If, in the immediate aftermath of the *Risorgimento* and the loss of the Papal States, Pope Leo saw Thomas chiefly as a weapon to beat back the flawed modern philosophies that had led so many people to hold God and his Church in such contempt, he did not ignore entirely the partial autonomy that Thomas granted to human reason.

As the Church in the second half of the twentieth century began to make its peace with the modern world, it was this latter

than Bonaventure, that human beings can only find ultimate fulfillment through the assent of faith to divine revelation. The difference is more one of relative emphasis.

19. Certainly, one factor in this favoring is the official approbation Thomas has received from the Church. See José Pereira, "Thomism and the Magisterium: From *Aeterni Patris* to *Veritatis splendor*," *Logos* 5, no. 3 (Summer 2002): 147–83.

20. Leo XIII, *Aeterni Patris* 18, August 4, 1879, vatican.va.

aspect of Thomas' thought that Catholic intellectuals came to value more. This can be seen in the Apostolic Letter *Lumen Ecclesiae*, which Pope Paul VI issued on the seventh centenary of Thomas' death in 1974:

> In the history of Christian thought, therefore, Thomas is regarded as a pioneer on the new road to be traveled thenceforth by all philosophers and scientists. The teaching in which he gave the prophetic answer of genius to the question of the new relation between faith and reason rests on a harmonization of the world's secularity with the radical demands of the Gospel. He thus avoided the unnatural tendency to despise the world and its values, while at the same time not betraying in any way the basic, inflexible principles governing the supernatural order.[21]

Paul VI sees Thomas embracing the world's "secularity"—a term that would have undoubtedly puzzled Thomas himself and horrified Leo XIII—without compromising the Gospel.

Thus, in the context of Catholics after the Second Vatican Council seeking to, as John XXIII put it, "throw open the windows of the Church," Thomas becomes something of a cipher for the new, harmonious relation of the Church and the modern world. His emphasis on the relative independence of nontheological intellectual pursuits allowed Catholic scholars to claim, and occasionally attain, a measure of respect in the secular academy. For if grace perfects and does not destroy nature, then "good Catholic scholarship" must first of all be good scholarship, just as "good Catholic art" must first of all be good art. Further, this approach has allowed Catholic intellectuals to be something other than theologians (which were, after all, rather rare in medieval universities), pursuing nontheological lines of inquiry into the

21. Paul VI, *Lumen Ecclesiae* 8, November 20, 1974, vatican.va.

nature that God has created, and that grace will perfect. Such scholarship does not deny the theological dimension, though it may not engage it directly. The Thomist approach has even allowed non-Catholics a place in the Catholic intellectual tradition by virtue of their engagement with the figures, texts, and cultural monuments that constitute the Catholic intellectual "canon," so long as that engagement recognizes its own limits with regard to the theological dimension.

And yet, in the years since the Second Vatican Council, we have perhaps seen among some Catholic intellectuals something of a revival of the Radical Aristotelian spirit: not primarily in a revival of interest in Aristotle, but rather in an insistence on the radical autonomy of purely rational inquiry. I suspect we can all think of those, in a variety of disciplines, who see any reference to a theological dimension of truth as undercutting the integrity of their scholarship, who associate faith with fideism and unreason. Like Siger of Brabant and Boethius of Dacia, some of these scholars are sincere Catholics, but also like Siger and Boethius they see their Catholic faith as something completely divorced from their intellectual pursuits. We might say that they are intellectuals who are Catholics rather than Catholic intellectuals. In some cases, the Catholic faith can even be perceived as a threat to their intellectual pursuits. For if secular truth is radically autonomous, then divine truth can only affect it by an act of sheer power, by which it cancels and overrides the truth arrived at by natural reason.

The approach of the Radical Aristotelians proved to be inadequate to the intellectual task of the thirteenth century, and I suspect their approach will prove inadequate today, at least if we want to develop and hand on the Catholic intellectual tradition. For this approach implicitly denies what I take to be the central conviction that underlies both what we include in our intellectual canon and how we read that canon: the belief that all truth is God's truth. There is not one set of criteria by which we ought to think about "natural" things and a second set of criteria by which we ought to think about "supernatural" things. Rather, there is a single, multi-voiced, ongoing conversation in which we together feel our way toward the criteria that will be adequate for this moment in the conversation, when the Catholic intellectual tradition faces these questions and can marshal these resources.

Yet there is perhaps a deeper difficulty that the Catholic intellectual tradition faces today. While some Catholic intellectuals might still concern themselves with the autonomy of reason and the threat of ecclesiastical impositions upon reason, much of the secular academy seems to have given up on reason, seeing it as at best a quaint Enlightenment notion and at worst a mask for the will to power.[22] "Reason" is increasingly seen as a strictly local phenomenon, entirely determined by language and culture. This might be seen as a good thing: if an insistence on the radical autonomy of purely rational inquiry is problematic for the Catholic intellectual tradition, then the secular dismantling of that autonomy might be greeted with joy. But the enemy of my enemy is not necessarily my friend. Catholics have a stake in reason and in the possibility of reasoned discourse across traditions. After all, we profess to believe that God is Logos, and that the Logos of God is somehow revealed in the order of the world, an order that our minds can grasp. The alternative to such faith in reason would seem to be the position that all disputes, intellectual and otherwise, are ultimately settled according to who has the most power. Thus, the Church, seen so long as the enemy of reason, now finds itself cast as the defender of reason against a certain strain of postmodern "irrationalism." This was a major emphasis in John Paul II's encyclical *Fides et Ratio* (1998) as well as Benedict XVI's now infamous "Regensberg Address" (2006)—a point that was almost

---

22. If Wippel is correct that the radical Aristotelian bifurcation of faith and reason ultimately issues in a fideism, then perhaps it should not surprise us if methodological atheism ends up in irrationalism.

entirely lost in the ensuing furor over what were seen as unflattering remarks about Islam.

So, the Catholic intellectual tradition stands poised between a rebirth of the Radical Aristotelian bifurcation of faith and reason, on the one hand, and the irrational erasure of reason, on the other. What path can lead us through? Perhaps the answer lies in a rediscovery of Thomas' approach to faith and reason, with its demarcation and balancing of nature and grace. Or perhaps it lies in a revival of the more prophetic spirit of Bonaventure; perhaps the proper response to a radical claim of the strict autonomy of secular knowledge is an equally radical claim of the unintelligibility of all things apart from divine revelation, the claim that faith in reason ultimately hangs on faith in revelation. It might be the case that the conversation that is the Catholic intellectual tradition will for our place and time turn out to be a conversation between the heirs of St. Bonaventure and the heirs of St. Thomas about how best to relate faith and reason, cult and culture. But what we must not do is to lose confidence in the Catholic intellectual tradition itself: in its ability to rise to new challenges, to help us see better and farther. Writing in the mid-twelfth century, John of Salisbury said:

> Our own generation enjoys the legacy bequeathed to it by that which preceded it. We frequently know more, not because we have moved ahead by our own natural ability, but because we are supported by the strength of others, and possess riches that we have inherited from our forefathers. Bernard of Chartres used to compare us to dwarfs perched on the shoulders of giants. He pointed out that we see more and farther than our predecessors, not because we have keener vision or greater height, but because we are lifted up and borne aloft on their gigantic shoulders.[23]

23. Quoted in Daniel D. McGarry, *The Metalogicon of John of Salisbury: A Twelfth-Century Defense of the Verbal and Logical Arts of the Trivium* (Berkeley: University of California Press, 1955), 167.

12

Startling Figures and Wingless Chickens

Flannery O'Connor's Postmodern Apologetic

The novelist with Christian concerns will find in modern life distortions which are repugnant to him, and his problem will be to make these appear as distortions to an audience which is used to seeing them as natural; and he may well be forced to take ever more violent means to get his vision across to this hostile audience. When you can assume that your audience holds the same beliefs you do, you can relax a little and use a more normal way of talking to it; when you have to assume that it does not, then you have to make your vision apparent by shock—to the hard of hearing you shout, and for the almost blind you draw large and startling figures.[1]

Anyone who has read any of Flannery O'Connor's fiction will have a sense of what she means by "large and startling figures": hermaphrodite circus freaks, prosthetic-stealing Bible salesmen, atheist prophets, and so forth. Likewise, readers will know how she seeks to "shock": sweet (or maybe not-so-sweet) grandmothers

---

* An earlier version of this essay was delivered as a lecture at the Catholic Information Center, Washington, DC, 2017 under the auspices of the Thomistic Institute.

    1. Flannery O'Connor, "The Fiction Writer and His Country," in *Flannery O'Connor: Collected Works*, ed. Sally Fitzgerald (New York: Library of America, 1988), 805–6.

are shot by serial killers; arrogant young sophisticates contract illnesses that confine them for life to their childhood homes; and respectable land-owning white ladies get themselves gored in the chest by someone else's bull (Wikipedia notes, presumably for the sake of students searching for the meaning of the story, "Some writers suggest that the bull symbolizes Christ").[2]

But O'Connor's reasons for populating her stories with such startling figures and such horrifying plot turns may not be so apparent. Many of her initial readers mistook her for a nihilistic misanthrope who crafted the most unappealing possible characters and gave them the most horrible outcomes in order to reflect her dim view of humanity. But, as O'Connor makes clear when speaking about her fiction, the large and startling figures are her attempt to speak as a Christian in a context in which we cannot presume a body of shared assumptions or a common commitment to unquestioned truths, even those of natural reason, from which arguments could be constructed. In other words, she felt that she lived in a culture in which the only way to convey the truth was via what she called the "shock" of narratives that subvert the presumptions of their readers so as to open up a new and unexpected kind of truth. This culture that O'Connor sought to address is what we today call "postmodernity," which already in the post-war 1950s and '60s was stirring into consciousness, and which O'Connor's sharp eye discerned. Despite the drastic cultural shifts of the past fifty years, O'Connor's writing retains its vitality and relevance in part because it speaks precisely to an intellectual culture that persists still in our day.

It is uncontroversial to say Mary Flannery O'Connor, born on the feast of the Annunciation in 1925, is one of the preeminent twentieth-century American writers. Prior to her death from lupus at the age of thirty-nine, she produced a small but finely

2. Wikipedia's "Greenleaf (short story)" entry, Wikimedia Foundation, last modified May 3, 2021, wikipedia.org.

honed body of fiction: two novels and two collections of short stories, one of which appeared only posthumously. Largely confined by her illness to her mother's house for the last thirteen years of her life, she was also a prodigious correspondent, whose letters are equal to her fiction in their literary value. But in addition to her literary achievement, she also suggests a way to offer a defense of the Christian faith in an age that rebels against the very idea of shared beliefs, even as it retains in fragmentary form values rooted in those beliefs.

APOLOGETICS ANCIENT AND MODERN
. . . AND POSTMODERN

First, let me make a few cursory remarks about the genre of "apologetics." The term itself, which in this context means "defense," crops up in early Christian writings, such as the First and Second *Apologies* of Justin Martyr in the second century, perhaps inspired by classical works such as Plato's *Apology*, which recounts Socrates's defense of his teachings in light of the charge that he was corrupting the youth of Athens. Faced with similar accusations, early Christian apologetics often took the form of simply recounting what Christians in fact believe and do—"you say we believe X when in fact we believe Y"—in an attempt to show that Christian belief and practice were not absurd or profane or subversive. Once Christianity became the dominant religion in the late ancient world, the need for such defenses seemed to diminish: no attack, no need for defense.

In the Middle Ages, we do find works that seek to defend Christian claims, particularly from the criticisms coming from Islam. Thomas Aquinas' *De rationibus fidei* would fit this description (though not, I would argue, his *Summa contra gentiles*, as is sometimes claimed, which is more an intra-Christian thought experiment in demarking the domains of natural reason and supernatural faith than it is a defense of Christianity). What many today would think of as apologetics—a defense of the Christian faith undertaken on purely rational grounds—does not really appear on the scene until the modern era. And this is because it is in the modern era that we begin to have increasingly widespread attacks on Christianity carried out in the name of reason. Beginning in the seventeenth century, apologetics becomes a kind of prelude to theology, establishing its rational credibility before proceeding to expound the faith.[3] Particularly after the mid-nineteenth century, this is often carried out in the name of Thomism, even though this is not how Thomas himself tended to go about doing theology. Indeed, such a project seems to share considerable similarity of approach to rationalist Enlightenment critics of Christianity, even though differing in its conclusions.[4]

Also in the nineteenth century, we see a different approach to apologetics emerging, one that reflects the Romantic reaction to the Enlightenment, what we might call the "second wave" of modernity, focused more on feeling and the yearnings of the human heart. The great Protestant progenitor of this approach is Friedrich Schleiermacher, whose *Speeches on Religion to Its Cultured Despisers* develops an approach of showing how "religion" (which is more akin to what people today would call "spirituality") answered human yearnings and further how Christianity was the highest expression of religion. In Catholic circles, this general approach did not really gain traction until the late nineteenth century, taking a form of dubious orthodoxy in such Catholic "Modernists" as the English Jesuit George Tyrell and a more orthodox form in the work of the French philosopher Maurice Blondel. For

3. It is perhaps an indication of the novelty of such an approach that Montaigne was spurred to write a mock "defense" of—which was in fact an all-out assault on—Raymond Sebond's *Natural Theology*. See *Essays* 2.12 in Michel de Montaigne, *The Complete Works: Essays, Travel Journal, Letters*, trans. Donald M. Frame (New York: Everyman, 2003), 386–556.

4. As an example, one might consult A.D. Tanquerey, *A Manual of Dogmatic Theology*, trans. Msgr. John J. Byrnes (New York: Desclee, 1959), of which the first part, running some 190 pages, consists of apologetic tracts intended to impart true certitude regarding the claims of religion, of Christ, and of the Church.

Blondel, there was a dynamism to human action that could only find fulfillment in revealed religion, in Christianity in particular, and the best defense of the Christian faith was not to be found in rationalist arguments for God's existence and the credibility of Christian claims but in showing how in every human heart there was a wellspring of desire that only Christianity could satisfy. This approach became known in some circles as "the way of immanence."[5]

Recently, Thomas Joseph White has argued that in the work of the French Jesuit Henri de Lubac we find a particular inflection of this way of immanence that focuses on the human yearning for unity. In his programmatic 1938 work, *Catholicism: The Social Sources of Dogma*, de Lubac presents the Catholic faith as answering to a universal human desire for the unity of the human race.

White points out that the claim that there is such a desire of unity gained credibility from the fact that de Lubac wrote at "a time when the West was overrun by urgent projects of social unity: fascism, communism, and nationalisms of various sorts."[6] That Catholicism was itself a project for social unity—indeed, *the* project for social unity—was a truth largely forgotten, even for Catholics. De Lubac writes:

> We are accused of being individualists even in spite of ourselves, by the logic of our faith, whereas in reality Catholicism is essentially social. It is social in the deepest sense of the word: not merely in its applications in the field of natural institutions but first and foremost in itself, in the heart of its mystery, in the essence of its dogma.[7]

5. See Maurice Blondel, "The Letter on Apologetics," in *Letter on Apologetics and History and Dogma*, trans. Dru and Illtyd Trethowan (London: Harvill, 1964).

6. Thomas Joseph White, "Catholicism in an Age of Discontent: The Need for Reason and Mystery in Catholic Apologetics," *First Things*, November 2016, firstthings.com.

7. Henri de Lubac, *Catholicism: Christ and the Common Destiny of Man*, trans. Lancelot C. Sheppard and Sr. Elizabeth Englund, OCD (San Francisco: Ignatius, 1988), 15.

De Lubac highlighted the communal nature of Catholicism to present the Church as a sign and cause of the unity of the human race. This approach, which White labels "inclusive triumphalism," found official expression at the Second Vatican Council, which taught that the Church was a "sacrament or instrumental sign of intimate union with God and of the unity of all humanity."[8]

White goes on to note, however, that such an approach faces new challenges today. As we move from the modern world—whether in its Enlightenment or Romantic mode—into what is widely described as the postmodern world, we can no longer assume that the human race is seeking unity. In his influential 1979 work, *The Postmodern Condition*, Jean-Francois Lyotard argued that the defining characteristic of postmodernity is what he calls "incredulity towards metanarratives," by which he means the attempt, whether grounded in universal reason or in universal feeling, to give a normative account of how the world is, of what is true and good and beautiful.[9] With a loss of faith in reason and the rise of identity politics, we face a situation in which projects of social unity are viewed with intense suspicion. Unity, it is thought, is inevitably bought at the price of particular identities and a constriction of individual freedom. We might think of the subtitle of the English translation of de Lubac's *Catholicism*: "Christ and the Common Destiny of Man." No doubt many today would see in that collective persona "man" not a salutary unity but an oppressive normativity that negates anyone who is not male or European or white or straight or cisgendered. In such a cultural situation, appeals to the human desire for unity are likely to fall on deaf ears or even be violently rejected. Whatever the truth of de Lubac's presentation of Catholicism as a communal phenomenon, it fails as an apologetic if it cannot be heard by Christianity's contemporary "cultured despisers."

8. Vatican Council II, *Lumen Gentium* 1, in *Decrees of the Ecumenical Councils*, ed. Norman Tanner (Washington: Georgetown University Press, 1990), 2:849.

9. See Essay 2 of this volume, "Aesthetics: The Theological Sublime."

Finally, White contrasts de Lubac's approach with that of the Swiss theologian Hans Urs von Balthasar.[10] Balthasar's theology focuses on the particularity of Christian revelation, found in the person of Jesus Christ. While not denying that the Church answers a universal longing for unity, Balthasar's apologetic strategy involves not arguing from that longing to the Christian faith but presenting Jesus as the one who awakens in us a sense of our own incompleteness by making present in highly particular form the universal fullness that is the divine life. Crucified love calls out to us and, in a sense, creates within us the space that it fills. White suggests that an adequate Catholic apologetic in our day involves a kind of dual strategy that incorporates the approaches of both de Lubac and von Balthasar, along with a healthy dose of Thomism, so that appeals to natural reason are not ruled out of bounds.

"WINGLESS CHICKENS"
O'CONNOR ON MODERNITY

Here I will not pursue further the particular strategy that White develops. Rather, I simply want to affirm that I find his account of where we now find ourselves fairly convincing in terms of defense of the Christian faith: appeals to the "common destiny of man" do not have much purchase and, indeed, repel many. Further, I would claim that this "postmodern condition" did not first emerge in the late 1970s, as it was being chronicled by Lyotard and others, but was a possibility latent within modernity itself and has been with us, at least incipiently, as long as modernity

---

10. It is worth noting that de Lubac and von Balthasar, who collaborated in founding the journal *Communio*, are often seen as kindred spirits, and contrasted with "progressive" theologians such as Karl Rahner, Edward Schillebeeckx, and others associated with the journal *Concilium*. White's presentation of de Lubac and von Balthasar as offering different apologetic approaches is a salutary reminder that theologians are often not easily sortable.

has. Flannery O'Connor discerned it during the 1950s. She wrote to a friend in 1955, "If you live today you breathe in nihilism."[11]

In another letter to the same friend, referring to something written in *The New Yorker*, she writes, "the moral sense has been bred out of certain sections of the population, like the wings have been bred off certain chickens to produce more white meat on them. This is a generation of wingless chickens, which I suppose is what Nietzsche meant when he said God was dead."[12] Our culture has bred its middlebrow intelligentsia not to attain a supernatural end, a common destiny for all people, but to be butchered for the market, and it is this denial of an end proper to human beings that constitutes the death of God. Despite what might seem like her dim view of such wingless chickens, these are precisely the ones for whom she is writing; as she says in yet another letter to the same friend, "My audience are the people who think God is dead."[13]

O'Connor was also prescient in seeing the consequences of having the moral sense bred out of human beings. Lacking faith, she writes, "we govern by tenderness." Our chief concern is not pursuit of the true or the good or the beautiful, but not giving offense, respecting difference, avoiding imposition. O'Connor is not, as some might think, opposed to tenderness. But she fears that what passes for tenderness is "a tenderness which, long since cut off from the person of Christ, is wrapped in theory. When tenderness is detached from the source of tenderness, its logical outcome is terror." Theoretical tenderness, respect for an abstract "other" and his or her or their abstract rights, can always absolve

11. O'Connor, "Letter to A," August 28, 1955, in *Collected Works*, 949. The correspondent identified as "A" in the published version of O'Connor's letters was later revealed to be Elizabeth Hester (1923–98). Hester, under O'Connor's influence, converted to Catholicism, though she left the Church after a few years, much to O'Connor's disappointment. Some of O'Connor's most probing theological discussions occur in her letters to Hester.

12. O'Connor, "Letter to A," July 20, 1955, in *Collected Works*, 942.

13. O'Connor, "Letter to A," August 2, 1955, in *Collected Works*, 943. Indeed, O'Connor herself identified with her audience; in the letter containing the "wingless chicken" remark, she described herself as "a Catholic peculiarly possessed of a modern consciousness."

us from showing tenderness to the particular other who stands before us, who can always be sacrificed for the sake of the theory: "It ends in forced labor camps and in the fumes of the gas chamber."[14] We need to think only of the destruction of life carried out in our own day in the name of justice and right, and even compassion, to come up with numerous examples of the kind of thing she had in mind.

O'Connor populates her fiction with precisely the kind of tender, wingless chickens who constitute her audience. She also populates it with rough and violent backwoods folks, who would be unlikely to ever read one of her books, but who believe in truth and goodness and beauty even when they are lying and being bad and acting ugly. These tough wild fowl serve as foils to their domesticated modern chicken cousins, revealing their captivity to the culture of ersatz tenderness. They do not typically embody true tenderness themselves; indeed, they are often quite wicked and cruel. O'Connor hated calls for Catholic authors to produce "positive novel[s] based on the Church's fight for social justice, or the liturgical revival, or life in the seminary."[15] She was much more interested in the encounter of wingless and wild chickens, in which their respective perversities are mutually revealing.

One such encounter can be found in her story "The Lame Shall Enter First." In this story, Sheppard, who is employed as City Recreational Director but who seems to see himself as something more like a combination of psychotherapist and social worker, seeks to save a juvenile delinquent named Rufus Johnson, whom he met while volunteering at the reformatory where Rufus was incarcerated. Sheppard had been impressed with Johnson's intelligence (measured by his 140 IQ), though he is dismayed that he would seek to explain his antisocial actions by saying, "Satan.... He has me in his power," and he seeks to release him from

14. O'Connor, "A Memoir of Mary Ann," in *Collected Works*, 830–31.
15. O'Connor, "The Catholic Novelist in the Protestant South," in *Collected Works*, 854.

such superstitions.[16] Sheppard is convinced that Rufus' problems stem not from Satan but from his club foot and his ill-fitting corrective boot, and that, given the proper attention, Rufus would blossom into a productive member of modern society, perhaps a scientist. In contrast, Sheppard has no such hope for his own ten-year-old son, Norton. "Johnson had a capacity for real response and had been deprived of everything from birth; Norton was average or below and had every advantage."[17] We see Norton through the eyes of Sheppard: "The boy's future was written on his face. He would be a banker. No, worse. He would operate a small loan company. All he wanted for the child was that he be good and unselfish and neither seemed likely."[18]

It emerges early in the story that Sheppard's wife, Norton's mother, had died a year before. Norton still dissolves into violent sobs at the thought of her, while Sheppard endures such displays "helpless and miserable, like a man lashed by some elemental force of nature."[19] Sheppard sees Norton's grief as just one more sign of his selfishness, his inability to feel anything for anyone other than himself. He sees himself, in contrast, both in his ability to master his grief and in his ability to see the objective superiority of Rufus Johnson to his own son, as embodying a kind of enlightened, dispassionate goodness. This does not escape Rufus' notice; after Sheppard brings Rufus to live in their home, Rufus comments to Norton, "God kid . . . how do you stand it?. . . He thinks he's Jesus Christ!"[20] As wicked as he is, Rufus is still outraged at Sheppard's pretensions.

Sheppard buys Rufus a telescope, a symbolic gesture indicative of his desire for Rufus to lift his gaze to the stars. O'Connor is no doubt thinking of how many a self-satisfied narrative

16. O'Connor, "The Lame Shall Enter First," in *Collected Works*, 600.
17. O'Connor, 599.
18. O'Connor, 595.
19. O'Connor, 597.
20. O'Connor, 609.

of modern progress associates humanity's first glimpse through the telescope with the collapse of the medieval worldview. Rufus professes to have no interest in the material heavens, noting that when he dies, he will go to hell. Sheppard responds to this with "gentle ridicule," noting that "nobody has given any reliable evidence that there is a hell." Norton, however, is only concerned that his mother might be there. Sheppard assures him, "Rufus is mistaken. Your mother isn't anywhere. She's not unhappy. She just isn't." When this only upsets Norton more, Sheppard tells him, "your mother's spirit lives on in other people and it'll live on in you if you're good and generous like she was."[21] Norton finds this reassurance utterly unconvincing. Sheppard eventually calls an end to the conversation, reflecting later that maybe talk about eternal reward and punishment wouldn't do Norton any harm: "Norton was not bright enough to be damaged much. . . . Heaven and hell were for the mediocre, and he was that if anything."[22]

Eventually, Rufus wears Sheppard down. He rejects the new corrective boot that Sheppard buys him, a sign of his rejection of the new and improved life that Sheppard wants to provide him. He continues his delinquent ways, and when the police bring him home one night, Sheppard tries to convince Rufus that he is not evil but only confused and trying to make up for his foot. This drives Rufus into a rage: "I lie and steal because I'm good at it! My foot don't have a thing to do with it! The lame shall enter first! The halt'll be gathered together. When I get ready to be saved, Jesus'll save me, not that lying stinking atheist." At this point Sheppard is broken. He assures himself, "I have nothing to reproach myself with . . . I did more for him than I did for my own child." As he says these words, "His heart constricted with a repulsion for himself so clear and intense that he gasped for breath. . . . His image of himself shriveled until everything

21. O'Connor, 611–12.
22. O'Connor, 613.

was black before him." As "a rush of agonizing love for the child rushed over him like a transfusion of life,"[23] overwhelmed with a desire to make his neglect up to Norton, he runs to his room, only to find that he has hanged himself in a search to find his mother beyond death's veil.

Beyond simply recounting the story, there is perhaps not a whole lot more to say. O'Connor is hardly holding up Rufus, the one Christian in the story, as an exemplary figure. Rather, he serves as a foil for Sheppard, bringing his flaws into relief. In a letter to Cecil Dawkins, she says that Sheppard is "the empty man who fills up his emptiness with good works," and admits that, unlike most of her characters, she doesn't like him all that much.[24] And in some ways Sheppard *is* a bit flat as a character. But perhaps this is because he embodies the one for whom goodness has been wholly reduced to a theory. When Norton tries to defend his father in the face of Rufus's criticisms, saying, "He's good. . . . He helps people," Rufus replies, "I don't care if he's good or not. He ain't *right!*"[25] Sheppard is one of those wingless chickens who seek to govern by tenderness, not truth. His tenderness, however, is wholly abstract. He turns Rufus, seemingly based solely on his score of 140 on an IQ test, into an ideal of the noble savage who needs only a bit of civilizing to make his native gifts blossom; Sheppard seems incapable of seeing the truth of the flesh-and-blood human being before him. This kind of blindness, this lack of moral sense, is even more at work when Sheppard looks at Norton; he cannot see the child grieving for his mother but only the disappointing offspring who fails to live up to his idea of what a son of his should be like. Sheppard's compassion is never for concrete flesh-and-blood human beings but only for abstractions, and he loses compassion for Rufus when he, by his repeated misdeeds, finally forces Sheppard to see him as something more than an abstraction.

23. O'Connor, 631–32.
24. O'Connor, "Letter to Cecil Dawkins," September 6, 1962, in *Collected Works*, 1174.
25. O'Connor, "The Lame Shall Enter First," in *Collected Works*, 604.

Sheppard is perhaps a bit of a caricature, an example so extreme that O'Connor can feel little sympathy for him, but there
are other exemplary modern people in O'Connor's writings for
whom she does evince more sympathy—the sullen Mary Grace in
"Revelation," the one-legged Hulga in "Good Country People,"
or poor Asbury in "The Enduring Chill." But while she may sym-
pathize, she never sentimentalizes; she never hides from us their
smug sense of superiority, though they may hide it from themselves. Yet despite the unsentimental gaze with which she views
them, O'Connor rarely forgets the truth that those wingless chickens who think God is dead, who live their lives as nodes of desire
caught up in a maelstrom of social and economic forces, whose
compassion quivers a hairsbreadth from genocide, are in fact created in the image and likeness of God and are called by their Creator
to eternal glory. The question is, how to overcome the blindness
that afflicts them? In a lecture, O'Connor contrasted the putative
"balance" found in a writer like Dante with the sensibility of our
age: "We live now in an age which doubts both fact and value,
which is swept this way and that by momentary convictions." In
such a context, ordinary beauty does not suffice: "There are ages
when it is possible to woo the reader; there are others when something more drastic is necessary."[26] Thus we return to the "large and
startling figures" with which we began.

O'CONNOR'S POSTMODERN APOLOGETICS

Let me offer some features of O'Connor's writing that, I would
argue, constitute her "postmodern apologetic" and what this
might suggest for how we make a defense of the Christian faith
in postmodernity.

First, as I have described, she saw her contemporary situation

---

26. O'Connor, "Some Aspects of the Grotesque in Southern Fiction," in *Collected Works*,
820.

with clear eyes, at least in some respects. She did not think that the world was filled with good-willed atheists who were Christian in everything but name and who were more or less on the lookout for divine grace. The effects of original sin are broad and deep, and when it is fallen human nature you are dealing with, grace only perfects nature by disrupting it. Jean Daniélou once wrote, "those who have seen farthest into human nature are all pessimists, like Augustine, Pascal, and Kierkegaard"[27]—and, we might add, O'Connor. The power of sin in the world is nothing new, but it does get inflected in particular ways in the contemporary West, and if you are going to make a defense of the Christian faith, it is a good idea to have some idea of who you are talking to. At the end of Christendom, we must confront the fact that we are not, as were the early Christian apologists, living among pagans, but rather among those who cling to deracinated shards of the Christian faith—ideas like equality and justice and compassion—that have become disconnected from the concrete truth of Jesus Christ. And these rootless abstractions can turn deadly. Julian, in "Everything That Rises Must Converge," seeks to teach his mother a lesson about racial justice and ends fleeing the guilt and sorrow that follows upon causing her to have a stroke; Asbury, in the "Enduring Chill," seeks to strike a blow for personal freedom and racial equality by drinking unpasteurized milk with the black workers on his mother's dairy farm, only to contract undulant fever. In some sense, frank paganism would be easier to deal with.

Second, O'Connor's pessimism is not restricted to the secular world. Those who bear the name Christian are also pretty immune to the gentle workings of God's grace, and they too require a sometimes-deadly whack in the head in order to get the message. As Alice Walker notes, "[O'Connor] perceived that not

27. Jean Daniélou, *The Lord of History: Reflections on the Inner Meaning of History*, trans. Nigel Abercrombie (Cleveland: Meridian, 1958), 342.

much has been learned by [Jesus's] death by crucifixion, and that it is only by his continual, repeated dying—touching one's own life in a direct, searing way—that the meaning of that original loss is pressed into the heart of the individual."[28] The Grandmother in "A Good Man is Hard to Find" can recognize her common humanity with the escaped convict known as the Misfit only when she is staring down the barrel of his gun in the moment before he shoots her; Mr. Head in "The Artificial Nigger" can only admit his depravity in abandoning his grandson in a strange city when confronted by a lawn jockey that somehow mysteriously represents the suffering both of Christ and of Black Americans; Ruby Turpin in "Revelation" must get hit in the head with a textbook entitled *Human Development* while in the doctor's waiting room before she begins to realize that her supposed virtues will not save her.

We might be tempted to think that O'Connor reserves her pessimism for Protestant Christians, who are the believers who feature most prominently in her stories. But Catholics are not exempt: the silly Catholic school girls in "A Temple of the Holy Ghost"—O'Connor's only story in which Catholics are the central characters—offer a good example of how someone can have all the right answers and still get things wrong. She noted to a friend, "It seems to be a fact that you have to suffer as much from the Church as for it."[29] As Augustine said, "Once you begin to follow [Christ] by conforming your life to [his] commandments, you will find many to contradict you, forbid you, or dissuade you, and some of these will be people calling themselves followers of Christ."[30]

Third, O'Connor suggests that in this particular moment, when we seek to defend Christianity from both its cultured

28. Alice Walker, "Beyond the Peacock: The Reconstruction of Flannery O'Connor," in *In Search of Our Mothers' Gardens: Womanist Prose* (New York: Harcourt, 2004), 55.

29. O'Connor, "Letter to A," July 20, 1955, 942.

30. Augustine, *Sermons* 96.4.

despisers and from the smug pretensions of Christians themselves, narrative becomes a particularly important genre. If we live in an age of abstractions, in which terms like "justice" and "equality" and "compassion" float free from any larger vision of the good, when we can love the other only in the abstract while overlooking the one who stands before us, then perhaps it is only the concrete particularity that narrative can render that can administer the shock needed to reground goodness in truth. Lyotard characterized postmodernity as "incredulity towards metanarratives." If this is the case, then we are in a situation in which we seek to speak to people who are blind and deaf to the grand story of creation and redemption. O'Connor does not suggest that we give up on that grand story, but that we create an opening for it by means of stories that are less grand but which contain within them the explosive potential to crack open postmodern complacency. Her own fiction, rooted in the concrete particularity of the mid-twentieth-century South, sought to open up, as she put it, "the possibility of reading a small history in a universal light."[31] Only such particularity can re-root the free-floating fragments of faith that still drift through the postmodern world: "Abstractions, formulas, laws will not do here. We have to have stories. It takes a story to make a story."[32]

This brings us back to Thomas Joseph White's suggestion that, in a world that finds appeals to unity and the universal at best incredible and at worst pernicious, a refocusing on the person of Jesus and the particularities of his story as this has been lived for two millennia in the Church may present the most credible apologetic option. O'Connor wrote, "Our response to life is different if we have been taught only a definition of faith than it is if we have trembled with Abraham as he held the knife over Isaac. Both of these kinds of knowledge are necessary, but in the last

31. O'Connor, "The Regional Writer," in *Collected Works*, 847.
32. O'Connor, "The Catholic Novelist in the Protestant South," in *Collected Works*, 858.

four or five centuries we in the Church have over-emphasized the abstract and consequently impoverished our imagination and our capacity for prophetic insight."[33] A recovery of such prophetic insight, and the capacity to convey it—to tell again the terrifying, disturbing, hilarious, large, and startling story of Jesus—may be our best hope.

Finally, O'Connor reminds us of the importance of hope. However pessimistic O'Connor may have been about both Christians and postmodern post-Christians, she was not, at the end of the day, a pessimist. The sheer violence displayed in many of her stories is a witness to how the disruptive grace of God could crash through any barrier human beings might erect. And we ought not forget just how funny O'Connor's stories are; her vision is, at the end of the day, comic and not tragic. And even though her pessimism did not stop at the gates of Rome, she still saw in the Church a resource for hope. Of course, this was a chastened hope, what I might call an "Augustinian" hope, that was rooted not in the goodness of individual Catholics but in Christ's promise and in the presence of holiness in the sacraments. She wrote in a letter to a friend, "I think the Church is the only thing that is going to make the terrible world we are coming to endurable; the only thing that makes the Church endurable is that it is somehow the body of Christ and that on this we are fed."[34]

O'Connor's convictions about the Church as Christ's body take perhaps their most powerful form in her story "A Temple of the Holy Ghost," in which two silly Catholic school girls, while visiting relatives, sneak into a freak show at the fair and see a hermaphrodite, who warns the audience not to laugh because God has made it this way. They recount this to their younger relative, whom they are visiting, and in the child's mind she imagines the freak, speaking as if at a revival meeting, proclaiming, "A temple

33. O'Connor, "Catholic Novelist," 859.
34. O'Connor, "Letter to A," July 20, 1955, 942.

of God is a holy thing. Amen. Amen. I am a temple of the Holy Ghost."[35] Later, taking the girls back to their boarding school, the child and her mother join them in the chapel for Benediction, and as the child looks at the host in the monstrance, she thinks of the hermaphrodite, the freak, the monster. Driving home, she looks at the setting sun, "a huge red ball like an elevated Host drenched in blood," which saturates the horizon with its redness.[36]

O'Connor wrote to a friend that "'A Temple of the Holy Ghost' all revolves around what is purity," which, she said, "strikes me as the most mysterious of the virtues."[37] The juxtaposition of the monstrous body of the hermaphrodite, put on display at the fair, and the Eucharistic Body of Christ displayed on the altar is certainly shocking (one reader from Boston wrote to inform O'Connor that she was herself a Catholic and she didn't know how anyone could even *have* such thoughts). But it suggests that, for O'Connor, the purity of the Church as the Body of Christ was not a matter of being a neat enclave with tightly policed borders but was the purity of the freak who is put on display to be mocked but also to bear witness through its shocking presence in the world and its acceptance of suffering.

Could it be that only some such shocking, freakish form of existence could draw the attention of a world satisfied with its own tenderness? Perhaps, even more than narrative, we need embodied lives of compassion, concrete acts of tenderness rooted in the truth of Christ and his sacrificial love, in order to shock and startle by making visible the folly of the cross. Maybe the best defense is found in giving offense.

---

35. O'Connor, "A Temple of the Holy Ghost," in *Collected Works*, 207.
36. O'Connor, "Holy Ghost," 209.
37. O'Connor, "Letter to A," November 25, 1955, in *Collected Works*, 970.

13

The Lamb of God in the Age of Mechanical Reproduction

PREFACE

As the religious or aesthetic pilgrim enters Sint-Baafs Cathedral in Ghent searching for the Van Eyck *Lamb of God* altarpiece,[1] it is possible to get confused. Looking in the Vijd chapel, for which the altarpiece was painted, one finds a full-scale reproduction, intended as a visual aid for those who want to give a lecture on the altarpiece before passing on to the real thing. I wonder how many people, not knowing that since 1986 the "real thing" has been housed in a special viewing room in the back of the cathedral, have taken the reproduction for the original and gone away disappointed, wondering what the big deal is about the painting. I wonder even more how many people have taken the reproduction for the original and gone away completely

---

* This essay was originally published as "The Lamb of God in the Age of Mechanical Reproduction," *Communio: International Catholic Review* 30, no. 4 (Winter 2003): 582–98. It should be noted that Van Eyck's altarpiece has since 2021 been relocated in a large chapel, though still encased in glass and detached from an altar.

1. Though I find intriguing Lotte Brand Philip's suggestion that Jan van Eyck was entirely responsible for the painted panels that we have today, while Hubert van Eyck carved the wooden and stone frame into which they were fitted, nothing in my argument hangs on determining who did what. Thus, when speaking of "Van Eyck" in relation to the altarpiece, one might read this as indicating either Jan or Hubert or both.

satisfied, having had their devotion—whether it be religious or aesthetic—stirred.

It is true that the original is incomparably more beautiful than the reproduction, and it is possible to be contemptuous of such touristic bumpkins, to sneer at their lack of spiritual or artistic sophistication, but perhaps we ought not do so. After all, is it really unsophisticated to expect an altarpiece to be located behind an altar in a chapel rather than in a museum-like space created in the back of the cathedral? At the very least, such a mistake, with a little help from Walter Benjamin's essay on "The Work of Art in the Age of Mechanical Reproduction," might prompt us to think about our notions of artistic "authenticity," the relationship of art to ritual, and, ultimately, about the fate of the Mystic Lamb in the long twilight of modernity. Put differently, what does it tell us about ourselves that we think it obvious that a fifteenth-century altarpiece ought to be housed behind two inches of bulletproof glass?

I

Benjamin's essay, first published in 1936, has become one of the canonical texts of cultural and literary studies. In it, he develops some theses that were foreshadowed by his Dadaist precursors regarding "the developmental tendencies of art under present conditions of production."[2] Like most of Benjamin's writing, the essay is allusive and ambiguous and does not submit itself easily to summary. His fundamental point—that the technology of mechanical reproduction has brought about a fundamental change in the nature of the work of art—is pursued along a number of different avenues, all leading back to the statement that he quotes from Paul Valéry at the beginning of the essay: "profound changes

2. Walter Benjamin, "The Work of Art in the Age of Mechanical Reproduction," in *Illuminations*, trans. Harry Zorn, ed. Hannah Arendt (London: Pimlico, 1999), 211–44, at 212.

are impending in the ancient craft of the Beautiful. . . . For the last twenty years neither matter nor space nor time has been what it was from time immemorial."[3]

For my own purposes I am less interested in what Benjamin has to say about the revolutionary impact of photography and film (which I think he overestimates) and more interested in his notion of the "aura" of the work of art, that aura's withering in the age of mechanical reproduction,[4] and in what he has to say about architecture as "the prototype of a work of art the reception of which is consummated by a collectivity in a state of distraction."[5] I do not, as Benjamin apparently did, think that reflection on these themes will offer a hedge against fascism or prove "useful for the formulation of revolutionary demands in the politics of art."[6] However, I will admit that my reflections are not without a certain political investment, though the *polis* of which I will end up speaking is that city that "has no need of sun or moon to shine on it, for the glory of God is its light, and its lamp is the Lamb" (Rev. 21:23).

II

Benjamin gathers under the term "aura" those elements in the work of art that are rooted in "its presence in time and space, its unique existence at the place where it happens to be,"[7] in short, those elements that constitute its "authenticity." Reflecting on various forms of reproducibility, Benjamin notes that the aura is precisely that which cannot be reproduced; it is what allows us to distinguish the original from the copy. In the case of manual

3. Paul Valéry, "The Conquest of Ubiquity" in *Aesthetics*, trans. Ralph Manheim (New York: Pantheon, 1964), 225. Quoted in Benjamin, "Work of Art," 211.
4. Benjamin, "Work of Art," 215.
5. Benjamin, 232.
6. Benjamin, 212.
7. Benjamin, 214.

reproduction, we sometimes call such reproductions "forgeries" and, no matter how painstakingly they are executed, they leave the authority of the original untouched. The presence of an excellent, hand-executed copy of the "Just Judges" panel of the Ghent Altarpiece has not led to any diminishing of interest in the location of the original panel, which disappeared in 1934. Why? While we ought not to underestimate the sheer impossibility of a modern artist reproducing Van Eyck's work because of changes in the way modern pigments are produced,[8] many of us are not so discerning, and we desire the original simply because the copy does not possess the aura and authority of the original. The copy of the "Just Judges" does not share with the rest of the altarpiece the duration of physical presence over time. It was not touched by the hand of Jan or Hubert van Eyck; it was not hidden from the iconoclasts in 1566 and again in 1578; it did not make the journey from Ghent to Brussels to Aachen to Berlin as the side panels changed hands over the years.

But, in Benjamin's estimate, it is precisely the aura that "withers" and "decays" in the face of mechanical reproduction. The original's stubborn spatial limitation is the condition for the possibility of distance, which Benjamin takes as essential to the original's aura. If one wishes to see the real *Lamb of God* altarpiece, one must occupy a certain, limited set of spatial coordinates. Reproducibility, however, takes what is distant and brings it close, makes it available. This is true in the relatively banal sense that one need not travel to Ghent to see the Van Eyck altarpiece but need only open an art history text or surf the web. Yet few would say that such reproductions in any way call into question the infinitely greater value of the original; they are without the aura on which the original clearly has a monopoly. Benjamin's point, however, is that technology has given us forms of art, such

8. This is the argument that Anita Albus convincingly sustains throughout her brilliant book *The Art of Arts: Rediscovering Painting* (Berkeley, CA: University of California Press, 2000).

as film and photography, that make it nonsensical to distinguish original from copy, works of which there *is* no original and thus art without an aura. No print of a Chaplin film has any more claim to authenticity than any other. One need not occupy any determinate set of spatial points in order to have an entirely "authentic" experience of *The Gold Rush* or *Modern Times*. And once authenticity becomes ubiquitous, one can no longer meaningfully distinguish between the authentic and the inauthentic. If everything is authentic, nothing is authentic. As Benjamin puts it, "To pry an object from its shell, to destroy its aura, is the mark of a perception whose 'sense of the universal equality of things' has increased to such a degree that it extracts it even from a unique object by means of reproduction."[9]

III

This crisis of aura is, in a sense, nothing new. Its roots lie in the notion of "art" itself, in the distinction between art objects and ritual objects. According to Benjamin, the work of art originates in cult, and it is from this "original use value" that the aura of the work of art derives.[10] It is during the Renaissance that a "secular cult of beauty" develops, which attempts to secure autonomy for the work of art by bestowing the aura of authenticity formerly bestowed by ritual. During the nineteenth century, under pressure from the advent of photography, the notion of art-for-art's-sake develops as what Benjamin calls "a theology of art."[11]

If art-for-art's-sake constitutes the modern "theology" of art, then Dada would be the village atheist, or perhaps Nietzsche's madman proclaiming the death of God. With a work like Marcel Duchamp's "Fountain" (1917)—a urinal that he bought, signed "R. Mutt," and entered in an exhibition—we have an

9. Benjamin, "Work of Art," 217.
10. Benjamin, 217.
11. Benjamin, 218.

all-out assault on the aura of the work of art. Duchamp and his so-called "ready-mades" pull back the aura's veil to reveal the work of art as in no sense autonomous, in no way dependent upon the formal qualities of the object or the creative skill with which it is executed. What makes an object "art" is its location in a museum or its association with a recognized artist. It is the museum that generates the aura, the name that secures authenticity. As Giorgio Agamben puts it:

> In front of the "ready-made,". . . in which the otherness of the formal-creative principle has been replaced by the alienation of the non-artistic object that is inserted by force into the sphere of art, critical judgement is, so to speak, immediately confronted with itself, or to be more precise, with its image in reverse: what it is supposed to trace back to non-art is already non-art on its own, and the critic's operation is limited to an ID check.[12]

One would think that the announcement that the emperor has no clothes would immediately dispel the aura, but it proves to be a durable creature. The cult of authenticity lives on and even Duchamp's "Fountain" can become an aura-saturated cult object. Having served its purpose, the original "Fountain" was lost or discarded, but in 1964 Duchamp authorized the Galleria Schwarz in Milan to produce a signed and numbered edition of his "ready-mades," including the now-lost "Fountain." In the proud announcement of their acquisition of one of the Schwartz ready-mades, the San Francisco Museum of Modern Art noted, "Each ready-made was refabricated by a highly exacting craftsperson to exactly replicate the original; the edition for each selection was limited to eight signed examples. The highly esteemed Arturo

12. Giorgio Agamben, *The Man Without Content*, trans. Georgia Albert (Stanford, CA: Stanford University Press, 1999), 50.

Schwarz edition of Fountain is the fourth full-scale version of the piece and the one that most closely approximates the lost original." But authorization is insufficient for authenticity in art; so the artist must be in some way involved. The San Francisco Museum of Modern Art announcement continues, "This is the only edition to be issued under the direct supervision of Duchamp at every stage of the project on the basis of a blueprint derived from photos of the lost original."[13]

Such an announcement is either a masterpiece of deadpan irony or reveals the power that notions of authenticity and craft retain so long as there remains an artist who possesses authority, an object that can be construed as "original" (even if that original is now lost), and money to be made from the combination of artist and object. Benjamin is correct to think that an art form such as film offers a more fundamental challenge to the artistic aura, and the possibility offered by digital technology of no degradation of quality from original print to copy raises this challenge to an even higher level. But the phenomenon of the "director's cut" of a film, which promises somehow a more original presentation of the director's artistic vision, one untainted by the commercially motivated meddling of the studio, perhaps shows that artistic authority and the original object can survive even digital technology.

Benjamin announced, "for the first time in world history, mechanical reproduction emancipates the work of art from its parasitical dependence on ritual."[14] Perhaps as a matter of principle, we should stop reading all sentences at the point where the phrase "for the first time in world history" appears, if only to save their authors from acute embarrassment. At least in this case, Benjamin's emancipation proclamation seems not to have taken effect. His announcement of the impending disenchantment of

13. The San Francisco Museum of Modern Art, acquisition announcement on their website, October 18, 2000. The announcement has now vanished from the museum website but can be retrieved at https://web.archive.org.

14. Benjamin, "Work of Art," 218.

the work of art, like all of modernity's announcements of disenchantment, has proved to be premature. No less than a prehistoric
cave painting or a medieval monstrance, the modern art object
remains a cultic object.

IV

However, Benjamin does point us to the interesting phenomenon
of the shift from ritual art to autonomous art. Whereas formerly the
work of art derived its aura from its ritual function in an ongoing
cultic tradition, with modernity there arrive forms of art that distance themselves and even break free from that cultic tradition to
varying degrees. In the case of European art, we are, of course, not
speaking of some generic "cultic tradition" but are speaking quite
specifically of the Christian tradition and its particular repertoire
of beliefs and narratives, images and institutions. It is these from
which European art emerges and which, in modernity, it abandons.
In pondering this shift, we might think in terms of the introduction of secular subject matter or the decline of the Church as the
principal patron of the arts. But perhaps the most vivid example is
the rise of the museum and the eclipse of the church building as
the paradigmatic site of the beautiful or, if not beauty, at least art.

The museum's beginning can be traced to the late medieval
collections of curios that wealthy and scholarly men kept in their
Wunderkammer. These collections were not limited to "art" but
contained all sorts of wonderful objects. For example, in 1576,
the *Wunderkammer* of Albert V of Bavaria contained not only 780
paintings but 2000 other items, including "an egg that a bishop
had found inside another egg, manna fallen from the sky during a
famine, a hydra, and a basilisk."[15] As Giorgio Agamben has noted,
what provided the glue that held these disparate collections together was a sense of the universe as cosmos; the *Wunderkammer* "was

15. Quoted in Agamben, *Man Without Content,* 29.

a sort of microcosm that reproduced, in its harmonious confusion, the animal, vegetable, and mineral macrocosm."[16] The collection of curiosities became intelligible because of its relationship with the cosmic whole.

However, the *Wunderkammer*'s offspring, the gallery and the museum, have no macrocosm in which they participate. To quote Agamben again, "art has now built its own world for itself."[17] In its autonomy, the museum possesses an almost sacramental efficacy, transubstantiating ordinary matter into art. The urinal is placed in the museum not because it is a wonder but in order to make it a wonder. The autonomous, aura-bestowing power of the gallery or museum reaches its apogee in a work like Yves Klein's 1958 Paris exhibit "The Void," which consisted simply of an empty, white-painted gallery.[18] The museum becomes the sacred space for the theology of art-for-art's-sake; it is the cosmos in which art can appear for its own sake as art. Indeed, the work of art is so entirely parasitic upon the museum that the object itself can be dispensed with. The apotheosis of artistic autonomy is the irrelevance of the crafted object.

In light of these reflections, one wonders about the decision in 1986 to move the *Lamb of God* altarpiece from the Vijd chapel, where it had stood off-and-on for over 500 years, to the museum-like space created in the cathedral's former baptistry. Lest one be tempted to cynically suppose that the altarpiece was isolated out of a desire to charge admission—a bargain, incidentally, at €2.50—I should note that there is evidence that, even in the fifteenth century, visitors were charged an entrance fee to the Vijd chapel.[19] And certainly, there were legitimate safety con-

---

16. Agamben, 30.

17. Agamben, 33.

18. See Klein's account of the exhibit's opening in *The Grove Book of Art Writing*, ed. Martin Gayford and Karen Wright (New York: Grove, 1998), 205–6.

19. Paul Coremans, *L'agneau mystique au laboratoire: Examen et traitment* (Antwerp, BE: De Sikkel, 1953), 14, cited in Lotte Brand Philip, *The Ghent Altarpiece and the Art of Jan van Eyck* (Princeton, NJ: Princeton University Press, 1971), 32.

cerns, a desire to protect one of the masterpieces of Flemish art, that would be sufficient to motivate the move. What is striking, however, is that the space into which the altarpiece was moved has the ambiance not of a chapel but of a gallery or museum. It is as if only such a setting can allow us to see the altarpiece as "art" rather than something else, such as decoration or architecture. As much as securing the altarpiece against theft or vandalism, its location also secures its aura as a work of art. It focuses on the artwork in all its autonomy, allowing us to contemplate it.

V

Benjamin links art to what he calls "contemplation" or the concentrated act of attention by which the viewer is "absorbed" by the work of art.[20] And certainly, the *Lamb of God*'s present location is one that facilitates absorption: the space is bare and there is no sound save the distant electronic mutter of the audio guides. If this were not sufficient to signal the artistic value of the work, the barrier of bulletproof glass creates precisely the "distance" that is at the heart of the artwork's aura. One can handle the reproduction in the Vijd chapel; one can open and close the wings and touch its surface. One can only encounter the original through a vision that is literally "through a glass, darkly," a vision that requires absorption.

Benjamin contrasts the concentration that characterizes our relationship to the work of art with the distraction that characterizes our relationship to architecture. He writes:

> Distraction and concentration form polar opposites which may be stated as follows: A man who concentrates before a work of art is absorbed by it. He enters into this work of art the way legend tells of the Chinese painter when he viewed

20. Benjamin, "Work of Art," 232.

his finished painting. In contrast, the distracted mass absorbs the work of art. This is most obvious with regard to buildings. Architecture has always represented the prototype of a work of art the reception of which is consummated by a collectivity in a state of distraction.[21]

Apart from a first viewing of a famous structure like St. Peter's or the Eiffel Tower, we do not normally contemplate buildings. Rather, we inhabit them; we use them. We absorb them not simply or even primarily through sight but also through touch and, as Benjamin notes, "tactile appropriation is accomplished not so much by attention as by habit."[22]

Benjamin's invocation of "habit" here is intriguing, not least because of the unstated connection between "habit" and "habitation." It is by dwelling in a structure that we acquire certain habits, even apart from conscious intention. I walk through my house in the dark without thinking, stepping around the obstacles that I habitually encounter. I instinctively open the correct drawer in the kitchen when looking for scissors. My habits guide me unfailingly so long as I remain distracted. But the minute I stop and think, "which of these drawers has the scissors in it?"—the minute I become aware of the room within which I am dwelling—I almost invariably choose the wrong one. The space of my house is "habitable" not simply because I dwell within it, but because by dwelling therein over time, I am formed and shaped in certain ways; I acquire certain habits.

But we need not restrict this to material structures; it is by dwelling over time within certain conceptual structures, certain narrative structures, certain institutional structures, that we acquire specific habits, specific patterns of behavior. And, like the physical structures in which we dwell, these conceptual and

21. Benjamin, 233.
22. Benjamin, 233.

institutional structures in which we dwell also normally operate on us in a distracted state; they form a kind of horizon against which we understand things but which we do not seek to understand itself. They, too, are habitable spaces.

VI

One thing that the moving of the altarpiece has accomplished has been to shift it definitively from the realm of architecture, which requires tactile appropriation through habitation, to the realm of the work of art, which requires visual appropriation through contemplation. Of course, this is simply the culmination of the long process by which *The Lamb of God* has become "art." If Lotte Brand Philip is correct in her hypothetical reconstruction of the original form of the altarpiece, the painted panels that we today think of as constituting it were in fact part of an elaborate architectural ensemble of painting and carving that Joos Vijd commissioned.[23] Whether or not Philip is correct in the specifics of her reconstruction, what is beyond doubt is that what Joos Vijd commissioned was not a "work of art" but part of a habitable space.

Though Jan van Eyck was famous for the portable paintings on oak panels that were the material precondition for the emergence of the autonomous work of art, the Ghent Altarpiece is not such a work. Of course, the work was executed with such skill that it immediately began to attract those who wished to see

---

23. Philip, *The Ghent Altarpiece*, 7–34. Philip proposes her reconstruction in part as a solution to the "Van Eyck problem"—i.e., what are the respective contributions of Jan and Hubert van Eyck to the altarpiece? Her solution is that Hubert was in fact the sculptor for the elaborate frame, which was largely destroyed in 1578 by troops billeted in the crypt of the church, while Jan did all of the painting. She also proposes her reconstruction as a solution to certain stylistic incongruities, particularly on the inside of the altarpiece, which have led some writers, such as Erwin Panofsky (see *Early Netherlandish Painting* [New York: Harper, 1971], 1:217–22), to question whether the altarpiece was originally conceived as a unified composition, or whether it was assembled out of disparate preexisting works (sort of a precursor to Duchamp's readymades). Philip's reconstruction is quite a detailed one. For a less detailed (and less conjectural) reconstruction of a possible frame, see Elisabeth Dhanens, *Hubert en Jan Van Eyck* (Antwerp BE: Mercatorfonds, 1980), 378.

this "wonder," but it was not yet "art." It was more akin to the curiosities collected in the *Wunderkammer*: a microcosmic concentration of the divinely ordered world.

One small indication of this is that when Jan van Eyck, returning from a diplomatic trip south to the Iberian Peninsula, decided to add Mediterranean trees and shrubs to the greenery on the lower register of the inside panels, he did so on what would have been the south side of the altarpiece as it was originally situated in the Vijd chapel.[24] This detail is now lost, since in its new location the orientation of the altarpiece has been reversed. Small loss, we might think. A tiny bit of artistic cleverness that most people would not have noticed anyway. But it is indicative of a larger loss: the loss of a connection between the world of the altarpiece and the larger world, which in the end is the loss of the altarpiece as part of a habitable place. And at the heart of this loss is the loss of the altar itself, or more precisely the loss of the Eucharistic action that takes place on the altar, which returns us to Benjamin's comments on art's "parasitic dependence on ritual."

In a deed registered in May of 1435, Joos Vijd and his wife established "to the glory of God, His Blessed Mother and all the saints . . . in perpetuity the office of a daily Mass for the salvation of their souls and those of their forbears, in the chapel and at the altar that they have caused to be erected at their own cost on the south side of the chapel."[25] Vijd did not commission a work of art but a ritual object, a Christian altar on which the Eucharistic sacrifice would be celebrated. As such it was to be beautiful, but it was not itself to be an object of contemplation. Rather, it was part of a space that, being inhabited over time, was to unobtrusively shape the habits of those within it. The true object of contemplation, the true artifact into which one was to be absorbed, was the Body of Christ, wrought by the priestly art upon the altar. Any

24. This detail is pointed out by Maurice B. McNamee, SJ, in *Vested Angels: Eucharistic Allusions in Early Netherlandish Paintings* (Leuven, BE: Peeters, 1998), 114–15.

25. Quoted in McNamee, *Vested Angels*, 103.

aura, any authenticity, that the altarpiece possessed was simply its reflection of the light cast by the true Lamb of God who takes away the sins of the world, Christ's Eucharistic body.

There is evidence that Joos Vijd's desire was for many years fulfilled, with the altarpiece fulfilling its liturgical function until the end of the eighteenth century when it was taken off to Paris by the French.[26] It is only when the altarpiece ceases to serve as a backdrop to the Eucharistic action and becomes an object of contemplation in its own right that it ceases to be architecture and becomes art. It ceases to be part of a place we dwell in and becomes something to look at.

VII

What, if anything, has been lost in this transition? One might perhaps think, as Adorno did in response to Benjamin, that there is still merit in the idea of autonomous art, that the work of art ought not be forever tainted with its origins in magic and ritual, that a properly dialectical understanding of the work of art and an attention to the technical processes of its production "brings it close to the state of freedom, of something that can be consciously produced and made."[27] From this perspective, nothing has been lost and much has been gained. In acquiring autonomy, the Van Eyck panels can be seen as the revolutionary advance in oil painting that they were. As something "consciously produced and made," the panels become what they ought always to have been, a testimony to the consummate skill of Van Eyck.

But why ought I be interested in the skill of Van Eyck? At best, the autonomous work of art tells me nothing about the world I inhabit. It is the invention of the artist, a world that I might inhabit for those few seconds or minutes that I contemplate it,

26. Dhanens, *Hubert en Jan Van Eyck*, 81.
27. Theodore Adorno, "Letter to Walter Benjamin," in *Aesthetics and Politics*, ed. Ronald Taylor (London: Verso, 1977), 121–22.

but which in the end I always leave for "reality." At worst, the autonomous work of art tells me that the world I inhabit is an abyss in which strong poets might create reality in which others must dwell. It tells me that there is no "reality." In either case, what is lost is the world as a habitable place, or at least the relation of art to the lives we actually live, the lives marked by the habits we acquire over time, in a state of distraction, through the daily rituals that constitute our lives.

Put differently, what is lost in the autonomous work of art is the politics of everyday life. This is what I think Benjamin was groping toward in his essay when he says that "the instant that the criterion of authenticity ceases to be applicable to artistic production, the total function of art is reversed. Instead of being based on ritual, it begins to be based on another practice—politics."[28] Benjamin is groping here because, while he recognizes that the autonomous work of art with its aura of authenticity is fundamentally apolitical and thus subject to fascist manipulation, he fails to see the sense in which ritual is not a separate practice from politics but rather is itself a form of politics.[29] Ritual is not the apolitical mystification of reality but the potential means by which we come to inhabit reality in a true and just manner. People are bound together in the world as a habitable space by patterns of action that are equally "ritual" and "political"; their habits are shaped over time by those repeated actions that write certain laws within them. Once we give up the illusion of the disenchanted work of art, freed from both ritual and authenticity by mechanical reproduction, we can see that the question facing us is not "ritual or politics?" but rather "which ritual?" and "which politics?"

28. Benjamin, "Work of Art," 218.
29. This is recognized by Thomas Aquinas when he classes *religio*, by which he means "offering service and ceremonial rites or worship to some superior nature that men call divine," as one of the virtues annexed to justice (*Summa theologiae* 2-2.80.1).

VIII

As I said earlier, in the case of European art in general and Van Eyck in particular, we are not speaking about some generic "cultic tradition" but specifically about Christianity and its beliefs and narratives, its images and institutions. These constitute the world inhabited by Van Eyck. They formed his habits, and it is this world that he seeks to render in the painted panels of the *Lamb of God* altarpiece. As rendered by Van Eyck, this world is above all a "Eucharistic" world, a world that has at its center the sacrificed Lamb of God. This is hardly a startling claim; many authors have noted the centrality of Eucharistic themes in the altarpiece, which is only to be expected, given its function.[30] However, if we see the altarpiece as part of a project to construct a habitable space, a ritual space, then we can extend this claim to say that the altarpiece forms the backdrop not only of the Eucharistic ritual but of a Eucharistic politics.

Perhaps what I mean by this can best be seen by looking at the painted panels themselves, focusing first on the interior panels. On the upper register [Image 1], we have a version of the traditional figures of the *Deësis*, an image more common in the East than the West, in which Christ the judge is flanked by Mary and John the Baptist, who plead for humanity. However, as several authors have argued, the upper register also carries overtones of another Eastern Christian theme: the cosmic or eternal liturgy that Christ celebrates to the praise and glory of God the Father. The cloth behind Christ's throne is figured with images of the mother pelican who pierces her breast to feed her young, a common medieval image for how Christ feeds his people with his Eucharistic body and blood. The angelic musicians on the doors [Image 2] minister at this liturgy, vested in splendid copes and dalmatics, traditional vestments for those assisting at the Mass. In contrast to the angels and their rich vesture, Adam and Eve

30. See, e.g., Philip, *Ghent Altarpiece*, passim, and McNamee, *Vested Angels*, 87–126.

stand scandalously naked on the far outer panels, seemingly in-
congruous interlopers in this heavenly scene. Panofsky calls them
"*ad hoc* additions,"[31] in keeping with his view of the altarpiece
as a not-very-artful assemblage of originally independent pieces.
But others have argued that they stand there as representatives of
redeemed humanity, ennobled and elevated to the heavenly realm
to share in the eternal liturgy.[32]

On the lower level [Images 1 and 2] we see another liturgy, an
earthly liturgy, which at the same time participates in the eternal
liturgy depicted above it by ordering the earth according to the
eternal pattern. The point around which this world is ordered
is the Lamb upon the altar, Christ, the celebrant of the eternal
liturgy, present on earth as the Eucharistic victim. Around this
altar kneel ministering angels in adoration, and streaming toward
the altar from the four points of the compass are the saints: patri-
archs, prophets, apostles, martyrs, confessors, and virgins. Further
out, on the door panels, are just judges and soldiers, hermits and
pilgrims. The multitudes gather in the verdant, park-like space of
the New Jerusalem. We have here a Christianized version of the
Old Testament theme of the pilgrimage of the nations. As the
prophet Micah presents this theme:

> In days to come the mountain of the Lord's house shall be
> established as the highest of the mountains, and shall be raised
> up above the hills. Peoples shall stream to it, and many na-
> tions shall come and say: "Come, let us go up to the mountain
> of the Lord, to the house of the God of Jacob; that he may
> teach us his ways and that we may walk in his paths." For out
> of Zion shall go forth instruction, and the word of the Lord
> from Jerusalem. He shall judge between many peoples, and
> shall arbitrate between strong nations far away; they shall beat

31. Panofsky, *Early Netherlandish*, 221.
32. McNamee, *Vested Angels*, 98–99.

their swords into plowshares, and their spears into pruning hooks; nation shall not lift up sword against nation, neither shall they learn war any more; but they shall all sit under their own vines and under their own fig trees, and no one shall make them afraid; for the mouth of the Lord of hosts has spoken (Mic. 4:1–4).

What Van Eyck depicts is what we might call the "Eucharistic Jerusalem": the nations on pilgrimage come to worship at the altar of the Lamb and to be judged by the liturgy's eternal celebrant, who orders them in peace. Its structure mirrors the heavenly scene depicted above it: Christ, surrounded by the angelic hosts and redeemed humanity.

In the foreground, the fountain of life flows out from the picture into the space of our world and, in the panel's original setting, would have appeared to flow out onto the center of the altar, where the Eucharistic ritual takes place. The painted panels, along with whatever architectural frame they were set in, would have served as a backdrop to the Eucharistic liturgy, supporting and reinforcing the ritual action while at the same time drawing their intelligibility from that action.

At the heart of this action is what we might call a form of reproduction that overcomes the anxiety of authenticity rooted in the dichotomy between archetype and copy. What Benjamin hopes technological advances in mechanical reproduction can accomplish is in fact accomplished by the Eucharistic *techne*, the liturgical craft. For Van Eyck, Joos Vijd, and countless others in their day (and now), the Eucharist is a representation of the saving death of the Lamb that, at the same time, without ceasing to be a representation, *is* the Lamb. In scholastic terminology, it is *signum et res*, both a sign and the thing signified. Through the work of the Spirit, who hovers at the top of the central panel, the Lamb is reproduced on countless altars through the instrument of human liturgical action, yet suffers no degradation save the self-willed abasement by which Christ becomes food and drink and habitation.

IX

But in what sense is this ritual also a politics? Again, Van Eyck's panels offer us a clue. The lower register shows a real world, painted in minute—some might say obsessive—detail. In comparing the *Lamb of God* to Grünewald's Isenheim Altarpiece, painted almost a hundred years later, Lotte Brand Philip writes, "The images of the Isenheim Altarpiece show the Heavenly Jerusalem as the vision of an enraptured mind. In a perfectly 'modern' way they depict religious truth as the experience of the human psyche but not as objective reality. This was the only form in which the great Apocalyptic idea could manifest itself once again in this rather late time. In the art of Van Eyck, however, reality and truth had still been one."[33] For Van Eyck, the Eucharistic Jerusalem is not simply a matter of personal vision but is a habitable space in this world.

It is habitable through the Eucharist's production of the very saints and virtues Van Eyck represents in his art. The poverty of the apostles, the purity of the virgins, the mercy of the just judges and righteous knights, the meekness of the hermits and pilgrims: all of these are concrete ways of inhabiting the New Jerusalem that he depicts.[34] What one modern critic, Craig Harbison, has called "strictly regulated religious and social groups" that led to a paradise "only accessible through the carefully mapped paths of traditional Church leaders and theologians"[35] would seem to Van Eyck and his contemporaries simply what Augustine called

33. Philip, *Ghent Altarpiece*, 220.

34. On the identification of the various groups in the lower registers with the Beatitudes, see Philip, 106, and Dhanens, *Hubert en Jan Van Eyck*, 103–6.

35. Craig Harbison, *Jan Van Eyck: The Play of Realism* (London: Reaktion, 1999), 195.

tranquilitas ordinis: the peace of order. Where the modern eye sees only strictly regulated social groups, the person who longs for Jerusalem sees diverse vocations, bearing in their own bodies and reproducing in their own ways the saving death of the Lamb. Where Harbison sees strict regulation by Church leaders, one who longs for Jerusalem sees a living tradition in which the past, present, and future overlap in the Eucharistic ritual of memory and hope.

But, of course, we who are Christians today cannot help but see with modern eyes, even as we long for the New Jerusalem. We cannot help but see the workings of human power and interest in the multitudes gathered to adore the Lamb. But the task of seeing the construction of the New Jerusalem as simultaneously a matter both of human historical processes and divine making is a labor that is not alien to Van Eyck himself. His art is one in which the angelic hierarchies have plunged into the very heart of the world. Indeed, the Lamb himself rules not from heaven but from the midst of the human world. Anita Albus suggests a parallel between Van Eyck's art and Nicholas of Cusa's philosophy, particularly in their ability to emphasize the role of human creativity without retreating from a fundamentally theological view of the world. Albus writes,

> the greatness of Van Eyck, like that of the philosopher, lies in the way in which this new view of humanity and the cosmos continues to accord with the basic religious ideas of the Middle Ages. The hierarchical order of the celestial and earthly spheres has been revoked, but everything in the sensory world is equidistant from the supersensory one; all things are therefore equally close to God.[36]

36. Albus, *Art of Arts*, 108.

Or, as Benjamin said in another well-known text, "every second of time was the straight gate through which the Messiah might enter."[37]

Van Eyck's *Lamb of God* is certainly an idealized depiction of the Eucharistic community. He was no doubt aware that those who gathered before the chapel altar would not be the examples of virtue that he depicted on the inside of the altarpiece. They were more likely to be like Joos Vijd, whom Van Eyck unflinchingly depicted on the outside of the altarpiece [Image 3] with a wart between his eyes: a man concerned enough about attaining the heavenly Jerusalem to endow a chapel but tied closely enough to the earthly city to have the considerable funds necessary to do so. The muted colors of the outside of the altarpiece, which is what would have been visible on most days, indicate the muted virtues of ordinary Christians. But the altarpiece also contains the promise, hinted in the Annunciation scene on the top of the outer doors, that behind the drab virtues of ordinary lives lie hidden the glorious virtues of the saints, and at their center, the Lamb who illumines them.

EPILOGUE

It would perhaps seem obvious that we no longer live in the world of Van Eyck. The medieval world and its ordered universe, its sacraments and magic, seem something past and gone. And if that is the case, it was necessary for *The Lamb of God* to leave its chapel. Ironically, in order to make *The Lamb of God* accessible, we had to put it behind bulletproof glass. By doing so, it becomes something we can understand: a work of art to be contemplated for a time while we clutch our audio guides like high-tech rosaries. Its

37. Benjamin, "Theses on the Philosophy of History," in *Illuminations*, 255.

current setting ensures that it will be protected and honored as the great work of art that it is.

And yet, is our world really no longer the world of Van Eyck? His world, as represented in his art, is one in which the past is never gone but is constantly borne into the future by ritual memory and hope. If the artwork is ultimately dependent upon the ritual, there is reason to hope; for the Eucharistic ritual is quite "portable." It is not tied to any particular sacred space, but itself makes space holy, makes memory and hope possible. Just as the vivid world of the heavenly Jerusalem lies behind the dimly colored doors of the altarpiece, awaiting the feast day when it will be revealed, perhaps too the doors of our world can be opened with the keys of memory and hope to reveal the city where the Lamb who was slain has already begun his reign.[38]

38. This essay began life as a lecture at the Hoger Instituut voor Wijsbegeerte at the Katholeike Universiteit Leuven. My thanks especially to Professor William Desmond for his invitation to give the lecture.

14

Masaccio's *Trinity*

Iconography, Spatial Construction, and Trinitarian Theology

INTRODUCTION

There is a view concerning what is wrong with the Trinitarian theology derived from Augustine, sometimes labeled "Western," that is nicely summed up by Catherine Mowry LaCugna in her book *God for Us*:

> The sharpened distinction between the triune God of salvation history and the Trinity of persons within God drastically transformed, under the influence of Augustine, the direction and substance of future Christian theology in the West. The doctrine of the Trinity gradually would be understood as the exposition of the relations of God *in se*, with scarce reference to God's acts in salvation history. After Augustine, in the period of scholasticism, the eternal, ontological relationships among Father, Son, and Holy Spirit would be viewed largely independently of the Incarnation and the sending of the Spirit. The divine processions—begetting of the Son, proceeding of the Spirit—would be understood as absolutely interior to

*A version of this unpublished essay was delivered as a lecture at the International Conference on Theological Aesthetics, Denver, CO, 2006.

God and explicated without reference to any reality "out-side" God.[1]

This view of what is wrong with Western Trinitarian theology is hardly peculiar to Lacugna. At least in Roman Catholic cir-cles, it finds its most influential modern proponent in Karl Rahner, who contrasts the "Latin" theology of the Trinity with the "biblical" or "Greek" approach.[2] For Rahner, "the basic Augustinian-Western conception" of the Trinity leads to "purely formal statements about the three divine persons" which "refer only to a Trinity which is absolutely locked within itself."[3] Rah-ner's solution to this locked-in Trinitarianism was encapsulated in his famous axiom "the 'economic' Trinity is the 'immanent' Trin-ity and the 'immanent' Trinity is the 'economic' Trinity."[4] That is to say, the relations of the persons *in se* ought not to be conceived as something apart from the persons active in salvation history.

In what follows, I want to use Masaccio's fresco of the Trinity in the church of Santa Maria Novella in Florence [Image 4] to argue that this putative separation of the immanent life of the Trinity from the economy of salvation in Western Trinitarian thought is a fiction. Masaccio's depiction of the Godhead in his *Trinity* is both thoroughly "Western" and a powerful presenta-tion of the Trinity as a mystery of salvation. Further, I want to argue that Masaccio's painting not only calls into question an unfortunate caricature of Latin Trinitarian theology but also, in its combination of the traditional Western iconographic scheme of the "throne of grace" with his innovative use of single point perspective, offers us insight into the Trinity as grounding the mystery of salvation.

1. Catherine Mowry LaCugna, *God for Us: The Trinity and Christian Life* (San Francisco: Harper, 1991), 81.
2. Karl Rahner, *The Trinity*, trans. Joseph Donceel (New York: Crossroad, 1997), 83–84.
3. Rahner, *Trinity*, 18.
4. Rahner, 22.

HISTORICAL CONSIDERATIONS

The fresco has had a somewhat complicated history, and certain questions about it and its painter are still debated. Tommaso di Ser Giovanni di Mone Cassai, nicknamed Masaccio or "sloppy Tom," was born in 1401.[5] We do not know with whom, if anyone, he studied art; the tradition that he was Masolino's pupil is almost surely wrong, since they joined the Company of St. Luke—the painter's confraternity—in the same year. He collaborated with Masolino on a number of projects, most famously the Brancacci Chapel in Florence. Masaccio had been active as a painter for only a few years when he died at the age of twenty-six or twenty-seven, shortly after leaving Florence for Rome, perhaps to collaborate with Masolino on another project. The greatest work that he executed by himself is undoubtedly the fresco that he painted in Santa Maria Novella.

The fresco was presumably commissioned by the donors who are depicted kneeling in the foreground. The fresco itself gives no clear indication of the identity of the donors.[6] It is not clear whether or not the fresco was associated with an altar (though most art historians think that it was) and, if it was, whether the altar was given by the same donors as the fresco.[7] With a bit of conjecture mixed in, here is a plausible history of the fresco: it was painted on the north wall of the church, probably in association with a marble slab denoting the place of burial of the donors and

5. For more on Masaccio's life (but not much more), see Diane Cole Ahl, introduction to *The Cambridge Companion to Masaccio*, ed. Diane Cole Ahl (Cambridge: Cambridge University Press, 2002), 3–5.

6. Rona Goffen argues for the donor being Domenico Lenzi, whom convent records indicate had a tomb slab near the fresco dated 1426. See her introduction to *Masaccio's "Trinity,"* ed. Rona Goffen (Cambridge: Cambridge University Press, 1998), 12–13.

7. Ursula Schlegel, "Observations on Masaccio's Trinity Fresco in Santa Maria Novella," *The Art Bulletin* 45, No. 1 (March 1963), 19–33; 19–25, in particular, argues for a freestanding altar. John Coolidge, "Further Observations on Masaccio's Trinity," *The Art Bulletin* 48, No. 3/4 (September-December 1966): 382–84, accepts Schlegel's argument and offers plausible arguments for the altar having been donated first, which means that Masaccio would have designed his fresco with the freestanding altar in mind. Charles Dempsey, "Masaccio's *Trinity*: Altarpiece or Tomb?" *The Art Bulletin* 54, no. 3 (September 1972): 279–81, argues that the altar was given later and Masaccio never conceived his fresco as in any sense an altarpiece.

possibly also an altar that stood free from the wall, under the aisle's arch. At some point, the altar was moved against the wall, destroying the marker for the tomb and covering over the bottom part of the fresco. In the mid-sixteenth century, Vasari, despite his high regard for the painting, covered over what remained of the fresco with another altarpiece during his redecoration of the church. In 1861 the upper part of the fresco was uncovered and moved to a place on the inner wall of the church's facade, suffering extensive damage in the process. Finally, in 1952 the art historian Ugo Procacci uncovered the bottom part of the fresco and moved the upper part back to its original location, where it is today.[8] It is only since 1952, then, that interpreters have had the fresco as a whole to work with. It is to the interpretation of this whole that I will now turn.

THE ICONOGRAPHY OF THE *TRINITY*

Iconographically, the central figures are, of course, the Trinitarian persons themselves. Masaccio's fresco contains as its central figure the so-called "throne of grace" or "mercy seat" image of the Trinity. More specifically, it contains what Sara Jane Pearman has called a "cruciform throne of grace," in which God the Father is depicted supporting the cross upon which hangs the Son, as the Holy Spirit, in the form of a dove, flies between them. She distinguishes this from the "*pietà* throne of grace," in which the Father holds the crucified body of Christ itself.[9] The cruciform throne of grace is an image, known only in the West, that first appears in the twelfth century, becomes very popular in the fourteenth century, declines in popularity in the sixteenth century, and virtually

---

8. For this history, see Goffen, *Masaccio's "Trinity,"* 12.

9. Sara Jane Pearman, "The Iconographic Development of the Cruciform Throne of Grace From the Twelfth to the Sixteenth Century" (Unpublished dissertation, Case Western Reserve University, 1974), 1–2.

disappears in the seventeenth century. In other words, it is a distinctly late-medieval, Western image.[10]

The earliest extant image using this iconography of the Trinity is found in a missal from Cambrai, dating from about 1120. In this missal, the cruciform throne of grace illustrates the *Te igitur* at the beginning of the canon of the Mass [Image 5]. Here we see a notably youthful God the Father holding the two arms of the Son's cross as the Holy Spirit flies between them, with one of the Spirit's wing tips touching the lips of the Father and the other touching the lips of the Son. The three figures are contained in a mandorla, which is in turn surrounded by the four Evangelists.

This early image suggests something about the origins of the cruciform throne of grace. Pearman argues that it was created by a combination of two images that were commonly found in missals on facing pages at the beginning of the canon of the Mass: one of Christ crucified and one of Christ in majesty, contained in a mandorla and surrounded by the four Evangelists.[11] By superimposing the image of the crucified upon the image of Christ in majesty, we end up with an image remarkably like the image from the Cambrai Missal, with the enthroned Father now taking the place of the exalted Christ, and the Spirit interposed between Father and Son. Pearman's thesis regarding the origins of the cruciform throne of grace becomes even more plausible when we further note that the Trinitarian image in the Cambrai Missal is located in the same place as the dual crucifixion-majesty images in other missals, at the beginning of the canon. Thus, we have in the throne of grace an image that combines abasement and exaltation so that the human suffering of Christ is located within the Trinitarian economy of salvation and, through the eternal Son's

10. For a catalogue of images, see Pearman, "Iconographic Development," Appendix 1.

11. Pearman, 14. Pearman quotes William Durandus's *Rationale Divinorum Officiorum*: "The Majesty of the Father and the image of the Crucified is painted in some books so that the priest saying the *Te igitur* sees—as it were in person—[Him] whom he invokes and addresses etc. and so that the passion, which is present in the heart is brought to the eyes" (38).

assumption of a human nature, in the eternal life of the triune God. We see the coincidence of the eternal serenity and peace of the persons of the Trinity with the historical event of Christ's suffering.

Masaccio's depiction of the cruciform throne of grace departs from the traditional pattern by having the Father standing rather than seated on a throne and having the eternal space defined by the "chapel" in which the persons stand rather than by the mandorla. But the same dialectic of majesty and abasement, eternity and history, is present. Eternal procession and historical mission coincide, giving visual expression to Thomas Aquinas' view that the sending of the Son and the Spirit in salvation history "includes the eternal procession, with the addition of a temporal effect."[12] Salvation history is nothing less than the eternal processions of the Son and Spirit "temporalized" within the tragic history of human sin. Furthermore, the volume and solidity that Masaccio gives to the persons of the Trinity, their "naturalism," make this coincidence of the eternal and temporal visually persuasive. His depiction of the crucified, which seems to be modeled on the famously realistic crucifix carved by Brunelleschi that was already present in the church of Santa Maria Novella,[13] resituates the story of the Man of Sorrows into the very heart of the triune God.

We do not typically associate Western Trinitarian theology with such images. If it is associated with any visual image, it is typically the "shield of faith" (*scutum fidei*) [Image 6]. This symbol seems to have arisen in the thirteenth century, perhaps out of reflection on Paul's remarks about the place of faith in the "whole armor of God" (Eph. 6). Commenting on this passage, Hugh of St. Cher explains how faith in the Trinity is like a shield: "faith is called a shield, because as the shield is one, and is a triangle,

12. *Summa theologiae* 1.43.3 ad 3.
13. On Masaccio's depiction of Christ compared to Brunelleschi's *Crucifix*, see Paul Joannides, *Masaccio and Masolino: A Complete Catalogue* (London: Phaidon, 1993), 366.

so is faith in the unity of substance and the trinity of persons."[14] Displaying the doctrine that each of the persons of the Trinity is identical with the divine nature but distinct from each other, it might seem that here we find summed up in picture form the "static" Western account of the inner life of the Trinity, disconnected from the economy of salvation. Of course, the *scutum fidei* is not really a picture but rather something more like a sentence diagram. It is not trying to capture a dynamic process but give us grammatical rules, telling us that everything truly said of God is truly said of each Trinitarian person, though the Father cannot be said to be the Son or the Spirit. As for the supposed divorce between this image and the economy of salvation, it is worth noting that in its earliest depictions, such as that found in the *Chronica majora* of Matthew Paris, the line connecting the name "Son" to the word "God" took the form of a cross.[15] But whether or not the *scutum fidei* can be justly charged with displaying the deficiencies of Western Trinitarianism, particularly the claims of LaCugna, Rahner, et al. about the "Western" emphasis on the immanent Trinity at the expense of the economic Trinity, the same charge cannot be plausibly leveled against the cruciform throne of grace in general, and Masaccio's use of it in particular, in which the cross is front and center.

In at least one respect, however, the throne of grace *does* express a distinctively Western theology of the Trinity, and this is with regard to the *filioque*. Though not universally the case, the cruciform throne of grace typically gives expression to the Western theology of the co-spiration of the Spirit by the Father and the Son, and of the Spirit as the bond of love between the Father and Son, by depicting the Spirit as flying between them. In

14. "*Fides dicitur scutum, quia sicut scutum unum est, et est triangulum, ita fide est de unitatye substantiae et trinitate personarum.*" Quoted in Michael Evans, "An Illustrated Fragment of Peraldus' *Summa* of Vice: Harleian MS 3244," *Journal of the Warburg and Courtauld Institutes* 45, no. 1 (1982): 14–68, at 24. Evans provides a brief account of the history of this image in the Middle Ages.

15. See Evans, "Illustrated Fragment," 22.

our very first example of the cruciform throne of grace from the Cambrai Missal [Image 5], the lips of the Father and Son are each touched by one of the tips of the Spirit's wings, symbolizing their common breathing forth of the Spirit. Likewise, Masaccio's fresco expresses this distinctively Western theology, with the dove of the Spirit visually linking the Father and the Son.

But the *filioque* too is viewed by many contemporary theologians as part of the degraded tradition of Western theology, which, as Catherine LaCugna puts it, obscures "the *proprium* of the Spirit by relegating the Spirit to an intradivine realm as the bond between Father and Son."[16] The *filioque*, on this account, is a species of speculation about the inner life of God, divorced from the economy of salvation, and it robs the Spirit of any distinctive role in that economy, its place taken by the scholastic notion of "created grace." LaCugna goes on to claim, not entirely accurately, that scholastic theology's designation of "passive spiration" as the "notion" by which the Spirit is known renders the Spirit "passive" because the Spirit has nothing of its own to do.[17]

But if we look at Masaccio's Spirit, we see something different. Rona Goffen notes that this is a heavily damaged part of the fresco, "so the Dove appears to be only a white silhouette." But, she continues,

If we look closely . . . and restore the image in the mind's eye, we see that Masaccio painted the Spirit not as a two-dimensional abstraction but as a powerfully volumetric form in space, a bird (probably based on observation of real

16. LaCugna, *God for Us*, 298.
17. Thomas Aquinas speaks of the "passive spiration" of the Spirit simply because the Spirit originates in being *breathed forth* (passive voice). It is true in terms of the Trinitarian "notions," by which we grasp the distinctness of the persons from each other, that the Spirit alone is distinguished by being wholly passive, since the Father is active (begetting and spirating) and the Son is both passive and active (being begotten and co-spirating). But to think that this identifies the Spirit as being characterized by idleness is to misunderstand the very specific and restricted role that such "notions" play in Trinitarian theology.

birds in flight) whose wings propel his downward motion and whose neck turns to suggest his responsiveness to the Son.[18]

The Spirit that Masaccio depicts as the bond between the Father and the Son is not "passive" but rather is the propulsive force in the sacrificial mission of the Son. It is as if the Spirit is the one who is impressing the image of the crucified Son upon our senses and, through our senses, upon our hearts. This depiction of the Spirit fits perfectly with Thomas Aquinas' understanding of the indwelling of the Spirit as the New Law of the Gospel.[19]

Let me make two further points regarding iconography. The first concerns the figures of the Virgin Mary and John the Evangelist. Though they were frequently included in Crucifixion scenes, their inclusion in the cruciform throne of grace, while not unheard of, is also not typical.[20] The effect of their inclusion is to heighten the connection between the eternal reality of the Trinity and the historical event of the cross. The figure of Mary is particularly striking. Though she stands at the foot of her Son's cross, she is not depicted as the typical *stabat mater*, the grief-stricken co-sufferer; if anything strikes us, it is her power and equanimity. Her face is turned toward us, not toward the cross, and her gaze locks onto ours. Her hand, in a gesture reminiscent of John the Baptist in traditional iconography, points us toward the crucified.

18. Goffen, Masaccio's "Trinity," 16.

19. *Summa theologiae* 1-2.106.1. One problem with modern interpreters of medieval theologians like Thomas is that they presume that everything that they have to say about the Trinity will be found neatly gathered together in a single comprehensive treatment. In the case of Thomas, for example, Questions 27–43 of the *Prima Pars* of the *Summa Theologiae* are treated as a "treatise" on the Trinity, when in fact one can only get a full sense of Thomas's understanding of the Trinity if one also examines, for example, what he has to say about law in the *Prima Secundae* or the gifts of the Spirit in the *Secunda Secundae*.

20. Pearman, "Iconographic Development," Appendix II (174), counts fifteen instances in which both saints are present, out of a total sample of 506 examples. The Virgin is present by herself in an additional 34 instances. Some examples from Tuscany include Luca di Tommé's *Crucifixion* (1366), which does not quite conform to the cruciform throne of grace model since the Father floats above the cross and is not supporting it, and Paolo di Giovanni Fei's *Trinity Altarpiece* (c. 1407). See Michael Mallory, "An Early Quattrocento Trinity," *Art Bulletin* 48, no. 1 (March 1966): 85–89.

Through this visual connection she serves as *mediatrix* between us and the divine persons who are depicted, replicating her role in salvation history.[21]

Masaccio's Mary is able to fix our gaze through her sheer imperiousness, and here we might see a connection between the fresco and the Dominican order that to this day occupies Santa Maria Novella and undoubtedly had a role in shaping the painting's iconography. As is perhaps fitting for a church operated by the Order of Preachers, Mary does not simply point out the Trinitarian mystery of the cross to us, but she commends this mystery to us for our emulation.[22] As Rona Goffen points out, this is the Mary of the wedding feast at Canna of Galilee (John 2:5): "Do whatever he tells you."[23] Mary is presented as, in a sense, the model Dominican, conforming to Thomas Aquinas' ideal of the religious life as "that form of active life in which someone, by preaching and teaching, delivers to others the fruits of contemplation."[24] She who "treasured all these things in her heart" (Luke 2:51; cf. 2:19) as she followed Christ even to his cross now shares her treasure with us. The eternal mystery of the triune life is extended into human history not simply by the missions of the Son and Spirit but also by the participation of the Church, exemplified by Mary, in the divine sending.

A final iconographical note: the lower third of the fresco is occupied by a "tomb" containing a skeleton with the inscription "I was once that which you are; and that which I am, you also shall be." This is the part of the fresco that was lost for nearly four hundred years, and in the years since it was uncovered it has occasioned considerable discussion as to its significance. Some

21. Dempsey, "Altarpiece or Tomb," 281.

22. On the significance of Christ as exemplar in Dominican theology, see Ulrich Horst, OP, "Christ, *Exemplum Ordinis Fratrum Praedicantium,* According to Saint Thomas Aquinas," in *Christ Among the Medieval Dominicans,* ed. Kent Emery, Jr., and Joseph P. Wawrykow (Notre Dame, IN: University of Notre Dame Press, 1998), 256–70.

23. Goffen, *Masaccio's "Trinity,"* 18.

24. *Summa theologiae* 3.40.1 ad 2.

have seen the skeleton as a kind of effigy marking the tomb of the donors.[25] Others, noting the inscription, have seen it as a sort of "Everyman" figure, reminding us of the common lot of mortals. Still others, pointing to the medieval legends of the cross being erected over Adam's grave, see it as the skeleton of Adam. This last possibility, of course, does not exclude the other two. Indeed, if we think of Paul's statement "as in Adam all die, so all will be made alive in Christ" (1 Cor. 15:22), then Adam *is* every man, woman, and child born into the mortal condition. But the identification of the skeleton as Adam, seen in light of Paul's statement, gives us another angle on the inscription: "I was once that which you are; and that which I am, you also shall be." For Christ *too* is Adam—the second Adam, "who became a life-giving spirit" (1 Cor. 15:45). Now the skeleton and its inscription are both a reminder of mortality and a promise of resurrection, for Christ, who was mortal as we are, now lives eternally in the Trinitarian life, and what he is—what we see depicted in the space above the tomb—we also shall be.

Thus, iconographically, Masaccio's *Trinity* offers us a tightly integrated Trinitarian theology, in which the triune mystery is presented not simply as a revealed "fact" about God but as encompassing both *theologia*—the eternal mutual indwelling of Father, Son, and Spirit—and *oikonomia*—the Father's sending of the Son and Spirit for us and for our salvation. The figures of Mary and John, the donors, and even the skeleton of Adam, serve iconographically to show the saving mystery of the eternal Trinity spreading forth into our human history. In creating this comprehensive visual theology of the Trinity, Masaccio draws on the theological resources of the Western Trinitarian tradition, resources that are sometimes rather cavalierly dismissed by theologians today.

25. Thus Dempsey, "Masaccio's *Trinity*," 280.

PERSPECTIVE, TIME, AND ETERNITY

While the iconography of Masaccio's *Trinity* draws creatively upon past traditions, it is not this iconographical creativity that has made it so celebrated. Rather, it is Masaccio's innovative use of perspective that continues to excite interest in the fresco. As Jane Andrews Aiken puts it,

> Masaccio's *Trinity* fresco has played a pivotal role in the history of art, both as a definitive example of early Renaissance linear perspective and as a kind of prophetic forerunner of the perspective method discussed nearly a decade later by Leon Battista Alberti. . . . The magnificent vault arching over the austere figures in Masaccio's fresco of the mid-1420's is an utterly convincing illusion of architectural form extending into space.[26]

In the final section of this essay, I wish to argue that Masaccio's use of perspective is not simply of art-historical interest, but, no less than the fresco's iconography, is of theological interest.

It is perhaps difficult to appreciate from pictures the fascinating and unsettling effect that Masaccio's *Trinity* has upon the viewer when seen *in situ*. The initial impression is of a real space seen through the pierced wall of the church. We seem to be looking into some sort of chapel in which the persons of the Trinity are located, along with Mary and John, who are slightly closer to us, and the kneeling donors poised on the frontier between our space and the space created by the painting [Image 7]. At the same time, the fresco is not simply a mechanical exercise in perspective construction or a simple attempt to trick the eye. As J.V. Field writes, "strongly illusionistic though the picture is,

26. Jane Andrews Aiken, "The Perspective Construction of Masaccio's *Trinity* Fresco and Medieval Astronomical Graphics," in Goffen, *Masaccio's "Trinity,"* 90.

Masaccio is a craftsman using a technique, not a mathematician displaying the scientific construction of a pictorial space."[27]

The technique that Masaccio used was single point perspective, learned from Brunelleschi, who used the principle of the convergence of orthogonals upon a central point of the horizon in order to produce three-dimensional architectural drawings of as yet unrealized spaces. It has been suggested that Brunelleschi derived this principle from the use of the planispheric astrolabe, an astronomic sighting device widely used in the Middle Ages, in which the bodies of the heavens are depicted as projected on the plane of the equator.[28] The metaphysical and cosmological implications of the use of principles derived from such an astronomic device in order to construct the visual space in which the persons of the Trinity are depicted were perhaps not lost on Masaccio. Richard Turner writes, "more than simply a continuation of the space of the church, the chapel in the fresco suggests another, celestial realm."[29] What better technique to construct a picture of the celestial realm projected upon a wall than that by which one maps the vault of heaven upon a flat disk? Masaccio's system of projection of spatial volume onto a flat surface, rather than being a simple triumph of rationalized mathematical construction, is something akin to alchemy. As Aiken notes, it "remained firmly linked to a traditional and highly suggestive religious interpretation of natural order in which mathematics functions as a bridge between concrete sensible reality and universal or divine truth."[30]

The naturalism of the fresco is therefore somewhat deceptive. The overall construction of the perspective is such that the depiction of the figures corresponds to the angle of view of a person of

27. J.V. Field, "Masaccio and Perspective in Italy in the Fifteenth Century," in *The Cambridge Companion to Masaccio*, 188.

28. On the astrolabe as a possible source for Brunelleschi's insights into perspective, see Aiken, "Perspective Construction," 96–103 and Field, "Masaccio and Perspective," 180.

29. A. Richard Turner, "Masaccio, Masolino, and the Brancacci Chapel Frescoes," in *The Art of Florence*, ed. John Daly and Constance Herndon (New York: Abbeville, 1988), 487.

30. Aiken, "Perspective Construction," 96.

average height standing under the arch of the aisle: one sees the skeleton in the bottom third of the fresco from above and the figures in the upper two-thirds from below.[31] But, in fact, while Mary and John are foreshortened to correspond with this angle of view, the persons of the Trinity are not. Indeed, rather than being foreshortened, God the Father seems to be pitched forward.[32] The crucified Jesus, on the other hand, is clearly seen from head on. Mary and John make sense in this space, but Jesus does not. The persons of the Trinity would seem to require a significantly higher viewing point in order for the angle of depiction to correspond with the angle of view. The result is that the divine figures, as one author puts it, "are not precisely locatable, appearing to hover indeterminately within the chapel."[33] In other words, Masaccio uses naturalism to indicate a realm that exceeds nature yet is not entirely discontinuous with it. From our earthbound perspective, we can see the transcendent "space" projected by the artist, but we cannot make everything square; to see the Trinity properly requires, in a quite literal sense, our "elevation."[34]

In our current state, we are bound to the earth and cannot see things from God's perspective. But, as the Letter to the Hebrews puts it, "we do see Jesus, who for a little while was made lower than the angels, now crowned with glory and honor because of the suffering of death, so that by the grace of God he might taste death for everyone" (Heb. 2:9).[35] Christ has passed through the veil, into the sanctuary not made with hands, the abode of the Trinity, yet in his incarnate nature, he remains in some sense "visible" to us,

31. See Schlegel, "Observations," 22. If there originally was an altar located under the arch, as some have speculated, then the priest celebrating Mass would have stood in the ideal position from which to view the fresco.

32. See Turner, "Brancacci Chapel," 486.

33. Joannides, *Masaccio and Masolino*, 365.

34. See Jonathan Goldberg, "Quatrocento Dematerialization: Some Paradoxes in a Conceptual Art," *The Journal of Aesthetics and Art Criticism* 35, no. 2 (Winter 1976): 154–68, esp. 154–57.

35. On some connection between Masaccio's fresco and the Letter to the Hebrews, see Rona Goffen, "Masaccio's *Trinity* and the Letter to Hebrews," in *Masaccio's "Trinity,"* 43–64.

offering us hope (Heb. 6:19–20; 10:19–22). Masaccio's *Trinity* conveys this sense of a temple not made with hands that is both accessible and inaccessible to us, something that is both a part of our world and in excess of it, something that is made available to us through Christ, the mediator of a new covenant (Heb. 12:24). Like the Letter to the Hebrews, Masaccio's fresco bids us to look "to Jesus the pioneer and perfecter of our faith" (Heb. 12:2).

Masaccio's innovations with regard to perspective give him a way in which to depict the transcendence of the eternal Trinity with regard to our space- and time-bound world while at the same time expressing Thomas Aquinas' conviction that the missions of the Son and Spirit are nothing other than their eternal processions joined to a temporal effect—that the temporal missions "include" the eternal processions. Far from positing an "immanent" life of God *in se*, that is, in Rahner's phrase, "locked within" and only extrinsically related to human history,[36] Masaccio's fresco depicts the Trinitarian life of God as simultaneously and seamlessly eternal and temporal. Masaccio gives visible form to the promise that just beyond the boundary of this world of time-bound mortality, there is the eternal life of love that is the unity-in-difference of the Father, Son, and Spirit—and that this eternal love is already dissolving that boundary, showing itself in Jesus crucified and drawing us into itself through the Spirit.

36. Rahner, *Trinity*, 18.

15

The Apocalypse of Peace

The chapel of the former St. John's Hospital in Brugge, Belgium, has been turned into a museum dedicated to the work of Hans Memling, the late fifteenth-century artist who is considered one of the greatest representatives of the so-called "Flemish Primitive" school of painting. The chapel is dominated by Memling's St. John Altarpiece, which he painted in 1479 to stand behind the altar of the very chapel where it is still located. In its central panel [Image 8], the triptych depicts the Virgin Mary and the child Jesus surrounded by saints engaged in "holy conversation." Kneeling on either side of Mary are St. Catherine of Alexandria, who is receiving a ring from the Christ child, and St. Barbara, who is engrossed in reading a book. John the Baptist and John the Evangelist, the two St. Johns from whom the hospital took its name, stand slightly behind and on the left and right, respectively, of Mary and the child. Mary is attended by two angels in liturgical vestments—one holds her book while the other plays a small organ—and two more who fly above her head holding a crown. This central panel conveys a sense of serenity and joy, a vision of the Church Triumphant eternally dwelling in peaceful communion.

Not so the side panels [Image 9], each of which is dedicated to one of the two St. Johns. The left panel records in gory detail

* This essay was originally published as "The Apocalypse of Peace," *The Sign of Peace: Journal of the Catholic Peace Fellowship* 1, no. 3 (All Saints Day 2002): 10–12.

the political murder of John the Baptist by Herod. In the background, we see Salome dancing before Herod, while in the foreground, we see John's decapitated body lying on the ground and the sword-wielding executioner placing John's head on a platter held by the oddly impassive Salome. The right panel shows us the vision of John the Evangelist, recorded in the book of Revelation. In the foreground, we see John on the island of Patmos, where he has been sent in exile. He looks up into a vision of the heavenly worship and sees the one seated on the throne and the Lamb, surrounded by the white-robed elders and the four living creatures. In the background, we see various scenes from the apocalypse: the four horsemen of war, famine, pestilence, and death; the woman clothed in the sun attacked by the dragon; and grotesque creatures and people fleeing in a futile search for shelter.

All three of these panels are painted in the same rich, vivid colors that are so characteristic of the Flemish art of the fifteenth century; as one walks into the chapel, one's eyes are irresistibly drawn to the altarpiece, which seems to glow with its own internal light source. The side panels, despite their darker themes, share the same brilliant colors as the central panel. The unity of the color scheme helps to make clear that the scenes of strife depicted in the side panels are in no way separable from the tranquil scene of holy conversation. Indeed, the peaceful repose of the saints is flanked by images of past conflict (John's execution) and conflict to come (the apocalyptic battle).

And as we begin to look more closely—which we must do, since medieval Flemish painting excels in the depiction of the minutest details—we begin to notice that the central panel itself is not free from conflict. Behind John the Baptist, we see the scene of his arrest and a depiction of John's body being burnt long after his death by the Roman emperor known as Julian the Apostate. In the distance behind John the Evangelist, we find a small depiction of him being boiled in oil in an unsuccessful attempt on his life. Then we notice that the large figure of John is holding a chalice with a snake in it, a traditional symbol of the Evangelist that reminds us of another attempt on his life by the high priest of Ephesus. Our attention shifts to the other saints and the symbols that surround them: Catherine with the wheel with which the emperor Maxentius first tried to kill her, and the sword with which she was finally beheaded; Barbara with the tower in which her father held her captive to prevent her from becoming a Christian.

As we study Memling's triptych, it becomes clear to us that the eternal peace of the Church Triumphant is hedged in on every side by the strife and conflict suffered by the Church Militant. The Baptist who stands serenely beside Mary is the same person whom we see violently executed by a foolish tyrant swayed by the dancing of a pretty girl. The Evangelist who sees the tranquil repose of the saints is the same person who saw the intensifying conflict suffered by the world as history strains toward its consummation. Catherine was broken on the wheel and Barbara was first imprisoned and then executed by her own father. The symbols of the saints remind us that, despite their peaceful repose, "These are they who have come out of the great ordeal; they have washed their robes and made them white in the blood of the Lamb" (Rev. 7:14).

Yet Memling's altarpiece also reminds us that even though Christ's kingdom is hedged by the violence suffered by his witnesses, that peaceable kingdom is in no way "contained" by violence. The sheer beauty of Memling's painted panels is an icon of the way in which the peace of Christ spills out into the world's conflicts through the lives of the saints. The scenes of John the Baptist's execution and the apocalyptic conflict seen by John the Evangelist reflect the colors of the sacred conversation. Conflict does not darken the scene of eternal peace; rather, it is eternal peace that illuminates the situations of conflict in which the witnesses of Christ refuse the violence of the world. The altar-piece's central scene of repose, and particularly the serenity of Mary's face, is the focal point from which radiates the illumination of saintly lives. The violence that frames this scene is transfigured into witness in the lives of the saints.

This transfiguration is most vividly enacted in interaction of the "inside" and the "outside" of the altarpiece. Normally, the altarpiece would have been closed, showing only the reverse side of the outer panels, which depict the four donors—two male and two female religious who were involved in the running of St. John's—each kneeling with their patron saints standing behind them [Image 10]. The outer doors are not simply a tribute to those who paid for the painting of the altarpiece. They also depict the link between the saints, represented by the patrons, and the everyday work of St. John's Hospital, represented by the donors. The colors here are much more somber, the radiance of the heavenly conversation muted by the sometimes-drab daily care of travelers, the poor, and the sick, to which the hospital was devoted. Yet on Sundays and feast days the doors would be opened, unveiling the true meaning of that daily work; it is the ongoing work of witnessing to the peace and communion of the heavenly city; it is a work whose drabness is transfigured by the communion between the Church on earth and the Church in heaven.

We see in the St. John Altarpiece an apocalypse—an unveiling—of peace. Peace is not something that we build by our own efforts and capacity for good will; peace is something that rushes toward us from God's infinite future; peace is something that arrives often in the distressing disguise of the suffering of Christ's witnesses, or the drab disguise of daily tasks of hospitality directed toward those who suffer. It is significant that this unveiling takes place on Sunday, the day of resurrection, for it is on this day that, as St. John Paul II put it, "every generation of believers hears the greeting of Christ, rich with the messianic gift of peace, won by his blood and offered with his Spirit: 'Peace be with you!'"[1] As the doors are opened with the arrival of the Lord's day, the vision of peace bursts upon us, not obliterating the history of suffering but transforming it into the beauty of witness.

In his book *Followers of Christ*, Johannes Baptist Metz point to the apocalyptic nature of the traditional religious vows of poverty, chastity, and obedience. These vows are unlivable for those whose perspective is shaped by profane time, time understood as a linear series of events stretching out endlessly before us. One might choose to live in poverty or chastity or obedience for a period of time, but when taken up for an entire lifetime they are an intolerable burden. Metz says that such vows are unlivable "if the time be not shortened" by the apocalyptic arrival of Christ's kingdom.[2] It is only the expectation of the immanent bursting forth of the kingdom that makes it possible for one to take up the freedom of these vows. As such, these vows become one of the signs of the "shortening" of time; they witness to the way in which the kingdom rushes toward us.

Much the same can be said about those who commit themselves to nonviolence. Seen within the perspective of profane time, nonviolence seems impossible. With infinite time stretching out before us, we may be able temporarily to resist the allure of violence, but eventually we must succumb to the very sensible logic of the world, a logic that says that it is only through recourse to violence that we can guarantee the security of all the things that we value. But disciples of Christ do not live within the perspective of profane time; they live within an apocalyptic time in which the peaceable kingdom of Christ hastens with infinite speed toward us. At every moment the doors are opening, showing that our drab little daily efforts at hospitality and nonviolence

1. John Paul II, *Dies Domini* 33, May 31, 1998, vatican.va.
2. Johannes Baptist Metz, *Followers of Christ: The Religious Life and the Church*, trans. Thomas Linton (New York: Paulist, 1978), 93.

contain within them all the splendor of Christ's kingdom of peace. Only such an apocalyptic perspective can sustain us in our commitment to nonviolence.

But how do we gain such a perspective? Again, Memling's St. John Altarpiece offers us an answer. It is by entering into "sacred conversation" with the saints gathered around their Lord that we learn to see in this apocalyptic way. The brothers and sisters who are depicted on the outside of the doors of the altarpiece do not kneel there alone; they are already accompanied by their patrons: James and Anthony, Agnes and Clare. And standing behind and between Agnes and Clare, not immediately visible, is the Lamb who is Christ, silently accompanying the brothers and sisters in their daily duties. It is in fellowship with the saints, and Christ to whom they point, that we begin to see from the apocalyptic perspective and the beauty of Christ illuminates our witness.

The exterior of the St. John Altarpiece only hints at the glories within, just as our refusal of violence only hints at the kingdom of peace for which we long. It sometimes seems as if the doors will never open to let the radiance of Christ shine upon our drab, suffering, violent world. But the opening comes, with a speed and a glory that surpasses all that we can imagine.

IMAGE GALLERY

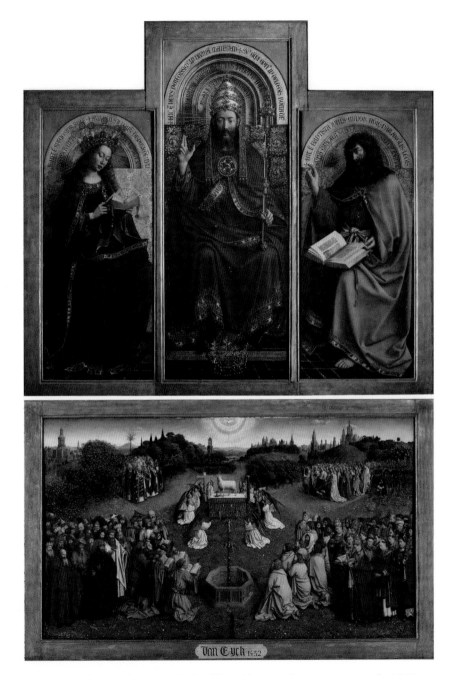

Image 1. Hubert and Jan van Eyck, *Ghent Altarpiece* (open, inner panel), 1432. Saint Bavo Cathedral, Ghent.

Image 2. Hubert and Jan van Eyck, *Ghent Altarpiece* (open, outer panels), 1432. Saint Bavo Cathedral, Ghent.

Image 3. Hubert and Jan van Eyck, *Ghent Altarpiece* (closed, after restoration), 1432. Saint Bavo Cathedral, Ghent.

Image 4. Masaccio, *Holy Trinity*, 1426–28. Basilica of Santa Maria Novella, Florence.

Image 5. Master of the Cambrai Missal, *Throne of Mercy: Miniature* in the *Cambrai Missal*, 1120.

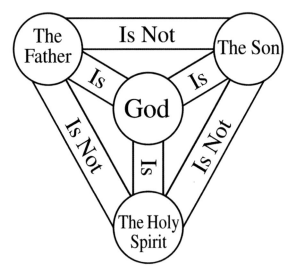

Image 6. Basic minimal (equilateral triangular) version of the "Shield of the Trinity" or "Scutum Fidei" diagram of traditional Christian symbolism, with translated English-language captions (in place of original Latin). Wikimedia Commons

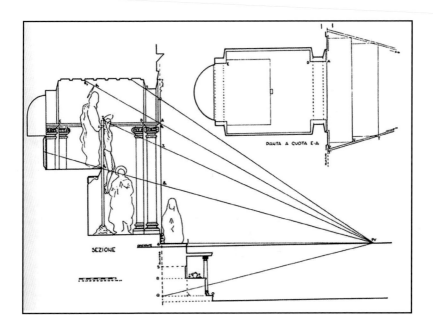

Image 7. Plan and elevation of Masaccio's *Trinity* as reconstructed by Piero Sanpaolesi.

Image 8. Hans Memling, *Saint John Altarpiece* (central panel), 1474–79.
Memlingmuseum, Sint-Janshospitaal, Bruges.

Image 9. Hans Memling, *Saint John Altarpiece* (interior sides), 1474–79.
Memlingmuseum, Sint-Janshospitaal, Bruges.

Image 10. Hans Memling, *Saint John Altarpiece* (exterior), 1474–79.
Memlingmuseum, Sint-Janshospitaal, Bruges.

BIBLIOGRAPHY

Adams, Marilyn McCord. *William Ockham.* Notre Dame: University of Notre Dame Press, 1987.

Adorno, Theodore. "Letter to Walter Benjamin." In *Aesthetics and Politics,* edited by Ronald Taylor, 121–22. London: Verso, 1977.

Agamben, Giorgio. *The Man Without Content.* Translated by Georgia Albert. Stanford, CA: Stanford University Press, 1999.

Ahl, Diane Cole. Introduction to *The Cambridge Companion to Masaccio,* edited by Diane Cole Ahl, 1–15. Cambridge: Cambridge University Press, 2002.

Aiken, Jane Andrews. "The Perspective Construction of Masaccio's *Trinity* Fresco and Medieval Astronomical Graphics." In *Masaccio's "Trinity,"* edited by Rona Goffen, 90–107. Cambridge: Cambridge University Press, 1998.

Albus, Anita. *The Art of Arts: Rediscovering Painting.* Berkeley, CA: University of California Press, 2000.

Al-Ghazālī, Abū Hâmid Muhammad ibn Muhammad. *Tahâfut al-falâsifa.* In *The Incoherence of the Philosophers,* translated by Michael E. Marmura. Provo, UT: Brigham Young University Press, 2000.

Alighieri, Dante. *The Divine Comedy: Paradiso.* In *The Portable Dante,* edited and translated by Mark Musa. New York: Penguin, 1995.

Anscombe, Elizabeth. "Modern Moral Philosophy." In *The Collected Philosophical Papers of G.E.M. Anscombe,* vol. 3, *Ethics, Religion and Politics,* 26–42. Oxford: Blackwell, 1981.

Aristotle. *Politics.* Translated by Benjamin Jowett. The Works of Aristotle, vol. 10. 2nd ed. Oxford: Clarendon, 1946.

Armstrong, Karen. *Visions of God: Four Medieval Mystics and Their Writings*. New York: Bantam, 1994.

Asad, Talal. "Anthropological Conceptions of Religion: Reflections on Geertz." *Man*, New Series 18, no. 2 (Summer 1983): 237–59.

Athanasius. *The Life and Affairs of Our Holy Father Antony*. In *Athanasius: The Life of Antony and the Letter to Marcellinus*, translated by Robert Gregg. New York: Paulist, 1980.

Augustine. *Christian Instruction; Admonition and Grace; The Christian Combat; Faith, Hope, and Charity*. Translated by John J. Gavigan, John Courtnay Murray, Robert P. Russell, Bernard M. Peebles. The Fathers of the Church 2. Washington, DC: The Catholic University of America Press, 1947.

———. *Concerning the City of God against the Pagans*. Translated by Henry Bettenson. London/New York: Penguin Classics, 2003.

———. *Homilies on the First Epistle of John*. In *Augustine: Later Works*, edited and translated by John Burnaby, 259–348. Philadelphia: Westminster, 1955.

———. *On Baptism: Against the Donatists*. Translated by J.R. King. Revised by Chester D. Hartranft. In Nicene and Post-Nicene Fathers, First Series, vol. 4, edited by Philip Schaff. Buffalo, NY: Christian Literature, 1887.

———. *Sermons*. Vol. 4. Edited by John E. Rotelle. Translated by Edmund Hill. Hyde Park, NY: New City, 1992.

Ayres, Lewis. "Augustine on God as Love and Love as God." *Pro Ecclesia* 5, no. 4 (Fall 1996): 470–87.

Balthasar, Hans Urs von. *The Glory of the Lord: A Theological Aesthetics*. Vol. 1, *Seeing the Form*. Translated by Erasmo Leiva-Merikakis. San Francisco: Ignatius, 1982.

———. *Love Alone is Credible*. Translated by D.C. Schindler. San Francisco: Ignatius, 2004.

Balthasar, Hans Urs von. *The Moment of Christian Witness.* 3rd ed. Translated by Richard Beckley. San Francisco: Ignatius, 1994.

———. *Mysterium Paschale.* Translated by Aidan Nichols. Edinburgh: T&T Clark, 1990.

———. *Razing the Bastions: On the Church in This Age.* Translated by Brian McNeil. San Francisco: Ignatius, 1993.

Barth, Karl. *Church Dogmatics.* Vol. 1.1, *The Doctrine of the Word of God.* 2nd ed. Translated by G.W. Bromiley. Edinburgh: T&T Clark, 1975.

Barth, Karl. *Church Dogmatics.* Vol. 1.2, *The Doctrine of the Word of God.* Translated by G.T. Thomson and Harold Knight. Edinburgh: T&T Clark, 1956.

———. *Church Dogmatics.* Vol. 2.2, *The Doctrine of God.* Translated by G.W. Bromiley et al. Edinburgh: T&T Clark, 1957.

Bauerschmidt, Frederick Christian. "Baptism in the Diaspora." In *On Baptism,* edited by Gerald W. Schlabach, 16–61. Kitchener, ON: Pandora, 2004.

———. "The Trinity." In *Gathered for the Journey: Moral Theology in Catholic Perspective,* edited by David Matzko McCarthy and M. Therese Lysaught, 68–87. Grand Rapids, MI: Eerdmans, 2007.

Baum, Gregory. "On the Modern World." *Commonweal* 83, no. 4 (October 29, 1965): 117–19.

Baumgarten, Eduard. *Max Weber, Werk und Person.* Tübingen: J.C.B. Mohr, 1964.

Baxter, Michael J. "'Blowing the Dynamite of the Church': Catholic Radicalism from a Catholic Radicalist Perspective." In *The Church as Counterculture,* edited by Michael L. Budde and Robert W. Brimlow, 195–212. Albany, NY: SUNY, 2000.

Benedict XVI. *Caritas in Veritate.* June 29, 2009. vatican.va.

Benjamin, Walter. "The Work of Art in the Age of Mechanical Reproduction." In *Illuminations*, edited by Hannah Arendt, translated by Harry Zorn, 211–44. London: Pimlico, 1999.

Blondel, Maurice. "The Letter on Apologetics." In *The Letter on Apologetics and History and Dogma*, translated by Alexander Dru and Illtyd Trethowan. London: Harvill, 1964.

Blumenburg, Hans. *The Legitimacy of the Modern Age*. Translated by Robert M. Wallace. Cambridge, MA: MIT Press, 1983.

Boff, Leonardo. *Trinity and Society*. Translated by Paul Burns. Maryknoll, NY: Orbis, 1988.

Bonaventure. *The Journey of the Mind to God*. Translated by Philotheus Boehner. Indianapolis: Hackett, 1993.

———. "On Retracing the Arts to Theology." In The Works of Bonaventure, vol. 3, *Opuscula: Second Series*, translated by José de Vinck. Patterson: St. Anthony Guild, 1966.

Bossy, John. *Christianity in the West: 1400–1700*. Oxford: Oxford University Press, 1985.

Bouyer, Louis. *Liturgical Piety*. Notre Dame, IN: University of Notre Dame Press, 1955.

Boyarin, Daniel. *A Radical Jew: Paul and the Politics of Identity*. Berkeley: University of California Press, 1994.

Boyle, Leonard E. *The Setting of the* Summa theologiae *of St. Thomas*. Toronto: Pontifical Institute of Medieval Studies, 1982.

Brown, Peter. "'A Promiscuous Brotherhood and Sisterhood': Men and Women in The Early Churches." In *The Body and Society*, 140–59. New York: Columbia University Press, 1988.

Bultmann, Rudolf. "New Testament and Mythology: The Problem of Demythologizing the New Testament Proclamation." In *New Testament and Mythology and Other Basic Writings*, edited and translated by Schubert M. Ogden, 1–43. Philadelphia: Fortress, 1984.

Burke, Edmund. *Reflections on the Revolution in France.* Harmondsworth, GB: Penguin, 1982.

Calvet, Gérard. "An Exhortation to the Restoration of Christendom." The Josias, October 31, 2014. https://thejosias.com.

Carlson, Thomas. "James and the Kantian Tradition." In *The Cambridge Companion to William James,* edited by Ruth Anna Putnam, 363–83. Cambridge: Cambridge University Press, 1997.

Cavanaugh, William T. *Eucharistie et mondialisation: La liturgie comme acte politique.* Geneva: Ad Solem, 2001.

———. *The Myth of Religious Violence: Secular Ideology and the Roots of Modern Conflict.* Oxford: Oxford University Press, 2009.

———. *Torture and Eucharist: Theology, Politics, and the Body of Christ.* Cambridge: Blackwell, 1998.

Certeau, Michel de. *The Mystic Fable.* Translated by Michael B. Smith. Chicago: The University of Chicago Press, 1992.

———. *The Practice of Everyday Life.* Translated by Steven Rendall. Berkeley: University of California Press, 1984.

———. "La rupture instauratrice." In *La faiblesse de croire,* 183–226. Paris: Editions du Seuil, 1987.

Chenu, M.-D. *Toward Understanding Saint Thomas.* Translated by A.-M. Landry and D. Hughes. Chicago: Henry Regnery, 1964.

Chesterton, G.K. *Orthodoxy.* New York: Doubleday, 2001.

Church, Forrest. "George Huntston Williams: Historian of the Christian Church 1914–2000." In *Notable American Unitarians 1936–1961,* edited by Herbert Vetter, 245–47. Cambridge, MA: Harvard Square Library, 2007.

Connolly, James M. *The Voices of France: A Survey of Contemporary Theology in France.* New York: Macmillan, 1961.

Coolidge, John. "Further Observations on Masaccio's Trinity." *The Art Bulletin* 48, No. 3/4 (September-December 1966): 382–84.

Courtenay, William. *Capacity and Volition: A History of the Distinction of Absolute and Ordained Power.* Bergamo, IT: Pierluigi Lubrina, 1990.

Cyprian of Carthage. *Epistles.* Translated by Robert Ernest Wallis. In Ante-Nicene Fathers, vol. 5, edited by Alexander Roberts, James Donaldson, and A. Cleveland Coxe. Buffalo, NY: Christian Literature, 1886.

Daniélou, Jean. *The Lord of History: Reflections on the Inner Meaning of History.* Translated by Nigel Abercrombie. Cleveland: Meridian, 1958.

Davies, W.D. *The Gospel and the Land: Early Christianity and Jewish Territorial Doctrine.* Berkeley, CA: University of California Press, 1974.

Day, Dorothy. *By Little and By Little: The Selected Writings of Dorothy Day.* Edited by Robert Ellsberg. New York: Knopf, 1983.

Deleuze, Gilles. *Kant's Critical Philosophy.* Translated by Hugh Tomlinson and Barbara Habberjam. Minneapolis, MN: University of Minnesota Press, 1993.

Delsol, Chantal. "Conclusion to *Qu'est-ce que l'homme?*" In *Lucid Mind, Intrepid Spirit: Essays on the Thought of Chantal Delsol,* edited by Lauren Hall and Paul Seaton, 11–18. Plymouth: Lexington, 2012.

———. *La fin de la Chrétienté.* Paris: Cerf, 2021.

———. "Introduction to *Qu'est-ce que l'homme?*" In *Lucid Mind, Intrepid Spirit: Essays on the Thought of Chantal Delsol,* edited by Lauren Hall and Paul Seaton, 3–9. Plymouth: Lexington, 2012.

De Lubac, Henri. *Catholicism: Christ and the Common Destiny of Man*. Translated by Lancelot C. Sheppard and Elizabeth Englund. San Francisco: Ignatius, 1988.

————. *Corpus Mysticum: L'Eucharistie et l'Église au Moyen-Age*. 2nd ed. Paris: Aubier, 1948.

————. *The Splendour of the Church*. Translated by Michael Mason. New York: Sheed & Ward, 1956.

Dempsey, Charles. "Masaccio's *Trinity*: Altarpiece or Tomb?" *The Art Bulletin* 54, no. 3 (September 1972): 279–81.

Derrida, Jacques. "Structure, Sign, and Play in the Discourse of the Human Sciences." In *Writing and Difference*, translated by Alan Bass, 278–93. Chicago: University of Chicago Press, 1978.

Dhanens, Elisabeth. *Hubert en Jan Van Eyck*. Antwerp, BE: Mercatorfonds, 1980.

Dod, Bernard G. "Aristoteles latinus." In *The Cambridge History of Later Medieval Philosophy*, edited by Norman Kretzmann et al., 46–48. Cambridge: Cambridge University Press, 1982.

Duffy, Eamon. *The Stripping of the Altars: Traditional Religion in England, 1400–1580*. New Haven: Yale University Press, 1992.

Dumoulin, Heinrich. *A History of Zen Buddhism*. Translated by Paul Preachy. New York: Pantheon, 1963.

Dupré, Louis. *Passage to Modernity: An Essay in the Hermeneutics of Nature and Culture*. New Haven: Yale University Press, 1993.

Epistle to Diognetus. In *The Apostolic Fathers*, vol. 2, translated by Kirsopp Lake, 347–79. Cambridge, MA: Harvard University Press, 1950.

Eusebius of Caesarea. *Oration on the Thirtieth Anniversary of Constantine's Reign.* In *The Early Church and the State,* edited and translated by Agnes Cunningham, 45–62. Philadelphia: Fortress, 1982.

Evans, G.R. *Law and Theology in the Middle Ages.* London: Routledge, 2002.

Evans, Michael. "An Illustrated Fragment of Peraldus' *Summa* of Vice: Harleian MS 3244." *Journal of the Warburg and Courtauld Institutes* 45, no. 1 (1982): 14–68.

Field, J.V. "Masaccio and Perspective in Italy in the Fifteenth Century." In *The Cambridge Companion to Masaccio,* edited by Diane Cole Ahl, 177–201. Cambridge: Cambridge University Press, 2002.

Figgis, John Neville. *From Gerson to Grotius, 1414–1625.* New York: Harper, 1960.

Flanagan, Owen. "Consciousness as a Pragmatist Views It." In *The Cambridge Companion to William James,* edited by Ruth Anna Putnam, 25–48. Cambridge: Cambridge University Press, 1997.

Florovsky, Georges. "Empire and Desert: Antinomies of Christian History." *The Greek Orthodox Theological Review* 3, no. 2 (1957): 133–59.

Foucault, Michel. *The Order of Things: An Archaeology of the Human Sciences.* Translated by Alan Sheridan. New York: Vintage, 1973.

Fowl, Stephen. Review of Boyarin, *A Radical Jew. Modern Theology* 12, no. 1 (January 1996): 131–33.

French, Roger Kenneth. *Medicine Before Science: The Rational and Learned Doctor From the Middle Ages to the Enlightenment.* Cambridge: Cambridge University Press, 2003.

Galloway, Andrew. "The Making of a Social Ethic in Late-Medieval England: From *Gratitudo* to 'Kyndenesse.'" *Journal of the History of Ideas* 55, no. 3 (1994): 365–83.

Garrett, William R. "Maligned Mysticism: The Maledicted Career of Troeltsch's Third Type." *Sociological Analysis* 36, no. 3 (Autumn 1975): 209.

Geertz, Clifford. *The Interpretation of Cultures*. New York: Basic, 1973.

Geffré, Claude, and Gustavo Gutiérrez, eds. *The Mystical and Political Dimensions of the Christian Faith*. Concilium 96. New York: Herder, 1974.

Geréby, György. "Political Theology versus Theological Politics: Erik Peterson and Carl Schmitt." *New German Critique* 35, no. 3 (Fall 2008): 7–33.

Giddens, Anthony. *The Consequences of Modernity*. Stanford, CA: Stanford University Press, 1990.

Gilby, Thomas. *The Political Thought of Thomas Aquinas*. Chicago: The University of Chicago Press, 1958.

Gobry, Pascal-Emmanuel. "Zombie Catholics vs. French Secularism." *America,* April 7, 2017. americamagazine.org.

Goffen, Rona. Introduction to Masaccio's *"Trinity,"* edited by Rona Goffen, 1–32. Cambridge: Cambridge University Press, 1998.

———. "Masaccio's *Trinity* and the Letter to Hebrews." In Masaccio's *"Trinity,"* edited by Rona Goffen, 43–64. Cambridge: Cambridge University Press, 1998.

Goldberg, Jonathan. "Quatrocento Dematerialization: Some Paradoxes in a Conceptual Art." *The Journal of Aesthetics and Art Criticism* 35, no. 2 (Winter 1976): 154–68.

Gramsci, Antonio. "The Modern Prince." In *The Modern Prince and Other Writings*, translated by Louis Mar. New York: International, 1957.

Gregory of Nazianzus. *Third Theological Oration*. Translated by Charles Gordon Browne and James Edward Swallow. In *Christology of the Later Fathers*, edited by Edward H. Hardy, 160–76. Philadelphia: Westminster, 1954.

Gregory of Nyssa. *Commentary on the Canticle*. In *From Glory to Glory: Texts from Gregory of Nyssa's Mystical Writings*, selected by Jean Daniélou, edited and translated by Herbert Musurillo. Crestwood, NY: St. Vladimir's Seminary Press, 1995.

Griffel, Frank. *Al-Ghazālī's Philosophical Theology*. Oxford: Oxford University Press, 2009.

Gustafson, James. Introduction to H. Richard Niebuhr, *The Responsible Self: An Essay in Christian Moral Philosophy*, 6–41. New York: Harper, 1963.

Gutiérrez, Gustavo. "The Limitations of Modern Theology: On a Letter of Dietrich Bonhoeffer." In *Essential Writings*, edited by James B. Nickoloff, 35–42. Minneapolis, MN: Fortress, 1996.

Harbison, Craig. *Jan Van Eyck: The Play of Realism*. London: Reaktion, 1999.

Harnack, Adolf von. *History of Dogma*. Translated by Neil Buchanan. New York: Dover, 1961.

———. *What is Christianity?* Translated by Thomas Bailey Saunders. Philadelphia: Fortress, 1986.

Hauerwas, Stanley. *With the Grain of the Universe: The Church's Witness and Natural Theology*. London: SCM, 2002.

Hegel, Georg Wilhelm Friedrich. *The Philosophy of History*. Translated by J. Sibree. New York: Dover, 1956.

Heiler, Friedrich. *Prayer: A Study in the History and Psychology of Religion*. Translated by S. McComb. London: Oxford University Press, 1932.

Henry, Patrick. "'And I Don't Care What It Is': The Tradition-History of a Civil Religion Proof-Text." *Journal of the American Academy of Religion* 49, no. 1 (Spring 1981): 35–49.

Hertzke, Allen. "The Theory of Moral Ecology." *The Review of Politics* 60, no. 4 (1998): 629–60.

Hollerich, Michael. "Religion and Politics in the Writings of Eusebius: Reassessing the First 'Court Theologian.'" *Church History* 59, no. 3 (September 1990): 309–25.

———. "Retrieving a Neglected Critique of Church, Theology, and Secularization in Weimar Germany." *Pro Ecclesia* 2, no. 3 (August 1993): 305–32.

Hookway, Christopher. "Logical Principles and Philosophical Attitudes: Peirce's Response to James' Pragmatism." In *The Cambridge Companion to William James*, edited by Ruth Anna Putnam, 145–65. Cambridge: Cambridge University Press, 1997.

Hopkins, Gerard Manley. *The Sermons and Devotional Writings of Gerard Manley Hopkins*. Edited by Christopher Devlin. London: Oxford University Press, 1959.

Horst, Ulrich. "Christ, *Exemplum Ordinis Fratrum Praedicantium*, According to Saint Thomas Aquinas." In *Christ Among the Medieval Dominicans*, edited by Kent Emery Jr. and Joseph P. Wawrykow, 256–70. Notre Dame, IN: University of Notre Dame Press, 1998.

Hütter, Reinhard. *Suffering Divine Things: Theology as Church Practice*. Grand Rapids, MI: Eerdmans, 2000.

Irenaeus. *Against Heresies*. Translated by Robert M. Grant. In Robert M. Grant, *Irenaeus of Lyons*, 57–186. London: Routledge, 1997.

Jaki, Stanley L. *Lord Gifford and His Lectures: A Centenary Retrospect*. Macon, GA: Mercer University Press, 1987.

James, William. *A Pluralistic Universe*. Lincoln, NE: University of Nebraska Press, 1996.

———. *Pragmatism*. Buffalo, NY: Prometheus, 1991.

———. *The Principles of Psychology*. New York: Henry Holt, 1890.

James, William. "The Social Value of the College-Bred." In *The Moral Equivalent of War and Other Essays*, edited by John Roth. New York: Harper, 1971.

————. *Talks to Teachers on Psychology and to Students on Some of Life's Ideals*. New York: Dover, 2001.

————. *The Varieties of Religious Experience: A Study in Human Nature*. New York: Longmans, 1902.

Janzen, W. "Land." In *The Anchor Bible Dictionary*, edited by David Noel Freedman et al. New York: Doubleday, 1992.

Joannides, Paul. *Masaccio and Masolino: A Complete Catalogue*. London: Phaidon, 1993.

John of Salisbury. *Metalogicon*. In *Medieval Political Theory—A Reader: The Quest for the Body Politic, 1100–1400*, edited by Cary J. Nederman and Kate Langdon Forhan, 26–60. New York: Routledge, 1993.

John Paul II. *Dies Domini*. May 31, 1998. vatican.va.

————. *Ecclesia in Europa*. June 28, 2003. vatican.va.

————. *The Gospel of Life [Evangelium Vitae]*. New York: Random House, 1995.

————. *Redemptoris Mater*. In *Mary: God's Yes to Man*. San Francisco: Ignatius, 1987.

Jones, David. "A, a, a, Domine Deus." In *The Sleeping Lord and Other Fragments*. London: Faber, 1974.

Julian of Norwich. *A Revelation of Love*. 3rd rev. ed. Edited by Marion Glasscoe. Exeter: University of Exeter Press, 1993.

Jungmann, Josef. *The Mass of the Roman Rite*. Translated by Francis Brunner. Notre Dame, IN: Christian Classics, 2012.

Kant, Immanuel. *The Conflict of the Faculties*. Translated by Mary J. McGregor. Lincoln, NE: University of Nebraska Press, 1979.

————. *Critique of Judgement*. Translated by J.H. Bernard. New York: Hafner, 1951.

Kant, Immanuel. *Religion within the Limits of Reason Alone.* Translated by Theodore Greene and Hoyt Hudson. New York: Harper, 1960.

Kaufman, Peter Iver. "Donatism Revisited: Moderates and Militants in Late Antique North Africa." *Journal of Late Antiquity* 2, no. 1 (Spring 2009): 131–42.

Kerr, Fergus. *Immortal Longings: Versions of Transcending Humanity.* Notre Dame, IN: University of Notre Dame Press, 1997.

Kilby, Karen. "Perichoresis and Projection: Problems with Social Doctrines of the Trinity." *New Blackfriars* 81, no. 957 (November 2000): 432–45. Reprinted in Karen Kilby, *God, Evil and the Limits of Theology*, 5–16. London: T&T Clark, 2020.

Klein, Yves. In *The Grove Book of Art Writing*, edited by Martin Gayford and Karen Wright, 205–6. New York: Grove, 1998.

Kolakowski, Leszek. *Modernity on Endless Trial.* Chicago: The University of Chicago Press, 1990.

LaCugna, Catherine Mowry. "God in Communion with Us: The Trinity." In *Freeing Theology: The Essentials of Theology in Feminist Perspective*, edited by Catherine Mowry LaCugna, 83–114. New York: HarperCollins, 1993.

———. *God for Us: The Trinity and Christian Life.* San Francisco: Harper, 1991.

Lago, Mary M. Introduction to *Imperfect Encounter: Letters of William Rothenstein and Rabindranath Tagore, 1911–1941.* Cambridge, MA: Harvard University Press, 1972.

Lakeland, Paul. *Postmodernity: Christian Identity in a Fragmented Age.* Philadelphia: Fortress, 1997.

Langland, William. *Piers Plowman: An Alliterative Verse Translation.* Translated by E. Talbot Donaldson. New York: Norton, 1990.

Lash, Nicholas. *Easter in Ordinary: Reflections on Human Experience and the Knowledge of God.* London: SCM, 1988.

Laurentin, René. "The Blessed Virgin Mary." In *The Historical and Mystical Christ,* edited by A.-M. Henry, translated by Angeline Bouchard, 266–69. Chicago: Fides, 1958.

Leo XIII. *Aeterni Patris.* August 4, 1879. vatican.va.

Lessing, Gotthold Ephraim. "On the Proof of the Spirit and of Power." In *Lessing's Theological Writings,* translated by Henry Chadwick, 51–56. Stanford, CA: Stanford University Press, 1956.

Lohfink, Gerhard. *Jesus and Community: The Social Dimension of Christian Faith.* Translated by John P. Galvin. Philadelphia: Fortress, 1984.

Lonergan, Bernard. *Method in Theology.* Minneapolis, MN: Seabury, 1972.

Loughlin, Gerard. *Telling God's Story.* Cambridge: Cambridge University Press, 1996.

Lyotard, Jean-François. *The Postmodern Condition: A Report on Knowledge.* Translated by Geoff Bennington and Brian Massumi. Minneapolis, MN: University of Minnesota Press, 1984.

MacIntyre, Alasdair. *After Virtue.* 2nd ed. Notre Dame, IN: University of Notre Dame Press, 1984.

———. "God and the Theologians." In *Against the Self-Images of the Age: Essays on Ideology and Philosophy.* London: Duckworth, 1971.

———. *Three Rival Versions of Moral Inquiry: Encyclopaedia, Genealogy, and Tradition.* Notre Dame, IN: University of Notre Dame Press, 1991.

———. *Whose Justice? Which Rationality?* Notre Dame, IN: University of Notre Dame Press, 1988.

Mallory, Michael. "An Early Quattrocento Trinity." *Art Bulletin* 48, no. 1 (March 1966): 85–89.

Marion, Jean-Luc. *A Brief Apology for a Catholic Moment.* Translated by Stephen E. Lewis. Chicago: University of Chicago Press, 2021.

———. *God Without Being: Hors-Texte.* Translated by Thomas A. Carlson. Chicago: University of Chicago Press, 1991.

Marion, Jean-Luc. "Metaphysics and Phenomenology: A Summary for Theologians." In *The Postmodern God: A Theological Reader,* edited by Graham Ward, 279–96. Oxford: Blackwell, 1997.

———. "Le phénomène saturé." In *Phénoménologie et théologie,* edited by Jean-François Courtine, 79–128. Paris: Criterion, 1993.

Maritain, Jacques. *Man and the State.* Chicago: University of Chicago Press, 1951.

Markus, Robert A. "Donatus, Donatism." In *Augustine Through the Ages: An Encyclopedia,* edited by Allan D. Fitzgerald et al., 284–87. Grand Rapids, MI: Eerdmans, 1999.

McCabe, Herbert. *God Matters.* London: Geoffrey Chapman, 1987.

McGarry, Daniel D. *The Metalogicon of John of Salisbury: A Twelfth-Century Defense of the Verbal and Logical Arts of the Trivium.* Berkeley: University of California Press, 1955.

McIlroy, David H. *A Trinitarian Theology of Law.* Eugene, OR: Wipf and Stock, 2009.

McNamee, Maurice B. *Vested Angels: Eucharistic Allusions in Early Netherlandish Paintings.* Leuven, BE: Peeters, 1998.

McNaspy, C.J. *Lost Cities of Paraguay: Art and Architecture of the Jesuit Reductions, 1607–1767.* Chicago: Loyola University Press, 1982.

McPartlan, Paul. *Sacrament of Salvation: An Introduction to Eucharistic Ecclesiology.* Edinburgh: T&T Clark, 2000.

Meeks, Wayne. *The First Urban Christians: The Social World of the Apostle Paul.* New Haven: Yale University Press, 1983.

Merton, Thomas, and Rosemary Radford Ruether. *At Home in the World: The Letters of Thomas Merton & Rosemary Radford Ruether.* Edited by Mary Tardiff. New York: Orbis, 1995.

Metz, Johann Baptist. "Christians and Jews After Auschwitz: Being a Meditation also on the End of Bourgeois Religion." In *The Emergent Church*, translated by Peter Mann. New York: Crossroad, 1986.

———. *Followers of Christ: The Religious Life and the Church.* Translated by Thomas Linton. New York: Paulist, 1978.

Midgely, Mary. *Can't We Make Moral Judgments?* New York: St. Martin's, 1991.

Mitzman, Arthur. *The Iron Cage: An Historical Interpretation of Max Weber.* New York: Knopf, 1969.

Montaigne, Michel de. *The Complete Works: Essays, Travel Journal, Letters.* Translated by Donald M. Frame. New York: Everyman, 2003.

Montoya, Antonio Ruiz de. *The Spiritual Conquest Accomplished by the Religious of the Society of Jesus in the Provinces of Paraguay, Paraná, Uruguay, and Tape.* Translated by C.J. McNaspy et al. St. Louis, MO: The Institute of Jesuit Sources, 1993.

Niebuhr, H. Richard. *Christ and Culture.* New York: Harper, 1951.

———. "The Doctrine of the Trinity and the Unity of the Church." In *Theology, History, and Culture: Major Unpublished Writings*, edited by William Stacy Johnson, 50–62. New Haven: Yale University Press, 1996.

Niebuhr, Reinhold. *An Interpretation of Christian Ethics.* New York: Harper, 1935.

Novak, Michael. *The Spirit of Democratic Capitalism.* New York: Simon, 1982.

Oberman, Heiko. *The Harvest of Medieval Theology: Gabriel Biel and Late Medieval Nominalism.* Durham, NC: Labyrinth, 1983.

O'Connor, Flannery. *Flannery O'Connor: Collected Works.* Edited by Sally Fitzgerald. New York: Library of America, 1988.

Origen. *Contra Celsum.* Translated by Henry Chadwick. Cambridge: Cambridge University Press, 1965.

Ozment, Steven. *The Reformation in the Cities: The Appeal of Protestantism in Sixteenth-Century Germany.* New Haven: Yale University Press, 1980.

Parker, Thomas D. "The Political Meaning of the Doctrine of the Trinity: Some Theses." *The Journal of Religion* 60, no. 2 (April 1980): 165–84.

Pascal, Blaise. *Pensées.* In *Pensées and Other Writings,* edited by Anthony Levi, translated by Honor Levi. Oxford: Oxford University Press, 1995.

Paul VI. *Lumen Ecclesiae.* November 20, 1974. vatican.va.

Pearman, Sara Jane. "The Iconographic Development of the Cruciform Throne of Grace From the Twelfth to the Sixteenth Century." Unpublished dissertation, Case Western Reserve University, 1974.

Peirce, Charles Sanders. "A Neglected Argument for the Reality of God." In *Collected Papers of Charles Sanders Peirce,* edited by Charles Hartshorne and Paul Weiss. Cambridge, MA: Harvard University Press, 1935.

Pereira, José. "Thomism and the Magisterium: From *Aeterni Patris* to *Veritatis splendor.*" *Logos* 5, no. 3 (Summer 2002): 147–83.

Perreau-Saussine, Emile. *Catholicism and Democracy.* Princeton: Princeton University Press, 2012.

Peterson, Erik. "Monotheismus als politsches Problem." In *Theologische Traktate,* 49–147. Munich, DE: Kösel-Verlag, 1951.

Philip, Lotte Brand. *Early Netherlandish Painting.* New York: Harper, 1971.

Philip, Lotte Brand. *The Ghent Altarpiece and the Art of Jan van Eyck*. Princeton, NJ: Princeton University Press, 1971.

Philip of Harvengt. "Letter to Henry, Count of Champagne." In *Medieval Political Theory—A Reader: The Quest for the Body Politic, 1100–1400*, edited by Cary J. Nederman and Kate Langdon Forhan, 64–66. New York: Routledge, 1993.

Portier, William L. "Here Come the Evangelical Catholics." *Communio* 31, no. 1 (Spring 2004): 35–66.

———. "Mysticism and Politics and Integral Salvation: Two Approaches to Theology in a Suffering World." In *Pluralism and Oppression: Theology in World Perspective*, edited by Paul F. Knitter. New York: University Press of America, 1988.

Power, David. *The Sacrifice We Offer: The Tridentine Dogma and Its Reinterpretation*. New York: Crossroad, 1987.

Putnam, Hilary. "James' Theory of Truth." In *The Cambridge Companion to William James*, edited by Ruth Anna Putnam, 166–85. Cambridge: Cambridge University Press, 1997.

Rahner, Karl. *Foundations of the Christian Faith: An Introduction to the Idea of Christianity*. Translated by William V. Dych. New York: Crossroad, 1987.

———. *Nature and Grace: Dilemmas in the Modern Church*. Translated by Dinah Wharton. New York: Sheed & Ward, 1964.

———. "Theology and Anthropology." In *Theological Investigations IX: Writings of 1965–1967 I*, translated by Graham Harrison, 28–45. New York: Herder, 1972.

———. *The Trinity*. Translated by Joseph Donceel. New York: Crossroad, 1997.

Ratzinger, Joseph. *The Theology of History in St. Bonaventure*. Chicago: Franciscan Herald, 1971.

Rawls, John. *Political Liberalism*. New York: Columbia University Press, 2005.

———. *A Theory of Justice*. Cambridge, MA: Belknap, 1971.

Rite of Christian Initiation of Adults. Prepared by International Commission on English in the Liturgy and Bishops' Committee on the Liturgy. Chicago: Liturgy Training Publications, 1988.

Robertson, Roland. "On the Analysis of Mysticism: Pre-Weberian, Weberian and Post-Weberian Perspectives." *Sociological Analysis* 36, no. 3 (Autumn 1975): 245–48.

Rorty, Richard. "Religious Faith, Intellectual Responsibility, and Romance." In *The Cambridge Companion to William James*, edited by Ruth Anna Putnam, 84–102. Cambridge: Cambridge University Press, 1997.

Rose, Margaret A. *The Post-modern and the Post-industrial: A Critical Analysis.* Cambridge: Cambridge University Press, 1991.

Said, Edward. *Orientalism.* New York: Pantheon, 1978.

Scheeben, Matthias. *Mariology.* Translated by T.L.M.J. Geukers. St. Louis, MO: Herder, 1946.

Schillebeeckx, Edward. *Christ: The Experience of Jesus as Lord.* Translated by John Bowden. New York: Crossroad, 1983.

———. *Christ the Sacrament of the Encounter with God.* New York: Sheed & Ward, 1963.

———. *Church: The Human Story of God.* Translated by John Bowden. New York: Crossroad, 1990.

———. "Eager to Spread the Gospel of Peace." Translated by David Smith. In *Church and Peace*, Concilium 164, edited by Virgilio P. Elizondo and Norbert Greinacher. New York: Seabury, 1983.

———. *On Christian Faith: The Spiritual, Ethical, and Political Dimensions.* Translated by John Bowden. New York: Crossroad, 1987.

Schlegel, Ursula. "Observations on Masaccio's Trinity Fresco in Santa Maria Novella." *The Art Bulletin* 45, No. 1 (March 1963), 19–33.

Schmitt, Carl. *The Concept of the Political*. Translated by George Schwab. Chicago: University of Chicago Press, 1996.

―――. *Political Theology: Four Chapters on the Concept of Sovereignty*. Translated by George Schwab. Cambridge, MA: MIT Press, 1985.

Shklar, Judith. *Ordinary Vices*. Cambridge, MA: Harvard University Press, 1984.

Smith, John E. "William James' Account of Mysticism: A Critical Appraisal." In *Mysticism and Religious Traditions*, edited by Steven T. Katz. Oxford: Oxford University Press, 1983.

Söderblom, Nathan. "The Role of the Church in Promoting Peace." In *Peace: 1926–1950*, Nobel Lectures: Including Presentation Speeches and Laureates' Biographies, vol. 2, edited by Frederick W Haberman. Singapore: World Scientific, 1999.

Steenberghen, Fernand van. *The Philosophical Movement in the Thirteenth Century*. New York: Thomas Nelson, 1955.

Stillingfleet, Edward. *An Answer to Mr. Cressy's Epistle Apologetical*. London, 1675.

Stout, Jeffrey. *Democracy and Tradition*. Princeton: Princeton University Press, 2004.

Tanner, Kathryn. "Trinity." In *The Blackwell Companion to Political Theology*, 2nd ed., edited by Peter Scott and William T. Cavanaugh, 363–75. Oxford: Blackwell, 2018.

Tanquerey, A.D. *A Manual of Dogmatic Theology*. Translated by John J. Byrnes. New York: Desclee, 1959.

Taylor, Mark. "Denegating God." *Critical Inquiry* 20, no. 4 (1994): 592–610.

Thomas Aquinas. *Compendium theologiae*. Translated by Richard J. Regan. Oxford: Oxford University Press, 2009.

―――. *Summa Contra Gentiles*. Translated by Vernon J. Burke. Revised by Joseph Kenny. New York: Hanover, 1955.

Thomas Aquinas. *Summa theologiae*. Translated by Fathers of the English Dominican Province. New York: Benziger Bros., 1947.

Tocqueville, Alexis de. *Democracy in America*. New York: Knopf, 1972.

Toennies Ferdinand, et al. "Max Weber on Church, Sect, and Mysticism." *Sociological Analysis* 34, no. 2 (Summer 1973): 140–49.

Toulmin, Stephen. *Cosmopolis: The Hidden Agenda of Modernity*. Chicago: University of Chicago Press, 1990.

Tracy, David. *Dialogue with the Other. The Inter-Religious Dialogue*. Grand Rapids, MI: Eerdmans, 1990.

————. "On Naming the Present." In *On Naming the Present: Reflections on God, Hermeneutics, and Church*, 3–24. Maryknoll, NY: Orbis, 1994.

Turner, A. Richard. "Masaccio, Masolino, and the Brancacci Chapel Frescoes." In *The Art of Florence*, edited by John Daly and Constance Herndon. New York: Abbeville, 1988.

Turner, Bryan. *Max Weber: From History to Modernity*. London: Routledge, 1992.

Turner, Charles. *Modernity and Politics in the Work of Max Weber*. London: Routledge, 1992.

Upjohn, Sheila. *Why Julian Now? A Voyage of Discovery*. Grand Rapids, MI: Eerdmans, 1997.

Valéry, Paul. "The Conquest of Ubiquity." In *Aesthetics*, translated by Ralph Manheim. New York: Pantheon, 1964.

Vatican Council II. *Dignitatis Humanae*. In *Decrees of the Ecumenical Councils*, vol. 2, edited by Norman Tanner. Washington, DC: Georgetown University Press, 1990.

————. *Gaudium et Spes*. In *Decrees of the Ecumenical Councils*, edited by Norman Tanner. Washington, DC: Georgetown University Press, 1990.

Vatican Council II. *Lumen Gentium*. In *Decrees of the Ecumenical Councils*, edited by Norman Tanner. Washington, DC: Georgetown University Press, 1990.

Volf, Miroslav. "'The Trinity is Our Social Program': The Doctrine of the Trinity and the Shape of Social Engagement." *Modern Theology* 14, no. 3 (Summer 1998): 403–23.

Vorgrimler, Herbert, ed. *Commentary on the Documents of Vatican II*. New York: Herder, 1967.

Waldstein, Edmund. "Integralism in Three Sentences." The Josias, October 17, 2016. http://thejosias.com.

Walker, Alice. "Beyond the Peacock: The Reconstruction of Flannery O'Connor." In *In Search of Our Mothers' Gardens: Womanist Prose*, 42–59. New York: Harcourt, 2004.

Wannenwetsch, Bernd. "The Political Worship of the Church: A Critical and Empowering Practice." *Modern Theology* 12, no. 3 (July 1996): 269–99.

Ward, Graham. "Introduction, or, A Guide to Theological Thinking in Cyberspace." In *The Postmodern God: A Theological Reader*, edited by Graham Ward, xv–xlvii. Oxford: Blackwell, 1997.

Watson, Nicholas. "Visions of Inclusion: Universal Salvation and Vernacular Theology in Pre-Reformation England." *Journal of Medieval and Early Modern Studies* 27, no. 2 (1997): 167–68.

Weber, Max. *Economy and Society: An Outline of Interpretive Sociology*. Edited by Guenther Roth and Claus Wittich. Berkeley: University of California Press, 1978.

———. *The Protestant Ethic and the Spirit of Capitalism*. Translated by Talcott Parsons. New York: Scribner's, 1976.

———. "Religious Rejections of the World and Their Directions." In *From Max Weber: Essays in Sociology*, edited and translated by H.H. Gerth and C. Wright Mills. New York: Oxford University Press, 1946.

Weber, Max. "The Social Psychology of the World Religions." In *From Max Weber: Essays in Sociology*, edited and translated by H.H. Gerth and C. Wright Mills. New York: Oxford University Press, 1946.

Weil, Simone. "The Love of God and Affliction." In *Waiting for God*, translated by Emma Craufurd, 117–36. New York: Harper, 1951.

Weisheipl, James A. "The Structure of the Arts Faculty in the Medieval University." *British Journal of Educational Studies* 19, no. 3 (1971): 263–71.

White, Thomas Joseph. "Catholicism in an Age of Discontent: The Need for Reason and Mystery in Catholic Apologetics." *First Things*, November 2016. firstthings.com.

Wilken, Robert Louis. *The Christians as the Romans Saw Them.* New Haven: Yale University Press, 1984.

———. *The First Thousand Years: A Global History of Christianity.* New Haven: Yale University Press, 2012.

William of Ockham. *Quodlibetal Questions.* Translated by Alfred J. Freddoso and Francis E. Kelley. New Haven: Yale University Press, 1991.

———. *Summa logicae.* In *Philosophical Writings*, edited by Philotheus Boehner. Indianapolis: Hackett, 1990.

William of St. Thierry. *The Golden Epistle.* Translated by Theodore Berkeley. Kalamazoo, MI: Cistercian, 1980.

Williams, George Huntston. "Christology and Church-State Relations in the Fourth Century (Part I)." *Church History* 20, no. 3 (1951): 3–33.

———. "Christology and Church-State Relations in the Fourth Century (Part II)." *Church History* 20, no. 4 (1951): 3–26.

Williams, Rowan. "Balthasar and Rahner." In *The Analogy of Beauty: The Theology of Hans Urs von Balthasar*, edited by John Riches, 11–34. Edinburgh: T&T Clark, 1986.

Williams, Rowan. *Resurrection: Interpreting the Easter Gospel.* Harrisburg, PA: Morehouse, 1994.

Winter, Art, with Elizabeth Dreyer. "Spirituality more easily found in the world than in churches." *National Catholic Reporter* 33 no. 7 (December 13, 1996): 9–10.

Wippel, John. *Medieval Reactions to the Encounter Between Faith and Reason.* Milwaukee: Marquette University Press, 1995.

Wolters, Clifton. Introduction to Julian of Norwich, *Revelations of Divine Love.* Harmondsworth, GB: Penguin, 1966.

Wright, N.T. *The New Testament and the People of God.* Minneapolis, MN: Fortress, 1992.

Yeago, David S. "The New Testament and the Nicene Dogma: A Contribution to the Recovery of Theological Exegesis." In *The Theological Interpretation of Scripture*, edited by Stephen E. Fowl, 87–100. Oxford: Blackwell, 1997.

Yoder, John Howard. "The Constantinian Sources of Western Social Ethics." In *The Priestly Kingdom: Social Ethics as Gospel*, 135–47. Notre Dame, IN: University of Notre Dame Press, 1984.

Zaleski, Carol. "William James: *The Varieties of Religious Experience* (1902)." *First Things* 101 (March 2000): 61.

Zilsel, Edgar. "The Sociological Roots of Science." *The American Journal of Sociology* 47, no. 4 (January 1942): 544–62.

Zizioulas, John D. *Being as Communion: Studies in Personhood and the Church.* Crestwood, NY: St. Vladimir's Seminary Press, 1985.

INDEX

over-beliefs (James), 163, 166,
176–77

Pascal, Blaise, 14, 258, 283
Paul VI, 266
peace
in the earthly city, 70, 210
in the kingdom of God,
327–30
Pentecost, 112, 118
perichoresis, 80, 83–84
Perreau-Saussine, Emile, 221–23,
229
personalism, 34–35
perspective in art, 96, 311,
321–24
Peterson, Erik, 85–88, 90–92, 94
Philo, 86
Piers Plowman (Langland), 141
Plato, 116, 180, 260–61, 272
polis, 100–102, 116–17, 187,
205, 208, 242, 290
political conception (Rawls),
214–17
Portier, William, 6–7, 10–11, 13,
18, 23, 200
postmodernity, meaning of,
24–31, 136–38, 275–76
potentia obedientialis, 9
power of God
in nominalism, 132–34
in occasionalism, 221
pragmatism, 156–57
prayer, 148–49
progress, meaning of, 21–22, 106
Promised Land, 237–38
*Protestant Ethic and the Spirit of
Capitalism, The* (Weber), 71,
159, 181–82, 194

Protestant Reformation, 71–73
psychology, 155
public morality, 212

Radical Aristotelianism, 267–69
Rahner, Karl, 4, 8–9, 36–37,
258, 311, 316, 324
rationalization, 180–84, 186, 188
Rawls, John, 214–17, 223,
225–27
religious experience
in James, 160–66, 169–71
in Schillebeeckx, 198–201
in Weber, 188
See also mysticism
religious freedom, 211–12
religious pluralism, 30, 165–66,
172, 211–12
religious violence, 172–73
res et sacramentum, 49
ressourcement, 17
Revelation (book), 23, 69, 110,
149, 326
routinization thesis (Weber), 162,
186–87, 201
Rublev, Andrei, 82, 96

Said, Edward, 190–93
saints
in art, 304, 325–28
as pattern of Christian life, 14,
17
Schillebeeckx, Edward, 198–205,
207, 209
Schleiermacher, Friedrich, 34,
166, 273
Schmitt, Carl, 90–92, 94
science of religion, 155, 157–58
secularity, 104, 106, 266

Sermon on the Mount, 78, 206,
208
sin, meaning of, 143–44
social Catholicism, 98, 102, 109,
121
social contract, 216, 223, 225,
242
social Trinitarianism, 81–82, 84,
96
St. John Altarpiece (Memling),
325–30
sublimity, 26–28
suspicion, 24, 27–32, 35, 39, 42,
52

Tagore, Rabindranath, 193
Tanner, Kathryn, 83–84
temple, 235–39
"Temple of the Holy Ghost, A"
(O'Connor), 284, 286–87
tenderness (O'Connor), 277–78,
281, 287
theology of art, 292
Thomas Aquinas
on morality, 60–62
on natural reason, 12–13,
263–66
on plurality of creation,
217–19, 221
on religion, 171
on Trinity, 315, 318, 324
toleration, 176
tradition
in art, 295
in Julian of Norwich, 138
in MacIntyre, 214, 216
in Rawls, 214–15, 225–26
transubstantiation, 49–50, 57

Trinity
and *caritas*, 46
cross and resurrection as icon
of, 42–43
economic and immanent, 40,
311, 316, 324
and *filioque*, 316–18
Julian of Norwich on, 138–39,
145–50
Kant on, 77
and modalism, 79, 84, 86
Niebuhr on, 78–80
Petersen on, 85–88, 90–92
perichoresis and 82–84
and *scutum fidei* (shield of
faith) 315–16
Aquinas on 315, 318, 324
Williams on, 88–90, 92–94
Trinity (Masaccio), 96–97,
310–24
typology, 110–12

universal call to holiness, 8, 10,
15
University of Paris, 260

Van Eyck, Jan, 288, 291,
299–301, 303, 305–9
Varieties of Religious Experience
(James), 153, 155, 157–60,
169, 174–76, 178
Vatican Council II, 3–6, 8, 19,
23, 55, 211–12, 266–67,
275
veil of ignorance, 216–17, 223,
225–26
Vijd, Joos, 299–301, 305, 308
violence and the state, 186–87